God Shall Wipe
Away All Tears

God Shall Wipe Away All Tears

A Mother's Journal of Caregiving,
Tragedy, and Hope
Insights into Life and Death

Colleen Curzon Openshaw

ARPress
ILLUMINATING IDEAS.
EMPOWERING VOICES

This material is neither made, provided, approved, nor endorsed by Intellectual Reserve, Inc. or The Church of Jesus Christ of Latter-day Saints. Any content or opinions expressed, implied or included in or with the material are solely those of the owner and not those of Intellectual Reserve, Inc. or The Church of Jesus Christ of Latter-day Saints.

Scripture taken from the King James Version of the Bible.

ARPress
45 Dan Road Suite 36
Canton MA 02021
Hotline: 1(888) 821-0229
Fax: 1(508) 545-7580

Ordering Information:
Quantity Sales. Special discounts are available on quantity purchases by corporations, associations, and others. For details, contact the publisher at the address above.

Printed in the United States of America.

ISBN-13   Paperback   979-8-89330-584-5
                 eBook   979-8-89330-586-9
                 Hardback   979-8-89330-585-2

Library of Congress Control Number: 2024902464

In remembrance of my husband Mike—we traveled this journey together and will be together eternally.

Also in remembrance of our sons Jonathan, Seth, and Michael—my angels in heaven,

And to all my living children—Jeremy, Jessica, Rebekah, Robert, Matthew, and Richard—who have loved and suffered with us.

Contents

Foreword

This book is a true story about a devoted couple with nine children and their commitment to their faith in God and to the teachings of The Church of Jesus Christ of Latter-day Saints. Yet it is a story within a story of this family's terrifying battle against the rages of a genetic immunodeficiency disease. For three sons—Jonathan, Michael, and Seth—this earthly battle was lost.

Mike and Colleen Curzon were dedicated to their values and the choices they made to fulfill their dream of having a large family. They were tested beyond mortal understanding, and *God Shall Wipe Away All Tears*, taken from excerpts of diaries and letters, chronicles their trials as their inspiring but heartbreaking journey unfolds.

This book details how the mother, who is the central figure, finds great comfort in her faith and convictions. There is the unspoken question, asked by the reader, whether the choices are defensible. This book documents the intense emotional responses of the author's parents, siblings, children, neighbors, and church members in combination with scientific information. It chronicles her and her husband's eagerness to have their ill children participate in experimental treatments and clinical trials. After many years, they begin to understand the prognosis and long-term outcomes for children born with this disease, and they learn the benefit of early intervention.

Although Colleen's husband, Mike, was often home to help with the children, Colleen relates in simply stated prose times of medical crisis when he was away in another state or country for army training. These were times of great loneliness and despair for Colleen. But this was the making of their eternal family, as they worked together to support each other both spiritually and financially.

Sadly, Colleen's husband, best friend, and love succumbed to death at age sixty-four after a battle with cancer, heart disease, and early dementia. The author continued to shoulder life's responsibilities and her memories alone. Always, this book is about love and how this powerful emotion can instill courage and bravery in all of us as we draw on support from our loved ones when needed.

This book begins at Christmastime when the author was seven years old and describes the warmth and love in her family of five sisters and one brother. Her family life was an atmosphere of strong religious belief and teachings that are core to the Mormon faith. With this childhood upbringing and background, the author began her own family to teach and to guide.

As I contemplate this very emotionally charged book, I think we all have our own stories of struggle and triumph we can relate to. This author was brave enough to put it on paper. I believe most of us are in the process of progression as we act on our own choices, and I believe we all have guardian angels who hover over us, just as the Curzon family are cheered on by angels Jonathan, Michael, Seth, and Mike from beyond the filmy curtains of heaven.

Above all, *God Shall Wipe Away All Tears* is a book about the ability to find solace and comfort in God, His plan of salvation, and faith in eternal families. The writer brings an innocence and freshness to this tragic but heartwarming story of unwavering faith.

Jayne A. Chaffin, MRC
(Master of Rehabilitation Counseling)

Acknowledgments

As church members in The Church of Jesus Christ of Latter-day Saints, we have received counsel from our church leaders to write in journals and record our life experiences. Recording and later reading what I have written of the ups and downs of my life has been a spiritually and emotionally strengthening process, allowing me to see how the Lord has guided and comforted me. I thank my wonderful parents who taught me important lessons and instilled faith and courage into my life.

My late husband, Mike, encouraged me in my writings and wrote some things of his own. In fact, parts of this book are from his journal. I also have included selections from my children's writings, letters, songs, journals, and poetry. I thank those of my children who have given me encouragement. I also thank my sisters and brother; my new husband, Gary; and other friends who have been very complimentary and have buoyed me up in my efforts to finish this manuscript. I thank Seth's doctor, Ulrike Ziegner, and other medical professionals, friends, and family who have written endorsements for my book or given permission to include emails sent to me. I thank Jayne Chaffin, an experienced therapist, for composing an objective and complimentary foreword to this book. I appreciate the careful editing and suggestions given by the Archway Publishing team. Most of all, I thank God, who for many years has impressed upon my mind that writing this book is part of my life's mission that must be accomplished. I hope this book will be a blessing to those who read it, as it has been a blessing for me to write it.

List of Abbreviations

B of M—The Book of Mormon: Another Testament of Jesus Christ

D & C—The Doctrine and Covenants of The Church of Jesus Christ of Latter-day Saints

P of GP—The Pearl of Great Price

Introduction

My sixteen-year-old son, Michael, had been in surgery for a couple of hours when the surgeon came out to see us in the parents' waiting room. I fully expected that there would be good news and that Michael would be on his way to recovery. At least, that was all I could stand to believe. The doctor said that Michael had done well in the operation and then asked us to follow him to a small private room adjacent to the waiting area where we could talk. I knew this had to mean bad news. We went in and shut the door.

Then the doctor said, "Michael is fine. He is in the recovery room. We did not take out his gallbladder, because we found tumors in his gallbladder, pancreas, and liver. We took a biopsy of the tumor, and it appears to be adenocarcinoma. It is malignant. This is a very difficult type of cancer to treat. There is very little we can do."

My head was reeling. *No!* my mind cried. *No, no, no!* I had always carried fears of losing another child sometime, and the doctor was telling us that the time was now. Michael wasn't going to go home and be well and free of pain. He was going to die. "How long?" I asked.

"Maybe two months," the doctor said. This was the most nightmarish day of my life. Michael had cancer? There was no treatment? My whole world was falling apart.

When Mike and I lost our first baby, Jonathan, at eight months old due to a rare genetic immune deficiency, hyper-IgM syndrome, it rocked our world. Even worse was to learn that the disease could occur again in future sons. But the doctors said there was a treatment, so we felt hopeful that we could still have the large family we desired.

After my baby's death, I felt that I wanted to write a book about the experience of loving and losing him, but as the years went on, more and more stories unfolded in my life—more chapters to add to my book. Twenty-four years later, after having eight more talented children, we were told that Michael had pancreatic cancer as a consequence of his hyper-IgM liver problems, and my heart broke. Losing Michael was torturous. The passing of our third son, Seth, after ten years of a downhill spiral was more difficult than I can express, and the death of my husband three years later was like losing half of myself.

Other serious events in my life include the tragic deaths of my best friend and my sister in car accidents. My father's life was taken by cancer. My husband and I both dealt with cancer, and my husband suffered from dementia before passing away at age sixty-four. My mother also died in her old age.

In the midst of "walking through the shadow of death" and experiencing the vicissitudes of raising a large family, the loneliness of my widowhood, the challenge of finishing college later in life, and the scare of cancer, I have felt God assisting me as a friend, mentor, and comforter. Thus came about the title of my book, taken from the Bible—*God Shall Wipe Away All Tears* (Revelation 21:4).

As I look back on my life, I feel it has been extraordinary. Although it has been unique and different from other people's lives and beliefs, it is my story. I was raised in a large and devout Mormon family in Utah. My father was a leader in The Church of Jesus Christ of Latter-day Saints. His church duties took us to Denver for three years to live in a mission home mansion where my dad served as a mission president. There I met my future husband. During our subsequent engagement in college, we talked about our desire to bring many children into our family. We believed that parenthood was a noble calling, a mutual creative experience with God to help His spirit children progress by experiencing and learning from mortal life.

Later, after marrying my sweetheart, our children began to come, but with the sad surprise that some had primary immunodeficiency disease (PI). Although the doctors told us it was very rare, it has now been "estimated that as many as one in every 1,200–2,000 people may have some form of primary immunodeficiency." There are "more than 250" such diseases, "which result from a defect in ... the normal immune system." Patients "have an increased susceptibility to infection ... anywhere in the body" (Immune Deficiency Foundation 2013, 11–12). Specifically, our affected sons had hyper-IgM syndrome, more recently called CD40 ligand deficiency.

This shocking turn of events brought times we never could have prepared for. The deaths of our three sons were tragic experiences. The silver lining in these dark clouds of our lives was that our sons had let their lights shine and had blessed the lives of many people. Although short, their lives on earth had not been in vain.

Thankfully, I have four sons who have survived, two of whom live near-normal lives with their disease and two who are unaffected. I also have two daughters and two granddaughters who are carriers of this defect and two granddaughters who are not carriers. (Most carriers do not display symptoms.) All of my posterity are precious to me.

Having given birth to nine children, I have experienced the ups and downs, the joys and heartaches of parenting, which all parents can relate to. I hope that writing about my family's experiences with this rare disease may be educational and inspirational for people facing similar trials in their own families and that they may be strengthened in illness or the loss of loved ones dear to them.

Most of my recollections in this book are taken from journals I have kept over the past four decades. I have also included excerpts from journals, poems, and emails from my husband, children, and doctors. I have lightly edited this material for clarity and to provide additional context where appropriate. The names of some people and locations have been changed to protect their privacy.

I give many medical details in this book as I explain the illnesses my family has experienced. Some of this information may be difficult to read, but I have included it because it may give important, even lifesaving information to others who may experience similar symptoms, especially people with an immune deficiency. I personally find it helpful to read what others have had to endure. It helps me to heal emotionally from the traumas I have seen my family go through. I hope that readers may also gain healing from my words and know that they are not alone in whatever trials they may be suffering.

As I chronicle my life in diary form, I explain the strong foundation of faith that I was blessed with from a young age and how that faith has given me strength to bring children into the world, to deal with the challenges of motherhood and wifehood, and to let loved ones go when the Lord calls. Birth and death are sacred doors to and from our mortal lives. In between, we experience many trials. But eternity is on the other side!

Although I am a religious person, I admit that I have not always acted nobly. I have been angry, terrified, and felt hopeless at times. I have not always been as prayerful and obedient in my daily life as I would have liked. But when I have tried to be faithful, blessings and peace have come to me. Being a pretty shy person when I first had children, it was only the horror of possibly losing them that brought me out of my shell as I had to argue with doctors about how to best treat their illnesses. I morphed into a sometimes feisty protector of my children and of ideas I believed to be right. I know there are others who have suffered in their lives far more than I have. But telling my story is important. I thank God for His great kindness and patience with me and for what I have learned in difficult times.

The true-life events that follow—including stories of tragedy, happiness, blindness, cancer, missions, Alzheimer's, deaths, widowhood, achievement, and new love—will pull at your heartstrings and hopefully strengthen your faith in a way few books do. This work includes the beautiful births of babies, the tragic deaths of loved ones, comforting messages from beyond the grave, the struggles of parenthood, and the comfort of faith. This book is a collage of powerful experiences all wrapped into one true story. Prepare for a roller-coaster read filled with tears and smiles.

1

My Blessed Early Life

DECEMBER 24, 1954

It's Christmas Eve, our most special time as a family. My daddy has built a fire in the fireplace, and we have the Christmas tree up with bubble lights on it. I'm seven years old now. Tonight I rocked my baby doll in the darkness and looked at the beautiful tree. Then we acted out the nativity story like we do every year. My dad was the donkey, and I was Joseph, with my long hair tied around my chin to look like a beard, since we don't have any boys in our family. My sister Wendy was Mary and held our baby sister, Rhonda, who was baby Jesus. My younger sisters Jackie and Paula were shepherds, using their new bathrobes as costumes. My mommy made us all new bathrobes for Christmas. She read the story of the birth of Jesus out of our Bible storybook, and then we turned out the lights, leaving just the fire and Christmas tree shining. Daddy told us with his tender, deep voice how much he loves us and how much he knows that Jesus really was born and is our Savior. It made me feel so happy and warm inside. Then we had family prayer. We put out fruitcake and milk for Santa to eat and hung up our stockings.

DECEMBER 25, 1954

Christmas has been wonderful. We all got great big teddy bears about as big as we are. Santa also brought a little blue kitchen set with table and chairs and a little cupboard. Mommy got a brand-new washing machine, and was very happy about it. Grandma and Grandpa and our aunts, uncles, and cousins came for dinner, which was spread out on the long dining room table and card tables. Grandma Scott made her special carrot pudding. I love it with the yummy caramel sauce on it. And of course we had turkey and pies and exchanged presents. There was a lot of snow outside, so we had a white Christmas.

APRIL 19, 1955

Today my mother, Arline Martindale Scott, picked me up from school early so that I could go downtown to the Mormon Tabernacle in Salt Lake City to be baptized, now that I am eight years old. My father, Verl F. Scott, who is also my bishop, performed the baptism. I was scared to be baptized because I can't swim and I had never put my face underwater before. After walking into the baptismal font in my white clothes, with warm water up to my chest, my father held me with his strong hands. I plugged my nose, and my father said in his resonating voice, "Colleen Scott, having been commissioned of Jesus Christ, I baptize you in the name of the Father, and of the Son, and of the Holy Ghost. Amen" (D & C 20:73). I was immersed in the water—and did not drown!

After coming up and walking into the changing room, where my mother waited with a fluffy white towel, I felt so exceedingly happy! I knew my sins had been washed away, and I had willingly decided to follow Jesus throughout my life. Afterward, I went out to eat with my parents at a restaurant. It was a very special day. I tried to be perfect after I was baptized, but I got mad at my sister later, so I had to repent.

JULY 1957

My sisters and I had a sleepover at our neighbor's house. We spread our sleeping bags out on the lawn and slept in their backyard. After we all fell asleep, I woke up at about three o'clock in the morning. The city lights were not as bright as earlier in the night. I was amazed as I looked up at the black night sky to see so many stars—more than I had ever seen before. Thousands of them shining against the darkness! It was just me and the universe! I felt awe and wonder at the millions of stars created by God—and to know that I was also His creation, His child. What great power and majesty I was witnessing in the sky! It was a special experience that I will never forget.

JULY 18, 1958

Today I was playing baseball in our backyard with some neighborhood kids and two of my sisters. I was up to bat, and I hit the ball hard. I was getting pretty good at batting. Then I heard a big crash. The ball had broken our bathroom window! I didn't get in trouble, because it was an accident. My sisters and I have a lot of fun with all the neighborhood kids. We play baseball and skate on the sidewalks and driveways. We make trains by tying all our wagons and tricycles together. It's usually my job to do that. We have lots of fun, except when our next-door neighbor's mother gets mad at us for no reason, and then our mother asks us to apologize, even if we didn't do anything wrong. We must keep peace with the neighbors.

We have to set a good example because Daddy is the bishop. We can't play outside on Sunday, of course, because it is the Sabbath day. On Sundays we go to church and then stay inside with our family and have a big dinner. My mom plays the organ at church, and my sisters and I have to sit quietly by ourselves in the second row. I like to listen to the speakers and sing the songs. It gives me a happy feeling inside.

DECEMBER 7, 1960

Today was the best day because my mom had a baby boy! After six girls, we finally have a boy, and my dad is so happy about it, although he loves all his girls too. My dad says that now he feels that everyone is here and that our family is complete. The only sad thing is that my baby brother, Richard, has clubfeet, which means they are turned inward, and he is going to come home with little casts on his legs to straighten them out. This is about the first time there have been any medical problems in my family, except when Barbara, my fifth sister, was born. She had to have a blood transfusion because she was turning yellow from the Rh factor my mom has. But she's okay now.

Now we also get to live in our dream house that my mom designed and my parents had built. It's big and wonderful, and it makes us feel really special to live here. We have a chandelier in the dining room and a big balcony out in the back where we can see the lights of Salt Lake City, and where we sleep outside in the summer. Oh, and we have a tennis court in the backyard.

SEPTEMBER 1962

What a sad time for our family! My dad, who is a major in the Utah National Guard, just left to drive to Fort Hood, Texas. He will be there for about a year because his unit was called to active duty due to the Berlin Crisis. The East Germans have just put up a wall in Berlin so that people cannot leave East Germany to go to West Germany. This is a national crisis that the US military is responding to by calling more troops to active duty. Last night, we had a special family home evening.

My dad gave each of us a father's priesthood blessing, laying his hands on our heads and speaking comforting words of love and guidance to bless us for the next year. Then we had family prayer with hugs and lots of tears. Mom and all the kids are staying here in Salt Lake so we can remain in our schools. I am in ninth grade now. We will miss our dad terribly! He is a wonderful husband and father.

NOVEMBER 1962

Guess what! We are moving to Texas! My dad missed us so much, and there is housing for families at Fort Hood, so we are all moving there! I'm excited and scared. I've never moved away from Salt Lake City before. So, I'm saying goodbye to all my friends.

JUNE 1963

Well, now that we've been here in Texas for seven months, I absolutely love Texas! I am in the ninth grade at school. I love the humidity and the wide-open spaces where you can look for miles across flat land. I love our church congregation and all the fun things we have been doing in the youth group. Every Tuesday we have Mutual, which is when the teenagers and soldiers get together at one of the buildings on post. We have spiritual lessons, but we also have lots of fun activities and dances. I love the dances! We had a sock hop, which was really fun, where we danced in decorated socks. I'm making a scrapbook of my time in Texas, with photographs and autographs. I will hate to leave. But I have learned not to be so shy in Texas, so it has been fun.

AUGUST 1963

This is one of the saddest days of my life. We are leaving Texas to go back to Salt Lake City. My dad's time at Fort Hood is over. As we drive away and I see the bluebonnets and the wide fields of grass, I think I will probably never come back here again in my life. I feel so depressed about it.

MAY 1965

I just graduated from Skyline High School in my cap and gown. I have a scholarship to Brigham Young University in Provo, Utah, and will be going there in the fall. One of my friends from Texas goes to

BYU, and I've visited her there in the dorms. It is so fun, and there are lots of dances. I will be majoring in English because I loved my AP English class in high school. I got a Yamaha guitar from Korea for graduation. My dad bought it when he went to Korea for a National Guard training. It's really nice. A friend has been teaching me some chords and songs.

APRIL 1966

I've had a wonderful time at Brigham Young University this past year. I met a very nice boy who was a friend of my Arizona roommates, and we started dating. Then he was called to be a missionary to New York. I'm proud of his desire to serve the Lord and to be worthy to do so by living righteously. So he is gone, and I am writing to him. School has been hard work, and I've spent lots of time in the library doing my homework.

We just had a big surprise as a family. My father has been called to be the mission president of about two hundred Mormon missionaries for the Western States Mission, with headquarters in Denver, Colorado. Dad called us all to come home, and we met in the living room so he could tell us of this very special calling from the general authorities of the church. He would like all of us to go to Denver. That means I will have to leave college for a year, but it sounds like a wonderful, inspiring adventure, so I'm excited to go. Our family will live in the mission home, which is really a big, old mansion. My dad is helping my sister Wendy and me to apply for full-time jobs as typists at the Denver Federal Center so we can work and save money for next year's college expenses.

JULY 1967

Well, I've been in Denver for a year living with my family in the mission home. It has been a great experience. This is a great place to live. The mission home mansion has a large stone porch with huge pillars in the front. Then you go into the foyer, which has a big grandfather clock and a wide, carpeted wooden staircase (with a stained glass window at the top of it) that winds up to the second floor. The first floor also has a ladies' sitting room with fancy, old-fashioned stuffed chairs; a men's sitting room with a big leather couch and chair and a big, tall fireplace; a huge dining room with an oval wooden table that seats about twenty-five people; a smaller dining room with a table that seats ten people; and a big kitchen. The ceilings are high and painted with gold leaf designs and flowers. There is also a big pantry and a sunroom with big windows on the first floor.

We have a jolly southern cook, Sister Stokes, who cooks most of the meals. We have great food and dessert every night, and we all take turns doing the dishes according to a chore chart.

Oh, by the way, our family lives on the second floor, which has four bedrooms, two bathrooms, and an office. About ten missionaries live on the third floor (where we never go), which has their bedrooms and a former ballroom which is now used as a study room. These missionaries are the office staff for the mission and also the assistants to the president, the best missionaries of all. We all eat dinner together around the huge table in the main dining room at 6:00 p.m. In the basement are the mission offices. The missionaries are fun to talk to, but they have to keep busy doing their missionary work and publishing the *WestState* magazine every month. I've had crushes on a couple of the missionaries, but of course there is no dating. I might see them when I return to BYU in the fall when they are off their missions.

The missionaries in the mission home have a football team named the 709ers. My sisters and I are cheerleaders for their team when they play against other elders in the area. It is really fun. In spite of these fun times once a week, there is a special, sacred feeling in the mission home as we observe the missionaries' dedication to preaching the gospel to people in Denver who are interested.

JULY 1967

I received a phone call telling me that my best friend from high school, Bonnie Barker, has been killed in an automobile accident in Blackfoot, Idaho. She was riding with her fiancé to meet his parents. While she was sleeping in the back seat, he drove upon some construction on the highway in the dark. Somehow the car swerved the wrong way and crashed. Bonnie was thrown out of the car, was taken to the hospital, and died the next day. When I heard the news, I ran into my bedroom and sobbed on my pillow. They were going to be married in just two weeks! I was going to be one of her bridesmaids in Salt Lake City! But instead of going to her wedding, I would be going to her funeral.

Bonnie truly had the gift of love as well as a pure faith in the gospel. She accomplished much in her life in learning the lesson of loving people. As tragic as her death was, it made me feel that somehow all was okay and that she had accomplished her mission on the earth.

OCTOBER 1967

Well, I'm back at Brigham Young University in Provo, Utah, as a sophomore. I am living in an off-campus apartment with one of my old roommates and her three friends from Arizona. It's fun. Guess what! Elder Michael Curzon and three other elders from the mission who are now going to BYU stopped by my apartment to say hi. (We called them elders while they were on their missions, but they are in their early twenties.) What a nice surprise! Later, I saw Elder Curzon (Mike) on campus, and he carried my books and walked me to class.

I don't know Mike very well. Even though he lived in the mission home and was an assistant to the president to my dad, we didn't talk much in Denver. Mike didn't spend time socializing with the Scott sisters, because he was a very dedicated missionary, so I have a lot of respect for him in that regard. He tells me how he misses his mission very much and even sheds some tears over it when he's going to sleep at night. I respect the fact that he loves serving the Lord so much.

OCTOBER 8, 1967

We've just had the most incredible meeting in the Joseph Smith Fieldhouse here at BYU. Hugh B. Brown from the church's First Presidency spoke to us. He told this story:

As he was leaving for his mission, his mother reminded him that when he was a little boy, he would sometimes have nightmares and call out to her in the night, "Mother! Are you there?"

His mother said something like, "Now when you have bad times, I will not be there, but you can always call out and say, 'Father, are You there?' Your heavenly Father will hear you and come to your aid."

President Brown said, "When each of you have problems in life, you can call out, 'Father, are You there?' You are His child, and He will answer your prayers. There will come into your heart a feeling of comfort and solace" (Brown 1967).

As he told this story, the Spirit of the Lord filled the huge arena, and we all felt the love of our Heavenly Father for us. It was a very special and memorable experience.

MAY 1968

Mike Curzon and I have been dating quite a bit this year, and I enjoy being with him a lot. He is a very good person, and he makes me laugh. I was attracted to him as he told me about being raised in the Idaho countryside and catching horses after school to ride. He was in the army before his mission for three years, serving as a medic. He told me a powerful story about treating all the officers for venereal disease and deciding that he would never be immoral as they had been, for he knew his dad would never have succumbed to such temptation. He was reading a lot of church books his mother had sent him in his spare time and saying his prayers. One night he walked a pretty Korean girl home after an army dance, and she invited him to come into her bed. He felt a powerful feeling from God saying, "Noooo!" He refused her offer and walked home with a wonderful feeling in his heart of having a clear conscience.

JUNE 1968

I have been in Denver visiting my parents at the mission home for two weeks before returning to summer school at BYU. Mike and I broke up because he was undecided as to whom he wanted to marry, me or another girl. I prayed a lot and told the Lord that I wanted to marry Mike and asked, if it was right, if He would please let Mike know. I returned to my apartment in Provo, Utah, and fasted for two days, eating dinner in between. I prayed that Mike would know whether he was supposed to marry me. How surprised I was when he knocked on my door and invited me to walk downtown with him to go see a movie. It was *Yours, Mine and Ours*, a story about a big family and a happy marriage.

I was so happy to be with him, and we went out the next two nights also. He acted extra kind, and I was wondering what was going on. Finally he said, "Colleen, have you been praying for me?" I said that I had. He told me that as he was walking to my apartment, the Spirit of the Lord rested upon him and told him that we should get married. It was a definite answer to my fasting and prayers! The warm summer night and the love in my heart for Mike, along with a special calm feeling that this was right, filled my heart with such joy and peace. It was a dream come true. His strong hands holding mine and a special kiss caused my heart to flutter. It was true love, and it was right.

AUGUST 1968

Mike and I have had a wonderful summer of being engaged, taking long walks in the evening summer air and talking about our future. We've talked about our mutual desire to have a big family, maybe eight children or more, and Mike set a rule that we have only one goodnight kiss each night during our engagement. He is so wise in making this rule so that we will have no problem keeping ourselves morally clean for our temple marriage, which is in November. He is truly a spiritual person who loves the Lord and strives to do what is right. That gives me so much respect for him. I also like that he is so outgoing and friendly to people and that he has a strong confidence about him.

NOVEMBER 14, 1968

This is our wedding day—a cold morning with the giant spires of the Salt Lake Temple reaching into the blue sky. I was nervous, but the ceremony was sacred and wonderful. We knelt, holding hands across the altar in the elaborate wedding room, and were pronounced husband and wife for time and for all eternity. I can't believe we are actually married! We had a wonderful reception with hundreds of people greeting us, including many friends of my parents who were general authorities in the church, since my dad has worked in the Church Office Building for the church magazines for many years.

FEBRUARY 1969

Marriage has been "real and earnest," as my dad always says. We live in a small, cheap apartment, and we are both going to college. We don't have a lot of money. I have to iron and cook and clean. It is an adjustment to be a wife.

But we have also had wonderful times together and have felt God's love surrounding us at times, telling us that we were meant to be together and that we were promised to each other in the pre-earth life. It has been a spiritual experience to be married. Also, it looks like I am now going to have a baby, something we have wanted. I'm getting morning sickness. My sweet husband is taking care of me, and he brought me a sweet booklet about baby boys. (He tells me he knows we are having a boy.)

SEPTEMBER 13, 1969

Today, our son, Jonathan Scott Curzon, was born! The labor did not go well, and after twenty-four hours, the doctors decided Jonathan needed to be born by cesarean section. I was relieved. Mike was sad that I had to have surgery. He had given me a priesthood blessing before we went to the hospital that all would go well. But all his sadness was swept away once he saw Jonathan. Things did go well, just not as we had expected. We feel blessed to have this special new baby from heaven.

NOVEMBER 1, 1969

Today Mike gave Jonathan his name and baby blessing in church, surrounded by other men who hold the priesthood. But Mike was unable to say much about our baby's future life, as usually happens in baby blessings. How strange. I wonder why his mind went blank. The congregation became uncomfortable as several seconds went by without any words being spoken. Finally, Mike quickly closed the blessing. After church we went home for a dinner with my parents, Verl and Arline Scott; my grandma Ruby Scott; and Barbara and Richard, my younger sister and brother. Life is just so perfect. Sometimes I feel like I need a new challenge to help me grow.

Honor the good things that your parents have taught you so that you don't have to reinvent the wheel in your own life. Spend quality time with your family in traditions that bring you together.

2

Too Pure to Stay

MAY 31, 1970

For six and a half months, our baby, Jonathan, was very healthy. He had no sickness whatsoever, except some colic in the early weeks that kept us up at night. In looking at him, there was a sense that he was somehow very wise. He seemed to radiate love and wisdom, as if he were an old spirit. More than one person commented upon this.

We enjoyed watching him grow and learn to eat solid food—he loved Gerber oatmeal cereal with bananas. We had fun watching him laugh at puppies, scoot around on the floor, say "Da-da," and get his first two bottom teeth. Mike would bounce Jonathan on his knee and sing songs about riding a horse. He would also play peekaboo with him.

I'll always remember how his dark hair stuck straight up no matter how it was wetted down. His eyes were a color you couldn't describe—first a sort of charcoal gray, then gradually getting specks of green and brown. He gained weight well, getting quite chubby by three months of age. We had a special mother-baby bond that formed as I nursed him at my breast. There is really nothing like such a bond in the world. He had complete and innocent trust in me.

Around the end of March, Jonathan began to have a slight cough, wouldn't eat well, and seemed lethargic. The doctor was not too concerned but gave him some medicine and said to bring him back in two weeks. I called the doctor, very concerned, before the two weeks, telling him that Jonathan's color was a little bluish. I somehow felt that he had a life-threatening illness. Jonathan seemed to have difficulty breathing, but Mike gave him a blessing and believed he would be okay.

11

The doctor was very alarmed when he saw Jonathan again and referred us to a pediatrician, who put Jonathan in the Provo hospital in an oxygen tent, saying he had viral pneumonia. Under the oxygen, Jonathan's color became pink again, and we were very encouraged. But this lasted only a few days, and then he became increasingly worse. When I held him, I was alarmed at how thin his little arms had become. He put his arms around my neck, clinging to me and crying when I had to go home. (In those days, parents were not allowed to stay with their children in the hospital.) I didn't know that these would be the last times I would be able to hold him in my arms.

Soon the doctor said he thought Jonathan had a rare kind of pneumonia, *Pneumocystis carinii*. He wanted to transfer Jonathan to the University of Utah Hospital in Salt Lake City. I was very afraid. I called my dad, and he said, "Colleen, have faith!" After I hung up with my father, I knelt by the couch and cried my heart out to God. I told him my fears and concerns. Suddenly a deep peace, like a blanket, came over me. I felt my Heavenly Father's love and concern for my sadness. In my mind, He explained to me kindly that Jonathan was His son before he was mine and that whatever happened would be the right thing in His infinite wisdom. From that time forward, I felt great strength to meet what was coming next. I suddenly knew a new definition of faith. It was *trust*. I trusted the powers of heaven to do the right and the eternally best thing for our lives.

After Jonathan was taken in the ambulance the next day to the university hospital, it wasn't long before my dad and Mike gave him a blessing. During the prayer, whereas before we had been so sad and afraid, the room was suddenly filled with a great, tangible feeling of love and peace that calmed our hearts. All of us felt it. Again, we knew that God was watching over us in this trying time. We assumed it meant that Jonathan would be cured.

The doctors did a lung biopsy on Jonathan and then put him on a respirator in the intensive care unit. They said they would treat him as if he had *Pneumocystis carinii* with a drug called pentamidine, but they weren't sure it would work, because the disease was advanced. This type of pneumonia is only seen in people with severe deficiencies of the immune system. With the respirator, there was no sound when Jonathan cried, as the tube was between his vocal cords. We tried to cheer him with some little rubber animal toys. His favorite was the giraffe, which he could hold on to with his little hand around the neck. We were only allowed to be with him fifteen minutes at a time. Then we had to wait in the hall. It was terrible! There was no good place to be. To see him so ill was unbearable. To be away from him was torture.

The doctors told us they did not expect him to live. It was so frightening to hear these words, yet we believed that there could be a miracle if it was God's will. The previous two months of his illness were a blur and a nightmare. I couldn't believe what had happened that had changed my life so drastically.

We stayed at my mom and dad's house in Salt Lake City. I remember sitting at the piano sadly leafing through the hymnbook. I found some wonderful hymns that comforted me. One went like this:

> Though deepening trials throng your way,
> Press on, press on, ye saints of God...
> Though tribulations rage abroad,
> Christ says, "In me ye shall have peace" (Snow 1998, 122).

I also found the following hymn:

> Come, ye disconsolate, where'er ye languish;
> Come to the mercy seat, fervently kneel.
> Here bring your wounded hearts; here tell your anguish.
> Earth has no sorrow that heav'n cannot heal (Moore 1998, 115).

I cried as I sang the hymns, but they gave me comfort and hope during this horrible time.

During those two weeks, Jonathan's heart stopped more than once. After he was revived by electric shock the first time, we could see that his bright, shining spirit was still there, looking out through his eyes. The second time that did not seem to be the case. The doctors told us that he was brain-dead. Within a few hours he died. The date was May 26, 1969. He was eight and a half months old.

It was death, the real thing—the thing you think will never come into your life on a firsthand basis. Our baby was gone! I remember his little gray body in the dimly lit hospital room, lying stiff on the white stretcher. There was no movement, no light in his eyes, no personality. Jonathan himself was gone. The spontaneous question came to my mind, *Where did he go?* The essence that had once made his body alive—that had given it happiness and sadness and responsiveness— the real little person inside had departed ... somewhere. My soul responded back with an answer. Jonathan was with God in the highest celestial spheres! He was happy. He was no longer suffering. And all was right and as it should be. All of this had been in the Lord's plan for him and was no surprise to God, although it had been a shock to my unsuspecting mortal mind. But, indeed, all was well.

The knowledge of these things was a tangible presence with me. It seemed, indeed, more real than the "real world" around me. It was true, and I knew it! What need was there for tears? Fear had been replaced by faith in my heart. All was well with Jonathan. The Mormon hymn "Come, Come, Ye Saints," which I had sung all my life, expresses it well:

> And should we die before our journey's through—
> Happy day! All is well!
> We then are free from toil and sorrow too.
> With the just we shall dwell (Clayton 1998, 30).

I knew I would see my baby again, would hold him and even raise him to maturity, after the resurrection, when the spirits of all men are reunited to become perfect, immortal bodies. I had been taught this all my life. But now it was more than an intellectual idea. It was a feeling, a faith, a knowledge. It was true, and I knew it.

We buried Jonathan in a little casket and a baby-blue outfit that had a little giraffe on it. He looked so sweet. We bought two burial plots for a payment of five dollars a month for several years, and were given a baby-sized plot for free. The plots lay across from a field with a white horse and beautiful tall mountains. (Little did we know how we would need those plots in upcoming years.)

It all seemed so unreal, but amid our sadness, Mike and I were upheld by our absolute faith. A great sense of peace enveloped us and kept us from feeling overwhelming sorrow. It is as if we were being lifted up on a cloud of comfort and peace before and during the funeral.

As hard as it has been, this has been a deeply spiritual experience. We know our baby was pure enough to not have to go through this trying mortal life, and our goal is to live in such a way as to be worthy to be with him again. The founder of our church, Joseph Smith, taught:

> The Lord takes many away, even in infancy, that they may escape … the sorrows and evils of this present world; they were too pure, too lovely, to live on earth. Therefore, when rightly considered, instead of mourning, we have reason to rejoice as they are delivered from evil and we shall soon have them again (Smith 2007, 176).

What a comfort it is to read these words and to know that if we are faithful, we will be able to raise Jonathan to adulthood after this life. He is sealed and promised to us in the temple to be our son for eternity. Our faith in these principles is absolute and gives us great strength to go on with our lives. I am so grateful for the immeasurable comfort God has given me in this terrible circumstance.

JUNE 1970

Jonathan's death has hit me harder now, and I cry as I pack his little clothes away in a box. My precious baby son is gone! I see now how painfully naive I have been when it comes to life-and-death situations and illnesses. Naive and unaware. I would now do things so much differently if it happened again. I would go to the doctor sooner. I would yell and scream that something was terribly wrong. Maybe it was my fault. Maybe I could have prevented this. But I just didn't know, and truly the doctors didn't know either. It was such a rare disease that it caught us all by surprise. Condemning myself or feeling guilty for what I was ignorant of won't bring him back. I suppose we could sue the doctor who didn't take Jonathan's illness seriously at first. But to do so is not in my heart.

Mike graduated from Brigham Young University with a bachelor's degree in child development and family relations. Because graduation was just a few days after Jonathan's funeral, we did not go or participate in it. It is painful when I see old friends and they ask me how my baby is. How awkward it is to have to tell them that he died.

15

I wrote a song about Jonathan:

> Jonathan, my son, when you came to earth,
> You were wanted. We had known
> You were a son, a special one.
> Jonathan, my son, your eyes were oh so bright.
> You seemed to know the wisdom you
> Had known in heav'n, but that you could not tell.
> onathan, my son, your time was oh so short.
> You brought us laughter. You brought us tears.
> Then your spirit left for years!
> Jonathan, my son, save a place for me
> With the angels, with the pure,
> With the Savior whose love is sure.

JULY 1970

Mike and I are moving to California to be home parents for Ettie Lee's Boys' Home. This will help us to move on and go to a new place. Maybe our sorrow will be relieved a little bit. Our job is to be parents for wayward teenage boys. It will be a challenge.

AUGUST 1970

We received the autopsy report from the doctor. Our baby, Jonathan, did have the rare *Pneumocystis carinii* pneumonia. This is something that only people with very poor immune systems get, as explained in the following medical paper: "*Pneumocystis carinii* pneumonia is relatively common during the first few months of life and its presence may be the first clue that the child has hyper IgM syndrome" (Immune Deficiency Foundation 2013, 63). The doctors tell us that our baby, Jonathan, had a very rare genetic immune deficiency that is carried on the X chromosome.

Any other baby boys I bear will have a fifty-fifty chance of having this immune deficiency, called hypogammaglobulinemia. The doctors say that this disease can be treated with gamma globulin shots, so that is good. This immune deficiency is something we will have to be very aware of with any other children that we have. We want to have another baby soon, but for now the crib is put away.

[*Note*: The doctors did not have the present name for my son's disease for several years. They first called it hypogammaglobulinemia, then X-linked agammaglobulinemia, the prognosis of which is promising: "Adults can have productive careers and families. A full active lifestyle is to be encouraged and expected" (ibid., 17). This is what the immunologists told us until after all my children were born. The true, more serious prognosis of their disease, now called hyper-IgM syndrome or CD40 ligand deficiency, was not known or told to us until the year 2000. Then the doctors at the National Institutes of Health informed us that statistically our boys had only a 20 percent chance of living until age twenty-five. The Immune Deficiency Foundation wrote in 2013 that hyper-IgM patients "may encounter additional problems including susceptibility to more dangerous types of infections as well as the development of autoimmune disorders and cancer" (ibid., 65). This was a shock to us. However, I do think that patients who receive the newer treatment, IV gamma globulin, from infancy will be found to have a better prognosis, as seems to be the case with my youngest son Richard, who has had thirty years of relatively good health.]

If you have experienced the death of a loved one, know that you can be strong, just as millions of others in the world have been strong. You can go on, with God's help.

3

Happy Years

NOVEMBER 1970

Last summer we got a job as a couple in Los Angeles, California, at Ettie Lee's Boys' Home, being home parents to troubled teenage boys. It was challenging and a little fun sometimes. It distracted us from the sadness in our hearts about Jonathan. At the end of the summer, we decided to return to BYU for Mike to work on his master's degree. We rented one side of a nice little duplex, and I got a job at BYU working as a secretary. I'm also taking some evening classes. We hope to pay some of Jonathan's $2,000 medical bill from the University of Utah Hospital. The bill is a big worry to me. We did have insurance when Jonathan was sick, but it didn't pay for the full bill. Because he was in intensive care for two weeks, his treatment was very expensive.

We are expecting our second baby in March! I have been sick at work, sometimes vomiting three times a day in the bathroom. I try to nibble on cheese and crackers and apples. We look forward to our new baby, but of course no one can take Jonathan's place. Each child is loved for himself or herself.

APRIL 1971

I quit work in March to get ready for our new baby's birth. It was a boy born the end of March. He is just so darling with great big eyes and dark hair. We have named him Jeremy Michael Curzon. He is so cute. I don't even mind getting up in the night with him. What a blessing he is! The doctor says his gamma globulin is a little low, so Mike is giving him gamma shots every week. (Mike was a medic in the army before we were married, so he knows how to do it.) But Jeremy is doing very well with no sicknesses.

OCTOBER 1971

We've been having a lot of enjoyable times with our baby, Jeremy. He is loved very much. He is crawling around on the floor now and is a lot of fun. Mike is teaching classes at school as a graduate student. We have some friends next door who also have a new baby, so we enjoy visiting with them.

JUNE 5, 1972

When summer came, Mike could not find a job, so we are living with my parents temporarily in Salt Lake City. Our third baby (second living) is due the end of this month. I want to have these children close together so that they can be playmates, as me and my sister, Wendy, were. These two children will be fifteen months apart. Mike is staying in California with some college friends to see if he can find a job down there. Today my mom and I took Jeremy to the zoo, and we walked around a lot. He loved seeing the animals. He can say a few words, like "Hi, Mommy!" He's very cute now with blond hair and hazel eyes. I wanted to have his picture taken, but he fell down and got a cut on his face, so I postponed it. Tonight I am worried because I seem to be having some labor pains. I hope they go away as I go to sleep. It's too soon. Mike needs to come back first.

FEBRUARY 1973

Well, Mike came home on the bus after finding a job in California as a salesman for an auto parts computer system company. When I picked him up at the bus station, he said he felt like I was going to have a girl. He was right—a beautiful baby girl with dark hair was born the last week of June. I had a C-section again. We named her Jessica after two weeks of trying to decide just the right name. Jeremy gives her kisses, but I think he is also a little jealous of the attention she gets.

We got a U-Haul trailer and drove across the hot California desert to live in Huntington Beach, California. Mom and Dad gave us a newer car. We live in a nice apartment just fifteen minutes from the beach. There is a little patio behind the kitchen. It is beautiful here with the palm trees and ocean breeze.

I stay home with my two little ones. I just love my little family—a boy and a girl. They are both healthy, although Jessica has a runny nose right now. We've been calling her "Jessicawa Running Nose."

Jeremy did get a fever after his immunizations but was soon okay again. He seems to be doing fine without gamma globulin shots, so he must not have the immune deficiency. I play ball and blocks with Jeremy. He likes his alphabet blocks the best and can build neat things and is learning his letters. We have family home evening with Jeremy and teach him about Jesus. Then Mike playfully throws him up in the air. Jeremy loves it and says, "Again, again!" Jessica scoots around on the floor and is so beautiful with her dark hair and eyes turning brown. She's a happy baby. I sing songs to my babies, like "Rhythm of the Rain" as we look out the window when it is raining. Sometimes we all go to the beach, and our children play in the sand.

Mike has been called to be second counselor in the bishopric of our ward congregation. He also teaches early-morning seminary religion classes to teenagers. We have also enjoyed attending religious classes taught by a friend we admire. Life seems complete and good.

Joy will come in the morning. The sun will shine again after the dark clouds of life have passed.

4

Transitions

NOVEMBER 1973

We have moved back to Salt Lake City and are living in a small apartment, preparing to return to college. Mike is working nights at Buehner Block Company running a huge kiln and train cars to make cement building blocks. He came close to being killed by a huge train car one night when he didn't turn a switch soon enough. But the Spirit warned him just in time, and he was okay.

I have been really sick lately with a lot of severe abdominal pain. I even had to stay at my mom's house for two weeks so that she could tend the kids while I was in bed. I thought it must be appendicitis, but the doctor said it was an infected fallopian tube. I got some medicine but still have had a lot of pain if I get out of bed.

DECEMBER 1973

The abdominal pain continued. I went back to the doctor, who did several tests, and before I knew it, I was in the hospital having emergency surgery at midnight after receiving two units of blood. It all happened so fast. The doctor said he thought I had a tubal or ectopic pregnancy, where a baby grows outside the uterus. He said that he would have to remove my fallopian tube and possibly my uterus, preventing me from having more children. This was very frightening to me. But then I remembered a special feeling I'd had a few months earlier while attending the Salt Lake Temple. I'd had the impression that there was another little boy waiting to be born into our family. With that remembrance, I felt more at peace as I went into surgery. Afterward, I was happy to find out that my childbearing abilities had not been lost. They found a blood clot as big as a grapefruit in my abdomen. I could have lost my life, but I'm home now, although very weak and tired. I'm taking care of my little ones, but we all stay in our pajamas all day and are taking it very easy.

JANUARY 1974

All of a sudden we find ourselves back in Provo, Utah. Mike found out in the first part of this month that he could get back into the master's degree program in child development and counseling at BYU. He is happy to continue his education. We live in an apartment house with a stream in the back and large areas of lawn (now covered with snow). I'm babysitting a little girl to earn more money. Mike is going to school and teaching child development classes as a graduate student. He sings to Jeremy and Jessica every night before they go to sleep, singing songs with lyrics like "Dearest children, God is near you, watching o'er you day and night" (Walker 1998, 96). He's a good dad.

JULY 1974

Summer is here, and the green grass around our apartment is beautiful. We recently had a party outside for Jessica's second birthday. She wore a pretty blue dress. She talks in complete sentences and is a real cutie with her long dark hair and big brown eyes.

DECEMBER 1975

A year has passed while Mike has worked on his master's degree. He also had a job as a painter at Primary Children's Hospital this past summer. We are happy to be expecting another baby in June. In fact, while he was in the hospital elevator one day, Mike felt the presence of the special spirit of the boy we are going to have. He felt such a kinship and bond of love with this spirit. It was a wonderful experience for him. I too feel the special spirit of this baby boy. I assume this boy is the one I felt was to be born when I was in the Salt Lake Temple.

A very exciting thing has happened! Mike is being hired to be an army chaplain. He was endorsed to represent the church after we were interviewed by one of the twelve apostles of the church. It was awe-inspiring to be in the apostle's office at the Latter-day Saints (LDS) Church Office Building and to have him ask Mike whether he was worthy to be a chaplain. Mike has been going through training by the church. We will be assigned to Fort Benning, Georgia in June after he goes through the chaplain training school at Fort Hamilton in New

York City. His master's degree training as a counselor has finally paid off! We'll make about three times more money than we do now and will have housing and medical benefits. What a blessing!

JANUARY 1975

This month we drove across the country to Hershey, Pennsylvania, where my sister Wendy and her husband, Tom, and their children live in a beautiful big house. My kids and I stayed with them while Mike went on to New York City to attend Army Chaplain School. We attend church here with them in a little old rickety white church. There is snow on the ground, and I feel homesick and somewhat out of place. Mike has been driving here on the weekends to see us, which has been nice. But now he is asking me, Jeremy, and Jessica to go with him to New York City for the last five weeks of training at Fort Hamilton. I'm scared, but we will go.

FEBRUARY 1975

We arrived in Brooklyn, New York, and stayed in a big army guesthouse for a few days. It was an old, wood building. We shared a bathroom with another family and cooked food in an electric frying pan we kept in our small, dark bedroom. Luckily there were some swings outside that the kids could play on. But I just felt anxious. We were referred to a ten-story hotel in Brooklyn that has kitchen suites, and we are now staying on the seventh floor in a pretty big room with two beds and a TV. It feels like a tenement building, and I feel fearful all the time. I fear that we will be hurt by criminals or that the building will burn down. A big, dirty city is not where I am used to living.

We watch *Little House on the Prairie*. We wash our clothes in the bathroom sink and hang them to dry overnight. The little kitchenette allows us to cook, and we have a small refrigerator. The water out of the tap has a rusty color to it. Kind of scary. I'm five months pregnant and starting to show. Mike goes to school every morning and doesn't get home until five. He is so happy to have us here. I can't bear to tell him that I am not thrilled to be in this situation, but it is only for five more weeks.

MARCH 5, 1975

After being here three weeks, I have become a little braver and have taken the kids to the beach, which is only two blocks away. We go to movies on post with Mike, and we went to see the American Museum of Natural History which has a huge squid hanging from the ceiling. We attend church on Sunday in a big, old redbrick building. The people are nice enough, but still, the dark depression I feel will not go away. I can't wait to leave this place.

MARCH 29, 1975

We have moved again, this time to off-post housing in Columbus, Georgia, near Fort Benning. It's beautiful here, and my depression has disappeared. There is green grass and little squirrels running up the trees. We live in a very small but nice house. I just needed to get out of the big city. It was such a culture shock to live there. But now I am back in more-familiar surroundings with small houses, grass, and trees. Even if it is two thousand miles from Utah, it feels good to be here. Mike is starting his job as a real army chaplain complete with fatigues, boots, hat, and all. He looks so handsome as a soldier!

MAY 1975

We're moving again! We have lived in five places in five months! I guess that's army life! Now we have been placed in officer housing at Fort Benning. It is a little nicer with shiny hardwood floors, and we can order furniture from post—a big, dark wooden dining table, chairs, cabinets, and beds. It has also been fun to go to a real furniture store and buy new things. We are in a subdivision of other similar redbrick houses surrounded by lots of green grass.

MAY 6, 1975 (MIKE'S JOURNAL)

My goal in keeping this journal is not to keep a daily record of all my family's doings. My goal is simply to record outstanding events, especially those which are faith promoting to my children and their children. My wife and I would like to make our inspired experiences more easily passed on to our dear children, whom we love with all our hearts.

JUNE 28, 1975

Today is Jessica's birthday. She is three years old and is finally potty-trained. She is beautiful with long brown ponytails, rambunctious and fun, and a good friend to her brother Jeremy. My third son, Seth Thomas Curzon, was born yesterday, June 27, in the hospital in Columbus, Georgia. The night before his birth, I sensed that he has a very special spirit and is known in the heavens as one of the great ones. I also felt Seth's love for me about a month ago, when I was discouraged trying to take care of my children. I felt he was telling me of his love and appreciation for bringing him into the world. He must have a mighty spirit to communicate with both Mike and me before he was even born.

Mike gave me a beautiful priesthood blessing the day before I left for the hospital. He said the angels of heaven would watch over me and that I would feel the comfort of the Holy One of Israel and would feel His arms around me. What a wonderful blessing. It gave me strength as I went into surgery for the C-section.

Seth has blue eyes and a touch of blond amid his dark hair. He has a calm spirit, and, just as with my other babies, it is a very precious experience to nurse him as he trustingly stares up at me.

Keep following your educational dreams. A whole new world of opportunity awaits you.

5

Chaplaincy—the Agony and the Ecstasy

AUGUST 16, 1975

Our little Seth, at six weeks old, suddenly stopped eating and was very weak, so we took him to the doctor on post here at Fort Benning. The doctor said that it is very dangerous for such a young baby to be so ill, so they put him in the hospital. After doing several tests, they said that he has aseptic (or viral) meningitis. He will be hospitalized for a few days, but they expect him to recover. I hope this will not cause him any kind of brain damage, which meningitis can do.

SEPTEMBER 6, 1975

Seth is fine now after his one-week stay in the army hospital. The experience scared us a little. Now he usually sleeps through the night. So chubby already! And he smiles a lot.

I've been holding "school" for my children this past week for a little while every day. It's so fun, and they really need the attention. I am trying to be much kinder and ignore their bad behavior. It is working wonders in my relationships with them. They are much more obedient and cooperative. I am so happy lately. Mike and I had family council last week, and it has had a far-reaching effect for good. We had a date last night, as we try to do every Friday now. We need that time together. Last week Mike performed a marriage for a couple in the chapel on post. I was so proud of him, as he gave them excellent advice and looked so handsome in his army blues.

OCTOBER 30, 1975

Although Seth recovered from the meningitis, he is sick a lot with fevers and coughs. I take him to the doctor a lot. They think he is allergic to milk and soy, so he is getting a formula called Nutramagen. It tastes awful, but Seth doesn't seem to mind it. We'll see if this works.

In spite of the difficulties we are having with Seth's health, I am so happy to have my three children. I feel they have been sent to me from heaven to perform wonderful things during their time on earth.

NOVEMBER 21, 1975

I told the doctor about the immune deficiency that Jonathan had. So they tested Seth's blood, and they said he is okay. I asked, "Are you sure?" The doctor said, "It is just as clear as it would be if he was born without a nose." Yes, he was sure. But Seth is sick so often! We'll just have to keep treating him with antibiotics.

JANUARY 4, 1976

Mike and I have been looking forward to having more children while we are in the army. It looks like I am pregnant again, and I'm very happy about it. I had a dream about having five children, and they were all so happy. I look forward to that. Seth still gets sick frequently, but he always recovers, and he is getting chubby and cute.

I find it challenging to take care of Jeremy, Jessica, and Seth while also keeping the house clean and going to church and army wives' activities. Sometimes I get down on myself and on the kids. But the Lord has told me it is a sin to be down on myself when I am trying my best. I must not constantly berate myself for what I can't get done. *Don't worry so much about the house*, I tell myself. *The family comes first! Do your best at the moment and then relax.* My family's happiness is the measure of my success.

MARCH 1976

I have not been feeling very sick with this pregnancy, and now I know why. I started bleeding very heavily a few days ago. I lay down on the bed, and even then I felt like I was going to pass out from loss of blood.

Mike took me to the hospital that night in the station wagon. The doctors said I was having a miscarriage and that the baby had died. So I have lost my baby, which we were looking forward to. My neighbor brought over a rosebud in a vase to cheer me up. It was very nice of her.

MAY 2, 1976

Seth was quite ill recently, and I was very worried. I didn't know what to do, so I prayed for guidance. I was impressed with the idea of keeping a log of his illnesses, to record vital signs, and so on. As I did so, I discovered he was breathing ninety times per minute. I called the doctor, who said breathing that fast was very dangerous. Seth was diagnosed with pneumonia but recovered with antibiotic treatment.

JULY 1976

We had a family reunion at my sister's house in Pennsylvania. It was fun for all the little cousins to get together. During the trip, Mike and I attended the Washington, DC, Mormon temple. It was a tremendous experience for me. I felt very close to my husband and wrote a song to him:

> I'll follow you, my love. I'll follow you wherever you wander.
> O'er mountain, plain, or sea, I'll follow you wherever you lead.
> The Lord has given me to you to be a wife so true,
> To comfort and bless all through our lives on earth.

I also felt very close to my Savior in the temple, more than ever before or since. This has been a very spiritual time of my life, as I have had to lean on the Lord while living in a new state away from my family and with Mike gone a lot with the military. I want more than anything to please God in my life and to be a good wife, mother, and missionary. I choose to follow the Lord's ways, and it brings me great joy to decide this and to feel His love for me.

SEPTEMBER 1976

Jeremy has started kindergarten for half a day and is doing very well. Seeing him leave on the bus while I stayed home with Jessica and Seth was sad. Earlier this summer Mike went on a three-week trip in the field with the battalion as their chaplain. He held nightly meetings in the tent and had some good experiences. But for me, not having him here for so long was about the worst time of my life. Jeremy was getting good at throwing temper tantrums, and it was very hard to know what to do. Kindergarten will be a good chance for him to get away and do something constructive in school. He is a very creative little boy. At Halloween he filled a whole ream of paper with pictures of pumpkins, which we hung all over his room. He loves to draw and make things. We also got a swing set in the backyard and a Saint Bernard–collie puppy! So cute! Jessica loves for me to swing her in the swing, and they all enjoy going down the slide.

OCTOBER 1976

One Sunday we went out to see a house in the country that a man in our church said was for sale. We fell in love with it and were able to buy it! It's a large brick house on two and a half acres of land and has three large bedrooms, two bathrooms, a living room, a dining room, a family room, and a big kitchen! We are so excited to move there and live in the country as a family. Since the kindergarten out here goes all day long, I've decided to keep Jeremy home for kindergarten. I hate to have him gone for so long at his age. It will be fun to teach him his numbers, letters, and so on. The kids love living out here and playing with the dog outside in the red Georgia dirt. We also found a tortoise and decided to keep it as a pet, since Jeremy adores it. We are so happy to finally own a house of our own.

Seth continues to be sick on and off. For about a week he had a mouth full of sores and a fever. After reading about the symptoms, I believe it was an initial herpes infection. After that he got cold sores around his mouth at times from fevers. But in between illnesses, he is fun and sweet. He has a rocking horse on springs, and he likes to play outside with his tricycle and toy gun.

JANUARY 1977

A new year. Mike is moving to the 269th Battalion and is looking forward to having his own chapel services and serving with greater dedication than ever before in his chaplaincy. I look forward to serving well in our home.

FEBRUARY 10, 1977

It is pretty warm today. The kids played outside without coats. Last week Mike took all of us across the street and down a hill to a pretty little lake and woods to hike in. The owner said we could come anytime to swim or picnic.

Last week was Mike's first "Protestant" service on post as a chaplain (the army mistakenly classifies Mormons as Protestants). Mike gave a sermon, and I played the piano and gave a little talk that introduced our family. Jessica and I sang a little song. Jeremy wouldn't give his planned talk, but eighteen-month-old Seth was talking all the time! There were about ten men there. Several of them said they enjoyed the simplicity of the service.

Mike is having tremendous experiences as a chaplain. Some of the soldiers he has taught the gospel to have decided to be baptized. He also teaches LDS religion classes at the post once a week, with great success. He is truly a gifted teacher, and the Spirit shines through him. As a chaplain, Mike also performs marriage ceremonies for couples as well as funerals for soldiers and their families. Sometimes I play the organ for these services, which are held in Protestant post chapels. One funeral was for a man whose wife had shot him. She sat in the front row in handcuffs during the service. Another was for a black soldier named Motel. The service was held far out in the country. I accompanied Mike to the little church and played the organ. As Motel's family and friends passed the casket, they literally shouted and cried, "Motel! Motel!" They were very demonstrative. His brother was named Hotel. The whole experience was kind of strange to us. What interesting experiences Mike is having as a chaplain!

Jeremy still draws a lot and wants to study everything! He asks so many questions. He still throws tantrums sometimes, however, which is disconcerting. Seth, on the other hand, has a mild disposition and is so frequently sick. Four-year-old Jessica and I are best friends, but she mostly plays (or fights) with Jeremy all day. She helps me make bread and makes a small loaf for herself. Seth is nearing his terrible twos and is starting to climb out of the crib. He plays with toy trucks outside. Overall it is such a joy to have these children! And it is wonderful to live in the country as a family.

APRIL 5, 1977

Today is my thirtieth birthday. I am happily expecting my fifth child, and I feel that this is the same spirit that tried to come to our family last year but was miscarried. I wrote a poem about his bright spirit coming down from heaven and preparing to be born:

A Life Begins

In all my life
The deepest love, the holiest joy of eternities past,
Is the oneness I feel with you,
We meet, and now and then the bright light from eternity's door
swings wide—
The light streams forth!
And in the brightness, much brighter than suns,
A spirit walks forth—in blazing light!
And now a seed begins to grow.
No need for fear; just sleep and grow.
We bring you here from realms of light.
Now sleep and grow.

I am also reminded of this passage from William Wordsworth's poem "Intimations of Immortality":

Our birth is but a sleep and a forgetting.
The Soul that rises with us, our life's Star
Hath had elsewhere its setting,
And cometh from afar:

Not in entire forgetfulness,
And not in utter nakedness,
But trailing clouds of glory do we come
From God, who is our home
(Wordsworth 1993, 190).

AUGUST 12, 1977
Seth is in the hospital today at Fort Benning with an ear infection and a boil on his leg. When the doctors lanced the boil, there was no pus. A blood test showed that his white count is very low. This condition is called neutropenia. Now the doctors think Seth might have the immune deficiency that Jonathan had after all! They should have figured this out much sooner! The doctors are going to put tubes in Seth's ears because he has been having a lot of ear infections, which have caused his eardrums to rupture. As a handbook for patients explains:

31

Patients [with hyper-IgM syndrome] are prone to infections because they lack antibodies. The infections frequently occur at or near the surfaces of the mucus membranes, such as the middle ear, sinuses and lungs... (Immune Deficiency Foundation 2013, 15).

I learned that babies have their mothers' antibodies for several months, especially if they are being breastfed. That might be why the doctors missed diagnosing Seth's immune deficiency. Now they want Seth to take sulfa drugs every day and to stay away from crowds. If he gets a fever, he should go to the hospital! This is such a shocking diagnosis, but in a way I suspected it all along. Why didn't the doctors see it sooner? My trust in doctors is definitely waning.

SEPTEMBER 1977

The doctors sent us to a hospital in Atlanta, three hours away, for Seth to see a hematologist. The hematologist confirmed that Seth has the immune deficiency, hypogammaglobulinemia, with neutropenia. He kept Seth in the hospital for a couple of days, waiting to see if he developed a fever. (We have a wonderful friend who lives near us who helped take care of Jeremy and Jessica while I stayed at the hospital with Seth.) I slept on a cot near Seth's crib. When the nurse came in the morning to check his blood, Seth would obediently stick his finger out to be poked. What a brave little man at two years old! He never did get a fever, so they let us go home. But Seth will need to have shots of gamma globulin weekly.

Patients ... can be given some of the antibodies they are lacking ... supplied in the form of gamma globulins given [by intramuscular injections at this date]. The gamma globulin preparations contain antibodies to a wide variety of microorganisms and are particularly effective in preventing the spread of infections into the bloodstream and to deep body tissues or organs. Recurrent or chronic infections of the mucus membranes, such as sinusitis, occur in some patients despite the use of gamma globulin (ibid., 17).

OCTOBER 1977

Mike has decided that he will not continue his service in the army as a chaplain after December 1977. Although it has been wonderful in many ways, this job has been difficult on our family, and his next assignment would be to go to Korea for one year without the family. We need our daddy here with us, so he won't be staying in the chaplaincy. Mike and I don't know what he will do next, however. He could stay here in Georgia and sell insurance or work as a counselor with the schools—both opportunities he has been offered. Or maybe we should go back to Utah, our home, to be with our families. As our little baby is to be born next month, we are concerned about the future and what to do next.

NOVEMBER 1977

On November 18, our new little son was born. Well, not so little actually: eight pounds thirteen ounces. I thought my stomach would pop the last month of my pregnancy! We are naming him Michael Leo because I saw in my mind's eye a little boy with blond hair about three years of age. I knew it was our son to be born and that his name was Michael. Leo is Mike's father's name. My husband goes by Mike, so we will call our son Michael.

Unfortunately, I had a bad cold before Michael was born, and he was born with pneumonia. They had to shave some of his dark hair off to put an IV in his scalp to give him IV antibiotics. I went home before he did. But now Michael is home, and we love him so. He is just darling! My mother and grandma Martindale are here to help us out for a while.

JANUARY 1978

Mike is officially out of the army now. The chaplaincy has been wonderful, but it has also been very difficult—the agony and the ecstasy, we call it. We are still worried about what we will do now that Mike is out of the army. Mike has a strong feeling that he should work with handicapped children. Right now, however, we don't know how that will happen. We are feeling drawn to go back to Utah to be with my family at April conference time. In the meantime, he is selling cancer insurance for Aflac.

These are trying times, but we feel the Lord's comfort as we pray and study the scriptures. We love this house and this country living, but we will probably need to leave it and go back to Utah.

MARCH 1978

Our little baby Michael has been very sick with difficulty breathing and a croupy cough. He also has a lot of stomach pain, cramping, and constipation. The country doctor took an x-ray and says he has bronchiolitis. With antibiotics he is getting better. The doctor also recommended starting solid foods, which is different from what they told us when Michael was born.

It's a scary time, but our little Michael makes us laugh so much now that he is feeling well. It seems he was sent to make us happy in trying times.

Family comes first. Make time to love yourself,
your children, and your spouse every day. Try to be
patient with yourself and family. Enjoy them!

6

A New Start

We took off to drive to Utah for the church's General Conference, looking forward to seeing my family and listening to inspired counsel. We've decided not to go back to Georgia. Our neighbor will help put the house up for rent or sale.

Jeremy and Jessica are attending the elementary school here near my parents' house in Salt Lake City. When Jeremy was old enough for first grade, he attended the public school in Juniper, Georgia and Jessica attended all-day kindergarten there. They rode together on the bus. Jeremy was the smartest in his class, but the school here in Salt Lake is far ahead of Georgia's schools, so my kids have some catching up to do.

MAY 1978
Good news! Mike is being hired to be an employment specialist for the LDS church in Renton, Washington! My dad helped Mike find this job opportunity through contacts at the Church Office Building and put in a good word for him. The pay is much less than we were used to in the army, but it will help us out a lot. We are flying up to Washington soon at the church's expense to see if we can find a place to live.

Our baby Michael is sick again. He's been breathing fast and has a gray color to his skin. I have seen these symptoms before in Jonathan! I think it is *Pneumocystis* pneumonia, and our pediatrician in Provo agrees with me. I took Michael to the University of Utah Medical Center to see the immunologist. Michael was put in the hospital. We learned that his immunoglobulin levels are low and that he is indeed immune-deficient. So he will have to have gamma globulin shots along with Seth. What a heartbreaker!

The doctors wanted to do a lung biopsy to determine for sure whether Michael had *Pneumocystis* pneumonia, but I refused, because that procedure caused Jonathan lots of problems. I said, "Please, just give him Septra [the new treatment for *Pneumocystis*]. I have seen this disease before, and Michael has all the symptoms. If you don't give it to him, I'm going to take him home and give it to him myself, because we have some in our cupboard!" (Seth takes Septra on a regular basis to prevent ear infections.) I was obnoxious, like a mother bear fighting for her cub. Finally the doctor gave in and consented to prescribe Septra. I feel certain it will cure Michael. (And yes, it did.)

> Because patients have a marked susceptibility to pneumocystis carinii pneumonia, [now known as pneumocystis jirovecii] it is important to initiate prophylactic treatment for pneumocystis carinii pneumonia by starting affected infants on trimethoprim-sulfamethoxazole (Bactrim, Septra) prophylaxis as soon as the diagnosis is made (Immune Deficiency Foundation 2013, 64).

However, our immunologist did not think it was a good idea for Seth or Michael to always be taking Septra, because of the drug's potential side effects.

JUNE 1978

We have moved to Auburn, Washington, for Mike's new job as an LDS employment specialist. It's nice he has a job, but it is pretty low pay, and we really struggle financially. With the help of church members we found a little blue house to rent in a neighborhood with lots of inexpensive little houses on top of a wooded hill. It is beautifully green and wooded here in Washington State with wild blackberries growing in the forests. It rains a lot. Once after three weeks of rain, I saw the sun for fifteen minutes, and it was the most beautiful thing I had ever seen!

The army moved our belongings here all the way from Georgia. That is a blessing, although they took every leg off of every table and chair, so we have to put it all back together like a giant puzzle. Jeremy and Jessica have started at their new school.

Seth loves to ride his big wheel around the neighborhood, and sometimes I can't find him. He's only three and has started to talk more. He has talked about how Jesus "killed him and he woke up in a hospital" (coming to earth from heaven?). Then he talked about a nice king and a mean king who were there. It seems he is remembering his pre-earth life. Later he didn't remember any of this. Seth continues to have frequent mouth sores and fevers due to his neutropenia, or low white cell count. He will often fall asleep at night with a fever but wake up the next day without one. He takes Septra often to prevent infections.

We take the kids to Puget Sound. The beach there is rocky but has some sand, and it is fun. Little Michael is almost two and is so funny and full of joy with his big brown eyes and blond hair. His health has been good since having the gamma shots, as his white count is normal, unlike Seth's. I am happy with my little family, although raising four kids is so much work. I find, however, that if I lose my selfishness in their service, things work out better, and we are all happier.

NOVEMBER 1978

Mike said he had a dream about a bird flying in the sky. The bird came down, and Mike caught it. Then he discovered it was not a bird but a baby! He told me he feels it's time for us to have another baby. Wow! I trust his inspiration, and so we will see what happens.

DECEMBER 1978

Well, it looks like I am pregnant. I have been a little bit sick but not as much as with my other babies, so that is a blessing.

FEBRUARY 1, 1979 (MIKE'S JOURNAL)

Seth is sick this evening. I gave him a blessing. It makes me so sad to see the suffering Seth goes through. He is so tough, so good about it all. His problem tonight is somewhat humorous, however. He ate half a can of beans and is having some discomfort from the gas. I had him up—half asleep—running around in the living room to relieve the gas.

Michael (fifteen months old) has diarrhea again but is very happy otherwise. He was walking from Colleen to me and then giggling, and when I clapped, he loved it and joined in too. He has been taking more to me since I started dancing with him. He has actually even squealed to leave his mother to come to me. Seth always did like me to hold him, but Michael has been a mama's boy. It makes me feel good to have the little cutie want to come to me sometimes.

FEBRUARY 17, 1979 (MIKE'S JOURNAL)
Today Colleen took Seth and Michael to the University of Washington Hospital. The doctor thought Seth was looking worse. He has lost weight and also has an ear infection, so we are going to intensify his treatment.

Dr. Hans Ochs and Dr. Fischer, immunologists at the hospital, asked if we wanted to participate in a clinical trial with Seth and Michael receiving the new intravenous gamma globulin (IVIG) instead of shots. It would all be paid for by the study. I said that sounded great, so I will be taking the boys monthly to receive IVIG in Seattle.

> [Hyper IgM] patients can be given some of the antibodies they are lacking … in the form of immunoglobulins [that] can be given directly into the bloodstream intravenously. Immunoglobulins contain antibodies that substitute for the antibodies that patients cannot make themselves … Immunoglobulin is prepared from plasma from a large number of normal individuals who have been carefully screened … [It] contains a broad range of … antibodies to many different types of bacteria and viruses. (Immune Deficiency Foundation 2013, 17, 147)

Lately Michael has been having frequent diarrhea. It has become almost commonplace for him. That is a worry. "Gastrointestinal complaints, most commonly diarrhea and malabsorption, have also been reported in some patients" (ibid., 62).

FEBRUARY 26, 1979 (MIKE'S JOURNAL)
Colleen took Michael and Seth to see Dr. Fischer again at the University of Washington Hospital. Seth has gained four pounds. He had strep throat before.

MAY 1979
The three-month clinical trial for intravenous gamma globulin is over, so now we will be going back to giving the gamma globulin shots,

which cannot provide as much of the protective antibodies. Perhaps intravenous gamma will become the normal treatment in the future, but not yet.

JUNE 1979

The LDS employment center where Mike works here in Washington will be shutting down at the end of June. We have agonized for months as to what we should do and where we should go when that time comes. After much prayer and scripture study, Mike feels that he is being told that if he returns to Brigham Young University in Provo, Utah, he will be able to teach religion there. I also feel that returning to Provo is the right decision, but it is scary to move our family again to another state. We will first go to Salt Lake City and stay with my parents for a while. Our baby is due in the middle of July, so the baby will be born shortly after we get there. Our health insurance will still be in force to pay for the birth, so that's good. Also, we sold our house in Georgia recently, which gives us some financial buffer.

Press forward when things are tough.
Follow your intuition!

7

Faith, Poverty, and the Shadow of Death

JULY 1979

We have moved to Utah and are staying with my parents for a little while in Salt Lake City. Mike drove Jeremy and Jessica from Washington in a U-Haul truck. I flew down with Seth and Michael on the plane. We are going to have the baby here very soon at LDS Hospital.

JULY 13, 1979

Today is the birthday of our beautiful daughter Rebekah ("Rosebud"). She has such chubby cheeks and is just beautiful! The doctor had a hard time getting my baby to breathe after the C-section, but after being suctioned to clear her airways, she began to cry and was all right. I feel very blessed that she is okay. How wonderful to have another daughter amid all the boys of the family. We chose her name partly because my dad suggested it, but we had also been thinking of naming her Rebekah, as spelled in the Bible.

AUGUST 15, 1979

I woke up about four this morning with Rebekah, and I have been up ever since. I feel such concern for each one of our children. We've found a three-bedroom house with a basement to rent in Provo. So far, Mike has three religion classes to teach as a graduate teaching assistant while he is taking classes in international studies. The classes he is teaching will give us only $750 a month, which is not enough, so we're selling some of the expensive furniture we bought in Georgia to help make ends meet.

SEPTEMBER 2, 1979

After a trying month of wondering how things will work out at BYU, Mike got a phone call from the religion department asking him to teach two additional religion classes. We are thrilled and grateful.

40

His teaching has ended up paying more than we expected. He has also been given five hours of free tuition! Moving to Utah with hopes that something would work out was a huge leap of faith, but we have learned that our inspiration was correct—Mike is teaching religion at Brigham Young University!

SEPTEMBER 1979

Jeremy, Jessica, and Seth are settled in their new school here in Provo. Seth is starting kindergarten. In a way, he doesn't seem ready to me. He has trouble speaking many words clearly. I have made a list of these words, and we sit on the couch and practice saying them correctly. I guess it is homemade speech therapy, but it is working. We also are practicing counting to twenty. We say the numbers over and over again. I never had to work like this with the other children. I wonder if Seth has a little brain damage from the meningitis or from all the fevers he has had in his life.

We don't have a lot of money these days. So we drink powdered milk and eat homemade bread, and I cook beans pretty often. Jeremy doesn't understand why we have to be so poor. I wish we had more money for his sake and for all of us. I have been tending some other children for some extra money.

We are giving Seth and Michael two gamma globulin shots every week. They are learning not to cry, and we sing songs to them while they get their shots. Seth takes Septra most days to prevent ear infections, but it doesn't always work. He still gets them pretty often. He just doesn't have enough white blood cells to fight them off. Sometimes I wonder if the Septra has caused the low white count from when he was a baby. It can be a side effect. My baby Rebekah is sweet, but she is also a little more emotional than the boys were. I guess that's just the way girls are. I feel that my hands are very full with my five children.

JANUARY 1980

The other day Jessica was taking a nap on her bed. I think she had been crying for getting into trouble. She said she woke up and saw Grandpa Martindale (who died before she was born) standing next to her bed smiling at her. He was wearing a plaid shirt and overalls. Yes, that was what he usually wore. I showed her a picture of him, and she said that was who she saw.

FEBRUARY 10, 1980

Right now we are doing better than we expected financially. As usual, the money keeps rolling in a little at a time sufficient for the day. The Lord is really blessing us.

MARCH 1980

I had the opportunity to get a temporary job as a census taker, which I did also in 1970. I was ready to go to some training and had a babysitter lined up, but that morning Seth was quite sick with bad stomach pains. He was really suffering, so I decided I better not take the job now and called to tell them I couldn't come. I felt it was the right thing to do, but I was very disappointed and shed some bitter tears because we really could have used the extra money.

The bishop arranged for us to have food from the church storehouse for a while, and that helped us out a lot even though we felt reluctant to accept it. We have always had what we need, and I'm sure God will continue to provide for us. "In every condition, in sickness, in health, in poverty's vale or abounding in wealth ... As thy days may demand, so thy succor shall be" (Keen 1998, 85). These words from the hymn "How Firm a Foundation" give me strength.

APRIL 18, 1980

I had so much fun playing with my nine-month-old Rebekah today. Then Mike and I took the kids down the street tonight to see a little colt that is five days old as well as some other horses. The children enjoyed it. Rebekah was so cute laughing in the car at the horses and playing peekaboo with her daddy. She has had a fever on and off today for some reason. I hate to see her sick.

JUNE 17, 1980

We had a sweet time tonight on the back porch with the kids at sunset. I read nursery rhymes and sang songs to them. It reminded me of similar times at our country home in Georgia. I cried a little over that. Will we ever have a home again that we love as we did that one? What a heartbreaker. I love my children so.

I try to start my day reading scriptures, as they give me so much strength and direction to make my family happy. With this determination for the past few days, I have felt more successful. I've started cleaning the house right before Mike comes home each night, and he's very happy about that. In the mornings I make the beds and do a quick straightening of the house. Then I spend time teaching and loving the children. Yesterday I taught Seth to tie his shoes and gave Jessica a piano lesson. I've been walking/jogging in the evenings. Last night the whole family went to the school grounds to jog around. It was so fun. I even climbed the jungle gym. I had so much energy! So unusual.

JULY 29, 1980
Seth had an earache tonight. I knelt by his bed and prayed that the pain would go away. I rocked him, and he asked me to sing to him.

AUGUST 27, 1980
I was worried about how to get money to buy the kids the clothes they need for school, but now I am babysitting three other children. It has been hard, but it has given us money we need.

Lately I've noticed that three-year-old Michael's tummy is getting to be so big! I was worried that he might have cancer, so we scheduled an appointment for him to have some tests at the University of Utah Medical Center in Salt Lake to see what is going on.

We took our family up to Mom and Dad's cabin in Midway for an overnight stay the day before Michael's appointment at the hospital. We had a good time at the cabin, but I was so worried about what the doctors would find the next day.

When we took Michael to see Dr. Shigeoka, she said, as she was feeling his tummy, "Well, his liver is just huge! He hasn't grown any taller in the last year because his liver isn't processing the food. We'll need to do a liver biopsy to see what is going on."

The biopsy showed that Michael has cirrhosis, and Dr. Shigeoka told us he might have only two years to live! No, it isn't cancer, but it's still a deadly disease. Dr. Shigeoka assumes it is hepatitis B, which could have come from the gamma globulin shots made from human plasma. His treatment has brought on his liver problems!

We're just devastated. He's still been playing around on the grass, laughing and having a good time, yet our little Michael is so sick inside of his body! It's heartbreaking. Of course he knows nothing about this diagnosis, and we aren't going to tell him.

Mike was gone to an Army Reserve camp in Texas at the time I got the final report from the doctor over the phone. Mike said that, after I told him, he walked around the base for a long time in the dark anguishing over the deadly diagnosis of our little boy. Finally, he just decided to put it in the hands of the Lord—He was in charge, and we had to trust Him and have faith in Him. This helped to calm his fears, and, as he told me his thoughts on the phone, it also brought comfort to me. What else could we do? We had no power over the situation. There was no real treatment except to give Michael extra vitamins to make up for the nutrients that his liver couldn't process. Although Seth was the one who had the most outward infections, which frequently took him to the doctor, Michael had a truly more serious condition.

SEPTEMBER 1980
Seth had an ear infection, so Mike gave him a blessing. Also, Michael has had diarrhea all summer, so I asked Mike to give him a blessing also. Well, he doesn't have diarrhea anymore! I am so surprised and happy. Seth was very ill last week, so I lost a lot of sleep one night. Almost right in the middle of vomiting, he looked at me and said, "Mom, I love you so much." He was so sincere and earnest that I couldn't help but get a lump in my throat. What a sweet five-year-old son!

OCTOBER 1980
Mike has been diligently looking for a house for us to buy. We have been looking at houses with a realtor, including a split-level home in a nice neighborhood in Salem, Utah, fifteen miles south of Provo. It is wonderful! We can buy it on a contract and refinance in four years when interest rates are better. It has a third-of-an-acre yard and is just what we need for our growing family. My parents are helping with the closing costs. I plan on doing day care in our home to raise some extra money, and I am working on becoming licensed to do this.

DECEMBER 1980

A few days ago while I was in the Spirit, I saw a little baby boy that is to come into our family. It was only in my mind. I saw him with my spiritual eyes, but the Lord truly showed him to me. It may be time to have another baby soon. I have felt several times lately that someone is missing in our family.

JANUARY 1981

I feel so grateful now for the Lord continuing to provide us with our daily needs. We love our new house with four bedrooms and a basement, and my child day care business is bringing in a lot of extra money coupled with a federal food program I am involved in similar to the hot lunch program for schools. This business is such a blessing, though very difficult at times.

Just recently, the liver doctor told me that Michael might not die in two years. His liver could regenerate, and the prognosis could go either way. I understood that things might be better than her original prediction, and I thought, *Why didn't you tell me this before? We have been agonizing about this for months!* But I didn't say anything to her. Haven't I learned before that doctors are not gods and cannot always be totally trusted? This is just another example of this truth. They are just humans making their best educated guesses. Her words did ease our fears, however, and we've been able to put Michael's liver disease into the back of our minds most of the time. He seems so healthy on the outside except for his little round tummy, his short stature, and some occasional mild jaundice. He is such a fun, happy little boy who makes us laugh and brings a lot of joy into our family. How can he be so sick?

Although I feel my "quiver" (Psalm 127:5) is very full of children, I often get the feeling as we sit at the dinner table that someone is missing. And I have little visions in my mind of another son who wants to come.

FEBRUARY 28, 1981

I have been so worried today about Seth, my kindergartener, and his seemingly constant horrible cough. He is always half-sick and has frequent fevers, poor appetite, and loss of weight. When we put him on antibiotics, the cough usually disappears, but it simply returns again when the antibiotics are finished, probably due to his low white count. When calling Dr. Robins's nurse today, I broke down in tears on the phone due to my anxiety about Seth. Also, our health insurance from Mike's job in Washington is raising the premiums above what we can afford. What are we going to do? My written patriarchal blessing, which I received when I was sixteen, says I will "pass through times of great uncertainty" in my life but admonishes me to "be calm and untroubled."

MARCH 17, 1981

I talked to Dr. Shigeoka at the University of Utah Medical Center today. She said that a fungus may be causing Michael's diarrhea as well as Seth's cough. I feel relieved that some headway is being made toward them becoming well. I will get prescriptions tomorrow.

MAY 3, 1981

Mike was at Army Reserve training this weekend in Provo. (He serves as a part-time chaplain, another source of income.) But I had two very good days as I've stayed home with my kids. It's been so wonderful. We've gotten along well, and the Lord has helped me to be patient.

MAY 12, 1981

I was at Mom's house on Mother's Day. I felt kind of depressed and even jealous of my sisters. Mike and I seem to have nothing in comparison to them materially. I'm also jealous of their new babies, and I feel I want to have another one. Rebekah is almost two years old now. But can I live happily with the children I have? And can I care for them? I have both feelings of frustration and joy in this calling of motherhood, which certainly has its ups and downs. But there is nothing I would rather be doing with my time than building and caring for my eternal family. Nothing is more important to me.

Even though in the world at large there is a push for population control and having only two children, it is not so in my family or in my neighborhood. In this rural Utah town, there are many Mormon families with five or six children and even some well-educated parents with eleven or twelve children! So I do not see it as so unusual for me to desire more children. We have a large home, a third-of-an-acre lot, and fields and mountains close by. We have enough to feed our family, although we feel a little money poor at times. I have instinctively felt some of my children asking me to let them be born, and I do believe what the Bible says: "Children are an heritage of the Lord ... Happy is the man that hath his quiver full of them" (Psalm 127:3, 127:5).

God will soften our sorrows and give us strength.

8

Long-Awaited Son

Something wonderful has happened. I am having another baby! We hadn't planned for it at this time. I don't know how we are going to pay for it. We are concerned. This will be my seventh cesarean section, quite a feat in these days when most doctors frown on more than four. (But my doctor in Georgia was more liberal in his views and said I could have all the children I desire.)

The Lord continues to let us know in dreams, impressions, and visions of the mind of another child to come and then another. How can I turn these children down when I know they are waiting to come to earth and are waiting for me to let them?

But financially, our situation has deteriorated lately. We bought this house, and the payments are high. Almost simultaneously, our health and maternity insurance premiums were raised and the coverage lowered. We could no longer afford to pay the premiums and so we had to discontinue the insurance.

On Mother's Day, as we drove home from visiting my family in Salt Lake, a minister on the radio said, "The ideal mother as portrayed in the Bible accepts her children as gifts from heaven. There is no such thing as an 'accidental' baby. Every child is sent to earth by Heavenly Father and with His knowledge." I agree with him. So when I "accidently" got pregnant this month, I was actually relieved. I think it is the little boy I have been seeing in my mind's eye. We are not sure yet how we will pay the hospital bill, but we trust that something will work out. Babies are more precious than money. My depression has lifted, and I am so happy to be expecting a child again. My youngest child, Rebekah, will be two and a half by the time the baby is born, so she is growing up. She is a sweet daughter.

SEPTEMBER 15, 1981

Mike was so sweet tonight, although burdened down himself. He took me out by the garden to enjoy the sunset, and he did the dishes for me. Later he took care of the children so I could watch the BYU devotional on TV. The speaker, Neal A. Maxwell, talked about how the routine of life can seem ordinary and mundane. However, it can become resplendent and meaningful under the influence of God. If life does seem mundane, if it seems that we should be doing something more important, "it is because we lack love … Love and patience is never wasted, though it may appear so" (Maxwell 1981). Good words for me to contemplate.

SUNDAY, JANUARY 17, 1982

Downs and ups this week. However, we have been greatly blessed. Mike is going to California for an army chaplain conference with the Army Reserve. This active duty time will give us enough money to pay for the hospital bill for our baby's birth! The baby's due date is in five days with a C-section scheduled for 11:00 a.m. next Friday. Mike flies to California tomorrow for the chaplain's conference and should be home for the C-section.

Our five-year-old Michael has been jaundiced for a while, and his appetite doesn't seem as good as it was. I wish there was some kind of medical cure, but there isn't.

Yesterday we took the kids to the Bean Museum at BYU and bought a black pet mouse for Seth and a goldfish for Michael—they love their new pets. We also have a cat, a guinea pig, and a nonvenomous bull snake, which is the pride of Jeremy's life. I guess kids need pets.

Tonight we had family home evening, and Mike gave me a blessing. He laid his hands on my head and blessed me that I would be patient with the children and remember that they are my most priceless possession—"Remember they are children," he said. He told me I should not be overly concerned with my weaknesses, for the Lord is merciful and understands, and I should just try to improve the best I can. He said, "I bless you physically, that you will be fine and everything will go well with the birth of the baby." At that moment, I knew clearly that I would have the baby while Mike was in California, but I felt a deep peace come over me. I knew the Lord would be with me, and all fears of not having Mike there disappeared. I felt I could go through it alone with no problem.

MONDAY, JANUARY 18, 1982

At four thirty in the morning I awoke with some mild labor pains, every fifteen minutes or so. I got up at five thirty and determined not to tell Mike so he wouldn't have to worry about it. He was going to California to earn money to pay the hospital bill. Mike left at seven that morning. We had a special prayer with the kids before he left. I hugged him and cried. I said, "I hope I don't have the baby while you're gone, but I might not be able to help it." He said he wouldn't feel too upset if I did. Things would be okay.

He left after a big hug and tears on my part. I had labor pains all day. I kept Jeremy home from school, and he helped me clean the house. After going to the hospital about six that evening, they took the baby by C-section at 9:50 p.m. I had an epidural for the pain. The surgery was a little difficult, but I truly felt close to the Lord and was not too afraid. The anesthesiologist was nearby telling me what was happening. When the baby was born, he said, "There's the head. It's got lots of hair. And it's a ... a boy! He looks good!" The baby cried from the moment they got his head out. The sound of that cry, which sounded so healthy, was wonderful to me. They put his face up to mine so I could kiss him. He was so sweet and cute. How I loved him! I just sobbed and sobbed for joy and thanksgiving to the Lord. I had now received the little boy so long awaited and promised to me.

Mike called me on the phone while I was in the operating room. I didn't think I could talk, because my mouth was so dry, but I did. They finished the operation and took me to the recovery room. My mom was there. She talked to me, kissed me on the cheek, and then went to my house to help with the family. It was over. What a blessing! My seventh C-section was the wonder of the maternity floor. Mike and I decided to name the baby Robert Verl Curzon (middle name after my father).

FEBRUARY 28, 1982

My heart is full of joy, gratitude, and awe as I look at my beautiful children. I am so grateful for them. I continue to wonder, however, how many children I should have and how I can care for them. After talking to my doctor about these questions, I went to the temple last Friday morning. Quietly, gradually, peacefully, answers came to my heart. Yes, there is another boy to be born. And as my patriarchal blessing promises, I will have strength in childbearing. I was full of peace and strength.

MARCH 12, 1982

Tonight I went for a walk in the dark with Michael, Rebekah, and Jessica. Pretty stars and moon. We saw our streetlight shadows as we walked along holding hands, and I felt special to be the one they look to for their needs. Later I prayed alone in the living room for charity, for joy in my life, for forgiveness, and for the ability to live a Christ-like life.

MAY 2, 1982

As in all families, we have our arguments and disagreements. I talked to Mike last night about the argument that happened with the kids. I admitted that it was my fault for getting mad at the kids' complaints about their chores that had started the whole fight. Then he jumped in to discipline them. He said, "We've got to change ourselves, not the kids." Mike was gone again to attend the Army Reserve drill today, his second job. I tried to watch myself carefully and to be calm and kind no matter what the kids did. I succeeded pretty well. Our attitudes are the key to harmony at home.

MAY 18, 1982

Mike was not accepted into the PhD program at BYU as we had hoped. So what do we do now? We need a permanent full-time job with benefits at some point. Should Mike go to another university or get another job? "Therefore take no thought for the morrow; for the morrow shall take thought for the things of itself....for your heavenly Father knoweth that ye have need of all these things" (Matthew 6:34, 6:32). The scriptures give me temporary comfort.

Jeremy, Seth, and Michael went with their dad to the fathers-and-sons outing at the sand dunes last week. And Jessica and Mike had a daddy-daughter date. These are yearly free events sponsored by our church congregation. Good times with their dad!

SUNDAY MAY 23, 1982

This morning I drove Mike to the Pleasant Grove Army Reserve Center. He's leaving for two weeks to attend summer camp in Virginia. I felt a deep ache of fear and loneliness as I left him there and drove home to my six children waiting for me. It scares me—the challenge of raising, teaching, disciplining, and caring for them all by myself. I lean on Mike a lot. Eleven-year-old Jeremy had the flu last night and today. He is not so lively and obnoxious that way—a blessing in disguise?

We went to church and had guitar singing time afterward at home, singing songs by the fireplace. The kids loved it, especially Jessica, Seth, and Michael. We're like the Osmond family! Not quite. But life is so good overall.

Children bring some of our greatest joys.

9

Daily Life with Immunodeficiency Disease

MAY 26, 1982

Today is one that will never come again—unique and commemorative. It's been twelve years since Jonathan died on this date, and I spent today in the same hospital—the University of Utah Medical Center—with Seth, Michael, and Robert to get their blood tested. My stomach had butterflies. As I went into the hospital, tears caught in my throat. The smells of the hospital, the busyness of the people, the elevators, and the same metal plaque on the wall—the hospital had grown and changed, but the same remnants remained.

Likewise, my family has grown and changed. In the doctor's office there were many student doctors asking us the same questions over and over. We were the center of attention—in the spotlight, under scrutiny. They took pictures of Seth and Michael to show to their medical classes. We were an oddity, a medical rarity—a family with X-linked hypogammaglobulinemia. The doctors are concerned about Michael's large liver and slow growth. They showed me how to do percussion on Seth's chest for the cough he often has. I feel that since we are such a rarity in the world, I need to write about our experiences in hopes that it will be educational and of help to someone else who may face similar trials.

MAY 29, 1982

Dr. Shigeoka called. She said Michael's liver function enzymes were really abnormal in the blood test. She wants to admit him to the hospital this week to have another liver biopsy because he is not growing as he should. Scared, I turned to our Mormon scriptures: "Have you any that are sick among you? Bring them hither and I will heal them … He commanded that their little children should be brought. So they brought their little children and Jesus stood in the midst" (3 Nephi

53

17:7, 17:11–12 [B of M]). "I am in your midst and ye cannot see me … Be ye strong from henceforth; fear not" (D & C 38:7, 38:15).

JUNE 30, 1982

A lot has happened in the past three weeks. I spent two days in Salt Lake City at my parents' home to take Michael to the university hospital for a liver biopsy. All went well.

Dr. Shigeoka called Friday. What a whirlwind of emotion I have gone through since then. The results of our little Michael's liver biopsy show that his liver has been damaged quite a bit by hepatitis B (chronic). It is very serious. There is nothing they can do about it. He may live a few years or twenty. I cried. I wanted to die, to move away and never see anyone again. It was an emotional roller coaster.

Jessica stayed at my mom's for a week. Jeremy took swimming merit badge lessons in Spanish Fork and enjoyed them very much. I picked up Mike at the airport following his army training. Afterward we went to my parents' cabin for a couple of days.

Later in the month I took five-year-old Michael to see the liver doctor. She repeated what Dr. Shigeoka had said, that Michael has hepatitis B and can be expected to live anywhere from two to twenty years. They don't know. I talked to a neighbor of my mom's, who said I should not cross that bridge in my mind unless I am forced to. In other words, try not to worry about Michael dying until the time it is happening. That seemed like good advice since the prognosis is so uncertain. Our feeling is that he will be all right for now. In the meantime, Michael has little understanding of this and continues to run and play and be the fun brown-eyed, blond-haired child in our family that he has always been. He doesn't seem very sick.

We bought a little puppy for Seth's and Jessica's birthdays.

JULY 28, 1982

Dr. Shigeoka called. It seems it is always bad news when she calls. This time was no exception. From the blood tests that were done on my baby Robert, it seems that he too has hypogammaglobulinemia. He was given a DT (diphtheria/tetanus) shot earlier, but he has produced no antibodies against these deadly viruses. This shows his body does not produce gamma globulin. I had suspicions of this a few weeks ago when we went up the canyon for a picnic. A biting fly landed on

Robert's forehead and bit him before I could shoo it away, but there was no reaction on Robert's skin. The fact his body didn't mount a response to the fly bite suggested to me that his immunity was low.

Dr. Shigeoka also said that Seth, Michael, and Robert should have the new intravenous gamma globulin (IVIG) preparations instead of the shots. The only problem is that they cost thousands of dollars each month and we have no health insurance. She said to think about it.

I'm very disturbed to think that we may just have to say no to the treatment the doctor recommends. Should the boys have this expensive gamma? I feel we should listen to the doctor and do all that is medically possible to save our boys' lives and improve their health, but where will the money come from?

AUGUST 2, 1982

I went to the Social Security office as suggested by the university hospital to apply for Supplemental Security Income for my three sick boys. It may mean nearly $900 a month in income if approved—a true miracle. If the boys are on SSI, they will also be automatically eligible for Medicaid, which would pay for medical bills and provide the expensive treatment our boys need. "I will make a way in the wilderness and rivers in the desert" (Isaiah 43:19). Truly, we can always trust the Lord to provide what we need.

SEPTEMBER 1, 1982

Now Seth, our seven year-old, has a liver function abnormality as shown in his blood tests. Dr. Book wants him to have a liver biopsy. I am numb about it all. How can so many things be going wrong? This disease is worse than we expected it to be. Seth also has a chronic cough. The chest x-ray showed infiltrates in his lungs. He is taking amoxicillin and must have his chest clapped three times per day. I am told that the chronic infection may develop into chronic lung disease. There seems to be no end to the problems we encounter with the health of these boys. I never realized their immune deficiency would be like this. I thought the gamma shots would cure it, but they really don't. They only help a little bit.

Feeling overwhelmed, I read my patriarchal blessing, the special written blessing I received from a patriarch of our church as a teenager. It lets me know I am a special daughter of God, that I can be strong in times of uncertainty. I am blessed with the spirit of wisdom and courage.

SEPTEMBER 8, 1982

I got up in the dark today at four fifteen to take Seth to Salt Lake City to see Dr. Shigeoka. They will do lymphocyte tests, another chest x-ray, and pulmonary function tests. I took all four younger children, but three stayed at Grandma's house.

At the hospital, Dr. Shigeoka listened carefully to Seth's chest, first one side, then the other, moving the silver metal disk from one spot to another. "Breathe deeply, Seth," she said kindly. "Now can you cough for me? Good." I like the way we get so much time and care here at the university hospital. "We will get another chest x-ray today. I don't really expect the x-ray to look any better," the doctor said. Seth went home on antibiotics for a chest infection.

SEPTEMBER 20, 1982

Seth's cough and fever continued even though he was taking antibiotics. He was in bed for a few days. Finally I called Dr. Shigeoka, and she said to bring him up to the hospital. It was discovered that he had a collapsed lung and pneumonia. He was put on a different intravenous antibiotic in the hospital, and his fever went down. Within a day he began to recover. The respiratory therapist would come in four times a day to pound his chest so he could more easily cough out the mucus. Eventually he got over his pneumonia and collapsed lung. Luckily, he did not end up with chronic lung disease, as the doctor had predicted may happen.

While Seth was in the hospital, I met the people who had a baby son in the next room. I learned that their baby had the same immunodeficiency disease as my boys and that he was fighting for his life against Pneumocystis pneumonia, the same pneumonia my Jonathan died of. The doctor said that their boy may not live, but they were treating him with both Septra and pentamidine. It was very sad and scary to see this happening firsthand to someone else. But it was somehow reassuring to find out that we were not the only family in the world fighting this disease. The mother and I became friends. She was someone I could call on the phone occasionally to discuss the disease, doctors, and the treatments our sons were receiving. Her baby did eventually recover from the Pneumocystis pneumonia. My baby Robert is the same age as her son—nine months old.

OCTOBER 1982

My little Robert has been having a lot of ear infections for a few months and taking quite a few different antibiotics for them. He is beginning to show signs of illness as the antibodies from me at birth are wearing off and he has to fight germs on his own. Lately, although his ears are okay, he has a poor appetite along with a low fever. It seems he can't get over this. The doctors don't know exactly what is wrong and cannot find a source of infection. He is beginning to lose his chubbiness and is becoming thinner.

In the midst of all this, I have all the signs of beginning a new pregnancy right now. We were using the Catholic natural birth control system, but I guess it didn't work. At the moment it is hard to believe that another baby is coming in June, as my heart and soul are so wrapped up in worrying about the children I already have. How will I take care of a new baby right now? However, lately I've felt in the temple that there are two more children to be born into our family, for a total of nine. This baby would be number eight and is a gift from the Lord to us. I'm sure we will love this child as we have all the others. I do feel another boy is coming to our family. Having no insurance right now is a big concern. I feel I have no time or money to go to the OB doctor, so I will get some vitamins and calcium to take and trust that this pregnancy will go well, as all my others have. That is indeed a blessing I have been given.

NOVEMBER 11, 1982

My dad wrote all his children a letter in his own handwriting. He said some special things:

Dearest People—

Veterans Day today with multiple memories of far-away grimmer times—and wildly happy ones when World War II ended. October General Conference of the Church—special, as always. Great men, great talks, always important to charge the spiritual batteries. Strange times in the economy. Time to cut down. Simplify and reduce—get back to basics. Remember families mean everything. Do all you can to have happy times, even with problems. Study, pray, love each other, speak well of each other. Have faith, live the gospel of Jesus Christ, and love one another.

My love to all of you. Dad

As always, his words melt my heart. I can hear his deep voice saying these things. My dad means so much to me. He is so strong and wise.

Don't cross bridges before you have to. Be grateful for the small blessings you receive. Love each other!

10

Trust in the Lord with All Thine Heart

JANUARY 1983

Since October my baby Robert has continued to lose weight and run a fever. Every time he goes to see Dr. Shigeoka, he has lost more. He drinks only about one bottle total per day. He is down to wearing newborn-sized diapers even though he is a year old. I cry myself to sleep over this. He was put in the Payson hospital, but since they can't find the answer, they have sent him home still sick. He is a beautiful baby with dark hair and big brown eyes. His eyelashes are sooo long. He is weak, and he sleeps a lot. I don't know what to do! A new pediatrician, Dr. Behrmann, is in Payson. I took Robert to see him one Sunday night. He was very kind, but he also had no answers for us.

FEBRUARY 1983

Because Robert is so thin, Dr. Shigeoka decided to put him in the university hospital. One doctor told me that he is within two weeks of dying from starvation! They test his body fat by pinching under his arm. He seems to be only skin and bones—like a starving child in Ethiopia. In the hospital they put a nasogastric feeding tube in his nose down to his stomach and taught me how to put it in and take it out and how to feed him formula through the tube. What a scary thing to have to do to your baby! Sometimes the tube goes into a lung, in which case he will cough and choke. When I think it is in the stomach, I have to blow air into it with a syringe and listen with a stethoscope to hear the bubbles in his stomach. Even though he is being fed a lot, he is also vomiting much of what we put into him, so I don't know if it is doing much good. Again we were sent home with Robert still sick and no good answers.

MARCH 4, 1983

Robert is still ill! To write about this breaks my heart. This has never happened with Seth or Michael. If they got fevers or infections, they got over them with antibiotics and were soon back to living their normal lives. Robert just sleeps all day and all night and has no energy. I continue to feed him through the tube. I guess it is at least keeping him alive. At fourteen months he has not learned to walk yet. He doesn't even crawl now. So he is very far behind developmentally at this time. Although he has been getting the new intravenous gamma for several months now, he continues to be so ill. And we don't know why. It is such a terribly sad burden. He has been in and out of the hospital a couple more times.

MARCH 20, 1983

This has been a horrific time. At about midnight, I went in the bedroom to check on Robert. I changed his diaper and found that it was filled with dark blood! I packed him into the car and drove to the emergency room of the Payson hospital. The other kids are in bed, but I let Jeremy and Jessica know that we were going to the emergency room. Mike, unfortunately, is in Korea at this time with the Army Reserve. This position in the Army Reserve helps us have extra money, but it seems Mike is often gone at the times I need him the most! So I must be strong and do this on my own.

In the emergency room, the doctor who looked at Robert said to me, "Your baby is very ill and emaciated." I said, "I know. He has been sick for months, and doctors cannot find out why." The hospital confirmed with a guaiac test that it was mostly blood in his diaper. They called the university hospital in Salt Lake and asked them to send down a helicopter to transport him. At four thirty in the morning the helicopter arrived. They put my little Robert on a papoose board and carried him into the helicopter with the wind from the propellers blowing and the sound so loud I couldn't hear. They told me I could not go with him and would have to drive up to Salt Lake. Such a horrible memory! I was standing in the dark sobbing, watching the helicopter take off with my sick baby inside. And there was nothing I could do to comfort or take care of him.

I drove home in the dark, and as the sun was coming up, I called my neighbor, to see if she could take care of my kids and help them get to school. Then I drove the sixty miles to Salt Lake City, almost falling asleep several times, as I had not slept all night. I couldn't get there fast enough!

When I walked into Robert's hospital room on the fifth floor, I saw him lying in a crib with an IV in him. They said he hadn't lost too much blood and they thought he would be okay. The doctor said that we should put him in a high chair and see if he would feed himself Cheerios with his fingers because children this age like finger foods. I thought that was a ridiculous strategy at this point of his illness, when he was eating nothing and vomiting what we were putting through the nasogastric (NG) tube. But we gave it a try without much success. Robert was there a couple of days, but no remedies or diagnoses were made. I took him home still sick.

MARCH 1983 (MIKE'S JOURNAL)
While in Korea, I received a call from the Red Cross. Robert has been put in the hospital. This upset me, of course, but they said he was not seriously ill and would be all right.

APRIL 12, 1983 (MIKE'S JOURNAL)
April has been a good month so far, as it was my birthday and Colleen's, so it has been a time of rebirth in a way. I have had some very difficult struggles due to Robert's hospitalization, the medical bills, and Robert's sickness at home. I dropped the two classes I was taking, as I was behind when I returned from Korea and with Robert's illness I doubted I could finish well with all I had to catch up on. The church's April conference centered on the family, it seemed to me. It gave both Colleen and myself a desire to improve on our family life.

APRIL 13, 1983
With my baby so sick and another baby on the way, my family and friends are naturally concerned and urging me not to have more children. I understand their logical reasoning, but it hurts my feelings. I know I have to trust in the Spirit rather than in people. In the temple I felt I was supposed to have nine children. This is number eight, so there is still one more to come after this. God's ways are not our ways.

61

I know I will be preserved in childbearing and be able to bear the nine children that I have been promised by the Lord in the temple. That is the path I have chosen to follow, and both earthly and eternal blessings will flow from this decision. People may think I am crazy, but I feel at peace.

APRIL 24, 1983 (MIKE'S JOURNAL)

Robert has been bleeding more from his bowels the last day or so. The doctor said to take him off the Pregestimil formula and put him on clear liquids for a while. Tonight (after twenty-four hours or more) we have started Robert on the formula again—though he is still bleeding some, it is less than before.

APRIL 27, 1983

Robert is still bleeding, so I called Dr. Shigeoka. She said to bring him to the hospital and that this time they would be keeping him in the hospital a long time and would find out what was wrong and try to get him well. Although I want him to get medical help, I no longer trust that the doctors can cure him. It has been months of no answers! I knelt down by the couch and prayed. It is so difficult on our family when Robert is in the hospital. I don't want to take him there if I feel no hope for a cure. I opened the scriptures, and my eyes fell upon the words "Trust in the Lord with all thine heart, and lean not to thine own understanding" (Proverbs 3:5, emphasis added). Yes, I can put my trust in the Lord that he will guide all the doctors to find a solution. I may not totally trust them, but I will trust the Lord! This gave me hope and courage to take him to the hospital again.

APRIL 29, 1983

The doctors here at the university hospital tell me that Robert's liver is very enlarged. He does have an enlarged tummy with skinny arms and legs. I can't believe how much trouble we have had with my sons' livers. They decided to do a liver biopsy, and it showed that he has a lot of fat in his liver, which can happen in cases of starvation. Some doctors want to put Robert on hyperalimentation, where he is fed through a central line put into a large blood vessel in his neck. Dr. Shigeoka, who is Robert's immunologist, says there is too much danger of infection to do that. I wish we could get it done. What we are doing is not working.

MAY 1, 1983

Our bishop has decided that the ward congregation will hold a ward fast for our son Robert and also for another baby in the ward who has been very ill. It is wonderful to have the support, love, faith, and prayers of many people.

Robert's head doctor is out of town for a few days, and the resident, Dr. Nielson, is taking over. She is a young doctor with a lot of compassion and courage. She feels we should start the hyperalimentation, or total parenteral nutrition (TPN) and with the approval of some other doctors, the central line was put into Robert's neck vein. Now he is receiving sugars, fats, and proteins—in their most basic form—directly into his bloodstream. They don't have to go through his digestive tract at all. He is also still being fed formula through the NG tube, and we are trying to feed him some food, such as yogurt, by mouth. Three ways of getting nutrition into him.

The gastroenterologist had Robert drink some barium and took x-rays to check out his intestines. The doctor also put a tube up inside Robert and found some bleeding sores inside his rectum. These he cauterized, putting silver nitrate on them to help them stop bleeding. Robert also received intravenous antibiotics, such as Flagyl, that are especially effective in the colon.

When I come to the hospital, I bring two large paper grocery bags full of medical bills to sort through while Robert sleeps in the crib. I made a list of all the bills and how much we owe and a timetable to pay them. The list included forty doctors, clinics, or hospitals. If we pay about $250 a month, giving each doctor between $5 and $40 a month, we could pay these bills in a year. It has been a big worry to me. But I talked to one wise grandmother in the hospital who had had a medically fragile child. She said to me, "The medical bills will go away eventually, and you will be able to pay them. If you pay a small amount on each bill, there is nothing they can do against you legally. Feed the monster every month, and it will be okay." That is how I keep my sanity about the bills. We can only pay what we can afford. Although we have applied to Social Security for Supplemental Security

Income (SSI) for Robert, he has not been approved yet, although Seth and Michael were approved a few months ago. Nevertheless, Robert is being covered by Medicaid insurance.

THURSDAY, MAY 5, 1983 (MIKE'S JOURNAL)

We had to put Robert in the hospital again (University of Utah Medical Center in Salt Lake) on Wednesday, April 27. Since then our life has been a bit hectic. Robert has been gaining weight, and his liver has been decreasing in size—yet he is less perky and throwing up more. Robert is being a good baby through all his problems. He hardly even cries when they take blood now. He gets along pretty well when he has to be there without Mommy or Dad, but he still wants us there. We usually stay with him during the day until midnight and spend the night at Grandma and Grandpa Scott's house. Colleen and I have been trading off. One stays with the children at home, and the other stays with Robert. Our ward members and neighbors have been very helpful. Yesterday I applied for a job as an interviewer at the state employment office.

MAY 10, 1983

I have had the impression that by May 26, the day that Jonathan died, Robert will be over his sickness. I don't know if that means he will be well or that he will pass away and no longer be sick. Because Robert has been suffering from starvation in spite of all we have tried to do to prevent it, I have been doing some studying about nutrition. I'm sure he is extremely deficient in all vitamins and minerals at this point. Low levels of zinc will cause lack of appetite. And all other vitamins and minerals are vital for a person to have a healthy body. I asked the doctor to check his blood levels for zinc, and the test results came back very low. Dr. Nielsen decided to add zinc powder and crushed-up adult Centrum vitamins to Robert's NG tube each day. I'm pleased that we're doing all we can to improve his nutrition.

Robert was still having diarrhea, although the bleeding had stopped. The doctor recommended that he be tested for *Clostridium difficile*, a bacteria that can cause diarrhea in people who are on antibiotics. The tests came back positive, so Robert is being given liquid vancomycin, a very powerful antibiotic, to combat the infection. He is also being given anti-yeast liquid to combat the yeast infection on his tongue

64

and in his digestive tract. He is gaining some weight and seems to be improving!

MAY 26, 1983

Today is the anniversary of Jonathan's death thirteen years ago but a day of great happiness for us today, as Robert is coming home from the hospital after five weeks! But he is still weak.

MAY 30, 1983 (MIKE'S JOURNAL)

Robert has been home from the hospital since last Thursday. He was doing well until we were about to take him home from the hospital. Then he had a gamma infusion, which started him throwing up again. He's been vomiting ever since then. We got a pump today to try to increase the caloric intake through his NG tube. He seems to be able to keep the formula down when it is pumped in slowly. Today the children and I (Colleen stayed home with Robert, as she had a migraine) visited Jonathan's grave in Holladay Memorial Park and put some flowers on it for Memorial Day.

JUNE 2, 1983

Robert has still been vomiting some. I felt that maybe it was because of a possible yeast infection due to all the antibiotics he has had. I started giving him the yellow medicine for yeast again, and he has been feeling better.

JUNE 14, 1983

A week ago, our new baby was born, Matthew John Curzon. He doesn't look like how our other babies have looked. He has much lighter hair. Our other babies were born with darker hair. Is he really ours? As I think about it, however, he looks like my side of the family instead of Mike's side. It is a joy to have him here healthy. I had a C-section again at about nine thirty in the morning. Mike was there for the birth this time.

Now I am back home with my sweet little Matthew. He is a very quiet, easy baby with blue eyes. He does not cry to be picked up but is content to lie in his crib. Maybe the Lord sent him with such an easy disposition because He knew this is what we needed in our family at this time. Matthew means "gift of the Lord," and truly he is.

Now I have two babies in diapers who cannot walk, since Robert is so far behind in his development at this time. A little like having twins. Thank goodness I have Mike and the older kids to help out this summer.

SUNDAY, JUNE 26, 1983 (MIKE'S JOURNAL)
This evening (11:20 p.m.) Robert was in pain and had been for some time. I anointed his head with oil and sealed the anointing in the name of Jesus Christ by the power of the Melchizedek priesthood, which I hold. Within five to ten minutes he had fallen asleep mumbling his favorite word—"Ball, ball." I am so grateful for the Lord's forgiveness of my sins that I could be the instrument to relieve the suffering of little Robert.

JULY 15, 1983
Robert is doing much better now, finally! He is gaining his weight back. He is, however, pretty afraid of strangers and wants to cling to me in public. It's understandable considering the fact that most of the adults he has come in contact with in the last few months have been doctors or nurses who poke him with needles.

AUGUST 14, 1983 (MIKE'S JOURNAL)
At this point, Robert is doing well. He is a fat, happy little baby. He still has to catch up on his development, such as walking and talking, but otherwise he is doing well. It is delightful to see him laugh and play after the long months of sickness.

SEPTEMBER 1, 1983
Robert is scooting around and beginning to crawl at nineteen months old. His greatest feat lately was to crawl up the carpeted stairs that go from our front door. He had to work at it, but when he finally did it, he was clapping and so happy, as was the rest of the family. His spunky personality is starting to come out again. What a joy! I am so, so grateful that he is regaining his health! I will never take this little boy for granted! The sun has finally come out after the terrible storms we have gone through with him!

NOVEMBER 1983
Robert is now twenty-two months old and is finally beginning to walk! Now that he is healthy, he is going through the developmental

milestones. He is chubby and happy and fun. He loves to play with balls, and my boys call him "Bobby Boscoe" after a BYU football player. Matthew is growing too and is almost six months old. We have learned to our great joy that Matthew has a normal immune system! What a blessing! These boys look like opposites—Robert with his brown hair and dark-brown, almost black eyes like bing cherries and Matthew with his blond (balding) hair and blue eyes. How fun to have different coloring in my children. These boys are buddies.

As I look back on this past difficult year with the miraculous healing of Robert and the birth of our healthy Matthew, I am reminded of Annie Johnson Flint's poem "What God Hath Promised," which expresses my feelings well:

God hath not promised
Skies always blue;
Flower-strewn pathways
All our lives through;
But God hath promised …
Help from above,
Unfailing sympathy,
Undying love (Flint 1919).

If we ask the Lord, He will help us, for we are His children. This I do know for sure!

When trials are long and hard, hold on to your faith and hope!

11

Carry On

FEBRUARY 19, 1984 (MIKE'S JOURNAL)
I continue teaching religion at BYU. I was accepted into their EdS (educational specialist) program with an emphasis in educational psychology.

OCTOBER 6, 1984
The past year has been full of blessings and not so many illnesses. From all the sicknesses our boys went through, we have received some financial blessings. The Social Security office has finally approved Supplemental Security Income for all three of my boys with the immune deficiency. Robert had to practically die for it to happen, unfortunately.

Because the boys were approved as being disabled, we now have more money to help pay for their medical and other needs. This frees up other funds for Mike to pursue the graduate program in educational psychology. I felt very strongly that it would be a good thing for Mike to go into the school psychology program because it would give him actual job skills. I thought this was a very good choice for him and for the future of our family. He will be able to have a stable career with health insurance provided for our family! We still have many medical bills, but everything will eventually work out. Otherwise, we are pretty stable financially and have avoided debt except for our house. We try not to use charge cards but to pay as we go. I'm also doing some babysitting again. It's going well.

Robert is now very healthy, as are Seth and Michael for the most part. I have been driving all three boys the sixty miles to the university hospital in Salt Lake City every three weeks for the IV gamma infusions. Once we nearly had a bad car accident as we drove up there during a snowy morning on the slick freeway. We escaped an accident by only inches. I had to wonder if it was worth risking our lives in a car accident to get the gamma infusions.

Once, Seth had a reaction to his IV gamma. His face started to turn red, and he couldn't breathe well. The nurse stopped the infusion for several minutes and then started it slowly again when his symptoms subsided. He was also given some epinephrine for the allergic reaction he was having. Allergic reactions can happen occasionally with intravenous gamma globulin infusions. Most of the time there is no problem, but sometimes reactions occur.

I am concerned right now about Michael—he has a very large lymph node on his neck that will not go away. So far we are treating it with antibiotics, seemingly to no avail. But he seems strong and healthy.

> Enlargement of the lymph nodes is seen more frequently in patients with X-linked hyper IgM syndrome than most of the other primary immunodeficiency diseases. As a result, patients often have enlarged tonsils, a big spleen and liver and enlarged lymph nodes (Immune Deficiency Foundation 2013, 62).

NOVEMBER 1, 1984

As I read over my journal, I feel that indeed the Lord is watching out for us, giving us the blessings we need, though at times we must go through trials to obtain the blessings. At times the progress seems so slow to us as mortals that it is almost imperceptible, but it is happening. And over time the patterns will be easily seen, and we will see that our lives do make sense—they're not just one big chaotic mess. There is an order to everything.

There are many defects and diseases in this world, as I have seen at the hospital. Our family has one of them. Some other people have diseases even worse than ours. Such hardships and struggles cause great concern, but we must not let them overwhelm us. They should be downplayed for the more grand purposes of life. Always we should seek to serve and to grow spiritually, just as Christ murmured not but bore his pain and suffering that the grand purposes of His atonement could be brought to pass. Pain and suffering also bring us the opportunity for spiritual growth if we turn to God.

DECEMBER 3, 1984

Today I took Michael to the very personable and competent Dr. Behrmann, our pediatrician in nearby Payson. This was one last effort before a biopsy on Michael's neck may be necessary. A month ago I put Michael's name on the prayer roll of the temple. He was on Septra, and the lump became noticeably smaller. I reported this to Dr. Shigeoka. I can't tell you how relieved and happy I felt, how full of gratitude and joy. But just when I thought the lump would continue to get smaller, I became alarmed by its increasing size. Was it just my imagination? No. It measured larger again.

Dr. Behrmann said we'll put Michael on a full course of erythromycin for ten days. "If there is no improvement, I think a biopsy is in order. It could be a malignancy. Cancer can cause this kind of thing," he said to me.

After I came home tonight, amid the bustle of fixing dinner and cleaning house, I started to feel a gnawing fear. "If it were my child, I'd want to know what was in there," Dr. Behrmann had said. I also want to know, although I will admit I have felt too afraid for the last week or two to face the issue of the growing lump—just when I had been so sure it was disappearing. Well, ten more days of antibiotics will tell. The lump must get smaller—yet I hardly dare to hope. On the other hand, I feel the Spirit reasoning with me that if the lump got smaller before on antibiotics, it is not malignant. I must exercise my faith that everything will be all right. I really believe erythromycin may do the trick. It has been our miracle drug several times in the past.

JANUARY 7, 1985

Michael's lymph node did get smaller on the erythromycin, but it seems to be growing again. Dr. Shigeoka says she definitely feels it is not malignant but some virus. Tests show it is supposedly some "serious" infection, whatever that means. She at one time said it could be AIDS! What a terrible notion. How would he get that? I don't think I believe it.

I feel like I am just one big ball of worries and fears about the kids' health, medical bills, making doctor appointments, and so on. Every morning I ask myself, *Who needs to go to the doctor today?* I find it hard to trust any one doctor. I always feel I have to come up with the right diagnosis and medicine, because I am more familiar with this disease than are the family doctors in this area.

Today Seth had a low fever and sore throat. Michael had the same tonight. Both are coughing, as was Robert last night. Robert and Seth got throat cultures today. I had a bad sinus headache today and went to the doctor to get medicine. My sinuses have been bothering me for a couple of weeks. One sweet note: Matthew is okay! I thought he had an ear infection, but the doctor checked his ears, and they are perfect. He got his measles shot. He's happy and has been walking the last three days.

The dryer doesn't work now, so I'm hanging clothes all around the house at night. And the vacuum is broken again. This is very upsetting to me. We did get the washer, toilet, and car fixed, however. There has got to be some silver linings in all my clouds, and I know I am looking on the gloomy side of things. At least none of us seems seriously ill right now. That is indeed a blessing.

FEBRUARY 19, 1985
I talked to Dr. Shigeoka about Michael. She said if the lymph gland on his neck is really as big as we say (golf ball size), it should probably be removed, as it may be a tumor. So we go tomorrow to Salt Lake City to see her. I have noticed that Michael is always running a slight temperature—something I hadn't realized before. Everything is so scary. He could have pre-AIDS, lymphoma, or leukemia.

FEBRUARY 20, 1985
I asked Dr. Shigeoka if we couldn't please put Michael on erythromycin again, since it seemed to work before, rather than have the lymph node surgically removed. She consented and also added Septra along with it. These two antibiotics are a good combination of drugs to cover many bacteria. So we will give it a try.

Count your blessings. See the silver linings in the clouds of your life!

12

Blessings in Career, Health, and Motherhood

APRIL 15, 1985

I must mention that after much anguish on my part, we have been very blessed with Michael's lump going away. After three weeks of erythromycin and Septra, and after some jaundice from a liver reaction, the lymph node has become very small. The jaundice is gone now, and he is feeling very well. It is a wonderful relief after worrying about this for almost seven months.

APRIL 19, 1985

I continue to struggle daily to be organized in my house and to be patient with my children and with myself. It seems this struggle goes on forever. I have been inspired in the temple and from books and talks I have heard lately. I am encouraged to be obedient, to sacrifice for my family, and to pray for help in my responsibilities. We cannot force our children but must go before them and show them how to live by the way that we live. Children should have clear rules and consequences that are applied without anger. Always mildness and love. Turn the TV off and tune into your family. These thoughts help me to know what I should be working on to become a better mother.

APRIL 21, 1985

Today my soul is being led "beside the still waters" (Psalms 23:2). I am filled with love for the members of my family. Jessica, who is thirteen, spent an hour with me today reading the book The Outsiders by S.E. Hinton. She shares so much of her life with me. I love her, and she is so special.

My parents are gone now to Manila in the Philippines as directors of the Missionary Training Center. They had a wonderful farewell meeting. It was very sad to see them go.

APRIL 21, 1985 (MIKE'S JOURNAL)

Since January I've completed the semester of teaching and taking courses. It was a trying semester in that I felt a lot of pressure from having too many things going on at once (teaching, school, trips to Vernal with the Army Reserve, family, and church assignments). The pressures have caused some disharmony in our home. This last week we took the entire family and three of the kids' friends to stay overnight at our grandparents' cabin in Midway. It was generally a good time for all the kids. They took a hike or two and went swimming at the Homestead Resort. I should mention my contract with the Nebo School District [to be an intern school psychologist with half pay]. I ordained Jeremy a teacher in the priesthood today, feeling a strong spirit assuring Jeremy of his importance to God.

MAY 19, 1985 (MIKE'S JOURNAL)

I have had more time lately, as the semester is over. I'm teaching Tuesday and Thursday evenings and have a lot of time at home. I've painted four pictures, spent a day at the church's meat-packing plant, and helped my neighbor put in a fence and unload some horse manure. There are some projects I need to work on around our house, but we need more money.

JUNE 27, 1985

This is Seth's tenth birthday. He has been such an obedient, conscientious son whom I am proud of. The other day as he was studying the scriptures, he asked me what one scripture meant. It was the one regarding that if a person has faith to be healed, he will be healed, if he is not appointed unto death (D&C 48:41). I had tears in my eyes. I think Seth is wondering if he could be healed from his immune deficiency.

AUGUST 23, 1985

The kids started school two days ago. It has been very stressful for me, although things have gone quite smoothly on the surface. I decided to take the morning off today, as I was just tied up in knots. I've exercised, played with Matthew and Robert, made brownies, and looked over my goals. This seems like a good year to work on writing my book, to get Jeremy into good study habits, and to work with Seth on his reading and math. Maybe I can give some piano lessons to my kids also. Not having a baby during this time gives me more time that I won't have later on.

My happiness and the happiness of my family depend on me becoming more organized. I need a house of order, a time for every purpose, a time to pray, meditate, study, work, have recreation, and give service. Also, my blueprint for myself is that I would like to be gracious, kind, efficient, beautiful, and strong.

OCTOBER 13, 1985 (MIKE'S JOURNAL)

This summer was quick in passing. We had a trip to Idaho to see my family. I taught religion classes at BYU, both spring and summer terms. Jeremy had a trip to the Virgin River in southern Utah—took a hike and came home with three lizards. I started my internship as a school psychologist and have enjoyed my first few weeks doing some testing and counseling. We are so glad that we now have health insurance for the family.

MAY 13, 1986

I was preparing to give a Relief Society lesson to the women of the church on teaching our children to work. After reading the lesson, I got up to a really messed-up house. I prayed for strength and assigned the kids chores. It turned out to be a wonderful day, and we accomplished so much!

I admit I was extra pooped at the end of the day, but I also felt peace and happiness. It is so worth it. I can do it! I can teach my children to be good workers! If I can do just half of what I did today, with my children's help, I will feel like a success. This is important because in five months I will be having my ninth baby! I want the house to be in better order before it comes!

Set achievable goals and work to accomplish them!

13

A Pleasant Surprise

SEPTEMBER 7, 1986

I haven't written in this journal all summer. We had a good summer, and I succeeded in teaching the children to work more than they ever have before. The kids each have a certain area of the house and the yard to clean up with a card of written instructions. Areas are rotated.

I feel I have a new self-image. I see myself as a successful worker, a good delegator—one who can accomplish in a day what I plan to accomplish. We can get to school and church on time with breakfast in our tummies. Weak things have become strong (or stronger) to me, with the Lord's help. Mike also tells me I am doing much better.

The time for the birth of our ninth child draws near in only about five weeks! All indications—both physical (ultrasound) and spiritual (dreams, feelings)—indicate it is a girl. It is so reassuring to know that now we have health insurance to cover this birth through Mike's new full-time job with Nebo School District.

OCTOBER 12, 1986
So much has happened since I last wrote, and my life has turned upside down, in a good way. The night before the birth of our baby, we got dinner done and the house cleaned up early. Mike gathered all the kids into the living room. He laid his hands on my head and gave me a husband's blessing. He blessed me that all would go well with the birth of the baby (by C-section) and that the baby would be healthy. He blessed me that I would have great joy in our new child. I had felt a lot of fear about the operation during that day, but during the blessing, all fear left me, and I felt peaceful and confident.

The next day Mike and I drove to Mountain View Hospital in Payson, Utah, around seven in the morning. They sent us upstairs to labor and delivery and took us into a lovely birthing room, which had a very homey atmosphere. They had me take a Phisohex shower and then put me in the bed and monitored the baby's heartbeat. I had very low blood pressure for a while after they gave me an epidural, but soon, our new baby boy was born, contrary to all my thoughts and feelings that it was a girl.

It has been a difficult decision for us to decide that this would be our last baby. I have prayed often in the past few weeks concerning the matter, and I did feel peaceful and confident that this could rightly be our last child. But the whole time I thought I was carrying a little girl. So it threw me for a loop when it was a boy. I didn't understand. Maybe the Lord is showing me that I am not as inspired as I think I am. He is in charge of my life.

But I love my new baby boy so much. He is so darling! He is definitely not a disappointment, just a surprise. We scrambled to choose a name and decided on Richard James Curzon. He's been crying a lot in the hospital nursery. The doctor says he appears to have a sore throat. I too have a sore throat as well as pain from the C-section. My parents called me in the hospital from the Philippines to wish us well. It was so good to hear their voices. They sent a pretty yellow quilted baby blanket.

OCTOBER 1986 (MIKE'S JOURNAL)

Tuesday of this week our ninth child was born—an eight-pound-thirteen-ounce, twenty-and-a-half-inch boy. He was healthy, and Colleen was fine except for a few minutes' scare when her blood pressure dipped low.

OCTOBER 26, 1986 (MIKE'S JOURNAL)

My work has been going well. I started full-time with Nebo School District as a school psychologist. The pay isn't great, but I enjoy the work, and to me that is very important. I have still been teaching religion classes at BYU for summer and fall semesters.

Tonight I sang some songs in the bedroom with Robert (four years, ten months) and Rebekah (seven years, three months). My children are wonderful. I need to spend more time with them having fun and sharing experiences.

OCTOBER 30, 1986

This has been a very good day, starting out with my prayer expressing my thanks for my new little son, Richard, and for all my children and husband. I also expressed my frustration at not being able to get things done with the baby so fussy and colicky. But he slept most of the day. I've felt a peace and quiet guidance in my activities. Two sisters from the church dropped by, and one brought dinner. I listened to devotional talks and cleaned the house. I'm grateful for a day of respite and relative peace.

NOVEMBER 27, 1986 (MIKE'S JOURNAL)

It's been a good Thanksgiving day. We had turkey and all the fixin's— apple, pumpkin, and mincemeat pie.

Since Richard was born, he has had some earaches and so on that have made him quite fussy. He's one and a half months old now, and I'm hoping he gets settled down and requires less total care in coming weeks. He's a cutie and probably will be fine.

I have been contemplating my many blessings, in spite of my many weaknesses.

DECEMBER 25, 1986 (SETH'S JOURNAL)

Today our family got a computer for Christmas, an Apple II. I got a Styrofoam airplane and book on bird-watching. I also got a parakeet. Tomorrow we are going to my grandparents' house. They just came back from their mission in the Philippines on the twenty-third of December for a little while, and then they are going back. We are playing Oregon Trail on the computer. It is a fun game.

JANUARY 6, 1987 (SETH'S JOURNAL)

Our grandma Ruth came from Idaho on December 26 and stayed until December 31. I am learning a lot about bird-watching now, and I am back in school. My bird is healthy and strong now.

JANUARY 17, 1987 (MIKE'S JOURNAL)

On December 7 Richard was blessed by me in church. Other brethren joined with me in the prayer circle. He was blessed with a strong, healthy body and that he would get along well with his associates, that he would be a blessing to his friends, and that he would have the fullness of the blessings of the gospel, including eternal marriage.

FEBRUARY 15, 1987 (SETH'S JOURNAL)

Today I went to church. I named the parakeet I got for Christmas Gorby. He is doing pretty well. And the baby Richard is smiling a lot, and he makes a lot of sounds. He is four months old now, and he can say "Hi" and make many sounds.

APRIL 12, 1987

My sweet baby Richard is six months old. I had pretty high hopes that he was a normal baby with no immune deficiency, but alas, his blood is not producing any antibodies to the DT (diphtheria/tetanus) vaccination, so it seems he does not have a normal immune system. I put off calling the doctor for a few days, as I was too afraid to find out—too afraid that my hopes would be dashed. I called the lab, and they said Dr. Behrmann had the results. I didn't want to call, so Mike did. The nurse said, "It looks like he is not producing antibodies." Mike had a shocked look on his face. He hung up and told me. I turned the other way and said nothing, wishing the last minute in my life had never happened—that I could turn the clock back to moments before when we'd been able to tell people, "We don't know yet. It could be either way." Now I knew it had turned out for the worst, and I wished I did not know.

APRIL 14, 1987

Our baby Richard will begin getting intravenous gamma soon along with the other three boys. They've been going to Mountain View Hospital in Payson, Utah, every three weeks to get their IVIG. It is a relatively short drive. Now that we have good group health insurance through Nebo School District, it is so wonderful that they can get these expensive treatments (which average around $2,000 per child per infusion). There is no way we could afford this without health insurance, so it is such a blessing. The boys love going to the hospital, lying in the beds, watching TV, and being served dinner. They are treated like royalty and don't mind being stuck with a needle to get such treatment. They know that getting their gamma is like a car getting gas. It has to be done so they can go forward and live their lives!

JUNE 15, 1987

My little Richard is not as happy as the other boys to be getting IVIG. The nurses tie him onto a papoose board to keep him still and then try to find a vein to stick the needle into. He doesn't understand what they are doing, of course, and he cries and kicks until the IV is in. He is lucky, however, to be starting this excellent treatment at such a young age, which the other boys were not able to do. Hopefully, he will have much-better health since he is getting the ideal treatment starting so young.

JULY 9, 1987

Last night I spent some time in the twilight pulling weeds out of the vegetable garden Mike has planted and enjoying my children, who were swinging and playing football. My sweet baby Richard was crawling around on his blanket on the grass. Such a darling! The moon was big and round with thin clouds covering most of the sky. The air was warm and soft. It was so beautiful. I suggested that the kids sleep outside in the backyard. It was one of the happiest days of my life— fear gone, joy and love all around. This is really a special time of my life. The kids are healthy, and life is good! I am so grateful!

Don't pity yourself or your children for their illnesses. Help them to accept their treatments as a necessary way of life and see the good in it.

14

When Ye Are in the Service of Your Fellow Beings

MARCH 25, 1987 (MIKE'S JOURNAL)

Tonight nine-year-old Michael ran his car in the Cub Scout pinewood derby. He and I carved and painted the small car from the kit he was given to race on the track. Afterward we went to McDonald's (Seth, Michael, Rebekah, Robert, and I). Today I passed my oral exams for my educational specialist degree at BYU. I met with three professors who quizzed me on my thesis and on course material from my school psychology training.

APRIL 1987 (MIKE'S JOURNAL)

I graduated from BYU for the third time—BS in 1970, MS in 1975, and now educational specialist (EdS). My mother came down from Idaho to attend the convocation. She gave me a Cross pen, the miraculous pen of the pen world.

MAY 24, 1987 (SETH'S JOURNAL)

School is almost out. I'm in the seventh grade now. Tomorrow is the last day of school for me in the seventh grade, and we get out at one o'clock because we are getting yearbooks.

MONDAY, JUNE 29, 1987 (MIKE'S JOURNAL)

Yesterday I was sustained and set apart as the first counselor in our congregation's bishopric by President Gibb, of the church stake presidency. I feel love for the great men I will be serving with. I feel that we will make a good team.

JUNE 28, 1987 (SETH'S JOURNAL)

Today is Jessica's fifteenth birthday, but she is not here. She went up to Oregon to help our aunt Paula, who just had twins.

Yesterday was my twelfth birthday, and I got an open-reel fishing pole. Today I got ordained to be a deacon in the Aaronic priesthood. I felt good being ordained, and I still feel good. The bishop told me that if I pray often, I will become very powerful in the Lord's hands.

JUNE 30, 1987
Mike was called to be first counselor in the bishopric, three men who work together as the administrators of our congregation. I know he is a good man and the right man for the job at this time. But I will need the Lord to give me strength to do my job better—taking care of the house and the children, being a better example in all ways. I have been stiff with fear. Being in the bishopric of the church requires my husband to attend many meetings in the evenings and on Sundays. He must go to church early, which leaves me to get all eight children to church on time by myself. It is challenging, but it's a blessing for Mike to serve the members of the church.

JULY 6, 1987
I've gone through a lot of self-doubt with Mike's new calling. I really need to organize myself more fully, although things are so much better than they used to be. I feel so inferior at times. But I have my own talents, and all I can do is my best, even if it's not as good as another person's best.

JULY 9, 1987
Yesterday, after receiving a priesthood blessing from Mike, I truly felt joy and love. I have enthusiasm for my new calling as choir director at church. I walked to the church, got some choir music, and enjoyed looking it over and seeing all the beautiful songs we can sing. I talked to my neighbor whose son was run over by a car and is in a coma. I tried to give her hope by telling her about Robert as a baby when we thought he would die from his long illness, but look at him now—a healthy, happy boy. I trust that her son will come out of this also.

Two nights ago Seth had a bad stomach pain for a few hours. He vomited, but still the pain persisted. At two thirty that morning, Mike gave him a priesthood blessing. Seth fell asleep right after and had no more complaints again. The Lord really is there. He really does answer our prayers over and over again. Why should I ever doubt or feel I am alone? I'm not!

AUGUST 27, 1987

I've been under mental stress as demands increase upon me from our church callings and kids starting school with their many activities. So I am taking a day off today, with the phone off the hook, so I can look at my life. I have had some great experiences this summer, going to the temple, going to part of BYU Education Week, visiting our neighbor's son at the hospital, seeing our nine-year-old Michael on BYU Kids Club on TV for winning an art contest, welcoming Jessica home from Oregon after she helped Paula with her twins, and so on. My first priority is to have a happy family and to raise my children to reach their potential. I need to cut down on my activities for a while until I can learn to handle the basics by following a monthly calendar.

OCTOBER 1987

Today was the General Conference of the church. We stayed home in the morning and listened to the conference on TV, had dinner between sessions, and then drove our kids to Temple Square in Salt Lake City. President Benson gave a beautiful talk titled "Come unto Christ." We walked around the temple grounds with many other people as the talk was broadcast over the loudspeaker. It was a beautiful, sunny autumn day. It was nice to see the beautiful Christus statue and to be strengthened and inspired.

DECEMBER 21, 1987

Yesterday I had a marvelous experience in my calling as choir director. It was our Christmas program. As I led the congregation in that last verse of "Oh, Come, All Ye Faithful," words fail to express the pure joy I felt. This calling has been a great blessing to me. There is no earthly pay, just heavenly pay when we serve the Lord.

Overall, as I look over the past year, we have been very blessed with relatively good health, no major illnesses in the family, and opportunities to serve the Lord in church callings and to help others to grow and learn. This is certainly the purpose of life.

MARCH 2, 1988

My parents, Verl and Arline Scott, came home from their three-year mission to the Philippines on February 12. All of us—cousins, aunts, and uncles—met them at the airport at two that afternoon. We all wore red, white, or blue and held balloons, and we had a sign that said, "Welcome home, Mom and Dad!" We shed tears as they came off the plane. There were hugs and kisses. They had never seen my baby Richard, so that was special. Later in the week there was a surprise open house for them and then their homecoming meeting. What great servants in the church they have been. How well they have used their lives to bless the lives of many people! "When ye are in the service of your fellow beings, ye are only in the service of your God" (Mosiah 2:17, B of M).

Later, however, we were concerned to learn that Dad has a lump on his jaw that has turned out to be a cancerous salivary gland. This showed up just two weeks before they came home. He will be having surgery and radiation. I hope all will go well with him.

JULY 1988

Richard (twenty-one months old) is darling. He's learning to talk and says, "Mom, a one" ("I want one"). He walks and runs all over and plays with the kids. I love him so, as well as the other little ones and big ones.

We have more big kids in the house right now because my sister Wendy sent her daughter, Jenny, from Louisiana to stay for a couple of months this summer. She is sixteen, the same age as Jessica. Of course, they are boy crazy. They are also working at the Payson cherry plant where the newly picked cherries are processed on conveyor belts and packed into buckets with sugar for cherry pies, etc. I have been driving them back and forth to work. It is a yearly ritual around here to work at the cherry plant to save money for school needs.

AUGUST 16, 1988

I saw Dr. Shigeoka yesterday with Michael and Richard. We are becoming better friends. She is also a Girl Scout camp leader, and she said something to indicate she was raised as a Quaker. How interesting. I feel love for her and somehow feel we are kindred spirits working to keep my boys healthy.

We had the Scott family reunion this month at East Canyon Resort in the mountains east of Salt Lake. The whole family was there, including my sister Wendy and her family from Louisiana and my sister Paula with her new twins. I was in charge of the relay races and prizes for the kids. We went to my parents' church on Sunday and sang our family's special song, "Oh, That I Were an Angel" by Wanda West Palmer. We had Sunday dinner at their condominium and stayed all day singing around the piano. Wendy and I sang with our two teenage daughters, Jessica and Jenny. So many tears flowed—tears of love and sadness, because Jenny was leaving after living with us all summer (although it was a challenge to have two rambunctious teenage girls in the house!) I felt so happy to be with all my family. It was like heaven to me.

FEBRUARY 4, 1989

Mike, Richard, and I drove to Salt Lake City to pick up Jeremy from a Washington DC trip paid for by the Senate Youth Program. I'm excited to have him back. We went to Mom and Dad's condo and visited for a couple of hours afterward. Jeremy told us about his African American roommate from Georgia, the tours of Washington buildings, President Bush taking off from the White House lawn in a helicopter, and meeting with Senators Hatch and Garn from Utah. We are thrilled to learn that Jeremy has received a four-year scholarship from BYU along with his $1,000 scholarship from the Senate Youth Program. He certainly has earned it by his hard work and straight A's in high school. We are very proud of him.

We had delicious homemade soup made by Grandma. Grandpa said how he would like to at least live to see the year 2000. They just had their physicals and are in apparent good health. I hope it's true and that the cancer Dad had treatment for last year won't return.

When you have a break in your life, try to give back to others in service and love.

84

15

Oh, Dad!

FEBRUARY 14, 1989
Valentine's Day. I called my mom and dad to wish them a happy wedding anniversary, their forty-third. Dad was not feeling too well and said that the night before he had felt a bad pain in the right side of his chest. That day he had been taken to the emergency room. A chest x-ray had shown a mass in his right lung. "It may not be too good and may be related to the surgery I had last year," Dad said, meaning the cancer surgery on his jaw. "We'll see the doctor next Thursday to have a bronchoscopy to get a biopsy. We've had forty-three years of marriage and a good life together," Dad said. I was in shock. It was the beginning of a nightmare for our family.

FEBRUARY 19, 1989
We spent Sunday evening with my parents in Salt Lake City (an hour drive from Salem) along with many of my sisters' families. Dad wasn't feeling too bad, just uncomfortable with a cough. We shared our love and tears, apprehensive of the biopsy to be done on Thursday. Jackie related to me that Dad said to her, "Jackie, I know that this could potentially be very serious. But I am prepared to take whatever comes. No one owes me anything. I've had a wonderful life, and I've never been more prepared to go than now."

FEBRUARY 23, 1989
My sister Jackie, who is a nurse at LDS Hospital, just called. Today we all fasted and prayed as a family because Dad had his bronchoscopy biopsy. Jackie was crying when she called. She said there's a tumor in each of Dad's lungs and they're beginning to block the airways. The doctor said the prognosis is bad. "Are we talking days, weeks, months?" asked Jackie. "Months," he said. Mom and Jackie both

burst into tears upon hearing the news. Dad goes to the oncologist next Tuesday to determine treatment. The doctor said that if there are family members who live out of town, they should come to visit soon.

After I hung up, one member of the family was angry that dinner was late (at five thirty instead of five). Then a man called just a few minutes ago saying, "We'd like to take care of this automobile accident." (I had backed into a car in a dark parking lot a week ago.) To top it off, Dr. Behrmann put Seth in the hospital today for pneumonia. He came home from school having difficulty breathing. He's alone over there at the hospital while all this crazy stuff is happening! He's fourteen, so I guess he can handle being alone for a while. We have been treating him with several antibiotics for the past twelve days, but he has continued to get worse and spiked a high fever. He's now on breathing treatments and intravenous antibiotics. He had a chest x-ray and blood tests. It may be just a virus. However, our immunologist, Dr. Shigeoka, has told us that we should always treat things like this as if they were bacterial because of the immune deficiency. I can't believe all the bad things that are happening today!

FEBRUARY 27, 1989

Seth has been having frequent illnesses lately. This week he stayed in Mountain View Hospital for a few days with his pneumonia. The doctor made us wear gowns to visit him in his room to protect him from germs we might carry. We had to do this because his white cell count was so low. Because of Seth's neutropenia, or low white cell counts, I've always had to explain to doctors that when he spikes a high fever, he may in fact have pneumonia, even though the chest x-ray may not show it. Since his body can't make pus without white blood cells, the infection may not show up on the x-ray.

After receiving the intravenous antibiotics, Seth's fever went away in about twenty-four hours, and the doctor said, "We need to get Seth out of here as soon as possible. A hospital is a bad place to be for someone who has such a low white count, because there are so many bad germs in hospitals." That seemed like a strange thing to say, but it must be true.

Seth was sent home with intravenous antibiotics, which I was to administer every six hours for several days into the IV catheter in his arm. At six in the morning, twelve noon, six in the evening, and twelve midnight, I infused the IV antibiotics dripping from a metal IV pole into his body. Such a schedule made it hard to get a good night's sleep, but it was good to see Seth recover.

Seth has also been getting frequent ear infections, so much so that his eardrums are scarred from the many times they have actually ruptured. He takes all these illnesses in stride as a normal part of his life and continues to work hard in school in spite of frequent absences or days of going to school half-sick. He was also on community football and basketball teams but was unable to continue due to his illnesses. Even though he is short and underweight due to being sick so often, he is a "trooper," as my dad would say. Such a great kid with a lot of faith and love!

FEBRUARY 28, 1989
Today Dad saw the oncologist (cancer specialist) to find out his course of treatment. My sister Jackie called sounding very cheerful after meeting with Dad's doctor. "Gee, I am really kind of encouraged," she said. "He said chemotherapy may give many more months to Dad's life. But he cannot promise a cure."

"We're going to fight this!" I said to Jackie. She agreed.

I called the Cancer Research Institute and they're sending me information on research currently being done on Dad's type of cancer.

MARCH 2, 1989
I received materials from the Cancer Research Institute. With Dad's stage 4 salivary gland cancer, the prognosis is poor. Chemotherapy has fair success. (They should have given him chemotherapy when he was first diagnosed a year ago!) Only about 5 percent of patients live past five years. Maybe Dad could be one of those five percent? Very depressing. I will not show this to my parents.

SATURDAY, MARCH 4, 1989
My sister Barbara called this morning. She said, "Colleen, we've found something that might help Dad!" She had heard on the radio about an American Indian herbal mixture called Essiac that treats cancer. It has supposedly cured some people with terminal cancer. Dad read some of the book and said we might as well try it. "Oh

good," I said, "because I also want to talk to Dad about some vitamins and diet recommendations."

Mike, Jeremy, and I drove to Salt Lake City to get Pyrex lenses for the laser Jeremy is building as a science project. Later we stopped in to visit Mom and Dad for a while. When I arrived, Dad was watching a BYU game with Barbara's husband, Russ, in the den. Dad was coughing some, and I noticed how his pants seemed to hang on him as he changed channels. He has lost some weight but seems strong and cheerful still.

While we were there, Barbara and I called health food stores to find the herbs for Essiac. We talked to Dad about trying everything—the chemotherapy, the herbs, the vitamins. Dad told us about a priesthood blessing he had received from Elder Ballard of the Council of the Twelve Apostles. We're trying every possible avenue to heal him.

MARCH 6, 1989
Dad started intravenous chemotherapy in the hospital along with nausea medicine. Mom called about ten o'clock this evening and said that Dad had done very well—no nausea. He had slept most of the day because of tranquilizers.

MARCH 7, 1989
More chemotherapy for Dad. Dad still doing well. He went home today.

MARCH 8, 1989
Dad went to the cabin to try to fix the toilet. He didn't tell Mom he had lost his breakfast until they got up there. Now Dad is taking oral chemotherapy pills instead of intravenous medication.

SUNDAY, MARCH 12, 1989
I've been afraid to call Mom and Dad for the past few days. I assumed Dad would be sick after the chemotherapy but have been hoping he would be better by today.

TUESDAY, MARCH 14, 1989
Mom called us tonight asking that both Mike and I be on the phone. It had to be bad news. Barbara and Jackie, my sisters, were on Mom's extension phones. They started to cry. My heart stopped. Mom said, "I'll let Jackie take over." Jackie said Dad was in the hospital again.

He had been very ill, had gotten dehydrated, and had choked on some food, causing him to pass out. The paramedics had taken him to the hospital, where the doctors concluded that the cancer had spread to surround his esophagus and larynx and he could no longer swallow. The chemotherapy wasn't working! There was nothing more they could do. Barbara had told the doctors about Essiac, and they'd said, "Sure, go ahead and try anything you want to." Doctors would put a tube into Dad's stomach through his nose to give him liquid food. I was in total shock. The cancer had grown so fast!

THURSDAY, MARCH 16, 1989
My dad has written a memo to us children and his grandchildren. I read it to the family around the kitchen table. The memo encouraged us all to be true to the gospel and to love each other. Jessica and Rebekah cried. Barbara called and said that Dad is much encouraged by the news of Essiac coming tomorrow and my brother, Richard, coming Saturday from Arizona to stay. I called Dad to say how much his memo meant to us. I am always worried that each time will be the last time I see or hear him.

MONDAY, MARCH 20, 1989
I spent an hour this morning reading the Bible and found a scripture in the Old Testament about King Hezekiah, who was granted fifteen more years to live when he was about to die. He was given an herb and lived a long time (2 Kings 20). Could Dad have this same blessing?

Jeremy, Seth, Rebekah, and I visited Dad at his home. The feeding pump has been running during the night, giving Dad two thousand calories per day. Barbara has also started giving him the Essiac herbs through the feeding tube. Dad seems tired. His weight is down to 144 from 155 a month ago. His blood pressure is down too, 90/54. He has been coughing up mucus.

There were several bouquets of flowers in the room. Like a funeral, I thought. Many people called on the phone to ask how he was doing. When I talked to Dad, I rambled about trivia, feeling great anxiety inside. I sat next to him on the couch and lay my head on my daddy's shoulder. But it seemed we could not really talk about what was actually going on. "I love you, Dad," I said as we left.

On the way home I worried about the process of dying my dad would probably have to go through and about the fear of death. The Spirit seemed to whisper, "Everything is under control." I could see in my mind's eye my dad surrounded by loving spirits at his death, taking him through this new but very natural experience. There was no need for fear. I felt a great relief and peace for the moment.

MARCH 31, 1989

We had an emergency family reunion for a couple of days, and it was wonderful. The first evening was a temple trip to the Salt Lake Temple for Mom and Dad and all their children and spouses who could make it. Wendy was here from Louisiana. Richard and Lee Ann were here from Arizona and Paula and Dave from Oregon. Dad was too weak to go through a temple session with us, so Richard took Dad to the celestial room in a wheelchair. Mom went with them also, and they waited there for us in their white clothes. In the session, we all stood in a prayer circle with a special prayer in our hearts for Dad. As we walked into the beautiful celestial room, Mom and Dad were sitting on the couch. With tears in our eyes, we each came up and gave them a hug and kiss. It was very touching, and we hoped that such a reunion could again occur for all of us in the celestial kingdom of heaven after death.

After attending the temple, we all went to Mom and Dad's condo and ate dinner, although Dad could not eat with us. We met in their bedroom later with Mom and Dad sitting on the bed and the rest of us circled around them in chairs. We went around the room and each expressed our thoughts and love to Dad in a farewell meeting. I was the first one to speak, being the oldest child. It was hard for me to open up. I said I hoped he could be healed with the herbs as Hezekiah was in the Bible. My brother, Richard, said that he felt Dad had "received his call" to go on a mission in the spirit world. And Dad never would turn down a call to serve the Lord.

There were lots of tears, but we all laughed when Dad said, "It's not very often a person gets to attend his own funeral!" The meeting ended with special words from Dad. He expressed his testimony of the gospel and the great love he had for all of the family. He admonished us to make sure that "l-o-v-e, the most important thing in this world," was paramount in our family relationships as husband and wife and told us how important it was that our kids especially know we love them.

He told us that he and Mom had recently purchased cemetery spaces in a mausoleum—"Because I want to be warm when I die!" he said. We laughed again. Dad has such a great sense of humor even when he is so ill, and he has such a special way of expressing his thoughts in his strong, deep voice. He said, "Symbolically I place my hands upon each of your heads and give you a blessing that you may be strengthened in your lives even though sometimes life seems so very difficult."

It was two of the most wonderful hours of love and unity I have ever spent in my life with "the Verl F. Scott forever family," as we call ourselves. This family meeting was recorded on videotape. Even though Dad seemed pretty strong, he had the feeding tube in his nose and continued to hiccup throughout the meeting due to the cancer in his esophagus—constant reminders of how very ill he really was. However, he claimed he was not in any real pain, just "uncomfortable." The Essiac is supposed to prevent pain. Maybe it has.

SATURDAY, APRIL 1, 1989
We had more of the family reunion with the kids having an Easter egg hunt outside and then the grandchildren having a talent show. It was fun. Then Dad asked Jeremy and Jeff to come forward, the two oldest grandsons, who had both just won scholarships to Brigham Young University. He expressed his pride in these boys as an example to the rest of the kids. Dad also showed us some special pocketknives, each engraved with an eagle, to be given to all the grandsons who get their Eagle Scout award in the future.

SUNDAY, APRIL 2, 1989
We all—Mom, Dad, kids, and grandkids—watched the General Conference of the church on TV together, just as we had always done growing up. After dinner we all gathered around for a special song, "God Be with You till We Meet Again" (Rankin 1998, 152). As the strains of the music "Till we meet, till we meet, till we meet at Jesus' feet, God be with you till we meet again" were sung, we knew this would be one of the last times to be with Dad before he was with

Jesus. Then we all knelt in a family prayer, the proper benediction to the great life Dad had lived.

FRIDAY, APRIL 14, 1989

Dad has been in the hospital for a few days in a last-ditch effort to give him some chemotherapy. Then he got pneumonia, so my parents decided to return home, as the chemo didn't seem to be helping. My sisters and I have been taking turns spending the night with them in their condominium. My turn was tonight. As I drove to Salt Lake alone to help take care of Dad, I was so afraid. I was afraid that I would meet Mom at the door to find her in tears. I prayed all the way that I would be able to be strong to help her. When I got there, Mom and Barbara did indeed meet me with crying, saying that they'd thought they were going to lose Dad just a short time earlier. I felt like I had to take over and be strong.

Dad was very weak. He complained of being hot even though the room was cool. We sprayed him with water from a spray bottle, and he had a fan blowing on him. Finally I suggested that we give him some liquid Tylenol through his nasogastric tube, which we did. It seemed to help him to not feel so hot. We were up and down with him all evening and night. He was very weak. Sometimes he choked up some dark-brown material and was very frustrated because he couldn't cough it out. He was getting panicky, and so was Mom.

Finally I told them how I had done postural drainage on my boys when they were sick with pneumonia. I told Dad to get down on the floor on his stomach. We put a pillow under his hips. I pounded on his back with a cupped hand for a while, like respiratory therapists do in the hospital. It helped the secretions to come out, and he could breathe a little better. Mom was very relieved and grateful that I seemed to know what to do at that time. Later I asked Dad if he wanted to get back on the bed. He said, "No, I'll stay here on the floor." Never have I seen my strong father so totally overcome by anything. It was alarming. He slept there on the carpet without any covers for an hour or two. He seemed like a physically defeated man. It hurt me so much to see him that way.

SUNDAY, APRIL 16, 1989

I returned home to my family knowing that Barbara and Jackie would be helping Mom to take care of Dad. It was obvious that the time of his death was near. Life was overshadowed with a heavy, dark cloud, as I knew that Dad was dying and we couldn't stop it.

TUESDAY, APRIL 18, 1989

My dad died last night, April 17. He was only sixty-nine years old. I never thought I would write this. It was my sister Jackie who called me about five this afternoon to tell me the sad news. He had been having difficulty breathing and was trying desperately to cough the phlegm out of his lungs. Finally my sister said to him, with her authority as a nurse, "Dad, you don't have to cough it out. Just relax."

"I don't?" Dad said, trying to be the perfect patient.

"No, you don't."

Gradually Dad lay back and tried to relax. Soon he seemed to be in a coma and was breathing very loudly and slowly. This went on for a few hours, but then Dad calmly stopped breathing. And it was over.

Oh, Dad! How I love you! How can you be gone? My dad has been my hero my whole life. I have always admired him and looked up to him for his strong faith and determination to do the right thing. He has loved us and encouraged us our whole lives. I remember when I was nine years old taking swimming lessons. On my first time to swim in the deep part of the pool, we were asked to dive in. I was absolutely terrified. Then I looked up in the balcony above the pool and saw my dad there. He gave me a thumbs-up, which gave me the courage to dive into the deep, dark pool. He's always been this sort of influence on me and my siblings.

Since I am forty-two years old and have lived away from Mom and Dad for a long time, I didn't think his death would hit me so hard. But it has! I will always be his little girl in my heart, no matter how old I am. I am so devastated and so surprised at my great sorrow. Tears flow freely.

Mike and I gathered our kids up after school to tell them the sad news and to drive them to their grandparents' place. When I walked into Mom and Dad's condominium, I hurried into the bedroom to see Dad. He was lying on the bed, his body already gray and somewhat stiff. I hugged him and cried and cried, wailing from sorrow, surprising myself with the grief I displayed. Where was my grown-up, dignified self? Buried under a little girl's tears. My daddy was dead! After a minute I realized the spectacle I was making in front of my siblings and children and calmed down. Dad had been deceased about two hours now. The mortuary was coming soon. Everyone said their individual goodbyes to Grandpa.

The doorbell rang. The man from the mortuary was here to take his body away. I was horrified when they took out a black plastic body bag, put my father in it, and zipped it up all the way so we could no longer see him. How could they be so inconsiderate? They carried his body out the door. He was gone, and now we were left in the emptiness of his house without him. It did seem empty, even though there were probably twenty people there. How could life possibly carry on without Dad? What were we to do now?

My mother was the most bereft of all of us. Dad's death was a terrible blow to her. She had been so dependent upon Dad's strength throughout her married life. Now she seemed like a sail without wind, a shadow of her former strong self. We would have to take care of her fragile emotional state. It had always been Mom and Dad. Now it was just Mom.

When we returned home to Salem that evening, I felt like Dad was there in our house watching over us. My son Jeremy counseled me about the importance of giving all the kids chores to do around the house instead of trying to do it all myself. Somehow, I felt that Dad was speaking through Jeremy to me so that my life could be happier and easier. I definitely felt my father's spiritual presence in my home that night.

APRIL 22, 1989

Today was my dad's funeral—a wonderful and sad occasion. General authorities of the church spoke. The grandchildren sang a song my mother wrote about the wonderful qualities of faith and love of their grandpa. My brother spoke and sang Deanna Edwards's song "I'm Glad That God Chose Me to Be Your Son." In his talk, he read some of the words my father had spoken in the special family meeting we'd had:

I hope you kids know that if it were to happen tomorrow, I wouldn't be any more ready than I am right now. I cannot believe any more strongly than I do that there is a God and Jesus Christ is our Savior and that there is a life beyond this one. I know with all my soul that the gospel is true. There is life after death. I would hope always and forever that this testimony will ring in your ears where I am concerned.

Dad's casket was placed in the mausoleum at Wasatch Lawn Cemetery after the dedicatory prayer on the grave and a 21-gun salute by the 142nd Linguist Battalion of the Utah National Guard, of which Dad had been a colonel and second commander. The flag draped over the casket was folded and given to my mother. It was a very solemn and impressive occasion. My father was such a great man and had an astounding influence in my life for good.

JUNE 18, 1989
Father's Day. I helped six-year-old Matthew learn a talk for Primary. He did very well. I helped the kids make a homemade Father's Day card for Mike. He and I have been so much closer lately. I love him very much.

I was very tearful tonight thinking of my dad. We got out the video of his talk to us at the family reunion. I was so comforted to hear it and was blessed by his counsel: "Face each new day with gratitude—each day is a new lease on life. Some things are more important than others—love is the greatest thing in this world." Dad is still alive. We just can't see him for a while.

SUNDAY, JUNE 25, 1989
We had choir practice tonight after church. As the director, I chose for the choir to sing "Families Can Be Together Forever." I told the choir about my father passing away. As I thought about Dad, tears caught in my throat when the choir sang:

I have a family here on earth. They are so good to me.
I want to share my life with them through all eternity.
Families can be together forever, through Heavenly Father's plan.
I always want to be with my own family, and the Lord has shown me how I can (Gardner 1998, 300).

The death of loved ones is devastating, but their bodies were too damaged to continue on in this life. They have transcended into a higher sphere, and we will see them again. Such understanding can bring us consolation.

16

They Are Not Far from Us

NOVEMBER 1, 1989

I was shocked this morning when my sister Barbara called to say that our grandma Ruby Palmer Scott had died during the night, October 31, Halloween. She was ninety-six years old. I felt very bad because I had planned on visiting her last Saturday while I was in Salt Lake. Mom and I had talked about going to see her in the nursing home but had changed our minds. I regret not saying goodbye to her three days before she died.

Grandma was a beautiful lady with a spotless house and fed us homemade bread with real butter. She smelled of perfume and was always so kind to me and my children. She would rock my babies sometimes and sing to them, "Rock-a-bye, don't you cry. We will go to Granny's. Over the hill, and far away, to see the little lambies." She had many years of ill health during the last twenty years of her life and had lived with my mom and dad for ten years and with Uncle Bob and Aunt Doris for a long time also. It was time for her to go to see her husband, who had died many years before. For the very old, death is timely and sweet.

NOVEMBER 4, 1989

Today was Grandma's funeral. During the funeral we learned that my sister Rhonda had had a dream about Grandma the night before she died. In the dream Rhonda met Dad and Grandma in a beautiful building. They were dressed in white, and she saw that Dad had come to get Grandma when she died. Rhonda said the dream was a revelation to her and very meaningful to her. Surely Dad did help Grandma have the courage to finally leave this life and go into the spirit world.

DECEMBER 6, 1989

I was feeling very sad today about my dad's death. I still cry about him, and it's been eight months. I happened to go into Jeremy's bedroom and saw some pictures he had taken on the top of his dresser. Amid the photographs were some he had taken of the Salt Lake Temple. As I looked at them, I felt very comforted to know that we would be a forever family even though death has separated us right now. What hope and joy and comfort these thoughts bestowed upon my soul! I dried my tears and went back to my daily duties.

APRIL 13, 1990

It's been almost a year now since Dad died. This morning before I woke up I had a wonderful dream about him. At the beginning of the dream, I was at a funeral. At one point it seemed like it was Mike who had died. I felt bad that there had been bickering between us at times. Now I knew I was really alone. I could not go to him when I needed comforting. But I also knew that we did love each other even now in his death and that our love would last forever.

Later I was in a large hall that seemed like the temple, and I was surprised to see my dad walking down the hall going in the opposite direction. I called to him, "Dad, I love you." He came and put his arm around me, and we walked together. He was dressed in white clothes— pants and shirt. His hair was grayish white. He looked healthy and happy. His form had a slight haziness and luster, so I knew it was his spirit, not his body.

Later we gathered in a room with about half of our family members— children and grandchildren. Dad started to teach us some things he had experienced and learned since his death. "You know," he said, "your life is only about three minutes long in eternity." He spoke very few actual words, but when he spoke, it seemed I was shown visual aids or movies that clearly presented what he was saying. (A picture is worth a thousand words.) I perceived that all the small incidents of our lives are recorded like on a roll of movie film, but the film is run by so fast, and what really matters is the overall theme or emphasis of our lives.

"What do you think is the most important thing in life?" Dad asked.

"Love people," I said.

"Yes, that's right," Dad said pleasantly.

I feel he meant that in all the little moments of our lives, in our family, church, or community service, it is most important that we have a feeling of love in our hearts for those around us and a desire to bless their lives. Words are really inadequate to express my experience.

Then Dad said, "Don't ever touch a cigarette in your life." I then was shown a spirit who had been addicted to cigarettes before he died. Now his prior use of cigarettes was causing him to be spiritually ill and in bondage in the spirit world. I assume that my father was referring to all kinds of addictive substances—alcohol, drugs, and so on. These substances leave our spirits captive and ill.

Next I seemed to see different places in the world and people that lived long ago. Dad said, "The people long ago said America differently than we do. They said Ameryeekah!" I could see the people that he was talking about. They had such love and hope in their faces, such longing for and joy in being able to come to America, the promised land! It was a dream come true for them to come to this land of freedom.

I could see the country of the United States as if I was looking down on it from space. I saw some of the people who live in America now who were totally oblivious to the blessing that was theirs to live in America, taking it for granted and blindly pursuing worldly pursuits. They were unaware of the grand scope of things around them in the heavens and the earth, past and present. They lived in their own self-centered worlds, oblivious to the great plan and creations of God. I feel that Dad was expressing admiration for those people of long ago while cautioning us not to become part of those who take these blessings for granted.

It was about then that I woke up. The most wonderful part of the dream was that I could really see my father in three dimensions. He was there! He was happy and loving. I felt his arm around my shoulder. Dad wanted to share what he had learned with us, but he wouldn't force himself upon us.

This experience taught me that at times we may come in contact with our loved ones who have died through inspired dreams. The spirit world is real! I have been crying often about my dad's death for almost a year, but I think my tears of sadness will stop now. I know he lives and is happy.

You may have special dreams or feelings that your departed loved one is near and wants you to understand his or her new reality and continued love for you.

17

Watching Our Kids Grow

NOVEMBER 4, 1989

A lot has happened the last few months. Jeremy moved to Brigham Young University and is living with his cousin in the dorms. I've missed him, but it's a great opportunity for him to be at BYU. I'm very proud of him. Finances have been a concern to us lately. I guess the best way to save money for Jeremy's mission next summer is in the food budget. My part-time job can be canning, baking bread, and cooking from scratch using basic, bulk foods—flour, potatoes, sugar, apples, powdered milk, and so on. I've been doing a lot of this lately.

DECEMBER 17, 1989

This weekend we've had a hospital in our house! All four boys with the immune deficiency—Seth, Michael, Robert, and Richard—have been ill with parainfluenza, a virus that has been going around almost like an epidemic. They have had high fevers and coughs. The rest of us are okay. This is where their immune deficiency really shows up. The gamma globulin is effective especially against bacterial infections and diseases against which many people have immunity, such as chickenpox.

I remember a few years ago, before the chickenpox vaccine came out, when Jeremy was about twelve, he had a very bad case of chickenpox with fever and his body covered with spots. This was with his normal immunity. Robert, on the other hand, who was getting gamma globulin on a regular basis, had only about five spots and did not feel sick at all. So sometimes gamma is better than our natural immunity, but not in the case of this flu virus.

[*Note*: In the following pages I include frequent excerpts from the journals of my teenage sons Seth and Michael, whose lives and trials

101

will be portrayed more fully later in this book. Michael loves to play the violin, and Seth is a falconer who has a license to capture and train hawks. Both boys suffer from the immune deficiency.]

DECEMBER 1989 (SETH'S JOURNAL)

I have been sick a lot this past year, so I have missed a lot of school. In one term I missed thirteen days. In the last few months miraculous things have happened. In many of the Communist countries, the government and the people have changed. In November the Berlin Wall came down.

APRIL 16, 1990 (SETH'S JOURNAL)

Jeremy has come back from BYU and is going to live with us another two months and earn money for his mission. The past day or so the USSR has declared that they will let missionaries come into their country. All the Communist governments are falling: East Germany, Hungary, Austria, Yugoslavia, and many other countries have been freed from Communist government. And many of them are letting missionaries in. I am in the ninth grade and have seventeen days left of school. Last Sunday some neighbor kids brought over two baby killdeer birds. I asked them to lead me back to the nest to put them back in.

I am getting good grades this term and will probably get a 3.9 this semester.

MAY 29, 1990

Today is a red-letter day. Jeremy got his mission call from the church to go to the eastern United States. The whole family was there when he opened the envelope (even the IV home health nurses were there, giving our four boys their IV gamma globulin infusions). He goes into the Missionary Training Center on July 5.

Jessica graduated from Spanish Fork High School on Thursday, May 24. She looked beautiful in her white cap and gown. Both grandmas came down, and we found a pretty good seat in the front bleachers. While at Spanish Fork High School Jessica participated in many dramatic plays and was awarded the Best Actress trophy. Friday she learned that she has been awarded a one-year full-tuition scholarship to the University of Utah and has also been accepted into the Actor

Training Program there. She is really talented in this area. My kids are really growing up now!

AUGUST 19, 1990 (SETH'S JOURNAL)

In late May our family went to St. George. We swam a lot, and I caught a foot-long chuckwalla lizard. It eats flowers and other vegetation, so it is easy to feed it. I also have a scorpion, Mr. Mahuta, which Jeremy and I caught last summer. He is still very healthy. I catch crickets for him in our neighbor's giant rock garden.

My brother Jeremy had his mission farewell on July 1 and went to the Mission Training Center (MTC) on July 5. Before we took him to the MTC, my dad gave him a father's blessing. My dad cried, and I almost did too. In the MTC, when it was time for Jeremy and us to go, it was the closest I came to crying of sadness with him leaving. Jeremy gave everyone a hug and left to do his missionary work in the MTC.

Near the end of July my Scout troop went on a two-day trip down the Green River. I caught a twenty-inch fish. We walked upstream and floated back down to camp on inner tubes. The water was about forty-five degrees. It was freezing cold. My legs and arms ached because they were so cold.

AUGUST 1990

Seth went on another Scout trip this summer up in the canyon. On a Saturday morning when they returned, the Scout leader knocked on our door with Seth with him. The first thing he said to me was "Do you want me to take him to the hospital?" I didn't know what he was talking about, but he soon explained that Seth had gotten wet from the dew on the grass. He'd started shivering and had gotten hypothermia. (Scout trips are always concerning to send Seth on because of his fragile health, but he loves to go. Even when the family goes swimming at Payson Pool, Seth is always the first to get out, because he starts getting very cold with bluish lips. He is so thin that he can't fight off the cold temperatures.) I told the scoutmaster I would take Seth to the doctor, which I did. He was okay.

However, after the Green River Scout trip, Seth began to have stomach pains in his upper right abdomen. After some stool testing, it was found that he had contracted giardia from the river water, so he had to take metronidazole pills to treat it. The pills, however, made him nauseated, so it was a tough few days to get him over this infection.

When Michael was about four years old, he was also found to have giardia after having diarrhea for two years. When the doctor discovered it, he said, "I am so sorry! I didn't suspect he would have this. I thought he just had common childhood diarrhea." Michael did get over his diarrhea with medication. Did he suffer needlessly for two years just because nobody knew what was wrong? How terrible! Michael didn't seem terribly bothered by it, however. He just took it as a normal part of his life. We gradually learned to be very leery of swimming in rivers and lakes and of drinking any water from the canyon streams, something that did not seem to be a problem when I was a child.

AUGUST 23, 1990 (MICHAEL'S JOURNAL)
Yesterday was the first day of school, and I'm in eighth grade. Mrs. Dunford, my orchestra teacher, said that our orchestra could go to Snow College this year for the String Festival and also for the String Ensemble Festival. We will also go to the Utah Valley Symphony again, and this time we get to go to Sizzler for lunch, and I'm really excited.

AUGUST 24, 1990 (MICHAEL'S JOURNAL)
Yesterday I went to school and had a pretty nice time. Then I came home and went to the doctor's even though I didn't want to. After that we zoomed over to Mrs. Dunford's house, where Bonnie (her daughter) gave me a private violin lesson, and that was fun. Then I bought some stuff for school, came home, ate dinner, did my homework, cleaned my room, and went to bed.

AUGUST 30, 1990 (MICHAEL'S JOURNAL)
Yesterday I got up, went to another regular day of school. But in art class we were doing a coat of arms, and in the mascot section I drew a castle. When I went home, I really felt like drawing another castle. It's probably the best castle I've ever drawn. Then I went to bed.

SEPTEMBER 30, 1990 (SETH'S JOURNAL)
On September 26, I caught an American kestrel hawk, which I've been training for the last four days. I took the falconry test to get my state

license, so I was allowed to do this. In school I got an A in Health, a B in Chemistry, an A in Geometry, and an A in World Civilizations. On the second day of my high school year, a couple of seniors and juniors made me push a penny with my nose along the floor.

OCTOBER 4, 1990 (MICHAEL'S JOURNAL)

Yesterday, almost the very second I got home from school, I had to change, stuff two biscuits in my pocket and one in my mouth. Then Seth, Richard, and I got in the car. We picked up Robert, and my mom drove us straight to the hospital, where we had our IVIG (five hours). I had to be poked three times, and my left arm got all puffed up. But we got to have the yummy hospital dinner and watch TV.

OCTOBER 5, 1990 (MICHAEL'S JOURNAL)

Yesterday I got up, went to school. When I came home, I watched some TV. Then I got a snack. Afterward I went downstairs and practiced my violin with Rebekah (she plays the cello.) Then I started on my homework while listening to some classical music. After that we ate a lamb chop dinner (gross). Then I watched TV and had a yummy snack. Then I did the dishes and went to bed after telling Richard a story.

OCTOBER 19, 1990

Michael has begun playing the violin in the junior high orchestra. He is short, so when the orchestra teacher came to his sixth grade class to invite students to take orchestra in seventh grade, Michael's small hands seemed perfect for the violin. He really loves playing and practicing it.

Although Michael seems to be doing well, he is very thin, and his stomach is still enlarged due to his liver. I decided he should go to a gastroenterologist to be checked out again in Salt Lake City. He was put in Primary Children's Hospital to have another liver biopsy. Before the biopsy, they first gave him platelets to prevent bleeding, because his platelet count was low due to an enlarged spleen (which often goes along with liver trouble.) The biopsy was performed successfully. It showed that he did have fibrosis of the liver but not full-blown cirrhosis, so that was somewhat good news.

The doctor was very concerned that Michael wasn't getting enough calories on a daily basis, as he only wants to eat half a piece of toast each morning and does not eat a lot the rest of the day either. (Liver problems cause the appetite to decrease.) She told Michael he had to start eating richer food in larger quantities. The hospital kitchen delivered a large grilled cheese sandwich for him to eat. He ate most of it, but it made him sick, and he vomited. His body isn't used to dealing with such high-calorie, rich food. Anyway, she urged us to strive to increase his caloric intake, for he will not be able to go into puberty until he reaches around a hundred pounds. So I set aside a special drawer in the bedroom with high-calorie treats for Seth and Michael to eat anytime they want to in order for them to gain more weight.

The younger children—Rebekah, Robert, Matthew, and Richard—are doing well. Matthew was a star reader in first grade. Rebekah and Robert are also doing well in school. Richard has learned to climb the walls, literally, in the hall. Unbelievable.

DECEMBER 25, 1990

Christmas. We went to visit Mom in Salt Lake City and met Marshall Brinton, a man my mother has been dating. He seems like a very nice man.

DECEMBER 29, 1990

Mom called to announce her engagement to Marshall. We were both glad for her and sad. It's been two years since my dad died, so it's nice that she will have someone to take care of her and she won't be alone. But nobody can begin to take my father's place in my heart!

JANUARY 3, 1991 (MICHAEL'S JOURNAL)

After school Rebekah, Heidi Bradley, and I went out and cleaned the camper trailer in the backyard while listening to *The Four Seasons* by Vivaldi. Then I went inside, cleaned my room, took a nap, did my homework, and ate dinner. Mom, Jessica, and Richard have to stay up in Salt Lake because Jessica had surgery on her sinuses and they had to stay for a doctor's appointment.

JANUARY 11, 1991 (MICHAEL'S JOURNAL)

Yesterday I got up, had yummy Indian fry bread for breakfast. Then I went to school, came home, and watched TV. Then I went down to my room and made my bed and cleaned my room after practicing my violin for about one and a half hours. Then I did my homework while listening to an opera by Mozart on tape. Then I sat around, read my scriptures, and went to bed.

JANUARY 11, 1991

My calendar is a sight to see with so many activities for all the children—violin lessons, Scouts, dance lessons for Rebekah, orchestra for Michael and Rebekah (she is learning the cello), Primary, high school plays and gymnastics for Jessica, karate for Robert, Matthew, and Richard, and, of course, doctor and dentist appointments. Matthew tends to get strep throat pretty often. Rebekah gets a rash at times when she takes antibiotics. They tend to have the normal illnesses of childhood which don't turn out to be very serious. But it makes me sad when they are sick also.

Life is certainly busy. I do a lot of driving back and forth to all the kids' activities. We strive to help the kids find and develop their natural talents and to encourage their education by watching educational shows on PBS. Robert and Matthew are obsessed with studying dinosaurs right now and have been drawing dinosaurs and making a book about them. Most of the kids, as well as Mike, are very artistic and talented in drawing and painting. Not me, however. I play the piano and encourage their musical talents. It is a joy to see them all so busy and happy in their lives.

MAY 13, 1991 (MICHAEL'S JOURNAL)

This weekend I went to my violin lesson, did my homework, and later Rebekah and I went and got a bunch of flowers and made a menu after buying Mom a necklace chain at K-Mart for Mother's Day. Sunday morning we did a restaurant thing for Mom and Dad (breakfast in bed). We took their orders and then cooked what they wanted. After church we went to Salt Lake to Aunt Barbara's house. We played, ate, talked to Jeremy on the phone from his mission, and goofed off. We listened to stuff about the summer family reunion.

107

[*Note*: This was a nice memory for me. They decorated our bedroom like a fancy restaurant with plants all around and then fed us a wonderful breakfast of bacon and eggs and pancakes. What sweet kids!]

People with immune deficiencies can have many normal activities in their lives. There are many good days among the bad days. They have special talents and interests. Encourage them to really live and enjoy life!

18

Dreaded Phone Call

SUNDAY, JANUARY 13, 1991

Terrible, fateful day. Mom called about ten fifteen this morning. She was crying and said, "Rhonda has been killed in a car accident on her way to the Tabernacle Choir broadcast!" Rhonda is my thirty-six-year-old younger sister. On Beck Street, her car had slid on some black ice, twirled around, and rammed into a telephone pole on the driver's side. She was killed instantly. I was just stunned. I always knew that sometime I would get a phone call like this—finding out that someone had died unexpectedly. My first thought was that out of all the people in my family, yes, she was probably the one most ready and worthy to enter into eternal life. *Of course she would be the first to go,* I thought. But it was such a shock.

We went to church, as Michael, my thirteen-year-old, was scheduled to play his violin. The whole meeting seemed surreal, but I knew there was nothing I could do at this point to prevent what had already happened. It was comforting to hear the gospel taught, to hear Michael's violin solo, and to sing hymns after learning of this horrible news.

We drove to Salt Lake after church and met at my mother's condominium with the rest of the extended family. Craig (Rhonda's husband) and their six children, ages five through fifteen, were there. There were many tears and hugs as we all tried to comprehend the news of Rhonda's death and to comfort each other. How could this be? The story was on the local TV news—a Syracuse woman on her way to the Mormon Tabernacle Choir broadcast was killed in a freakish accident caused by black ice.

JANUARY 14, 1991

More information about Rhonda's accident has been trickling in and shared through our family grapevine. Apparently someone who lived across the street from the accident saw it happen. They ran over to the car and saw Rhonda with a smile on her face right before she collapsed and died. (Why was she smiling? Did she see my dad coming to get her?) The neighbors called the paramedics, who took her body to the hospital. The doctors determined that she'd had her seatbelt on, which may have made it worse. Her chest had slammed into the pole, breaking an artery that goes to the heart. She had bled out in a matter of seconds, and there was nothing that could have been done to save her.

Her family decided to donate the corneas of her eyes. This gives us all a small bit of solace to what seems such a senseless death. I went with my sisters to the mortuary to see her and help dress her. She was slim and beautiful. She was only thirty-six but had borne six children—three boys and three girls. I know she was wonderful at teaching her children.

I remember one time when all the family was staying overnight at Mom and Dad's cabin. In the midst of the vacation-mode frenzy of multiple cousins, Rhonda gathered her children around her knee to say their personal prayers before the cousin sleepover and then made sure they brushed their teeth. I don't think any of the rest of us parents thought of doing these simple things with our own children in that situation. But Rhonda knew prayer was important no matter what the setting.

Rhonda was also a very fun person. She was very active in church callings and creative service to others. She sang solos in church and created beautiful crafts for her home. So full of love, testimony, and fun. Her marriage with Craig seemed to be ideal. She had valiantly fulfilled her purpose on earth. How interesting now to remember the dream she had of meeting Dad and Grandma Scott in the spirit world. It must have been a premonition of what was to come for her.

I drove down to Beck Street to see where the accident had happened. The heavy metal pole that the car had struck lay on the side of the road. Broken glass covered the street in the lower-class neighborhood. How sad to realize my sister lost her life there!

JANUARY 14, 1991 (SETH'S JOURNAL)

The United States is preparing for war against Iraq for invading Kuwait. The United Nations set a deadline for Iraq to pull out by tomorrow.

My first hawk got away, and I've had about four or five after that. All of them escaped except one. That one died by freezing in the subzero weather. I have another one now, and I think I'll be keeping it for quite a while.

JANUARY 15, 1991 (SETH'S JOURNAL)

Tomorrow, when I come home from school, our family is leaving for Syracuse, Utah, to attend Rhonda's viewing and to stay overnight at Grandma's for the funeral the next day. I feel very bad about the death of my aunt. I remember the fun times she made for us at family reunions and the like. You never really appreciate people until they're gone. I feel bad for her kids and her husband, Craig.

I received a microscope for Christmas. It's really neat. It can go up to 1200 power. I've been doing exceptionally well lately in school. I'm in tenth grade, 5 feet 5 inches tall, and weighing just under a hundred pounds. My grades this year have been 3.75, 4.0, and the third term I think I'm getting a 3.9.

JANUARY 15, 1991 (MICHAEL'S JOURNAL)

This Sunday and Monday have been good and bad. To start out with I got up and was practicing Bourrée on the violin when Grandma called and gave us the bad news. Aunt Rhonda got killed in a car accident. When I went to church, I performed my solo. Everyone said that it was absolutely wonderful. We went to Grandma's house and saw them talking about Rhonda's accident on the news. It is so sad, especially for her family.

JANUARY 19, 1991

My sister's funeral was amazing. The chapel was filled all the way back to the stage in the cultural hall. A portion of the Tabernacle Choir sang. I helped choose one of the congregational hymns—"Each Life That Touches Ours for Good." One part says, "When such a soul from us departs, we hold forever in our heart, a sacred, hallowed memory, bringing us closer, Lord, to thee" (Davidson 1998, 293). That hymn will always remind me of Rhonda. She was a beautiful person in every way.

I feel that Rhonda was well prepared to meet God. We all have our time to go, and there are definite reasons for our being taken in death when we are. So there is nothing to fear in all this (although we do anyway). All is well. There is no tragedy in death, only in not being ready, with our lives in order, when death comes to us.

The day after the funeral, my mom and Marshall Brinton decided to get married early since so many family members were here from out of town for the funeral. We feel that Dad sent Marshall into Mom's life, especially to help her in this sad time of Rhonda's death.

Some people just seem to shine! And sometimes those special people are taken from us earlier in their lives than we think they should be. Only heaven knows why.

19

Cancer Scare and Confirmations of Faith

MARCH 25, 1991

For a few months I have had a feeling of discomfort and pain in my left breast and collarbone. I intended to see the doctor about this after Christmas, fearing it was cancer. But when Rhonda was killed in January, I thought, *I can't see the doctor now. If it is bad news, I couldn't do this to my family, especially my mom. We can't have so many tragedies all at once.*

One day the discomfort was so noticeable that I called Dr. Clark right then to make an appointment for the following week. The doctor didn't feel anything but suggested I have a mammogram soon. When I went for the mammogram, at first it all seemed pretty routine. The mammograms were taken, and I was about ready to get dressed when the technician came back into the room. "The doctor wants to take another shot. He's found a lump in your left breast. Is that the one that you said has been bothering you?"

"Yes," I replied. Suddenly all my silent fears that I had cancer and that I was going to be the next to die avalanched upon me. My mind was overtaken with fears.

While waiting for the doctor to come in, I spent a few minutes looking over a pamphlet on breast disease that was in the mammography room. One chart showed the average sizes of lumps found by a first mammogram. Mammograms could find lumps the size of a pea, which people might not be able to feel. That's okay, I thought. *I can live with a pea-sized lump. It should be no big problem.*

When I walked into Dr. Green's office, he greeted me kindly, then put four x-rays on the screen for my observation. Two of the x-rays were mammograms done in 1989, showing fibrous changes but no lumps. The second set were today's mammograms. "See how the right-breast films show no real changes? But your left breast shows a new lump that was not present in 1989," he said. I stared in disbelief. This was no pea-sized lump but a whitish circle about the size of a quarter. "The thing that concerns me is that this is a totally new formation that we did not see before," the doctor said. "I would strongly recommend that you have it removed right away and that we not wait. Do you have a history of breast cancer in your family?"

"No," I answered.

"Well," the doctor said, "like I said, we should take it out and have a look at it to make sure it isn't cancer. Are you okay?"

I nodded, and the doctor left the room. I ambled toward the soft pink couch. It was nice of the hospital to have such pretty surroundings to tell you horrible news. It did somehow make it more tolerable. I sat there alone for a half hour. How could I go home now and tell my husband? I dreaded telling my mom. I was shaking slightly, but I wasn't cold. I was just afraid, so afraid.

I had been on a diet for a couple of days—whole grains, no sugar, healthy foods, and vitamins. Maybe if I hadn't eaten all those chocolate candy bars in the past year, if I had eaten more nutritiously for the last two years instead of the last two days, this wouldn't have happened. Or maybe it was from stress. Maybe if I had lived the Word of Wisdom (the health code of our church) to the tee, the destroying angel would have passed by me as promised. If only I had eaten less fats and more fruits and vegetables! But if all this was God's plan for me, then I could take it. For a moment I felt a sweet peace in that thought. So many thoughts whirling in my head! So afraid. So afraid. So cold. How could I go home and act like everything was normal when my life had turned upside down in the last hour? It was a nightmare come true.

JUNE 7, 1991

Seven weeks have passed since I last wrote in my journal and was convinced I had cancer. As it turned out, I had a biopsy, healed quickly, and the lump was found to be benign—no cancer. All the fear was for nothing, except that it actually has had quite a profound effect upon me. Thinking I was going to die caused me to look at my life more carefully. I have had too much contention in my heart. I have had envy of other people's money. I was not spiritually ready to meet my God. I decided I want love and peace and freedom from anger more than I want to have a clean house or to lose weight or to have a beautiful yard. Those things seem to not be terribly important anymore. I want to be a better person than I have been in the past.

JULY 7, 1991 (SETH'S JOURNAL)

Today I was ordained to the office of a priest in the church. I am sixteen now, and I will be a junior in high school this coming fall. I have started driver's training course. Well, anyway, today has been a very special day for me because of my ordination. My heart swelled with joy today as I tried to listen to the Spirit and gain a spiritual experience, which I did. I love the Lord and know He lives and have had experiences that have testified this to me.

JANUARY 5, 1992 (MICHAEL'S JOURNAL)

Today has been rather eventful because I set my goals for this year, which include writing in my journal. I'm happy just because I feel fresh and new, like my future is unblemished and I can keep it that way!

JANUARY 6, 1992 (MICHAEL'S JOURNAL)

Today has been rather uneventful, unlike yesterday. I went to school, came home, slept (because I had a bad headache), and then ate and practiced the violin, did my homework, read my scriptures, and now I'm going to go to bed.

JANUARY 8, 1992 (MICHAEL'S JOURNAL)

Today I had another headache. Every day this week I've had one. I went to the string choir. It was fun.

MARCH 7, 1992 (MICHAEL'S JOURNAL)

Today started at six in the morning when we got up to get ready for the stake priesthood meeting at seven. Everyone was tired, but I got some good things out of the meeting. It's too bad I can't seem to remember things like that very well. I then came home and slept for a few more hours, then went to church.

The last few weeks have been quite eventful. First of all, on November 18 (my birthday) Grandma and Marshall (my step-grandpa) went on a mission to Palmyra, New York. For Christmas I mainly got a wonderful Sony stereo that I've been wanting for a long time. Back to the last few weeks—I'm now working for an older lady who owns a kennel. I feed dogs, mix food, wash and dry puppies, sweep, mop, and my favorite—poo scooping. But so far I've made about seventy dollars in the last two to three weeks. The first thirty dollars was spent when Kendall, Rebekah, Heidi, and I went to the mall for a day. I got a J. R. R. Tolkien poster, some tapes, and two fish, a beta (Poserdo) and a little goldfish (Triton).

I also competed in our school music competition. My solo and ensemble won on Tuesday, and the ensemble and I played for the whole school. Everyone says my violin solo sounded good, but I know I made many mistakes. Maybe they didn't hear or notice them. Today my older goldfish, Aquarius, died. We also have another cat, Pumpkin. We got her in about September. I'm looking forward to playing the beautiful music I'm listening to now, The Four Seasons by Vivaldi.

By the way, last summer Rebekah and I went to summer orchestra. I swear that it is the most fun thing in the world (even though it's at 7:00 a.m.). Denise Willey, our director, is the funniest person who ever lived. Mrs. Dunford (the orchestra teacher) is great! I am now enjoying Triad English and US History (honors) in school. And "The Book" that my friend Kendall and I are writing is great! I also have an A+ in art, and String Choir is so fun.

MAY 7, 1992 (MICHAEL'S JOURNAL)

Today I fasted and got a headache, but it was worth it because I got a great patriarchal blessing, an inspired prayer for me and my life. It talked mostly about service, opportunities, and some missionary work. Afterward, Mom and Dad took me out to eat at a Mexican restaurant.

JULY 1992

Mike and I, with Seth, Michael, and Rebekah with us, drove to the eastern states in the station wagon to pick up Jeremy from his mission. (Robert, Matthew, and Richard stayed at my sister Barbara's house.) It was a great, inspiring trip. We picked up Jeremy at the mission home and met the mission president. Then we were able to attend a missionary meeting where Jeremy spoke and the missionaries sang "Called to Serve" (Gordon 1998, 249). It was the most beautiful, inspiring moment of my life to hear these missionaries sing this rousing song and to know that my son was among them. We also visited a family that Jeremy had taught.

After that, we took off to visit my mother and her new husband, Marshall, in Palmyra, New York, where they are serving a mission. There are many Mormon historical sites in the area. We saw the Joseph Smith home, the Sacred Grove where he had his first vision, and the Whitmer home, where a lot of the Book of Mormon was translated. Later we drove to Liberty Jail and Carthage Jail, where Joseph Smith was martyred. We visited the city of Nauvoo, Illinois, which was built by Mormons, and looked across the Mississippi River where the pioneers crossed on ice to leave their beautiful city, escaping from their enemies. All these church historical sites were very strengthening to my faith.

JULY 1992

We returned to Utah and picked up Robert, Matthew, and Richard from my sister Barbara's house. I wish they could have come with us, but there was no room in the car. They will have opportunities in the future for more trips when they are older.

AUGUST 1992

Robert's appetite seems to have gone down. He will often leave food on his plate and go off to play. I suppose he is just too excited to play rather than eat. Probably nothing serious.

> *It pays to take time to grow spiritually and to look*
> *inward to improve our character traits.*

20

Chronic Illness

SEPTEMBER 1992

My son Robert, age ten, went on an overnight camping trip at the end of the summer with the scouts. After coming back, he got a low fever and reduced appetite and complained of a sore in his mouth and of his ear hurting. We went to see Dr. Shigeoka, our immunologist at the University of Utah Medical Center in Salt Lake City. She said he had swollen, red tonsils and thought he might have strep throat. He was put on amoxicillin, and she also raised his gamma globulin dosage from twelve grams to fifteen grams every three weeks. She said nothing was visibly wrong with his ear.

After a few days at home on the amoxicillin, Robert continued to have a fever and earache. The medicine was not working. It should have worked if he indeed had strep throat. So we switched him to Pediazole, a liquid antibiotic that is a combination of erythromycin and Septra. It seemed to help his ear feel better, but his fever and swollen tonsils continued. His appetite was poor.

A terrible fear began to grow inside me. As a baby, Robert had very similar symptoms that had ended up with nine months of illness, malnutrition, intestinal bleeding, and weight loss accompanied by almost constant fever. Surely it wouldn't happen again! No! Please, no!

NOVEMBER 1992

Robert has lost a lot of weight and is still sick with fever and poor appetite. I bought him some new skinny pants and a little belt because his clothes had become much too big and baggy for his thin torso. I am afraid that Robert will die within a few months, so I arranged to have a family picture taken. Will it be our last picture all together?

118

DECEMBER 1992

I continue to take Robert from one doctor to another. After waiting for two hours to see our family doctor, he recommended that Robert take hot lunch at school so he could gain weight. What a ridiculous idea! He already did take hot lunch. We made meals for him all the time. The problem was not the availability of food but that Robert just would not eat it. He always said he wasn't hungry. The doctor said, "Well, I'll do what I do with little old ladies. I'll give him amitriptyline, an antidepressant that also increases appetite." So we have tried that, and it seems to have helped a little. Robert has gained a little bit of weight.

The doctor also found that Robert has giardia in his intestines. So glad to find an answer. I trust that when we get this treated, he will be well!

JANUARY 1993

Robert is still ill. The Flagyl medication, for giardia, has made no difference in his health. So I guess the giardia was only a piece of the puzzle. Robert has been missing many days of school, so the school has arranged for him to be on home/hospital instruction. Once a week, a kind older male teacher comes to bring Robert schoolwork and helps him with it. This has been very helpful so that Robert can pass fifth grade. He is still doing well academically and learning what he needs to learn.

Robert has had a lot of painful mouth sores lately on his gums, tongue, and so on. I fear that he has sores in his esophagus and stomach also. The doctors have not given us any good answers or cures. They have given him a special mixture of yeast medicine, Maalox and Benadryl to help his mouth feel better. We've also used liquid lidocaine to numb his mouth before he tries to eat. Rinsing with salt water every hour has also been helping. In looking things up in my medical book, it sounds like it could be trench mouth. The book recommends a variety of vitamins.

JANUARY 13, 1993 (SETH'S JOURNAL)

I just got back from a trip to California with my debate class. I have been in Lincoln-Douglas debates. We left on Thursday the seventh and drove until we got to the Peppermill Hotel, where we stayed. The palm trees we saw were awesome. After swimming and playing around we went to bed, and the next morning we left for Anaheim, California, where we stayed for four days.

FEBRUARY 2, 1993

Being very distraught with Robert's trials, I decided to read the book of Job in the Bible. He was a righteous man who had terrible things happen to him and his family. Maybe I could find some insight to help me in my agony over Robert's illness. The book of Job was long and tedious reading. But there were a few gems of wisdom and inspiration that stood out to me and put our suffering in perspective:

> Man that is born of a woman is of a few days, and full of trouble. He cometh forth like a flower, and is cut down: For there is hope for a tree, if it be cut down, that it will sprout again, and that the tender branch thereof will not cease … If a man die, shall he live again? Thou shalt call, and I will answer thee (Job 14:1–2, 14:14–15).

> When he hath tried me, I shall come forth as gold (Job 23:10).

> Oh, that I were as in months past, as in the days when God preserved me; when his candle shined upon my head, and when by his light I walked through darkness … When the Almighty was yet with me (Job 29:1–3, 29:5).

Job said to God, "I know that thou canst do everything" (Job 42:1–2). And the Lord gave Job twice as much as he had before and "blessed the latter end of Job more than his beginning" (Job 42:12).

So in spite of losing his family and being covered with boils, out of Job's deep trials eventually came blessings and joy. I hope that Robert and our family will someday experience the same and come out of this deep trial. I cry myself to sleep often. All I can think about is how to get Robert well from this nightmare.

MARCH 1993

Since December Robert has had a severe case of laryngitis, along with enlarged tonsils. Will we ever hear his voice again? In January I decided to take him to Dr. Gibb, an ear, nose, and throat specialist. He used a special instrument to look down at Robert's larynx. Dr. Gibb determined that Robert had a sinus infection along with lots of small white sores on his tongue, throat, and larynx. He put Robert on an antibiotic as well as antiviral Zovirax capsules.

Robert was put in the hospital to get a closer look at his vocal cords under anesthesia. After the procedure, Dr. Gibb said that he'd had to cut out part of Robert's vocal cord! He could not predict how Robert will be able to talk in the future. Dr. Gibb also had to cut off Robert's epiglottis because it was hanging by a thread due to a large sore there. The epiglottis is what keeps food and water from going into the lungs when we swallow. (Although Robert can still swallow without severe problems, he did develop a chronic cough around that time.)

Something amazing happened after the operation: Robert was ravenously hungry! He ate a sweet roll in the hospital and other things. He hadn't eaten like that in months! I asked Dr. Gibb what had happened to temporarily increase his appetite so dramatically. He said that Robert had been given a shot of steroids to control swelling. Steroids increase appetite. I said it was a miracle drug and asked, "Could Robert have more steroids to help him out?" He was put on a low dose of steroid pills for January and February, and he ate much better during that time. However, he soon had the puffy red cheeks that come with prednisone. Dr. Shigeoka was also worried about other long-term effects, like muscle weakness and osteoporosis, as well as increased risk of infection.

We saw a rheumatologist at the university hospital who postulated that Robert might have some sort of autoimmune disease like lupus that was making him so ill. In that case, steroids or cortisone would be the proper treatment. However, the immunologist thought we should take him off the steroids by tapering them down over a week's time. So we reluctantly took Robert off the steroids, and he again became a sickly child with fever and no appetite.

Although our local doctors recommended that Robert get his tonsils out, the immunologist said that is a bad idea. "We should never take out any organs that can help the immune system such as tonsils," she said. So we didn't do it. The doctors continue to check Robert's white cell count, but it is always in the normal range.

Robert went to Primary Children's Hospital to have a barium swallow test. He had to drink a huge amount of chalky white liquid as they took live, moving x-rays of his swallowing mechanism and the motility of his esophagus, stomach, and small intestine to observe if food could go down properly. I sat in the corner and watched it all with great interest, hoping they would find a clue to his illness. The doctors didn't find any huge problems in the scan, so we are back to square one, not really knowing what is wrong with him.

Because Robert isn't eating much, he has again been losing weight. He is very weak, and we take him in a wheelchair down the hospital halls when we visit the doctor now. We've finally admitted to ourselves that he will probably need to have a nasogastric tube through his nostrils down to his stomach to get calories into him, just as when he was a baby. It is so painful to reach this conclusion. I've been having him drink a lot of eggnog, which is very high in calories and protein. But he drinks such small amounts that it isn't enough.

This month Robert was put in the hospital and had an NG tube placed into his stomach, and I was taught again how to change it. It stays in for a few days taped to his cheek. I wish we didn't have to do this. Even though he has formula going into his stomach, he often vomits and always feels nauseated. He will only tolerate about 1,200 calories per day. That is with a constant twenty-four-hour drip with a pump. My poor son! He can't even swallow his own saliva without feeling sick, so he has a cup that he spits in all day.

APRIL 1993

Now we have new problems. Robert is beginning to have bloody diarrhea, and he is becoming very pale and anemic from loss of blood and from not having enough nutrients to make red blood cells. So we will have to start taking him to the university hospital every few weeks for blood transfusions. He has been on doxycycline for a month, and it seems to have stopped his 104-degree fever spikes. Now he just has low fevers. He was also on Septra and other antibiotics for his sinuses.

MAY 1993

Robert has been in and out of Primary Children's Hospital several times but always returns home still sick. How long will this last? He still has no voice. I've been reading a lot about vitamins. Vitamin C can get rid of fevers, so I have been putting large amounts of vitamin C in his NG tube. It does seem to make the fever go away temporarily.

Robert lies on the couch and watches TV or sleeps all day and night. He always has a bowl at his side in case he needs to vomit.

I took Robert to an alternative medicine doctor in Provo, Utah, who recommended liquid vitamins, huge amounts of vitamin C, and liquid iron to build red blood cells. So we have been using those. He gave Robert an infusion of vitamins also. It's good Robert can get these through his NG tube. Of course, he continues to receive his intravenous gamma globulin infusions every three weeks. In spite of all we do, he is still very ill. Will this ever end? Chronic illness that goes on and on is one of the most *difficult trials I have ever been through*!

JUNE 5, 1993

A few glimmers of happiness in our sorrow. Seth graduated from Spanish Fork High School and has been accepted to go to BYU. We are proud of his good grades and accomplishments. He is raising rabbits out under our balcony to feed the hawk he has trained. They are so cute, and they do multiply quickly!

Michael held a personal violin concert at the Springville Art Museum. He played several numbers by himself with piano accompaniment by myself and his violin teacher, including the very difficult "Summer" from The Four Seasons by Vivaldi. He played wonderfully, and he is so handsome! We couldn't be prouder of him. His health seems good, and he has accomplished so much this year. He is still thin and his liver and spleen are still big, but he has been doing well. He and Rebekah are best friends, and she plays her cello with him. Matthew has been taking karate lessons, but Robert had to quit because of his illness.

JUNE 25, 1993

I have been desperately worried about Robert, and I told the Lord I would do whatever he wanted me to do if only Robert could get well. I felt prompted to give Dr. Shigeoka a copy of the Book of Mormon. Although I felt reluctant to do so, I decided to obey this prompting. I took Robert to her office. As usual, he was very ill and had lost more weight. She told me that sometimes kids with immune deficiencies just get ill and end up dying and the doctors don't really know why. After that cheery news, I told her I still had hope that he could get better and that I had felt impressed that I should give her a copy of the Book of

Mormon. She was nice and said that in her religious upbringing as a Quaker she'd also been taught to witness to people.

She had Robert admitted at Primary Children's Hospital again in Salt Lake City. After doing what I'd felt inspired to do, I was looking for a miracle. A couple of days later, I went down to the medical library of the hospital and was looking for anything that was similar to Robert's illness. The librarian came up to me and asked what I was looking for and offered to help me in my search. She looked on the computer for "immune deficiency," "bloody diarrhea," "anorexia," and so on. In doing so she came across an article about an immune-deficient boy with many of Robert's same symptoms. The boy in the article underwent an abdominal CT scan, and doctors found an infection and were able to treat it successfully. I was very excited to find this. Maybe this was my miracle.

The doctor consequently ordered a CT scan, which showed some narrowing of the ileum, a portion of the small intestine. With this knowledge, it was decided that Robert should undergo surgery to explore and fix the problem in his abdomen. Before surgery, Robert also had an upper endoscopy, which involved putting a tube and scope into his stomach, as well as a colonoscopy. These procedures showed many sores and lesions in his digestive tract. He was given some medicine, Versed, to help him not remember these procedures. I felt so sad and helpless waiting in the hall knowing what Robert was going through.

I also pushed the doctors to include the pediatric gastroenterologist on Robert's care team. This was the doctor who had recently seen Michael. When she came in and observed that Robert was so underweight and was vomiting a lot of what we were putting in the NG tube, she looked at him and said, "Robert, I want to get you well so you can go outside and play baseball!" She had a very optimistic attitude and decided that Robert should get a central line (intravenous tube into his chest that would go into a major artery). Through this central line he could get total parenteral nutrition (TPN)—proteins, fats, and carbohydrates—directly into his bloodstream. This is exactly the treatment he had received as a baby. I was thrilled that we were going to be making some progress and trying new things.

Robert did undergo surgery. A section of his small intestine was so infected and damaged that the surgeon removed it. The surgeon also took out Robert's appendix for good measure. The doctor said that it appeared Robert had Crohn's disease, which can affect the whole gastrointestinal tract and cause sores throughout. Later, however, after the tissue was observed under a microscope, we were told it was not actual Crohn's disease, but a Crohn's-like condition caused by his immune deficiency.

After the surgery the nurses attempted to put a large green NG tube through Robert's nostril into his stomach to suction out blood oozing from the operation. It was so painful, and Robert was crying and crying. We asked them to stop. Mike gave him a priesthood blessing to calm him down, and after the blessing, Robert had the courage to allow them to put the NG tube in. It seemed like the worst day of Robert's life. It was the only time he had really cried from all he was going through. The memory of that huge green tube and him sitting in the hospital bed trying to be brave as they put it in his nose is etched in my mind as a painful memory. Robert continued to have bloody diarrhea after the operation, and it seemed that he would never get better!

Robert is now also being given several intravenous antibiotics that are especially good for the digestive tract—ampicillin, Flagyl, and gentamicin. Surely all this treatment should get him well. I wish they had done this months ago.

JUNE 27, 1993 (SETH'S JOURNAL)

Now that I'm eighteen, I can get my general-class falconry license. I found a Cooper's hawk nest just yesterday, and if I don't find a goshawk nest, I'll get a Cooper's hawk. I hope I can find a goshawk nest before that time comes.

I'm really not very happy today even though it is my birthday. My little brother Robert, who is ill, is in the hospital. He's been sick on and off ever since September. Doctors are going to give him nutrient IVs and antibiotic and antivirus for the virus in his liver and against the bacteria attacking his body. My mom has been up with him at the hospital for the last four days. We're going up later on today.

JUNE 29, 1993

I will backtrack a little here to talk about a problem Seth has been having. About a week ago, Seth was on a hike in the mountains looking for bird nests. The next day he complained that a spot on the bottom of his foot was hurting. We looked carefully to find a sliver, but we saw nothing. His tennis shoes had a hole in them, so his socks were full of weeds. We figured he must have some little piece of a weed in his foot.

After a day or so his heel was becoming swollen and red. It was time to go to the doctor. There was some fluid coming out, and the doctor cultured it. The culture came back as being Pseudomonas, a potentially dangerous infection. The doctor decided Seth needed to come to the office every day for a shot of Rocephin, a broad-spectrum antibiotic. He went in every day for six days with gradual improvement of the infection. On the last visit, it appeared to me that the infection had not fully cleared up, but the doctor said Seth had received enough shots and that the infection was gone. I did not agree with him, but I hoped he knew what he was doing.

JULY 1, 1993

Seth has spiked a high fever just as he always does when he gets pneumonia. He will need to go into the hospital. Since Robert is in Primary Children's Hospital, the doctor arranged for Seth to also go there and be placed across the hall from Robert. I've never had more than one son sick in the hospital at one time. What a crazy life!

JULY 2, 1993

Tonight I am sleeping in a cot in Robert's hospital room. He is not doing well. Seth is also doing poorly. Usually Seth's fever will go away within twenty-four hours of starting intravenous antibiotics, but not this time. He still has a high fever. The doctor believes that his foot infection got into the bloodstream and caused pneumonia. They assume it is *Pseudomonas* pneumonia, which requires very strong antibiotics, a combination of ceftazidime and gentamicin.

I am at the end of my rope! All our efforts do not seem to be working. Does God want to take these boys home to Him? I need to be willing to say, "Thy will be done" (see Luke 22:42). Lord, please take these boys in Your arms and nurture and take care of them—heal them if it is possible, for we are not succeeding as mortals here on earth. I ask

126

that Thy will and whatever is best for my sons be done. May their suffering be over soon.

JULY 4, 1993

Independence Day. However, we are not independent but are shut up in this hospital. My poor sons are so ill. I wanted to do something special for them. I asked Robert and Seth if they wanted to go outside the hospital and watch fireworks in the city from the high, grassy hill on which the hospital stands. Seth was too sick to go, but Robert wanted to go. So, with the nurse's permission, he got in the wheelchair carrying a vomiting bowl with him, and I wheeled him out onto the lawn around the hospital. We saw many fireworks being shot off throughout the city. It was a nice, warm evening. And for a few minutes, life seemed just a little bit better. After about ten minutes, Robert felt sick and wanted to go back inside. Maybe this break was more for me than for him.

JULY 7, 1993

The hospital lab looked at Robert's white cells under an electron microscope, and they found that, although he has a normal number of white blood cells, the cells are very slow in their movements, perhaps because of the steroids he had in earlier months. Dr. Shigeoka said she would try giving Robert Neupogen shots, or granulocyte colony–stimulating factor (G-CSF), which promote the growth of neutrophils, white blood cells that fight infection. It might also help Robert's white cell function. Sounds like a great idea.

JULY 8, 1993

Today is my father's birthday. He would have been seventy-four years old. Today they will be giving Robert a Neupogen shot, which may increase and invigorate his white blood cells. We hope this is the miracle we've been seeking. I feel that my dad is helping us from the other side to get Robert and Seth well.

JULY 9, 1993

A miracle is beginning to happen! Robert is swallowing his saliva now instead of spitting it out. He was also able to swallow a little bit of juice and keep it down. He went to the hospital playroom today for a while and played instead of staying in his bed. I think he is really starting to feel better!

Seth's fever from his pneumonia has also come down, and he is feeling better. What a blessing!

JULY 12, 1993

Robert and Seth are both going to go home today! Robert is still on the TPN machine to give him intravenous nutrition. Seth will receive intravenous antibiotics at home as well as Biaxin so that he can return to BYU summer school soon.

JULY 13, 1993

Today is Rebekah's fourteenth birthday. She is definitely a teenager now, bringing challenges and fun into our lives. She has a great sense of humor. She has braces now and beautiful green eyes.

Seth has been getting intravenous antibiotics contained in round plastic balls delivered by a home health company to treat his pneumonia. Every six hours he receives the two different medicines, gentamicin and ceftazidime. Robert continues to get the total parenteral nutrition containing proteins, fats, and carbohydrates. It is pumped into his Broviac, the tube into his chest. An automatic pump delivers the nutrition in the proper time and dose. We are continuing Neupogen shots on a regular basis, every other day. It has been our miracle cure.

JULY 14, 1993

Seth is beginning to get very nauseated. I don't understand what is happening. He is losing weight and can't keep much food down. He must be reacting to the high-dose antibiotics.

JULY 16, 1993

We took Seth up to the university hospital to see Dr. Shigeoka. After taking some blood tests, she found that Seth is ill because his kidneys are failing! His blood urea nitrogen (BUN) and creatinine levels are very high. How horrible! The doctor assures us that the kidney failure is probably temporary and is due to the combination of gentamicin and ceftazidime along with becoming dehydrated. They are placing Seth on a low-potassium diet since his kidneys are not getting rid of potassium. We will stop the gentamicin. When I got home, I discovered that about all he can have on the low-potassium diet is white bread, bologna, and Kool-Aid. Anything that we would normally consider healthy has a lot of potassium, so he can't eat much variety.

JULY 20, 1993

Seth is beginning to feel slightly better, and his BUN and creatinine levels are coming down, showing that his kidneys are beginning to work. He's continuing the low-potassium diet and is still quite weak. I am upset that Seth was sent home with the IV antibiotics without instructions to drink a lot of fluids for the medicines to be safe.

JULY 22, 1993 (SETH'S JOURNAL)

This summer has been a real challenge. I started summer school at BYU, but then I got sick with pneumonia, was put in the hospital for a week, and missed a lot of school. The medicine caused my kidneys to be damaged, so I was nauseated for a month and had to withdraw from school. I have lost a lot of weight and need to gain twelve pounds to be the person I was before.

JULY 24, 1993

My mom, siblings, and cousins had a family reunion today where we celebrated Pioneer Day by going downtown, doing a tour of Brigham Young's home, and then walking to a restaurant to eat. It was a very hot day. Robert went with us even though he is still recovering. I was thrilled to see him drink a glass of orange juice and to enjoy being with his cousins. It has been such a long time since he was able to do this. We also attended the Manti Temple pageant last night, driving with the family to Manti with Robert's feeding machine in the car. After he receives his nutrition, he is unhooked from the machine so he can walk around just like anyone else, hiding the Broviac tube under his shirt. He is gaining weight quickly. We are also beginning to hear Robert's voice again after seven months of him whispering. So that is also a great blessing. Seth is beginning to feel better too.

JULY 25, 1993 (MICHAEL'S JOURNAL)

I haven't written for more than a year, so I have a lot to catch up on. I won first place in the school music competition again this year (third time) with my violin. I played Vivaldi's "Summer." I was in all the same classes as Kendall Hulet, my best friend. Mrs. Gottfredson's English class was quite an experience—very difficult. I was in Honors

English, Triad Physical Science, and Triad Geography. I have been in String Choir for two years now, and we have all had a good time. We performed in Symphony Hall in the foyer. I went on tour to Las Vegas with the high school orchestra. It was very fun. We had a very interesting experience with our host family, if you can call it that—a Dad and some kids. It was exciting and life-threatening—no food! I also won first place in the school and BYU science fairs (with coaching from my brother Jeremy, a physics major)! My project was entitled "The Particle-Wave Nature of Light." Ninth grade has so far been one of the best years of my life.

Don't give up hope, even when circumstances are bad for a very long time! Try to be optimistic and continually search for solutions to problems and for new doctors to assist you. Pray for strength and guidance.

21

Colorado

JULY 26, 1993 (MICHAEL'S JOURNAL)

It looks like we are going to be moving to Colorado so Dad can go to school. I really don't want to leave all my friends here. But I am trying to be optimistic and think that moving to Denver will be a good experience. It will almost definitely be good for me concerning musical education and opportunities. But I don't want to miss out on our orchestra tour, string choir, summer orchestra, private violin lessons, etc. My best friend, Kendall, and I will at least be staying in touch.

AUGUST 1993

We are moving to Colorado. I can't believe it. Mike has applied to several different colleges in the past year to do some more graduate studies, but the University of Colorado at Denver is the only school that has accepted him. We said to ourselves that we couldn't go unless Seth and Robert got better. They are on the mend, and it feels right. The doctor is putting Seth on Neupogen shots to help prevent more infections and to boost his white blood cell count. This should help him out a lot to not have frequent mouth sores, gingivitis, ear infections, and pneumonia—things he has been dealing with his whole life. The doctor also ordered that whenever Seth gets his IVIG, the nurse must bring pizza or some kind of food so that he can gain weight. He doesn't complain about that!

OCTOBER 10, 1993 (SETH'S JOURNAL)

So many things have changed since I've written last. My dad got accepted to the University of Colorado. He is on a sabbatical leave from Nebo School District, so he is getting half pay. I'm going to BYU. My brother Jeremy is also going here and lives three blocks away

131

from me. My sister Jessica is still up in Salt Lake working and going to school at the University of Utah. School is hard, but I am doing okay. My dad came back from Colorado in the middle of September to ordain me to the office of an elder. It was a great experience. For General Conference Jeremy and I went to visit our aunts, uncles, and cousins and my grandma Scott and step-grandpa Brinton. They came home from their mission in Palmyra, New York.

I wasn't able to find a goshawk nest, and I wasn't able to get a Cooper's hawk, because I had to come and live in the apartments. I'll have to wait until after my mission to get another bird, I guess.

NOVEMBER 14, 1993

Our twenty-fifth wedding anniversary. We are living in Littleton, Colorado, while Mike is working on his degree in marriage and family therapy at the University of Colorado at Denver. He is also working half-time as a school psychologist in Greeley, Colorado—a one-and-a-half-hour drive. I am working at Euclid Middle School in the kitchen as a food services worker four hours a day while the kids are in school.

We were able to find a very nice house to live in here in Littleton very close to a river with a walking trail alongside. It is beautiful, and the kids love to spend time there. We were very blessed in the move. Still, our finances are tight.

Richard is now in first grade. He and Matthew (fifth grade) attend Centennial Elementary. Robert (sixth grade) attends Goddard Middle School. Robert got his Broviac central line taken out of his chest. The doctor just pulled it out! The doctor has lowered Robert's Neupogen shots to every other day, .2cc, and next week to every three days. Robert is doing very well and is healthy. What a wonderful blessing!

Rebekah (ninth grade) and Michael (tenth grade) are attending Heritage High School. They are both in the orchestra, with Michael playing violin and Rebekah playing cello. Michael will be going to Carnegie Hall in New York City in March with the orchestra. He is also playing with the Littleton Community Symphony. The school orchestra is very big and amazing. These are great opportunities for their musical education that they did not have in Utah. Maybe that is why we really came to Colorado. We have had our spells of homesickness, especially Rebekah, but we are getting adjusted now. It has been a good opportunity to become closer as a family.

DECEMBER 1, 1993

We have had a lot of fun opportunities living in the Denver area for the past few months. Our family has been to visit the Denver Museum of Nature and Science with dinosaurs and mummies, as well as the Denver Art Museum, an amazing five-story museum of art from around the world, from Asia to Alaska. We've also been to the Denver Zoo.

Tonight was another enjoyable experience. Michael wanted to attend the Littleton City Christmas tree–lighting ceremony. Because it was so cold outside, no one else wanted to go. So just Michael and I went alone. We bundled up with gloves, hats, scarves, and boots; parked a long ways away; and walked together in the dark to the magical streets of shops, carolers, bands, and Christmas smells. We went into a little art shop, bought a few Christmas presents, and then witnessed the lighting of the giant Christmas tree. It was a magical night for me to spend with my son Michael that I will always remember. He always has a spirit for adventure.

DECEMBER 15, 1993

Tonight we attended the Christmas concert of the combined bands, orchestras, and choirs of Heritage High School. The school is huge. We sat in the balcony. The concert was absolutely amazing. Michael and Rebekah played violin and cello in the orchestra. The most outstanding musical number was Beethoven's "Hallelujah" from *Christ on the Mount of Olives*, with the wonderful phrase "Hallelujah, hallelujah unto God's almighty Son!" They will be performing this in March when they go to Carnegie Hall. What a great opportunity for my kids to participate in such a high-class performance as we saw tonight. The orchestra at Spanish Fork in Utah does not compare to Heritage High School's orchestra.

DECEMBER 26, 1993

We had a nice family Christmas with my Utah college kids home to visit. Today Michael has been complaining that his stomach hurts and feels "spleeny," meaning that it feels like it is his enlarged spleen hurting. That is somewhat concerning. He also says he has an earache, which is so unlike him. He has had very few infections with his immune deficiency, just liver problems. Guess we'll have to go to the doctor soon.

JANUARY 5, 1994

Michael is being treated for an ear infection and is going to a gastroenterologist to see why his stomach continues to hurt.

JANUARY 25, 1994

Today Michael had an endoscopy—a scope into his stomach—to look for an ulcer or something that could be causing his increasing pain. Afterward he told me it was so wonderful to be given the medication beforehand, because it took away his pain for a little while. The doctor did not find anything seriously wrong with Michael's stomach, just a little gastritis. She suggested to me that this could all be psychological since he is under a lot of stress at school right now along with working at Pizza Hut and doing his music. I cannot believe this could be true. This much pain does not seem like a psychological problem to me. It has been increasingly difficult for Michael to keep up with schoolwork and his job. He has called me a couple of times at my work to pick him up from school. This did not make my boss very happy, as I had to leave early.

Last week Michael had an abdominal ultrasound. There were some spots on his liver, but the doctor said it was probably just due to his liver cirrhosis, and he discounted my question as to whether it could be cancer.

FEBRUARY 5, 1994

My daughter Jessica married Rob today in the Salt Lake Temple! We drove from Denver a couple of days early—left about three thirty in the morning so we could get to Salt Lake by two in the afternoon for a CT scan of Michael's abdomen. (His stomach pains are getting worse. Ulcer medications aren't helping. The CT scan showed spots on his liver that Dr. Shigeoka attributes to cirrhosis. No definite answers. Michael is taking Tylenol with codeine every few hours for pain so he can visit his friend Kendall, have a sleepover, and go to school with him the next day, then a cousin sleepover Friday night.)

The wedding was at ten thirty today on a beautiful sunny day. We picked up Jessica and met Rob at the temple. I helped Jessica with her gown. We went to the sealing room for their marriage. It was wonderful to see her married in the temple!

Later we attended a wedding breakfast at Della Fontana. The reception/party that evening, with dancing, was at the Pioneer State Park social hall. It was very fun. Even Dr. Shigeoka came and stayed a long time.

SUNDAY FEBRUARY 15, 1994

We are back in Littleton, Colorado, again. Today Michael stayed home from church because of his abdominal pain. He was recently ordained to be a priest but was not able to bless the sacrament (like Communion). In sacrament meeting we sang "How Great the Wisdom and the Love" about how Christ came to "suffer, bleed and die" (Snow 1998, 195). It made me think of Michael's present suffering. Tonight I visited with him. I felt the Lord guiding my words to him. I said, "Michael, I think that the Lord has a different path for you to take in your life right now. You need to stop worrying about your schoolwork and your job and take some time off. You will probably need to go into the hospital until we can find out what is wrong. You may have to suffer, just as Christ had to suffer. Let things go and take this new path for a while." I knew that I was being inspired in my words to him. How I appreciate the Lord's guidance and calming influence to my soul right now. He is with us in these trials.

FEBRUARY 17, 1994

Michael is not going to school now. I have called the school and his workplace, Pizza Hut, to tell them. The manager at Pizza Hut said that he needed to have two weeks' notice. I replied that I was sorry but Michael was just in too much pain to come into work anymore. He said he hadn't noticed Michael being in pain. The codeine has helped Michael in the past but doesn't seem to be working too well now.

FEBRUARY 22, 1994

Last night I heard water running in the middle of the night. I found Michael in the tub of hot water trying to get rid of his abdominal pain. That's it! I have had it with these once-a-week tests on Michael. I called Dr. Hayward, his immunologist in Denver, and demanded that Michael be put in the hospital immediately. They must find out what is wrong with him now! He is suffering too much. Dr. Hayward said okay, so we are taking Michael to Children's Hospital Colorado in downtown Denver right away.

FEBRUARY 23, 1994

Michael got to the hospital in the late afternoon yesterday. He was put into a small, dark private room and was soon hooked up to some intravenous pain medication. We were so grateful he could get this, but as it turned out, it didn't work that well, and it also made him nauseated. He ordered lots of fruit plates and said he was craving melons, but most of the fruit remained uneaten. Mike came to see him after work.

This morning they began a series of tests on Michael. The first was an ultrasound. As the technician was scanning, she said to herself, "What is that?" That scared me as I was watching from the corner of the room. She said she would have to go get her supervisor. The supervisor went to get the doctor after looking at the screen. All of them seemed to be puzzled by what they were seeing. It was very scary to me. I feared they were seeing tumors, but they would tell me nothing.

FEBRUARY 25, 1994

The last couple of days Michael has had a CT scan and a radioactive scan. He has also had numerous blood tests. Finally, the doctor told us that they would be operating to remove his gallbladder, as it did not look right. Michael is still nauseated and still in pain. He is always feeling hot and wants a fan blowing in his face all the time.

FEBRUARY 26, 1994
5:00 p.m.

In an hour or so Michael will be operated on to take out his gallbladder. This is a strange time of day to do surgery. Mike has arrived from work. The intern came in the room to say that if they found something else when they operated, they might not take out his gallbladder. I said, "What? You have to take it out! He needs to get well and go home!" The intern repeated what he had said before. Then I understood his meaning.

Mike gave Michael a blessing. We gave Michael a hug and walked down the hall with him as he was wheeled to surgery. *His weeks of pain will soon be over,* I thought.

> **If you have physical ailments that will not resolve, do all you can to find answers. Be brave and assertive with your doctors until the correct diagnosis is found.**

22

Nightmare

After Michael was in surgery for a couple of hours, the surgeon came out to see us in the parents' waiting room. I fully expected that there would be good news and that Michael would be on his way to recovery. At least, that was all I could stand to think. The doctor said that Michael had done well in the operation and then asked us to follow him to a small private room adjacent to the waiting area where we could talk. I knew this had to mean bad news. We went in and shut the door.

Then the doctor said, "Michael is fine. He is in the recovery room. We did not take out his gallbladder, because we found tumors in his gallbladder, pancreas, and liver. If we had taken out his gallbladder, it would have made his recovery from surgery much more difficult. We took a biopsy of the tumor, and it appears to be adenocarcinoma. It is malignant. This is a very difficult type of cancer to treat. There is very little we can do."

My head was swirling. No! my mind cried. No, no, no! I had always carried fears of losing another child sometime. I didn't know whether it would be from being hit by a car or what. I had just always felt I would lose someone. The doctor was telling us the time was now. Michael wasn't going to go home and be well and free of pain. He was going to die. "How long?" I asked.

"Maybe two months," he said.

This is the most nightmarish day of my life. Michael has cancer? There is no treatment? My whole world is falling apart.

"Michael will be in his room in about half an hour," the doctor said. "You can see him then. We can do it however you want. You can tell him, or we can tell him—whatever you decide."

138

After the doctor left the room, I cried and screamed with anguish. I felt horrified, angry, and afraid. How could this be happening? We didn't come to Colorado to lose a child! Maybe if we hadn't come, this wouldn't have happened. Mike and I were both in such a state of shock. Even though I had often wondered whether Michael did indeed have cancer, the reality was so much worse than I had ever imagined. This couldn't be happening! After a half hour, I finally calmed down. We had to go see Michael in his room. We had to be strong.

When we came into Michael's room, it was dark outside the windows, and the lights were turned low. Michael was in pain. We patted and kissed him. He was very drowsy. I decided to stay overnight while Mike went home. A wonderful nurse cared for him all night and tried to make him comfortable. She was an angel. All the nurses seemed to know what his diagnosis was. They gave me hugs, shed tears, and said kind words to me. They were wonderful.

About four in the morning, Michael asked, "Mom, what did they do?"

My heart froze. I wasn't ready to tell him the terrible news. I simply said, "They did not take out your gallbladder."

"Oh," he said and then fell asleep again.

FEBRUARY 27, 1994
Bishop Weaver showed up early this morning to see Michael. I stopped him in the hallway and told him what the surgeons had found and explained that Michael didn't know yet. We talked for about twenty minutes. He was so gentle and understanding. He went into the room and visited with Michael, talking in general terms about the surgery, and then gave him a blessing of comfort, as Michael requested.

My husband, Mike, came around ten in the morning after taking care of things at home and taking the day off from work. He had told the kids at home the sad news, but Michael still didn't know. We decided that we would like to be the ones to tell him his diagnosis rather than have the doctors do it. When everyone had left the room but the three of us, Mike stood at Michael's bedside. He spoke the hardest words of his life with a quivering chin and tears in his eyes: "Son, the doctors did not take out your gallbladder, because they found that you have cancer inside of you. They tell us it is a very hard kind of cancer to treat, and, unless there is some miracle, you are probably going to die. We are really sorry, Son, that we have to tell you this."

As we talked about it with him, we told him that the doctors had said he may have only two months to live. We talked about what he wanted to do during the time he had left. I said, "You don't have to do any more homework!" (He has been under a lot of stress at school lately trying to keep up in very challenging classes while being in pain.) We planned that maybe he could still go to orchestra and seminary, his two favorite classes, and that maybe he could still go to Carnegie Hall with the school orchestra on Easter. He said he felt sad and disappointed but that he feels sadder for us, his family, than for himself. He said he is getting the good end of the deal.

Michael seems to fully believe he will be going to a better place in the spirit world while we have to stay behind in this difficult world and miss him. The place he wants to visit most before he dies is Utah—to see his family and friends. He also wants to see the Utah Symphony, get the music CDs he has wanted (Handel's Messiah), and enjoy what time he has left. I haven't seen him cry about his plight. He seems very calm. He requested that his CD player be brought into the hospital. Wonderful, somber classical music now plays almost constantly. Michael has no interest in watching TV. It is like a sanctuary in his hospital room, preparation for the greater life beyond.

Later, as Michael slept, I looked back on Christmastime and the book I'd bought then, *Beyond Death's Door* by Brent and Wendy Top. I marvel now that I was so unknowingly wise to read many selections from the book to my children. These selections spoke of the beauty and order of the spirit world after death, of how righteous spirits have so much freedom of movement and increased knowledge and understanding and are engaged in important work for the Lord. It was very interesting to all of us.

We also watched as a family a video of the television movie *Go toward the Light*. It is a true story of a young boy who contracted AIDS from blood factor he received as a hemophiliac. His parents helped him set goals to accomplish for the rest of his short life. They lovingly prepared him with faith for the next stage of his existence after death.

How amazing that these things have somehow prepared Michael and us to better deal with his cancer and upcoming death. They have given us some strength to know what to do and what to expect. Likewise, having watched my dad die of cancer has also given us some mental and spiritual preparation. Sweet blessings in the midst of a horrible trial.

FEBRUARY 28, 1994

Michael has developed a fever, and I can't help but think that it is some sort of infection from the surgery. Most of the doctors don't seem worried about it and say that this can happen with cancer. But I was finally able to get Dr. Linda Stork, our petite, confident, and compassionate oncologist, to agree to put Michael on some intravenous antibiotics for a while. Michael says we should treat the things we can treat, and I totally agree.

MARCH 2, 1994

Michael's fever has disappeared, so he did have a treatable infection. The people in our church congregation (Littleton Ward) have heard about Michael's cancer. Several people have come to the hospital to visit him. The Young Women's group brought him flowers and balloons and stayed and talked and laughed with Michael. He really appreciated it. The bishop has come almost every day. Sometimes there are so many visitors that Michael hardly has time to rest or use the bathroom. His home health nurses also came—Beth and Mary Ellen—and they were very sweet. They noted with sadness that his tummy was beginning to swell due to ascites or fluid buildup in the abdomen due to his liver cancer.

Since the doctors learned Michael had cancer, they have put him on morphine—a more effective pain reliever. But it has side effects, including nausea, constipation, and urinary retention. He is becoming very thin, so he was given total parenteral nutrition (TPN), or food into his veins.

MARCH 3, 1994

Sister Barker from our congregation came to visit Michael. She brought a book called *In the Eye of the Storm* by John H. Groberg, a general authority of the church. I have been reading some of it to Michael.

It takes our thoughts to a Pacific island where Elder Groberg served on a mission as a young man. Some parts have been very touching and appropriate to this terrible ordeal we are going through. One time Elder Groberg almost starved to death over several days because there was no food on the island due to a hurricane that had delayed the supply ship. During this time of near starvation, he had some very spiritual experiences where he visited the spirit world and learned that there is nothing to be afraid of in dying (Groberg 1993, 114).

Another chapter tells of one native's death from tetanus. It was a horrible death, but Elder Groberg wrote that he feels all people have things to learn by how they die that may be important for them to learn before going to the other side. The fellow islanders of the boy who died said, "How come he is so lucky to die so young, and we still have to live and work and sweat and hurt? It doesn't seem fair. What does God have against us?" (Groberg 1993, 101). I feel this applies to Michael very much. He gets to die young. The book seems to say to us that it is okay to starve and even okay to have a difficult death. In God's eternal plan, all these terrible trials we are going through have purpose and will end in Michael going to a wonderful place. I truly feel this book was a gift from the Lord to make what Michael will go through more bearable and understandable to us.

MARCH 4, 1994

We brought Michael home from the Denver Children's Hospital today, but not until my husband and I had a heart-wrenching conversation with his oncologist, Dr. Stork. She said she had called the University of Colorado Hospital to ask their advice regarding Michael's pancreatic cancer (which the doctors had determined was the source of the cancer). She said, "We don't know anything about adenocarcinoma of the pancreas at the children's hospital, because children don't get it. It is more a disease of men in their fifties." She was told that there is no chemotherapy or radiation that has been found to be effective in this type of cancer, and the cancer has already spread too far to be treated with surgery. So Michael may have two months to live or much less, depending on what happens. (Less than two months? Oh, no!)

She told my husband and me that Michael could die from bleeding as liver clotting factors fail or from infection or from liver failure.

She said Michael's pain will be aggressively treated with morphine. The main goal is to keep Michael comfortable, and whatever amount of morphine he needs, he will be given, even if it slows down his respiration. She instructed us that if anything happens, we are not to call 911, because paramedics are required to resuscitate. She wrote do-not-resuscitate orders. This was horrifying to me. She also said Michael needs to be put on hospice. I at first was opposed to this. Couldn't we wait longer for that? "No," she replied. "Michael will need hospice nursing and social work services now." It was very shocking to hear her say these things about our sixteen-year-old son.

I expressed my concern to Dr. Stork that Michael has lost so much weight and was thin to begin with. I requested that he be given more TPN treatments to receive nutrition intravenously. He had a Broviac central line placed in his chest into his main artery during surgery through which he could get TPN. I was shocked again when she told us that TPN does not usually work well with cancer patients. It actually helps the cancer to grow, as the cancer takes most of the nutrients. I could not imagine such a terrible thing. But she gave us permission to try the TPN if we desired.

Dr. Stork said that she was so impressed with the courage and faith we and Michael have displayed during the hospitalization. We told her it was because of our faith, our Mormon religion, and our belief that families can be together forever. She commented, "There really is something special about your beliefs." I told her that another reason I may appear so calm is that I already lost one son to the immune deficiency and have gone through many diseases with my boys. One thing I have learned through all these experiences is that the sooner I accept things that truly cannot be changed, the sooner I will feel peace. I feel in my heart that this is one time that fighting will not help. Now is the time to accept what seems to be the inevitable. This is Michael's call home to God. I know that he is sealed to our family in the temple and that we will see him again after this life. Dr. Stork said she is amazed at our strength.

A little later a pain specialist came to talk to my husband and me about the morphine pills for Michael as well as liquid morphine that can be placed under his tongue if he has severe "breakthrough" pain. She was very helpful at explaining everything.

I also spoke to the social worker, who said she would contact the school where I work and let them know of Michael's condition and my need to miss work for an extended period of time. She said the federal Family and Medical Leave Act will allow me to keep my job while caring for Michael and be able to keep the life insurance I have for him through my job. That was a big relief to me. She would talk to my boss, and I wouldn't have to.

MARCH 5, 1994

It has been quite an ordeal to bring Michael home and have everything ready for him so he can be as comfortable and well cared for as possible. I am giving him intravenous antibiotics and also Lasix into his Broviac under doctor's direction. The Lasix is a diuretic to help him get rid of the fluid that is collecting in his abdomen (ascites). He is taking MS Contin (morphine pills) several times a day for pain, as well as the liquid morphine to put under his tongue in emergencies. Morphine has so many side effects, so there are pills to treat those. He has pills for nausea (Zofran), pills for constipation (Senokot-S), and mint oil to smell for urinary retention. There are other medications also. It is a constant challenge to keep them all in balance, and it seems almost impossible for him to take all the pills that have been prescribed. Every hour or so he has several pills to swallow. I also am giving him vitamins. He is constantly drinking water out of his water bottle, as his mouth is so dry due to the morphine. The morphine also makes his skin itchy, so he's always scratching.

We bought a new mattress as well as an egg-crate foam pad for his bed since he will spend most of his time there. We also bought a sheep-skin for him to lie on to prevent pressure sores and a big special pillow to help him sit up in bed when he wants to. We also bought a big fan to blow on him all the time, as he is always hot. Is it because cancer speeds up the metabolism? My father had the same symptoms.

In trying to arrange for Michael to have the TPN, we have discovered that the insurance won't pay for him to have it at home. Even though it costs $700 a day, we decided to try it anyway. But the first time I began infusing it as he lay in his bed, he complained that it made him feel awful, and he asked me to stop the infusion. Perhaps his body just can't handle it for some reason. So I guess he will just keep losing weight. It is so scary! Nothing goes as planned with this cancer. It is the boss.

Overall, it's great to have Michael home again and for him to sleep in his own bed. We have chosen to have him die at home (rather than in the hospital), where we can all be here to love and support him with the help of hospice. We, of course, would choose for him not to die anywhere, but that is not a choice we have been given at this time. My heart cries within me.

Nothing is worse than being told your child is dying!
Do your best to be strong, treat the symptoms,
and show your love amid your fears.

23

Ministering Angels to Our Aid

MARCH 5, 1994

As soon as our college kids in Utah learned of Michael's illness, they wanted to come to Colorado. I told them that they needed to wait till Michael felt a little better, so they came as soon as he got out of the hospital. Jeremy has been helping us buy the bed supplies I mentioned. Jessica has been wonderful in giving Michael back rubs and massages to help him with the pain. Jessica's husband, Rob, along with our son Seth are a big boon to cheer up Michael. They won't let him stay in bed feeling sorry for himself. They took him to his favorite spot—Cherry Creek Mall in Denver. His favorite store there is the Nature Company, which has interesting rocks and nature things as well as beautiful music, pictures, and so on. They took a video of him shopping. Michael was temporarily feeling pretty well with the help of his pain medication. Jessica also took him to get his hair cut, which he needed. In the back of my mind, I thought that this haircut would also be getting him ready for his funeral. Such heartache!

Michael's cousins from their Dutifully Awesome Scott Cousins (DASC) club have sent a big basket full of treats, cards, CDs, and balloons that say "Get Well." What a kind thing for them to do.

MARCH 6, 1994

A brother from the Salem Ward congregation in Utah surprised us today by showing up on our doorstep. He was here in Denver on a business trip and dropped by our home to give us a very generous gift of $1,200, which had been collected from our neighbors in Salem, Utah. It was a very thoughtful thing for them to do, as it seems a lot of money is needed at this time of our lives.

146

MARCH 8, 1994

Michael has not been eating well for days. But tonight Jeremy and Michael went to a Mexican restaurant, and Michael ate a lot. That gives me some hope that he'll eat better in the future and won't need the TPN. Our refrigerator is being filled with good food from ladies who attend our church. One sister begged me to tell her what she could do to help. I asked her to buy some flexible-waist pajamas for Michael to wear and Levi's for Robert, as his are getting holes in the knees. She has lost a child in death and knows that any service she can give is very helpful.

MARCH 9, 1994

Michael's nurses, Beth and Mary Ellen, paid a special visit to Michael today. They have come to our home for several months to administer IVIG to my sons. They brought him a tape of beautiful piano music to listen to. Secretly they told me how sad they are to see that his tummy is full of fluid. This is an ominous sign of serious liver failure. But they shared their love and cheerfulness with Michael. We appreciate their kindness.

Jessica, Rob, and Seth will be leaving tomorrow to return to college, so we decided to have a special family meeting to share our love and bond together in this trying time.

MARCH 10, 1994

The family meeting didn't start last night until eleven o'clock, because Michael was in too much pain before that time. We had to get the right balance of pain medication so that the pain was pretty well under control but Michael was not too drowsy from the medicine. Jessica and others spent a lot of time massaging Michael's back and stomach to help him feel better. He really appreciated it. In the meeting we each took turns saying how we felt and expressing our love to Michael, just as my family did before my dad died. Rob recorded it all on the camcorder. It was a wonderful time together.

Mike, my husband, conducted the meeting and expressed his love for Michael and our collective sadness that this is happening to him. (We are still in such shock. Can this be real?) He asked Michael to watch over us from heaven and visit us if he can. We sang a hymn and had a prayer. We sat in a circle in the living room on the couches and chairs. The love and pathos was thick in the air. When we asked Richard, who is only seven years old, if he wanted to say something, he sat silently on his chair with big tears falling from his eyes. Mike told him to go give Michael a hug, which was very touching to see. "That says it all, Richard," said Mike.

Jeremy spoke of good times he and Michael enjoyed in doing an art project together last summer, drawing a raccoon in a tree. He gave the framed picture to Michael and expressed his love for him. Rob, Jessica's new husband, knelt close to Michael and related a poem about Jesus's empty tomb, which gives us all hope for a resurrection. Jessica said how amazed she was at Michael's faith and strength in this tragedy. She reminisced about the fun times they had when Michael visited her in Salt Lake City and was happy for their joint love for the arts.

I said that Rob and Jessica's wedding had been timed perfectly, before we knew of Michael's cancer. I quoted from Thoreau, who said, "I went to the woods because I wished to live deliberately, to front only the essential facts of life … and not, when I came to die, discover that I had not lived" (Thoreau 1854). "Michael has lived life to the fullest," I said, and I expressed my appreciation for the good son he has always been. Robert and Matthew, ages ten and twelve, shyly and briefly expressed their love and sadness to Michael. Seth said how much he admired Michael's many talents in music and art and how he would really miss him. Rebekah tearfully said how she and Michael had always been best friends and she would miss him so much. Mike expressed the love he has had for Michael ever since he was a little boy. He spoke of the hope we have from the scriptures, which say, "In my father's house are many mansions … I go to prepare a place for you" (John 14:20).

It was then Michael's turn to express his feelings and thoughts to us. He had been lying on the couch, but he sat up straight and looked around at all of us. He had a nasal oxygen cannula on his face because his swelling belly made it harder for him to breathe. He expressed his love to Mike, his dad, for being there when he needed him, thanked me for doing so much for him and the family and told me not to worry so much, expressed his admiration for Jeremy and the hardworking student he has been, told Seth he never expected to be even sicker

148

than Seth had been so many times, and said he admired both Seth and Robert for their bravery in all their illnesses. Michael said how much he loved Richard because he was always so cute and nice. He told Robert and Matthew, his two younger brothers, that he was sorry for getting angry with them so often for "bugging" him. "I love you, and I hope to get to know you better in the time I have left," he said. He told Jessica how he had enjoyed visiting her in her apartment in Salt Lake. He looked at Rebekah and started to cry. They were closest in age and had been best friends throughout their lives. He said, "Rebekah, we have always been a team! Now I won't be here to be your buggy older brother. Just remember you have great talents and to use them." He cried and said he would really miss her.

Then Michael said some profound things that we will always remember: "About my feelings, I'm not afraid to die, and I'm happy to do what the Lord wants me to do. I just feel really bad for everyone else—that you have to lose me and stay here. Just have great lives and live them the best you can, because I want to see all of you again. If I do die, I'm looking forward to it, to seeing Grandpa and having many opportunities and things that aren't possible here. So don't worry about me. And I promise that if I can, I'll always be watching you." We were all deeply touched by this. It still seemed all so unreal that we were going to lose him.

After we had all said what we wanted to say, we sang "God Be with You till We Meet Again" (Rankin 1998, 152). "When life's peril's thick confound you, put His arms unfailing round you. God be with you till we meet again!" We meant it.

We have had angels around us in the form of friends and family and even strangers, to hold us up in these trying times. Sometimes it seemed that the phone rang too often and the knock at the door was too frequent. But we could not hold back the outpouring of love that we received from others during Michael's illness.

Michael said that he was not afraid to die and that he was looking forward to seeing his Grandpa and having many opportunities in heaven that are not possible here on earth. It was wonderful to see his faith.

24

Michael's Last Trip to Utah

MARCH 11, 1994

When Michael was done with all the antibiotics at home, we left as soon as possible to go to Utah. This was his last wish. Quantum, our home health company, offered to pay for the flight.

Michael and I flew from Stapleton International Airport in Denver. We rode the cart in the airport rather than having to walk the long distances. He looked very sick, pale and thin. Luckily, the one-hour flight went fine.

When we arrived in Salt Lake, a lot of cousins were there with Grandma and Grandpa Brinton. We went straight to their house, and Michael had oxygen delivered. Later he went up to his cousins' house for a sleepover but ended up not staying overnight. After playing games for a while, he came back to sleep at Grandma's. He was too ill to stay.

SATURDAY, MARCH 12, 1994

This morning I drove Michael to Salem, Utah, to visit his best friend, Kendall Hulet. They had been buddies in middle school. After visiting other friends, we drove to Kendall's house, where Michael would stay overnight. Michael and Kendall had hoped to go to the mall later (their favorite hangout), but Michael's stomach kept hurting too much. We kept waiting for him to feel better, but by the time he did, it was too late to go.

I went to K-Mart to buy some Sunday clothes for Michael, as we had forgotten to bring some with us. While I was gone, Michael and Kendall had a good visit. Michael told me later that Kendall said he didn't see how Michael could be so brave and didn't think he could be that brave in similar circumstances. Even though they didn't get to do anything "fun" that night, Michael said it was still worth it to visit Kendall and talk to him. The Hulet family were very gracious to us, although I'm sure they felt awkward under the circumstances. I was often busy with Michael making sure he had the right medicine at the right time. We had a small yellow suitcase filled with meds we had brought. I had to be with him wherever he went. We stayed at Kendall's that night, each of us with our own bedroom.

SUNDAY, MARCH 13, 1994

Michael's desire today was to go to church at our ward (congregation) in Salem. My husband, Mike, and the family met us there. The people in the ward knew of Michael's situation, and we felt very on the spot when we came in and sat down. Michael was not feeling very well, but he wanted to be there anyway to see many of our old friends. After the service we went into the foyer and were greeted by the bishop and his counselor and several other people. It was good to see all the kind faces.

After church we drove to Salt Lake City to go to Grandma's house. All the cousins were there. We had a nice dinner, and Michael ate pretty well and talked and laughed. We had some pictures taken and had a short family meeting where Grandma expressed everyone's love to Michael and our faith in the gospel. We sang a hymn and had a family prayer. It seemed too much like our farewell to Grandpa Scott.

MONDAY, MARCH 14, 1994

Today Mike and I took Michael to downtown Salt Lake City with his sister Rebekah and his cousin Brittany. We went to see Legacy at the Joseph Smith Memorial Building, a film about the Mormon pioneer trek to the Salt Lake Valley in 1847. It was very good. Then we walked around the beautiful building with its huge columns and chandeliers. Michael bought some beautiful pictures that depicted Christ's life and death at the Distribution Center downstairs. I thought that it was really wonderful that Michael wanted to have them at this time when he will be leaving this world soon.

Later we went to the Nature Company, Michael's favorite store, at the ZCMI Mall. I bought a camera to take pictures. We bought big soft pretzels to eat. Michael got a little bit sick. It is so hard to balance the morphine pain pills, which make him nauseated, with the Zofran pills to treat nausea. After the mall we met other members of the family at the restaurant on the top floor of the Joseph Smith Memorial Building. We had a delicious dinner, and the leftovers were given to us in tinfoil, from which the kids sculpted swans. It was overall a very good day because Michael felt quite well for several hours.

TUESDAY, MARCH 15, 1994
Mike and the kids left today to return to Colorado for work and school. All the cousins near Michael's age got together to have a group picture taken. It turned out very nice. Rebekah felt bad that she couldn't be there for it, but she needed to return to Colorado.

Tonight I gave Michael a back rub. It scared me very much to see how thin he is getting! I became very tearful and went into my mom's bedroom to talk to her and Marshall about it. They suggested letting nature take its course rather than doing too much "heroic treatment," such as intravenous nutrition. After much prayer, I feel that Michael should decide what treatment he wants. I feel I have to leave things in the Lord's hands and entrust Michael to his care.

WEDNESDAY, MARCH 16, 1994
I went for a walk alone around Grandma's condo among the big trees, trying to feel some peace and comfort. Michael and I had also walked there earlier that day. I had talked to Michael about what he wanted to do—have a nasogastric tube, take herbs, or do TPN (feeding through his veins)? He wants to do what will make him comfortable and what he feels like having at the time. Maybe we'll do TPN when we get back to Colorado. Michael has been eating a lot of Captain Crunch cereal. I'm glad he has found something he enjoys eating. But my heart is breaking inside. This is all a big nightmare.

THURSDAY, MARCH 17, 1994
Today I drove Michael to Spanish Fork High School to visit his orchestra class and his orchestra teacher, Mrs. Dunford. Everyone hugged him and cried. We watched a video of their orchestra tour last year to Las Vegas showing Michael playing games, trying to throw girls in the swimming pool, and so on. I drove Michael and his best friend, Kendall, to JB's to eat and then to the mall. I stayed with them, although Michael and Kendall went off by themselves for forty-five minutes. I bought Michael a nice card with a picture of Christ in a

columned temple, and Michael bought a CD case to keep his music CDs in. It seemed a little strange to me, but I'm sure we will be glad to have it. We pretty much get Michael anything he wants to buy or eat these days. Kendall's parents picked him up at the mall to take him home. I think we all knew that it was the last time these best friends would see each other.

FRIDAY, MARCH 18, 1994
Michael was in bed most of the day until four. He went to look at the proofs of the cousin pictures that were taken and then went with his cousin Brittany to Symphony Hall to go to a concert, his favorite thing to do. My sister Jackie invited me to see the movie Shadowlands, a very touching movie about C. S. Lewis and his wife, who died of cancer. It was very good and appropriate for what we are experiencing right now. Michael bought a Utah Symphony T-shirt and enjoyed the concert very much but vomited his dinner when he got home. I don't want him to suffer too much or too long. Please help us, Heavenly Father!

SATURDAY, MARCH 19, 1994
Michael slept most of the day. I went to the Jordan River Temple with Mom and Barbara while Grandpa Marshall stayed with Michael at the condo. In the temple, my impression about Michael was that he is definitely going to die. All things on this earth die. It is part of the plan. Later in the evening, several members of the family came to say goodbye to us at Mom's condo. Then we rode to the airport to return to Colorado. Michael was very weak as we rode on the airport shuttle. At the gate we said sorrowful goodbyes to our family members.

The airplane trip was uneventful, and Mike and the kids picked us up at the airport. It was early evening. It was good to get home to Littleton and to be in our own house again. Michael thought so too. His own bed is more comfortable. His room is so nicely decorated with his pictures and posters. A fan is always blowing on him because he is so hot. And he has his classical music playing most of the time. This is like a movie—so poignant. So much love in our family. So much heartache.

Our faith in God, the beauty of nature, our extended family, and close friends carried us in our hard times.

25

Final Days

MARCH 20, 1994

I made up a potion for Michael to drink with Essiac, the anticancer herbs Grandpa used, along with grape juice, vitamin C powder, and vitamin A and E from capsules. He likes it pretty well. I hope I can do something to help his body fight the cancer.

MARCH 24, 1994

Michael has gone days and days without nearly enough calories. I can't stand to do nothing about it. Even though the doctor said that total parenteral nutrition (TPN) would not work, that the calories would just help the cancer grow faster, we decided to try it for a few days to give Michael more strength. I think he gained a little weight while he was on it in the hospital. So we got three bags of TPN from Quantum, our home health company. We ran the first one all night. Afterward, it seemed that Michael had a lot more pain than usual. The next night when I started it running into his Broviac central line in his chest, he said it just made him feel so awful. That was the end of the experiment with TPN

I feel sad. We are definitely coming toward the end of his life. He is skin and bones and getting weaker every day. It is such a letdown after being in Salt Lake, where there were things to do and people to see. What can be our goal now? We have to have a goal. I guess the new goal is to keep him as comfortable and free of pain as possible. That is all we can do. And to give him all the love we can.

A couple of nights ago the Young Men organization from the church came to visit him for a short time. I think it was very thoughtful of them.

The Heritage High School orchestra has offered to have Michael go with them to Carnegie Hall and to let me go with them for free, even if Michael isn't strong enough to play the violin. A sister from our church is coordinating this effort. It is so sweet. But I had to tell them he is way too weak and sick to go, which is definitely true.

FRIDAY, MARCH 25, 1994

I took Michael for a car ride today to get him out of the house and to drive past the high school. It was kind of a bumpy ride due to the roads. When we got home, a sister in our ward and her daughter, Courtney, visited Michael. The sister insisted that she take home some of our laundry to wash. She was very sweet. After Courtney had visited for a few minutes, Michael said he felt nauseated, so he left the room. I went back to see how he was doing and found that he had vomited blood.

I was so scared! I thought I would take him to Littleton Hospital first. I didn't know who I should call, so I just called everybody—Dr. Stork, hospice, Dr. Rosenbaum. This was about five thirty. Dr. Stork was the one who called back. She said to bring him to the emergency room at the Denver Children's Hospital. They would give him some blood. Luckily, my husband, Mike, came home shortly after this, and we drove Michael the half hour to the hospital.

After we got there, they took some blood tests, and then Dr. Stork came in. Michael seemed to be pretty strong with no more vomiting. Dr. Stork said that he hadn't lost enough blood to warrant a transfusion. She said something very scary, however. She said we need to decide what we will do if this happens again—whether to do a lot of heroic treatments or just let things go the way they will. At some point, she seemed to be implying, we would have to let him go. She gave us vitamin K tablets to help prevent further bleeding as well as some shots of morphine that we could put into his Broviac. She also ordered a morphine pump for him.

SUNDAY, MARCH 27, 1994

Michael had no more vomiting over the weekend. Bishop Weaver came to visit him and gave him another blessing because Michael requested it. He said that Michael seemed to be more at peace than ever before.

I have noticed that Michael seems to be needing less of the morphine pills for pain. In the literature that hospice gave us, I noticed that needing less pain medication is one of the signs that death is getting closer, as it means the liver has shut down and is not synthesizing the medicine so quickly. Oh my goodness! We express our love to Michael often. Waiting and watching. Wondering and worrying. So scary. How will it happen?

I stayed home with Michael while the family went to sacrament meeting today. Mike said he bore his testimony that we know Michael is going on a mission and that gives us some comfort. Many people in the ward said what a wonderful testimony it was. After church several people from the church came to our home to visit and comfort us. Their kindness was really appreciated. Everyone is giving us so much love and support.

Yesterday I asked hospice if Michael could have some IV fluids and dextrose to give him a little more strength since he is eating and drinking so little.

Michael is beginning to look very jaundiced, with yellowish skin and eyes. Apparently his liver is really shutting down. This may mean that in a week or so he will go into a coma before he dies. Michael took a shower today and washed his hair. I had the thought that he was washing for the last time before his death. I prayed that, however his death occurs, it will happen at the best time and with the best possible circumstances for him and for the family.

He walks between his bedroom and bathroom with a walker to hold him up. He is so very weak now. We wonder and worry about what will happen. He has continued to eat and drink little (except for his ever-present water bottle to wet his mouth). Last night he did, however, have a plate full of chicken and rice, which he enjoyed. That was nice to see.

During most of his illness, Michael has listened for hours to his music on his CD player. I feel he is such an example of a rare, choice young man who loves the greatest classical music of the centuries— only the finest music for one of the world's finest young men, who has such a short time to spend on earth.

MONDAY, MARCH 28, 1994
This was a pretty quiet day. I read some of the book In the Eye of the Storm to Michael (see Groberg). It takes our minds to a far-off tropical

island and the spiritual experiences of the author while he served as a missionary. The other kids went to school, which is their work and task at present.

At about four in the afternoon, Michael began vomiting blood again! This time it was so much, and it just kept coming. (I caught it in a bowl and flushed it down the toilet.) I was so scared. I got him in the back of the car and raced to Littleton Hospital, just a few minutes away. Mike wasn't home from work yet. Michael and I went in the emergency room doors. I was frantic, telling them quickly that my son had cancer in his liver and was vomiting blood profusely. They put him in a private examining room, took off his stained clothes, and put a hospital gown on him.

[*Note*: It is so difficult to write about the next twenty hours of Michael's life. It has been two years now since it happened, but I still have a feeling of dread at recording these events. But I also have a feeling of obligation that everything be written down as a tribute to Michael for bravely enduring all that he did to leave this world.]

The nurses proceeded to unwrap a thick, greenish plastic tube and then inserted it into Michael's nose to go down into his stomach. The tube would suction out the blood. They told him to swallow as it went down. He tried to be cooperative. I was silently cringing, remembering when nurses had done this same thing to Robert a year earlier and how he'd cried and begged them not to do it. Suddenly Michael was coughing and choking violently because the tube had gone into his lungs accidently. "Do you have to do this?" he asked.

The nurse answered, "This tube will draw the blood out of your stomach. If we don't do this, you will continue to vomit blood."

I asked if I could talk to the doctor about what was happening. After a minute the doctor came. We went into the hall so I could talk to him privately. He said if we wanted to save Michael's life, we would have to do this and other painful procedures to stop the bleeding. But, he said, the bleeding might start again in a few days. I asked if they couldn't just give Michael some blood, since he had lost so much. The doctor said it wouldn't do any good, because it would just bleed out again.

I went back into the white, sterile room where Michael was and explained to him what the doctor had said. "What do you want to do, Son?" I asked.

He said, "I just want to go home."

I said, "You know if we don't do something to stop this bleeding that you will probably die today."

Michael said that he had been through enough suffering and didn't want to go through any more, so let's just go home.

What can I possibly say to express the agonizing emotions I felt! A temporary stopping of whatever was causing his bleeding would be effective for only a few days. Then we'd have to go through this all over again. It seemed certain that he would die of liver failure in a few days no matter what. (Uncontrollable bleeding is a sign of liver failure, I later learned, since the liver manufactures clotting factors to make blood clot.) His body just could not live with the cancer's onslaught no matter what we did to try to prolong his life for a few days.

The medical staff and I helped Michael back to the car to lie down in the back seat of the red Pontiac. His vomiting had slowed down or stopped at that point. I called Rebekah and told her to make a bed on the couch for Michael. I explained that the doctors were doing nothing and that Michael had chosen to come home to die. As we drove home, probably a ten-minute drive, I expected that Michael might be dead within an hour, as I had read how ruptured esophageal varices (varicose veins in the esophagus, which Michael did have) could take someone's life very quickly. I assumed that was what was happening to Michael. I also assumed that when someone bled to death, they rather quietly slipped away, as if falling asleep. I was wrong.

We got home. Mike and I carried Michael upstairs to the living room as Mike was home from work. I was so glad to have his support. The kids were also home from school. We waited for the terrible end to come. Surprisingly, there was no more vomiting, or only very small amounts. Michael had lost perhaps two or three cups of blood and was considerably weaker than before. We called Jeremy and Jessica in Utah, and they decided to come with Seth on the first plane they could catch, which was to arrive in Denver about eleven o'clock that night. It was about six o'clock at this time.

159

Michael lay on the living room couch with his oxygen and his IV fluids going. He was weaker than he had been before and spoke very softly and weakly when he did speak. Mike called his brother Dick, who lived in Idaho, and told him to have his son Scottie call Michael. Scottie and Michael had been "best cousins" during our trips to Idaho and had had a lot of fun together. I called my mother and asked her to let everyone know that the end was near. Soon cousins were calling from Idaho, Salt Lake, and Louisiana. Michael smiled and nodded and occasionally said "yes," "I love you," and "uh-huh" but spoke very little, mostly listening. This went on for an hour. His bleeding had apparently stopped, but he was still so very weak. I commented to Michael, "We won't even let you die in peace, will we?" His life had been too short! We didn't want to waste a minute of it but to cling to all the people who loved him.

Around nine or ten o'clock, Michael was having some rattling in his chest that he was unable to cough up because of his weakness. This was the death rattle I had read about in the literature that hospice had given us. It was one of the signs that death was near. Around this time, I dared to talk to Michael about what I had never mentioned to him before, even though I had thought about it and made plans. "Michael, who do you want to speak at your funeral?" I asked.

"I don't know. Whoever wants to," he replied.

I said, "We're going to bury you in Salt Lake City next to Jonathan. Is that okay?"

He nodded. My heart was breaking. What do you say to your dying son? Rebekah, Michael's closest sister, gave Michael a big hug. He said, "I love you," and she began bawling and couldn't speak. "I know," he said to her, to indicate that he knew how she was feeling.

Mike and Rebekah left to go to the airport to pick up Jeremy, Jessica, and Seth. They had a scary ride back home in a snowstorm on the freeway. When they arrived home about midnight, they all came into the living room to see Michael. Around this time, it seemed that he was beginning to hallucinate or to see into the spirit world. He said, "I've got to paint all the people."

"What people?" Rebekah asked.

He got kind of a funny smile on his face and said, "The sick people." Later he talked about seeing "the apostles."

TUESDAY, MARCH 29, 1994

Around one in the morning, things seemed pretty stable, so we all went to bed—Mike and I in our room, the younger boys in their bedroom, and Jeremy, Jessica, and Rebekah on mattresses in the front room with Michael. They spent a restless night. If Michael coughed, they would wake up in alarm. Around five o'clock I woke up to check on them. I was surprised to find them all awake. Michael had been asking for sugar, so Jessica had fed him straight sugar with a spoon, and he had swallowed it. Now he seemed to want more, but as I put the spoon in his mouth, he seemed as if he didn't even know what a spoon was for. He was almost unconscious. At some point we took him back down to his bedroom downstairs, his beautifully decorated room with posters, pictures, and memorabilia of all the things he loved—his music, his artwork, his family, and his faith. It was like a sanctuary to all of us.

I began to wonder if I had been wrong in my estimation of when Michael might die. It seemed as if he had started into sort of a birth process, but this time it was the process of dying. As much as we wanted him to go on living, we knew that now was his time to die, and we had to help him through it. Just like going through labor to be born, it seemed that he must go through a sort of labor to die. How could we be thinking this? How could this possibly be happening to our Michael? But it was, and we needed to help him in the process of leaving his mortal body.

Around nine in the morning Mike, Jeremy, and Seth gave Michael a priesthood blessing that he would be able to pass away without too much discomfort or pain, and Mike expressed to him the love we all had for him.

Within a half hour or so, Michael began to vomit blood again in large amounts. We knew that this was probably the beginning of the end. We called the hospice nurse, Caitlin, as we had been instructed to do. Michael was close to unconsciousness, it seemed. It was heart-wrenching to watch our Michael bleeding to death before our eyes.

Over the next two hours, Michael probably lost three quarts of blood. Still he was alive. The nurse suggested that we unhook the IV fluids and take off the oxygen mask to speed things along. She also said we should tell him that it was okay to go, that we would be okay. How contrary all this was to what a mother wants to do—to save her child!

161

Around this time, my husband asked the nurse if she could leave for a while so that we could be alone as a family. She did so. We told Michael it was okay for him to go and that we loved him. I do think that Michael was pretty much unconscious at this stage.

Michael's breathing was becoming rapid. He seemed to be gasping for breath. We kept pushing the button on his morphine pump, hoping that he would be out of his suffering soon. His body was desperate for air, gasping for breath. Then he took about three breaths where no air would go in.

And then it was over. No more breathing. No heartbeat. He was still and peaceful. The time was twelve noon. We were relieved that his suffering was over, but now we would suffer from losing him. His precious body was still warm, his swollen abdomen, his perfectly formed feet, his thin legs and arms. We caressed him. How we loved him! Our Michael! How could he really be dead? We closed his mouth, closed his jaundiced eyes as best we could, laid him straight in bed, washed the blood off, and combed his hair. How precious his body was, but his spirit was gone. He was finally free! There was peace.

Michael died at exactly twelve noon on Tuesday, March 29, 1994. We found out later that at twelve noon that day the Heritage High School orchestra was beginning their Easter concert at the capitol building rotunda in Denver. This was the orchestra that he had been a part of and enjoyed so much. At the beginning of the concert, probably right near twelve o'clock, the master of ceremonies dedicated the concert to Michael Curzon. Students in the orchestra told us that never had the orchestra played with such spirit. All the players felt it—even more than when they later played at Carnegie Hall. I like to think that Michael's spirit went there to witness this inspiring Easter performance.

All morning as Michael had struggled, still alive, it had been a dark and cloudy day, snowing lightly. At noon, after he died, it became sunny outside. Our nurse, Caitlin, returned. She called the doctor and the mortician. She told us what a good job we had done with Michael. Even if Michael had been in the hospital, the medical professionals could not have done any better at taking care of him, she said. I was feeling upset that all my kids had seen Michael die a very rough death, not the peaceful falling asleep I had hoped for. I apologized to Jeremy

162

that he had to see this, but he said he had wanted to be with Michael when he died.

As we waited for the mortician to come and get Michael, I was worried that they were going to put his body in a black zippered bag as had happened with my dad. I so much did not want that to happen. When the mortician came, they carefully put his body on a narrow stretcher and placed a beautifully colored light-blue blanket over him up to his chin, leaving his face uncovered. I was so glad. As they rolled the stretcher outside, the sun was shining through the clouds, and tiny, sparkling snowflakes landed on his face. It seemed almost magical. They placed him in the back of a station wagon. No neighbors were out to see the terrible, touching drama. It seemed strange that none of them knew what was happening to our family. The car drove away as we watched. They would prepare the body and then take it to Utah for the funeral. We were left alone to contemplate what we had just witnessed, the final hours of our beloved Michael's mortal life. How could this have happened to my sixteen-year-old son? We missed him already.

JUNE 1994

In thinking back on all I went through with Michael's illness and death, I'm struck by how often I felt during that time a divine providence guiding us in our decisions, comforting me, helping us to make the last weeks of his life the best possible. I know it was a time of great soul-searching for Michael as he was so unexpectedly forced to deal with his upcoming death. When he was in the hospital, he said to me one day, "Mom, what kingdom do you think I will go to?" I told him that even though he was not perfect, I felt he would go to the highest level of heaven, the celestial kingdom, because he did believe and had been trying his best to live the right way, even before he knew about the cancer. He would continue on the path he was already on into the next life.

The difficult death that Michael went through was not so unusual, as I found out in later readings about the process of dying. I guess it is not so important how one dies but how one lives. I feel that Michael lived in dignity, not perfectly, but very well. He tried very hard to live the best life he could, and he accomplished more in his short lifetime than most people do in decades. He proved his industry and faithfulness. An old saying seems to fit his life and death: "The good die young." Michael, you were good, and you died young. We love you very much.

Michael died at twelve noon, when his orchestra was dedicating their concert to him. His life was too short but full of accomplishment.

26

Michael's Funeral

MARCH 29, 1994

The last entry in Michael's journal was written by his sister Rebekah, age fifteen:

> Michael died today. He was diagnosed with pancreatic cancer on February 26. He had been having pain in his abdomen since December of '93. During the middle of February he left school and did not go back …
>
> Mike, I know you can probably hear what I'm thinking, and I want you to know how much I love you, how much we all love you! We'll miss you a lot, but it's all for the better! We know how much happier you are and that you aren't hurting any more. Well, I guess that's about it.
>
> Love always,
>
> Rebekah
>
> PS: We did move to Littleton, Colorado, in August of '93, only seven months ago. (When Michael died he was sixteen years, five months, and eleven days, or 197.33 months.)

MARCH 29, 1994

We made phone calls to people in the ward and to our relatives in Utah and Idaho to let them know of Michael's passing. Later in the afternoon, the home health nurses came to give Robert and Richard their IVIG infusions so that we could leave the next day to go to Salem, Utah, where the funeral would be. The nurses, Beth and Mary Ellen, brought so much love with them. It was like seeing some good counselors to talk with them about Michael's death. Beth said that she would have done just as we did to prolong Michael's life and then to let him go. She said I couldn't have done it any better. I really appreciated that. It was so nice to have someone to talk to who was so intimately acquainted with the events that had occurred. They wished us well on our trip and hugged us.

MARCH 30, 1994

We drove to Utah today. A couple of the kids rode with Jeremy in another car and a couple rode with us. All the way there Mike and I planned and talked about what we wanted for the funeral—who was to speak, the songs to be sung, and so on. It took several hours to figure it all out. We had to make it as perfect as possible.

Before we left, a sweet sister from the ward, the compassionate service leader in the Relief Society, brought a basket full of sandwiches, cookies, books, and magazines for the kids to read on the way. She was so cute—a tall, young, blonde mother who was so very spiritual, strong, and in tune with our needs. She also brought a copy of a letter from her uncle that had been written to their whole family. In the letter, he revealed to his family his special spiritual gift of being able to see spirits or angels from time to time. The first time it happened was in a stake conference meeting. He could see angels dressed in white robes in the aisles, on the stand, and assisting the speakers. Another time he saw hundreds of spirits at a funeral. Although this was a private family document, she gave it to us to read to bolster our faith in the reality of the spirit world.

This letter reminded me of another sister in our church who told of her grieving for many years over her baby boy, who had died very young. Years later, when she awoke one morning, she saw the spirit of a young man sitting on her bed. Instantly, she knew it was the spirit of the baby she had lost years before. He told her he had work to do in the spirit world that she was making difficult for him to do with her continual grieving. He told her he was all right and happy in his spiritual duties. After that she felt peace in her heart concerning this son who had died. These stories helped increase our faith that Michael's spirit was alive and well and would be doing important and wonderful things.

We arrived at Grandma's condo in Salt Lake City around nine at night. It wasn't until then that we realized it was Jeremy's birthday, March 30. It definitely wasn't a very happy birthday, but we gave him some Hostess cupcakes.

I had prayed that Michael's death would come at a time that would be best for the family. At least as far as the school schedule in Denver, it did work out well, as he died during the week of spring break. The kids would not miss any school.

MARCH 31, 1994

Mike and I spent the day going to the funeral home in Spanish Fork where Michael's body had been transported after being embalmed. We asked if we could see his body, and the funeral director said we had to bring in clothes for Michael. I had most of his clothes, and we later bought him a gray suit coat to wear with his white shirt, tie, and dark pants. A viewing had been announced in the paper for that evening. We quickly went downstairs and chose a casket. It didn't take long to choose one that was reasonably priced but also very pleasing to us—a shiny silver-colored metal coffin that looked elegant and very nice.

We spent some time in the office to choose a funeral program. I chose one with the sun coming out from the clouds because it reminded me of the day Michael died when the sun came out after snowing all day. Also, it represented to me coming into the brightness of the spirit world after suffering pain and death, as well as the hope of a glorious resurrection. The light of the sun reminded me of Michael, who had always brought sunshine to our lives. We also picked out flowers—blue, yellow, orange, and red—to symbolize Michael's youth and his enthusiasm for life.

At the cemetery office, we showed them our deed and contract to the grave sites we owned. The contract stated that if a child in the family died under eighteen years of age, a free plot would be given to us. They were surprised to see this in the contract, but they did give us a free plot next to the plots for Mike and me. We could afford all the funeral expenses because both Mike and I had life insurance for Michael through our jobs. It was just enough to cover all the funeral expenses. We also had cancer insurance through Mike's part-time job—something we have never had before or since. These were blessings at this difficult time.

Tonight there was a viewing in the mortuary. We arrived early to be able to spend some time alone with Michael, whom we hadn't seen since he died. His body was cold but soft and flexible. He looked very good, though thin. His hair was shiny. His face was peaceful. His hands were folded over his chest. He still wore his CTR ring on his third finger. How could we ever let him go? He was so precious to us. I wished we could keep his body with us forever. We kissed his forehead and patted him. But the real Michael wasn't there. I felt empty.

Most of the family came, as well as many fellow students from Michael's school, many of whom I did not know. His school also sent a plant. I was very touched by these expressions of love.

APRIL 1, 1994

Today was Michael's funeral at the Salem Seventh Ward chapel in Salem, Utah, our old home. I wrote this eulogy, which Michael's uncle Larry read:

> Michael Leo Curzon was born November 18, 1977, at Fort Benning, Georgia, the fifth child out of nine children in his family. He brought great joy and laughter to his family as a baby and a young child with his impish smile and antics. Life was a party with him around. As he started school in Salem, Utah, he excelled in all subjects. He was especially known for his very creative artwork of dragons, elves, castles, and nature.
>
> At twelve years of age, Michael began playing the violin in the Spanish Fork Intermediate School orchestra. He loved it from the beginning and never had to be told to practice.
>
> When his grandfather died of cancer in 1989, Michael observed what it meant to die with dignity and faith. He had his own health problems throughout his life but learned to endure discomfort and pain without much complaint.
>
> Michael and his sister Rebekah joined the Utah Valley String Choir and the Youth Symphony Guild in Salt Lake and enjoyed

168

volunteering at the Salt Lake Children's Museum in Salt Lake City.

The Curzon family moved to Littleton, Colorado, in August 1993, and Michael saw it as a new adventure. He especially appreciated the big orchestra at Heritage High School. The music was very challenging. He was thrilled to learn they were planning to perform at Carnegie Hall in New York on this Easter Sunday. Michael was chosen from his school to participate in Weekend for Strings in Greeley, a statewide event. He found a violin teacher and was invited to join the Littleton Community Symphony. He got a job at Pizza Hut to finance his musical goals.

In school Michael was a straight-A student in Spanish Fork and received a letter in academics at Heritage High School. In everything he did, he gave a 100 percent effort. He worked hard, and he played hard. His bedroom was immaculate. His life was in order.

Michael was faithful in the church. He enjoyed scouting activities, seminary classes, and doing his duties in the Aaronic priesthood. Michael always wore his CTR ring and was happy to tell many people what it meant—choose the right.

Michael received the news of his cancer with feelings of sadness, especially for his family, but also anticipation for what he was to experience beyond the grave. God must want him for a special purpose, and Michael was willing to do whatever the Lord required of him. He was not afraid of death, and he endured his illness with great courage.

The closing song at the funeral was "Abide with Me" (Lyte 1998, 166). The following phrase from the song meant a lot to me: "Change and decay in all around I see. Oh, Thou who changest not, abide with me."

After the funeral, I had a feeling that Michael had not only died but graduated to a higher state of life. I felt very comforted with this thought and totally believed it was true. It was raining outside as we went to our cars and drove the fifty miles to Salt Lake City to the cemetery. The Relief Society prepared sack lunches for the family to eat on the way instead of a luncheon.

As we arrived at the cemetery, the clouds parted, and the sun came out as my husband, Mike, pronounced the dedication of the grave. The weather seemed to be giving us a constant reminder that although this event was as sad and gloomy as the dark clouds, yet there was a joyful silver lining as Michael entered the glorious spirit world to begin his new life!

We'll miss you a lot, but we know you are happier and not in pain anymore. You have graduated to a higher sphere!

27

Aftermath

APRIL 3, 1994
Before leaving Utah, we chose Michael's gravestone, a carved granite block engraved with "Beloved Son, Michael Leo Curzon. Nov. 18, 1977–Mar. 29, 1994." The gravestone contains a carving of the Salt Lake Temple and one of a violin and bow. It expresses his love and talent in music and our belief in the eternal state of his soul and his part in our eternal family.

We drove home from Utah with deeply wounded hearts from losing our Michael. Yes, we have faith in the spirit world and the resurrection, but living without him in our family is unthinkable! I cling to every thought of hope. On my refrigerator is a quote from President Hinckley, our prophet: "Every temple, be it large or small, old or new, is an expression of our testimony that life beyond the grave is as real and certain as is mortality" (Hinckley 1993, 74). I read these words over and over and hope and pray it is all true. I cry several times a day. This is the greatest loss of my life—my sixteen-year-old son who has carved such a deep place in our hearts.

I walk into Michael's bedroom, which is so beautifully in order and artistically picturesque with many posters and pictures displayed—the raccoon drawing he did with Jeremy, a colorful poster of a coral reef with all the underwater fish and creatures, a large etching of a medieval knight, get-well balloons from his cousins, a mountain painting from *The Lord of the Rings*, an exquisitely painted papier-mâché fish he made hanging from the ceiling, a long poster of Utah Symphony Hall above his closet, another large poster of a violin, his desk with a picture of Christ, a vase, paintbrushes and pencils in an artistic mug, his bookcase with classic books and statuettes of *The Thinker* and of several elves, a glass container full of seashells. All things he loved and that represent him so well. We cannot move anything. This is Michael's room.

APRIL 4, 1994

This morning I went into Rebekah's room to wake her up for school. She was crying and said she didn't want to go. She told me about a wonderful dream she had just had. Michael had come to get her and said, "Do you want to go see where I live now?" After goofing around for a while, as they always did, they flew up into the sky on a cloud. On the cloud they came to a door. Michael opened the door, and Rebekah saw a beautiful green meadow with beautiful flowers of many different colors, even colors we do not have on earth. It was a wonderful place. Michael said, "I have to go now." He went through the door and was gone, and then Rebekah woke up. She said she felt it was actually a real experience, not just a dream. How wonderful that her best friend and closest brother could give her this experience. I let her stay home from school.

APRIL 7, 1994

We have been going through some boxes of Michael's keepsakes and school papers. We have found something very meaningful to us. On November 2, 1991, Michael wrote a letter in which he was practicing his skill of calligraphy. Maybe he was just goofing off at the time, but as we read it now, it seems that he must have had some kind of premonition that he would be dying and leaving us:

Dear Family,

I regret to inform you that by the time you read this manuscript I will be gone to another world far from our own. It is a world beyond the farthest horizon. Where unicorns run freely through the forest and faeries play in the silver moonlight.

I will never forget you and I will always be happy here. Goodbye.

Love,
Michael L. Curzon

Outside Michael's basement bedroom window I've noticed a single tulip blooming as spring begins. No other flowers bloom in the yard, only this one. Is this a sign?

I ran across the following poem by John Donne (written in England in the 1600s):

> Death, be not proud ...
> Nor yet canst thou kill me ...
> One short sleep past, we wake eternally,
> And death shall be no more ...

APRIL 9, 1994

Today we held a memorial service for Michael for the people who know our family here in Littleton, Colorado. We had a display outside the chapel of Michael's things—his violin, his artwork, and so on. The program had his picture on the front and this Book of Mormon scripture inside: "They never did look upon death with any degree of terror, for their hope and views of Christ and the resurrection; therefore, death was swallowed up to them by the victory of Christ over it" (Alma 27:28).

Michael's seminary teacher spoke and said, "Good for you, Michael!" What a positive statement for Michael, who has graduated to a higher sphere. Michael's orchestra teacher spoke of Michael's talents as a violinist and said that he feels everything in life happens for a reason. A fellow student from the orchestra played "Ave Maria." A girl from the ward spoke, and a youth choir from the ward sang "I Feel My Savior's Love" (Rodgers, Dayley & Huffman 1989, 74). Rebekah spoke and referred to Janice Kapp Perry's song "The Test," which says "After the trial, we will be blessed. But this life is the test" (1985). Our bishop, who had been so close to Michael and had given him several priesthood blessings, also spoke. There was quite a large crowd of people from our ward and people that we work with. It was a very nice service. Michael's life touched two groups of people—those in Utah and those in Colorado.

MAY 19, 1994

I attended a memorial service put on by Hospice of Metro Denver, the hospice company that assisted us in Michael's death. It was for families to remember their loved ones and share a brief thought. I shared the following scripture from the Book of Mormon:

> Now concerning the state of the soul between death and the resurrection—behold ... the spirits of all men, as soon as they are departed from this mortal body, are taken home to that God who gave them life ... [They] are received into a state of happiness, which is called paradise, a state of rest, a state of peace, where they shall rest from all their troubles and from all care, and sorrow (Alma 40:11–12).

The program said, "We honor the memory and celebrate the lives of those whom we have loved." A girl sang "Wind beneath My Wings." Names of those who had died were read. On a table of some displays I saw a poem that touched me deeply and expressed what Michael might be saying to our family at this time:

I Am Free

Don't grieve for me, for now I am free.
I am following the path God laid for me.
Perhaps my time seemed all too brief,
Don't lengthen it now with undue grief.
Lift up your hearts and share with me.
God wanted me now. He set me free.
(Jackson)

I put this poem on my refrigerator, and I read it often. I try to believe it, try to tell myself not to grieve too much, try to realize that Michael is in a better place. But it is hard. For a long time I cried several times a day. Finally one day I said to myself, "Don't cry anymore! It will not bring Michael back, and it doesn't do any good." I did stop crying for the most part and have not been able to cry too much ever since.

MAY 22, 1994

I returned to my work in the lunch kitchen of Euclid Junior High. The work was still hard, but everyone was so nice to me. I'm sure they felt sorry for me and also sorry that they had given me a bad time when I missed work to take Michael to the doctor. They couldn't understand why I didn't come back to work sooner. I just couldn't. I had also spent

174

many hours going through the numerous medical bills. I cried when I was on the phone with Littleton Hospital, which was where Michael was in the emergency room vomiting blood the day he came home to die. They waived the bill for that ER visit, which was very nice.

On Sunday I ran out of church into the ladies' room and sobbed about Michael. Too many reminders of suffering and death in the sacrament songs, I guess. I miss him so. I cling to every word or phrase or thought that can bring me some comfort for a while. It's a constant effort to overcome grief and have faith. God is in charge, not me.

JUNE 1994

I stood in Michael's bedroom today and felt him near my side. Soft sunlight filled the room. I had an overwhelming feeling of great peace. I felt he was telling me that he was happy, that everything was all right with his dying. It was all in the plan for him, and all was well.

Our neighbors across the street, whom we had never met, somehow learned of Michael's death. They invited our family over for a Sunday barbecue dinner, and we got to know them. They're an African American couple with some teenage children. They also gave us a beautiful plant with purple flowers. It's amazing how much these simple gestures mean when your heart is breaking.

The Young Men and Young Women of the church had a tree-planting ceremony on the front lawn of the church to remember Michael and someone else in the ward who had died. Someone also gave us a rose-bush with peach-colored roses to plant in remembrance of Michael. The Primary girls recently presented me with a quilt they had made to remember Michael by—dark green, his favorite color. So many kind gestures that mean so much.

One Sunday Sister Fisher spoke at her son's missionary farewell. She said there were several missionaries going out during this time from our congregation, "but the first one of the group that was called to serve was Michael Curzon." She said she could never complain now about letting her son go on a mission for two years after seeing our example. That was so nice.

JULY 1994

I took my boys with the immune deficiency to see Dr. Hayward, the immunologist at the University of Colorado Hospital in Denver. He told me that although patients with hyper-IgM syndrome sometimes get lymphoma, the fact that Michael had a solid tumor in his abdomen was unusual. He said he would be reporting this in a research paper he was writing. He felt it had happened because of the years of having an inflamed liver and cirrhosis. My sons are making medical history that is being reported worldwide in medical journals.

AUGUST 1994

My daughter Rebekah wrote a beautiful poem about Michael's death:

Quietly

Quietly he enriched our lives, filled our home with angelic music, Brightened my days with true companionship.
Quietly he endured the pain, overcame his fear in the face of eternity, Smiled as his life quickly dwindled from him.
Quietly he made his peace, said goodbye to those he loved, Put his exemplary life into God's hands.
Quietly he closed his eyes. Quietly, I screamed inside.
My silent tears fell on his face. He never did belong in this imperfect place.

Michael, we love and miss you so much! You were a joy to raise. You made me so proud with all your wonderful accomplishments. Thank you for being my son and trying to raise our family to a higher level of living with your beautiful music and orderly ways. It was fun trying to teach you how to drive in our neighborhood. But you never got your license. I guess you won't need it where you are going.

I need to express my sorrow to the Lord and let Him heal me. I need to trust Michael to His care. He knows what is best for Michael. I believe that in eternity Michael will not lose out on any blessing. What would Michael say to us? "Have great lives! Don't be afraid to live life to the fullest! Get in and do what you want to do! Live fully! Don't grieve for me. Do great things! Move forward!" That is what he would say. I will try to do so.

Don't grieve! Do great things. Move forward!

28

Seth's Trials

[*Note*: I am backtracking a few months to record Seth's experiences. Seth moved to Provo to go to BYU when the rest of the family moved to Colorado. He was receiving Neupogen shots to raise his white count and was much healthier than he had been for a long time. Jeremy was also in Provo but in a different apartment. Seth had trouble with his roommate criticizing him for sniffing his nose and only taking twelve credit hours. Seth was doing the best he could in life with his poor health and some possible brain damage from his early meningitis. It seems that some college kids are just not terribly understanding of those who have disabilities. Or maybe Seth didn't appear to have disabilities, which made it even harder.]

MARCH 27, 1994 (SETH'S JOURNAL)
Winter semester is almost over. I am taking twelve credit hours like last semester. I did have fifteen hours with my humanities class, but with spraining my ankle in February and with my brother Michael getting sick, I fell too far behind in my classes, so I dropped my humanities class. I'm excited for this semester to end so I can get out in the mountains more often to bird-watch and study the animals. I'll probably go back to Colorado to get a job to help pay off my car and to pay for my mission.

MARCH 29, 1994 (SETH'S JOURNAL)
Yesterday I got a call from Rebekah in Colorado informing me of Michael's situation. I drove back to my apartment later so I could speak with Michael for the last time on the phone. I told Michael that I loved him and that I was sorry for anything I had done that may have hurt him. I also told him that I forgave him for any harm he had done to me.

After talking to Michael, Jeremy and I called Jessica and had her buy three tickets to Denver that night for 10:15 p.m. We met Jessica at the airport and left for Denver. When we got home to Littleton, Michael was in the upstairs living room on the couch. We tried to talk to him, but he was too tired to talk. The next morning he was throwing up blood a lot, and we were helping him. For the most part he was incapable of any movement or speech at all. He was more in a comatose state. The whole family came in the room and cried. His classical music and hymns were playing in the background. We all expressed our love to him before he died. His death was very hard, full of pain and anguish.

Michael was absolutely the best guy. He had so many talents and great attributes. He was a great artist, and he had a love for classical music. He played the violin masterfully. He was a righteous person. I love him very much.

MAY 1, 1994 (SETH'S JOURNAL)

Before my finals were over, I got to go to Ryan Oldham's mission farewell. We've been friends ever since the sixth grade. After the farewell and the luncheon afterward, Ryan and I talked for a couple of hours about his grandpa dying recently and about Michael. We talked about how blessed we were to have strong families and the gospel of Jesus Christ to guide us. It was really special for me to be able to talk to him about some of these things close to my heart.

Now that I'm here in Colorado I need to get a job to pay for my mission. I'm getting a shot of Neupogen every day to boost my white blood cell levels up so I can be healthier.

[*Note*: Seth was much healthier. He was getting fewer infections and gaining weight. He looked great!]

MAY 3, 1994 (SETH'S JOURNAL)

Since I've been home I've been able to spend a lot of time with my brothers Robert, Matt, and Richard. Down by the river by our house we found a couple of great horned owls. Today we found a bunch of owl pellets, which we collected and dissected to find out what the owls ate. We found bird, mice, vole, and other small animal bones.

JUNE 1994 (SETH'S JOURNAL)

Many things have happened to me since I wrote last. One of the most significant is my health got really bad. Around Wednesday, June 22, I started noticing that my throat was getting sore. I was working at Taco Bell on Broadway in Littleton, Colorado, and I wasn't feeling good. When I got home that evening, I had a low fever. I started to take amoxicillin for two days when my throat felt worse and my fever went higher. I saw the doctor, and he admitted me into the Swedish Medical Center in Denver. This was on Friday, June 24. I was on intravenous antibiotics for two days, and my fever was gone on June 27. They released me to go home from the hospital on oral medication for my birthday that day. Later that night I was readmitted for a fever. After an examination, the ear, nose, and throat doctor thought I had an infection farther down in my throat. So they did an MRI scan and found a tonsillar abscess at the base of my tongue. They continued the intravenous Unasyn for seven days.

JUNE 26, 1994

I'm sitting here in the hospital while Seth is sleeping while being treated for the abscess behind his tonsil. During the physical exam on Seth, while looking into his eyes, the doctor discovered that his right eye has a pale optic nerve, meaning that it is atrophying or shriveling up. The doctors are very concerned about this and have decided to do a CT scan of his brain and orbits (eye sockets) to see if a tumor is pushing on his brain and optic nerve. Life is too much, too hard. I'm very worried. Also, the doctors keep mentioning things like leukemia and Hodgkin's disease because his blood count is abnormal with low platelet count (69,000) and enlarged spleen. He also has little red growths, like moles, all over his chest and back. They are pyogenic granulomas, maybe due to his Neupogen shots. Also, Seth has lost ten pounds since coming home from BYU. He has no diarrhea, but the weight loss could mean he has giardia, which he may have gotten from swimming in the river near our home.

Although Seth's white count is much higher than it used to be without Neupogen shots (2,800, which is still low), it seems the Neupogen (granulocyte colony–stimulating factor [G-CSF]) is not quite the panacea we thought it was. It seems to have some unwanted side effects—enlarged spleen, skin granulomas, maybe even his optic nerve atrophy? How scary. What's next?

JUNE 28, 1994

After Seth had his brain CT, we were relieved to hear that they did not find any tumors. Then the doctors started questioning me about how Seth is doing in school. I told them he has been going to college and getting Cs and Bs but taking less than a full load of classes. They were somewhat surprised to hear of his relative success in college, because the brain CT scan showed some atrophy of the brain as well as the optic nerve. They assumed this atrophy would cause him to struggle in school. They want him to see a neuro-radiologist. This sounds very serious. I don't know what to think about it. Seth has always struggled in school somewhat but has learned to work hard for his grades. Has he always had this atrophy, or is this something new? Is it related to his immune deficiency, to his meningitis as a baby, or to the Neupogen? We're not sure. But we know it is more bad news for Seth. However, he can still see pretty well, though with some diminished peripheral vision and a little nearsightedness.

AUGUST 28, 1994 (SETH'S JOURNAL)

I was released from the hospital and went on a trip to Utah with my family the first week of July. We celebrated the Fourth of July at the cabin with my grandparents and cousins. My cousin Kris Mulcock and I went on a hike and found the same Cooper's hawks I had seen the year before. We also found a nest of long-eared owls.

After finishing seven days of the intravenous meds and returning to Colorado, I was feeling a lot better and returned to work. But about ten days later, I started feeling a sore throat and fever coming back. I was put back in the Swedish Medical Center but later transferred to the National Jewish Hospital, which specializes in immunology and respiratory problems. The doctors there continued me on the Unasyn because it had worked before. After I felt better, they sent me home, where I continued my intravenous treatments for another two weeks. So I had a total of three straight weeks of the antibiotics. My energy was down, but I was overall feeling a lot better. It was now around the first part of August, and my family was preparing to move back to Utah.

AUGUST 1994

We are moving our family back to our home in Utah to recover from this terrible blow to our family of Michael's death. My husband's sabbatical year is over, and he will return to work full-time for Nebo School District. I feel like I don't want to see anybody or talk to anybody but just hide in a hole and not come out. I wish we had a private fenced backyard in Utah, but we don't. I need time to heal in privacy.

AUGUST 1994 (SETH'S JOURNAL)

My whole family and I moved back into our old house in Salem, Utah. Rebekah and I drove up to our old home in the Honda Accord at eleven thirty at night on August 12. I just lay in the living room with the cooler blowing on me while our cat reacquainted herself to the surroundings. It wasn't until one in the morning that the next Curzon caravan—Mom and kids in the station wagon—came home, and later, at three o'clock, my dad arrived in the U-Haul truck. The next day a lot of our neighbors helped us carry our stuff into the house. Later our relatives came to help. Now that I'm here, I'm working at Taco Bell in Provo, and I hope to find myself a Cooper's hawk or goshawk.

OCTOBER 31, 1994 (SETH'S JOURNAL)

Many faith-building experiences have happened to me in the past month. On September 6, 1994, I was put in the University of Utah Hospital up in Salt Lake City for hemolytic anemia and low platelet counts (thrombocytopenia). My hematocrit (red blood cell count) was down to 22 percent (normal is 40 percent), and my platelets went down to 13,000. Normal platelet counts are 150,000 to 300,000. My spleen was very enlarged. The doctors believe that was the reason why my red blood cell and platelet levels were so low. My spleen was so big that it was eating up my red cells and platelets. They were planning to take my spleen out to correct the problem, but before they could do that, I got very sick with a high fever. They found it was *Pseudomonas* bacteria in my bloodstream, or sepsis, something I could have died from quickly. I was put on intravenous antibiotics, and the operation was postponed.

The doctors were also concerned about me having some kind of malignancy, because my CEA levels were really high. CEA is a blood factor that can be related to colon cancer. They did a bone marrow biopsy and took a bone core sample to see if there were any indications of lymphoma. They found some fibrosis in my bone marrow. Fibrosis is scar tissue and means the bone marrow isn't working right. They believe 10 percent of my marrow is fibrosis, but the rest is working fine. Dr. Shigeoka thinks I have myelofibrosis, which is fibrosis or scar tissue in the bone marrow. It can get worse, where more of my marrow won't work to make blood cells, and then I would have to have a bone marrow transplant to save my life. Having a bone marrow transplant is very risky and dangerous.

I was in the hospital for ten days, and on September 16, I was released to go home. I was still on intravenous medication to treat my bacterial infection. Once my meds were done, the doctors were thinking of putting me back in the hospital to take out my spleen, but my mom and I wanted to try stopping the Neupogen (G-CSF) since it can cause enlarged spleens.

We stopped the Neupogen, and I started eating healthy (lots of liver and spinach) and taking vitamins. My spleen got smaller, and my blood counts got better after I stopped bleeding from the colonoscopy. Now my blood levels are pretty well normal, and I'm regaining my strength. I believe it is because of my prayers of faith and priesthood blessings that I got better. Now I hope to fully recover to serve a mission in a few months.

OCTOBER 1994

When Seth was in the hospital with enlarged spleen, sepsis, and hemolytic anemia, the doctors did a colonoscopy on him because his CEA was so high. Dr. Shigeoka told me in a private room that she thought he probably had colon cancer. When she told me that, I just couldn't believe it. In fact, I did not believe it for some reason. I have been told too many horrible things about my sons' health, and I was just numb. As it turned out, they found no cancer. When Seth was in the University of Utah Hospital, my extended family held a family fast, and I think it helped to get Seth on the road to recovery.

OCTOBER 1994 (SETH'S JOURNAL)

During Labor Day weekend, our family went to Idaho to have a family reunion with my dad's side of the family. I got to visit with my cousin

Scott Curzon. It was fun. Around the first week in October I trapped a male red-tailed hawk, but he escaped when I had him perched outside and his jesses slipped out of the swivel. But, only a couple of days later, I was lucky enough to catch another male redtail. Now I have him flying on the line outside. Today I might fly him free for the first time, and by the end of the week, I should have him catch a rabbit. I've had this hawk for nearly three weeks now.

JANUARY 19, 1995 (SETH'S JOURNAL)

In the past couple of weeks, I had my wisdom teeth pulled out, which was a painful experience. My friend Jared gave me his Cooper's hawk to fly. This past month I went on a couple of dates. The first was a double date with my cousin Kris. Later I took a girl out to Chuck-A-Rama, then to the BYU recreational center to play two rounds of pool, a little Ping-Pong, and air hockey. Then we went to see *The Jungle Book*.

JANUARY 29, 1995 (SETH'S JOURNAL)

Today was stake conference Sunday. I was also called today to meet with a high councilman, who told me I was called to serve a local mission. I felt overwhelmed from the great responsibility that lay before me. I know it will help me to be a spiritually stronger person, to strengthen and bless me before I can serve a full-time mission. I haven't been able to serve a full-time mission like I've wanted to because of the illnesses I've had. I hope I can help bring others into the light of Christ.

MARCH 19, 1995 (SETH'S JOURNAL)

Time goes by so fast. In my missionary work I have one guy who wants to take the discussions. I just got a job at the Story Teller, where they make felt boards of dinosaurs, space, Book of Mormon stories, and many other things with felt cut-out figures.

Almost all the people my age are out on missions out of state. And now the people who are a year younger than me are going. I might be going back to BYU for spring term. I released both my Cooper's hawk and my redtail, so I don't have any bird now. But I got a dog, a German shorthair mix named Bo. He's chocolate brown with a white spot underneath. He's a pretty neatlooking dog.

APRIL 1995

Seth is starting to wear glasses because his vision is deteriorating some due to the optic nerve atrophy. His left eye has been able to be corrected to 20/20 but with some diminished vision of color intensity. Red looks more like pink. His left eye is correctable to 20/25 with diminished color vision and a small blind spot that he doesn't notice much. He has been seeing the neuro-ophthalmologist at the Moran Eye Center at the University of Utah.

MAY 24, 1995 (SETH'S JOURNAL)

In my missionary work, Ross Christensen and I go out visiting families two to three times a week. We also go out with the full-time missionaries to teach a Vietnam vet. I was able to answer some of his questions. He was really excited to learn.

NOVEMBER 12, 1995 (SETH'S JOURNAL)

I'm going to school part-time taking only health, PE, and religion classes in the evenings. I quit my job at the Story Teller, and now I have a job at Systems Connections in Provo where I fill orders for OfficeMax Company around the United States. I work with a few neat guys. I went out with my neighbor with his red-tailed hawk and caught a rabbit.

FEBRUARY 1996 (SETH'S JOURNAL)

One day Mark Whiting came over to my house about three in the afternoon. He said, "Let's drive to Arizona and find some snakes." Doing one of the most spontaneous things I've done in my life, I packed up all I could think of and was off with Mark by five o'clock to Arizona, driving my red Ford Pinto station wagon. We drove to Nephi, got some food and a map, and enjoyed a discussion about the cute girls we passed by. Then we drove all night until we got to Page, Arizona. We slept there on the side of a dirt road.

The next morning was beautiful with the sunrise showing the silhouette of the red sandstone rock formations that surrounded us. We went to the Hoover Dam and looked off the edge; it was a splendid sight. We went looking for snakes by turning over rocks but never found one. Later we were told that snakes don't come out in February, even though it was ninety degrees. We ate out of cans of food, camped in a ponderosa pine forest near Flagstaff, heard an animal outside our tent, and found deer, elk, and cougar or bear tracks around our camp. We explored a nearby cave. Later we also saw the Grand Canyon and the Petrified Forest.

SUNDAY, MARCH 24, 1996 (SETH'S JOURNAL)

I recently sent my mission papers in. I just got an answer about whether I could go or not because of my health problems. The church has released me from serving a full-time mission because they think my illnesses are too serious to risk sending me. I still have a great desire to teach the gospel. I may be able to go out with the full-time missionaries. All my friends are out on missions, and some are returning soon. The past few years have been very lonely and trying for me because of the absence of my friends. I'm excited to see them return.

JUNE 30, 1996 (SETH'S JOURNAL)

On June 27 I turned twenty-one years old. While at work my fellow workers bought me a German chocolate cake with "Happy Birthday, Seth" written on it. It made me feel really good to know that they cared enough for me to buy a cake. After work my mom had secretly invited a lot of my friends from work and neighbors to a pizza-and-pop party in the backyard. It made me happy to see that they could take time to come and wish me happy birthday. After the party, I went to a wedding reception of Robert Oldham. I was able to see my best friend, Ryan, for the first time after he got off his mission! It was a great day.

AUGUST 1996 (SETH'S JOURNAL)

I went to the eye doctor at Moran Eye Center in Salt Lake. My vision is stable right now, and with contacts I can see 20/20 with one eye, so I'm pretty content with that. Still I can tell my vision isn't what it used to be.

DECEMBER 1996 (SETH'S JOURNAL)

My glasses prescription changed, so I went to the eye doctor to check it out. He checked my left eye, and I could see 20/20. Then he switched to my right eye, and I couldn't make anything out. It's like I have a big blurry spot in my line of vision. I can kind of make out things out of the corner of my eye but not straight ahead. My eye doctors at the

Moran Eye Center, who have seen me many times before, commenced numerous tests to determine the cause of the large change in my vision in the last four months. So I had to miss a class (history) on Thursday. The doctors did the usual visual fields, color, and acuity tests, but they also wanted more. So they took blood and did a retinal test (with large contacts in my eyes) and a spinal tap. I was really nervous when I found out they wanted a spinal tap to check for viral inflammation of my nervous system. It was nerve-racking. I had to lie flat on the way home and when I got home to avoid a bad headache. I ended up being okay. They also biopsied the purple moles on my chest that I got when I was on Neupogen. They are checking them for bacteria or viruses that could have caused my vision loss.

DECEMBER 1996

The eye doctors gave me a copy of a medical article about chronic viral meningoencephalitis, which Seth might have and which can cause eventual blindness and even death. Could it be true that this is what is wrong with Seth? It is very scary. Seth seems to have diminished night vision now also. The other night he was carrying his youngest brother, Richard, down the hall to put him in his bed. Richard sleeps on the top bunk, and the bedroom light was out. Seth lifted Richard up to put him on the top bunk but missed it and dropped Richard on the floor instead. Seth just couldn't see well enough in the darkened room to see the bunk bed. His eyesight is becoming a worry.

MARCH 22, 1997 (SETH'S JOURNAL)

I moved from home and live in Miller Apartments in Provo to attend BYU again. I moved in January 3, 1997. I played basketball with my roommates and hung out with them for a couple of days. I was able to feel a part of the group. On January 6, school started. The last few months being in school have been pretty rough. I bombed my first, second, and third tests in my History 202 class. I also had to completely miss taking my first music tests because I got some kind of flu with laryngitis and a high fever. I had to go home to Salem so Mom could help me get better, and I missed a week's worth of school. I went to the emergency room and got a shot of steroids that made me better.

APRIL 10, 1997 (SETH'S JOURNAL)

I had to go home again because of a cough, sore throat, and ear infection. My eardrum ended up rupturing, with the process being very painful. The doctor pulled a whole ball of wax out of my ear later. It's still healing. School is nearly over for winter semester. I've done a bad job of keeping my grades up. I just haven't had the motivation this semester to do well. I think my study skills and work ethic has diminished since I've been out of school for so long. I need to find some driving force in my life so I can be happier and motivated to do good in school or whatever I choose to do. I am having a hard time deciding what direction I'd like to take in my life.

JULY 1997

I took Seth to see Dr. Shigeoka for his annual checkup and blood tests. She said that his liver function tests are abnormal and she doesn't understand what has happened to his liver. She wanted to have a liver biopsy done on him. When he went for the liver biopsy, it went pretty well, but when he stood up to go home, he fainted on the floor. His sister Jessica and I were there. I just started screaming and crying. For some reason, I thought he was dying or something serious. He came to, and we got him home.

The next couple of days he started looking increasingly pale and weak. His skin was so white he looked like a ghost. I thought he must be bleeding internally from the biopsy. I took him to the doctor, and they found his red cell count was 22, about half of normal. So he was immediately put into the Provo hospital to get a blood transfusion. His skin started to look a little pink again, and he was feeling much better afterward.

AUGUST 1, 1997 (SETH'S JOURNAL)

This summer Jeremy worked in Salt Lake City, so I was able to see him quite often and go fishing and hiking. I also went with him and his friend on a backpacking trip to the High Uinta Mountains near Red Castle Lake. Round-trip was twenty-five miles. Our feet were killing us. We did it in three days. It was rocky with red rock and pine and aspen trees. There were also marshy areas where we saw a few moose. It was overall a fun experience but very trying to the physical body.

I also worked at Payson Fruit Growers part of the summer doing the graveyard shift from 5:00 p.m. to 5:00 a.m. getting six dollars an hour. That job soon ended, and I used the money I got to pay for fall semester tuition.

I was able to get a Cooper's hawk this last summer from a friend. The bird was a great hunter. He was able to catch a sparrow or two almost every day. He was a fun and tame hawk. But while perched outside my apartment one day, he got away.

From hospital bed to flying with hawks,
Seth had an indomitable spirit.

My parents, Verl and Arline Scott, with me and my sisters, 1958.

Colleen as a senior in high school, 1965.

The mission home mansion, Denver, Colorado.

Salt Lake Temple where we were married.

Colleen and Mike Curzon wedding reception, 1968.

Colleen and son, Jonathan, 1969.

191

Jonathan Scott Curzon, six months old, 1970.

Mike and Colleen with Jeremy and baby Jessica, 1972, visiting Idaho.

Colleen holding Seth, 1976, Ft. Benning, Georgia.

Michael's first birthday, with Jeremy, Jessica, Colleen and Seth, 1978. Auburn, Washington.

Colleen with Rebekah, Mike with Michael. Seth, Jessica and Jeremy in front, 1981, Utah.

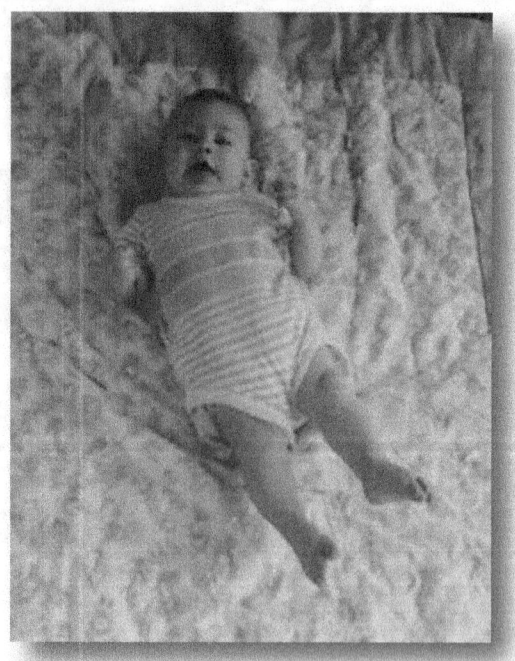

Robert Curzon, 1982, Salem, Utah.

Curzon kids playing in backyard, Salem, Utah, 1983

Curzon family with new baby, Matthew, 1983.

Front: Rebekah, Robert, Michael, Seth; back: Matthew, Jeremy, Colleen, Mike, Jessica, Salem, Utah. 1985

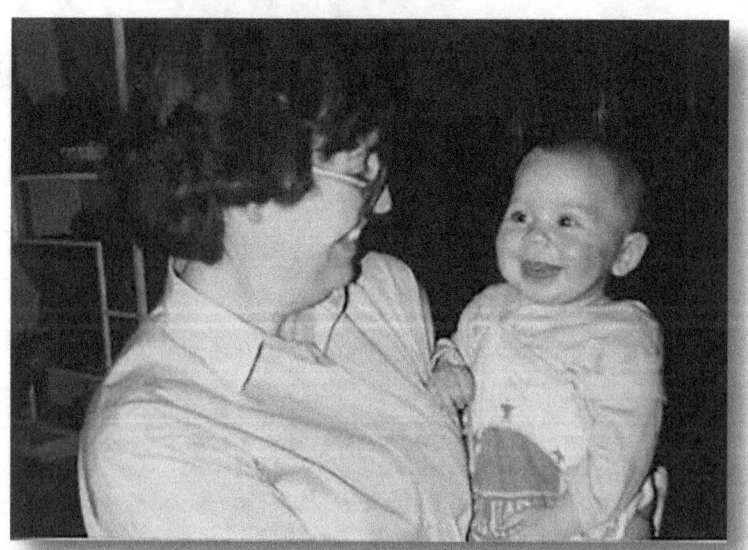

Colleen holding baby Richard, 1987, Utah

Mike's Ed.S. graduation, with Jessica, Michael, Colleen, Rebekah, Seth and Jeremy, 1987.

Scott family- Paula, Colleen, Richard, Verl, Arline, Wendy, Barbara, Jackie, after Mom and Dad's mission in the Philippines, 1988.

Curzons at East Canyon Resort, Utah, family reunion, 1988.

Christmas music at home- Jessica, Colleen, Michael and Rebekah, 1990.

Seth with trained red-tail hawk, Salem, Utah, 1992.

Colleen and Hyper IgM sons at U of U Hospital- Richard, Seth, Robert, Michael, 1993.

Michael playing violin at his concert, Springville Art Musem, 1993, Utah.

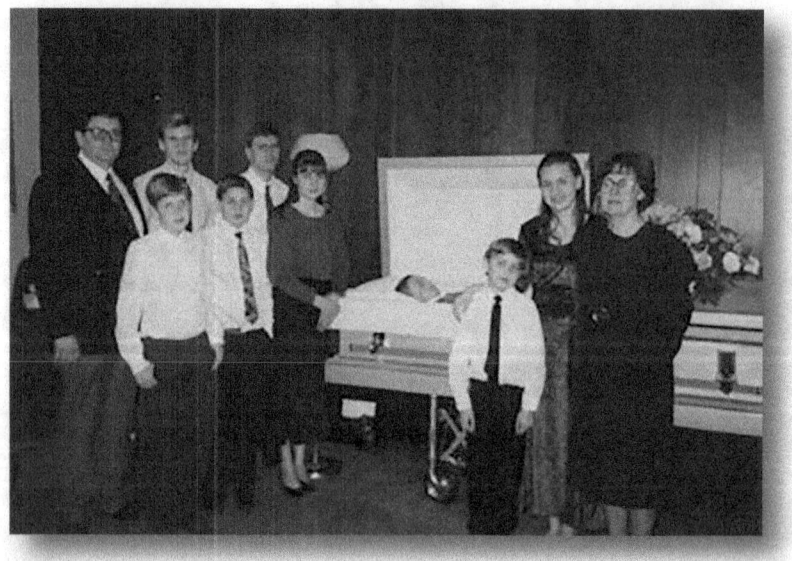

Family at Michael's funeral, Utah, 1994.

Jessica and Rob's wedding, 1994

Rebekah ready to walk down the aisle with her Dad, 2001.

Seth, Grandma Scott and Colleen at Devil's Punchbowl where Seth worked. California, 1999.

Richard, Mike and Seth in Yosemite, California, 1999.

Seth reading with low vision, 1999.

Little Ally with "Uncle Boys," Richard, Seth, Robert, and Matthew.
LA Zoo, 1999.

Mike and Colleen in Israel after cancer diagnosis, 2000.

California family- Rob, Rich, Matt, Seth, Colleen and Mike after chemotherapy, 2000.

Jessica and our sweet granddaughters, Leah and Ally, 2002.

Mike and Colleen at Lake Tahoe, California after Mike's stem cell transplant, 2002.

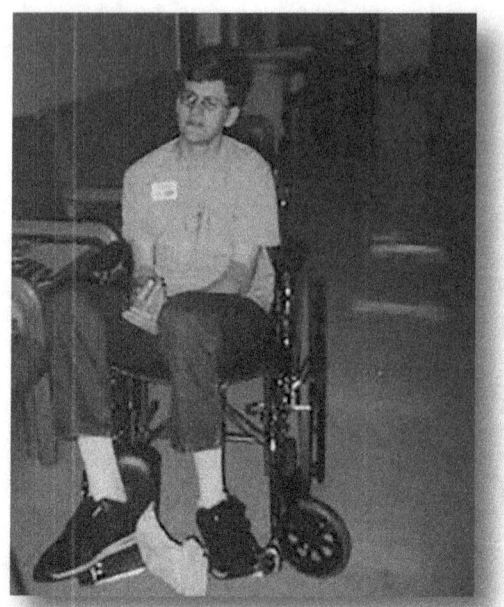

Seth at National Institutes of Health, 2003.

Seth about 2004, a year before his death.

Richard's missionary farewell with Rebekah, Colleen, and Mike. Provo, UT, 2006.

Christina and Matthew's wedding, Toronto Temple 2007.

Our kids, spouses and granddaughters at Rob and Stephanie's wedding, California, 2008.

Our last dance, Colleen and Mike, April 2008.

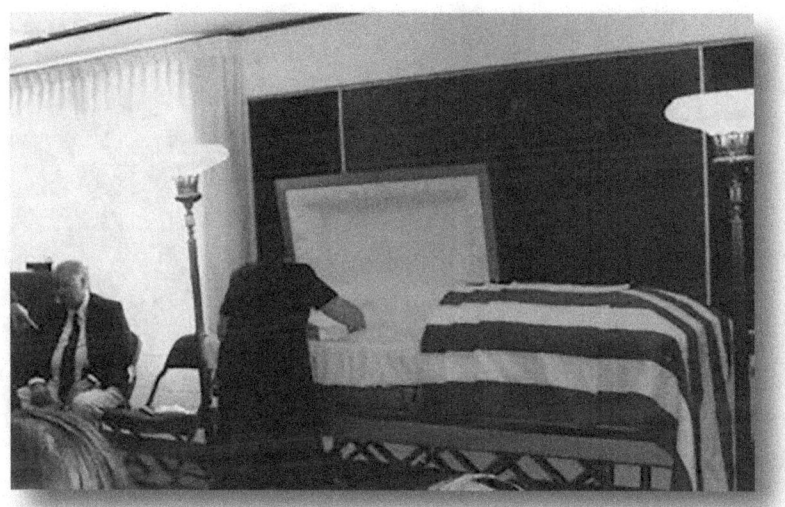

Colleen saying goodbye to Mike, October 2008.

Mike's side of the family with Colleen at cemetery, October 2008.

My darling new granddaughter, Mala! October, 2008.

My sweet mother, Arline's, 90th birthday party, 2008. Three years before her death.

In New York City Chinatown with Jessica, Rebekah and missionary Richard. March 2009.

Colleen's Brigham Young University graduation, April 2009.

Visiting with Maya and Mala. About 2011 and 2013.

Little Susanna with her Dad, Robert, 2013.

Me and my new hubby, Gary Openshaw, 2013.

Colleen and Gary on vacation in North Vancouver, Canada, 2014.

Christmas lights with Susanna, Rob, Rebekah, Colleen, Christina, Matt, and Rich, 2016.

Rebekah's nursing school graduation with me, Leah, Jessica, Ally; Susanna in front. 2017.

Abby, Noah, Zak, Ally, Jessica and Leah, 2017.

Robert and Nicole, 2021

Rich, Siru and baby Maija, 2022, Tennessee

Robert, Susanna and Nicole, 2023.

Richard, Siru and baby Maija, 2023.

29

Emotional and Spiritual Consequences

JULY 1994

I will backtrack a little here to mention some trials of faith that have begun to find their way into our family's lives. When we had our last family meeting with Michael, it seemed that all of us were united in the belief that the gospel of Christ was true and that we would see Michael again. We believed he was going to a better place in the spirit world. It was a wonderful sacred time in our family, though so sad.

Now I see in some of my children some disturbing signs of deep depression and beginnings of doubt and despair because of Michael's death. Yes, I too have been very sad, and my faith has been tested also, but I have reached out to God, and I have been comforted on almost a daily basis. Perhaps they haven't been able to do that and have let their sorrow overcome them. I see evidence of shrinking belief in God in some of my children as they are struggling as to why God would allow Michael to die and suffer as he did. This has caused me to feel a lot of anguish and sorrow.

CHRISTMAS 1994

We had the usual family meeting on Christmas Eve and talked a lot about Michael, who died in March. We sang our family song "If We Hold on Together" (Diana Ross). Robert said he felt Michael's presence as we were singing. My sister Paula gave me some wonderful gifts—two ceramic angels to represent Jonathan and Michael, as well as a book titled *The Christmas Box* by Richard Paul Evans, about a woman who lost her little daughter in death. These helped my heart to heal more.

APRIL 1995

Mike and I attended a regional church conference at the BYU Marriott Center with our son Jeremy. Elder James E. Faust spoke about a daughter-in-law of his that was killed in a car accident. "Why did this have to happen?" he asked. According to my notes, he said something like "Don't try to figure out why. You will see that good has come of this tragedy. And we have seen good from this tragedy. My counsel is to be still and know that God is God, and as we meet our challenges, think of the eternities. In the eternities, so many things in this life really aren't going to make that much difference." (See also James E. Faust, "The Good That Can Grow out of Tragedy," *Stories from My Life,* 21). He then pronounced a blessing on the congregation, and then we sang "Faith of our fathers, holy faith. We will be true to thee till death!" (Faber 1998, 84). It was a very inspiring meeting. My feeling was that God is in charge and Michael is in His care, as are all spirits. Everything is fine and in order. Trust in the Lord. Let Michael go. Such a hard thing to do!

Brother Faust's experience is just what I needed to hear. I hope it will increase my son's faith also. Elder Faust has also said:

> For some, the refiner's fire causes a loss of belief and faith in God, but those with eternal perspective understand that such refining is part of the perfection process ... If there were no night, we would not appreciate the day, nor could we see the stars and the vastness of the heavens. We must partake of the bitter with the sweet. There is a divine purpose in the adversities we encounter every day. They prepare, they purge, they purify, and thus they bless. When we pluck the roses, we find we often cannot avoid the thorns which spring from the same stem (Faust 1999, 250).

Michael's life and spirit were like a beautiful rose given to our family. Unfortunately there were also the thorns of his illness and death. But the memory of the beautiful rose will be with us forever. In the suffering I have experienced, I have felt God's love and compassion and guidance. My faith in Him is stronger now than it was before this tragedy.

219

MAY 1995

I have had many arguments and hard feelings toward my daughter Rebekah in the past few months for her teenage antics of skipping school and not coming home. She is a sophomore in high school now. Although she is very intelligent and excels in orchestra and drama, she has not been serious about a lot of her schoolwork. It has caused me a lot of heartache. One day I opened the scriptures and read, "Of you it is required to forgive all men" (D & C 64:10). "If ye have not charity [love], ye are nothing" (Moroni 7:46, B of M). I definitely need to change and do better. I need to show love to my daughter in spite of her actions. Our conflicts have not been helpful.

SEPTEMBER 29, 1995

It has been one and a half years exactly since Michael died. I visited my family in Salt Lake City and then went to see Michael's and Jonathan's graves. I asked them to please help my other kids to increase their faith. I also prayed to the Lord with sadness for my children. Later I felt impressed to pick up the Bible, and I turned to Isaiah. It was very inspiring where the Lord says, "I will save thy children ... and all flesh shall know that I the Lord am thy Savior and thy Redeemer" (Isaiah 49:25–26).

OCTOBER 10, 1995

I had an incredible discussion with Rebekah tonight. She told me of the many spiritual experiences she has had in her life. She saw Jonathan (as a grown-up spirit) when she was a little girl. She dreamed about Grandpa Martindale, whom she had never seen. Her incredible dream of being with Michael after his death and the scripture she read that helped her understand the reason Michael died—all these experiences have meant a lot to her. I'm so glad to see that Rebekah seems strong at this time. On the other hand, my son Jeremy seems a little lower and more depressed over Michael's death every time I talk to him.

MAY 1996

Rebekah has been struggling in school, being sick at school and missing classes while hanging out with her friends. She is also very busy in drama—*West Side Story*, in which she plays an important role. It seems we must let her mostly stumble in her schoolwork if she chooses to. She would run away from home if we put too much pressure on her. "Try not to worry. Just love her." That is what her friends have told me to do when I asked their advice.

JUNE 1996

We recently drove to Salt Lake City to see Jessica graduate from the University of Utah with a bachelor's degree in therapeutic recreation. She decided that this would be a more practical major than drama was. It was a great day, and we are very proud of her. Her husband, Rob, was at her side as we took pictures on the grassy hill at the U of U. She will work as a recreational therapist at the Neuropsychiatric Institute of the University of Utah. This is a great accomplishment!

APRIL 1997

Now that Rebekah is almost through with her senior year of high school, we found out that she has been experiencing severe depression from her brother's death. We did not know this, as she did not seem sad. She was often laughing and smiling with her friends or else being angry with us as parents as we tried to get her to follow the rules. She has seen a counselor and has been put on antidepressants. She is suddenly a different person. She is nice, respectful, and even her stomach problems have disappeared. I have learned that teenagers often do not show the classic signs of depression and that it may manifest itself as anger or rebellion.

Rebekah has been working hard in school now to make up work so that she will be able to graduate, something we were beginning to think might not happen. I guess this has been another aftermath of Michael's death. I thought Rebekah had handled his death well, but underneath she has still been wrestling with a lot of sadness, even three years later. The immune deficiency has not only robbed some of us of physical health and life but has also caused others in the family to struggle with their spiritual and emotional health as well because of the chronic sorrow we have experienced.

As James E. Faust said, "You will see that good has come of this tragedy." But first comes the sorrow.

30

Gold in California

A lot has happened in our family in the past few months. I've written numerous pages in my journal but will only summarize here. Grandma Ruth, Mike's mother, came for Thanksgiving last year and didn't go back home until April. I endeavored to be of service to her, but it was difficult with her poor health.

Exciting news! Jessica is expecting a baby girl in December. She went to Philadelphia to have a special medical procedure to learn the sex of the baby and whether it has hyper-IgM syndrome. Because it is a girl, there is no worry that the child will have this illness! We are all very excited. Other medical news that is not so good is that Seth can no longer read with his right eye. We've been to the neuro-ophthalmologist several times with no real answers. But he is still going to BYU and living in Provo and doing well in school and in church. I am proud of him. My kids are progressing in the right directions.

Rebekah graduated from high school with the help of counseling and Prozac and some hard work to catch up. Her oldest brother, Jeremy, started at Yale Law School last fall! Life has been exciting but also hard. We've been worrying about having enough money. In fact, we seem to be going into debt $500 every month now. That is why we began to look around for other jobs. With kids in college and the increased expenses as our children grow older, we need to bring in more money.

After going to the temple together, Mike and I felt strongly that he should take a school psychology position he learned about in Southern California. It will pay almost twice as much in salary, and the housing market in the Palmdale, California, area is depressed at the moment, so we can buy a house there for about the same amount as we are paying now. I think things will work out. We need to remember our responsibility to Seth and Grandma Ruth, who still need our help. Rebekah also will need our assistance, as she has declined to go with us, wanting to be on her own here in Utah now that she is eighteen.

OCTOBER 1997, LITTLEROCK, CALIFORNIA

Well, we moved to California in August for the new school psychology job. The move itself was very challenging, with us bringing stuff from our six-bedroom house. Mike drove a big U-Haul truck, which broke down, and I drove the old station wagon. After spending a week in a Motel 6, we have landed in Littlerock, California, which is a small town in the desert fifty miles northeast of Los Angeles. We are renting a three-bedroom house right now and have our three youngest sons with us—Robert, Matthew, and Richard. Rob and Matt are not happy at their new high school, and Richard is not happy at his elementary school, which is two blocks away. There is sand, sand everywhere. This is really a desert!

Mike's job is much different here and much more challenging also. He works longer hours than he did in Utah. The schools are challenging, multiethnic, and strict. Early-morning seminary for Rob and Matt at 6:00 a.m. before school is almost unbearable because they are so sleepy. Then they have school all day and homework later. Matt especially is getting sick a lot, I think because he just hates to go to school so much. We have learned that a lot of people in our church here do homeschooling. There seems to be a lot more flexibility in education than in Utah. We'll have to look into that.

The boys have had some good times here going fishing in the canal, watching Star Wars movies, and having some good discussions with us. If we can just hang in here for a few more years, it will work out. We mustn't lose hope and faith just because it is strange and scary right now.

NOVEMBER 9, 1997 (SETH'S JOURNAL)

Since I've written, my parents moved from Salem, Utah, to Littlerock, California. My dad wasn't making enough money as a school psychologist in Utah. He was led by the Lord to find another job.

223

This semester at BYU I signed up for classes like zoology, statistics, chemistry, sociology, and religion. Being out for the summer seemed to have a greater effect on me in having no desire or motivation to do my schoolwork. I went to a doctor, and he diagnosed me with severe depression. So I asked him to give me a letter of discontinuance from school. Now I have nothing to do but read, play Sega, and vegetate. I've been telling myself to get a job, but I don't have motivation for that either. I'm debating whether to stay in school next semester or not.

DECEMBER 1997

Seth is not doing well in school at BYU. After performing many neuropsychological tests on Seth, a psychologist at BYU told us that Seth's IQ has decreased and we shouldn't expect him to be able to do college-level work. I guess his brain atrophy is showing itself more in his life. Since he has failed classes and dropped out of school, we persuaded him to come with us to California and begin a new life there rather than trying to get back into school again. I feel we need to watch over him a little more now that his eyesight is getting worse.

Seth has such high hopes and expectations for his life but is simply unable to live the normal life of the twenty-two-year-old that he is. It is heartbreaking to see this. His brain atrophy and poor vision are getting worse. He also seems to be having a little trouble with his balance as he walks. Like the neuro-ophthalmologist told us, he could have a degenerative atrophy of his central nervous system, which will continue to worsen. Just in the past few years, there have been reports of such deterioration occurring with some patients who have primary immune deficiencies such as Seth has. I have never heard of this until a few months ago as being a possible scenario with this genetic disease. It is very frightening. Oh God, help us to press forward.

We went to Utah for Christmas and stayed with my mother. On December 29, Jessica had our first grandchild in Salt Lake City—a girl, Ally Michael! I can't believe I am a grandma! We were happy to be in town at that time. Jessica began her labor as a home birth but ended up going to the hospital for a forceps delivery. Ally is very sweet, and Jessica and Rob are doting parents.

JANUARY 1998

We've had some happy changes in our life situation here in California. We just purchased and moved into a nice big house that makes this area feel like a whole new world! The boys have also changed their school situations. Robert and Matthew are now doing a home study program through the high school, and Richard changed elementary schools to one where he is not being bullied by other students. The boys are making some friends at church, and we are all happier now. It just took some time to work things out in this new state.

MAY 1998

We are really beginning to enjoy living in California and have had lots of visitors who want to visit us here and take advantage of going to the beach, the Los Angeles Zoo, Disneyland, the San Diego Zoo, Tijuana, and so on. Richard is enjoying Cub Scouts, and he went on a whale-watching trip with his school. You can't do that in Utah!

Mike's mother came to live here for about two months. Again, it was very difficult for me, but I did try very hard to be patient and loving with her. Mike drove her back to Idaho in April.

MOTHER'S DAY, MAY 1998

A very quiet day of reading, thinking, writing, and going to church. I got flowers, a card, and breakfast in bed from Mike and the four boys. I think about my motherhood—things that have gone wrong, things to improve.

Jeremy called recently from Yale to say that he is engaged to a girl from India named Maya. I'm sure she is a sweet person, and I am happy Jeremy has found someone to love, but I am saddened that he is marrying out of the church. I look back on Jeremy's life and think about the mistakes we made as parents, being too strict with him at times, and thinking about what we can do in the future to do better. I think about my boys here at home. I nag them too much to get work done, but it seems necessary. I seem to spend my whole life coaxing them to stay busy and get their schoolwork and chores done. I think about my Michael, who passed away, and my dad. Please, dear God, give me strength to be the mother I should be.

I am happy with Seth's opportunities here in California. He has been volunteering at the Devil's Punchbowl, which is a Los Angeles county park area in the mountains. He is helping to take care of an injured hawk up there and really enjoys the work. He has been called to be a stake missionary along with my husband, Mike, and was able to help teach and baptize a man they met on the street. Seth has also been attending religion classes here and dances and parties with the young people. So this is turning out to be a good experience for him, although he still has lonely times and sadness about his health issues. All his life he has jokingly said, "I'm going to California!" and now he is here.

AUGUST 1998

After volunteering at the LA County Parks and Recreation's Devil's Punchbowl for a few months, Seth has actually been hired there. It is such a perfect job for him to work in this natural canyon of rock formations. It is a slow-moving job, working with animals and nature, which is ideal for Seth. He has made several friends up there and is able to have some opportunities to share the gospel. So, even though he has only had two years of college in wildlife biology, he has found his career. I had to fill out the applications for him, as it seemed he could not do it himself, but I am so happy he got this job.

NOVEMBER 1998

Jeremy, my oldest son and Yale Law student, has married Maya, another law student from India. In August we had a family party for them in Salt Lake City at my mother's condominium clubhouse. Maya is vegetarian, so we didn't quite know what to serve, but we had rice and vegetables and dessert, along with meat for the rest of us. They had flown to India to have an actual Indian Hindu wedding with her parents. Afterward they came to our home here in California with souvenirs from India and a video of their Indian wedding. Now they have had another American wedding ceremony in downtown Salt Lake City. Most of Jeremy's Utah relatives were able to come, as well as Maya's relatives from India. So Maya is officially part of the family. She is a very charming and fun girl and we like her a lot. I am glad Jeremy has found someone to spend his life with!

This time of our lives has become a high point. We are happy about so many things. Our children are doing well for the most part. Living in California is very enjoyable with the blue skies, sunny days, wide deserts, mountains, palm trees, and expansive ocean.

Happy days in sunny California gave us a lift!

31

Cancer!

OCTOBER 18, 1998

I had a mammogram a month ago. The day I was to get the mammogram was pretty inconvenient, and I almost decided not to go, but it seemed the Spirit whispered that I should, so I did. After the mammogram, the technician motioned for the receptionist to come in and see my mammogram. I had the feeling there was something wrong with it. A few days later, I got a note in the mail saying I needed another mammogram in three months.

I called the doctor's office after getting the note in the mail. They told me I had a small nodule in my left breast and needed to see a surgeon. I went to see my doctor to get the referral, and I saw the report of my mammogram. It said there were three microcalcifications in connection with a three-millimeter nodule that was quite well defined. There had been no such growth two years ago. All I have read indicates that microcalcifications are usually associated with malignancies. I have been really scared.

I have decided that if I have cancer, I will do my best to fight it and to live to raise my kids. It may mean a lot of sickness, though, if I have chemotherapy and so on. The cancer is probably at a very early stage, which means I would have a 95 percent chance of living five years and less than a 10 percent chance that the cancer would recur in ten years. (I got lots of books at the library about this.) I have to totally stop taking estrogen, which I have been taking since my hysterectomy in 1996. Estrogen is fuel for breast cancer. I should see the surgeon in a week or two. Mike forgot to ask me about my doctor appointment, but I brought it up later that night. He is being very sweet to me.

JANUARY 5, 1999

I had a second mammogram. There were more microcalcifications, so I went to get a stereotactic needle biopsy, which is guided by x-ray. However, they couldn't make it work, because the nodule is too close to the chest wall. So I will have to have a regular biopsy done at the hospital.

JANUARY 10, 1999

I went to see the surgeon today at High Desert Medical Group. He did a physical exam and said he felt a hard "ridge" in my right breast. It hurt quite a bit when he pushed on it and continued to hurt afterward for several days. The left breast was the one they were concerned about from the mammogram. It scares me that he felt something in the right breast. Is it possible to have cancer there without it showing up on the mammogram? The plan is that I will have a regular operation biopsy on January 23. It is so hard to keep waiting and wondering. I am so afraid that I have breast cancer.

I've been reading lots of books about diet and breast cancer lately. They suggest to eat brown rice, tofu, fruits, vegetables, and very little milk and meat. It seems I need to say no to myself on almost everything I want to eat so I can live healthily and live long enough to raise Richard, who is only twelve years old. I am probably being silly to be so afraid. My emotions are like a roller coaster. I hope I can remember the joy and peace I felt in church.

JANUARY 28, 1999

I went to have the biopsy on my left breast at Antelope Valley Hospital a few days ago. Before the operation, I asked the surgeon to at least do a needle biopsy on my right breast where he had felt the ridge. He agreed, so that is what happened. Mike was with me and took me home afterward. I was really groggy and didn't eat the rest of the day. I learned the results of the biopsy today, and they were just the opposite of what I had expected. The microcalcifications on the left are benign, but the needle biopsy on the right came back "suspicious" for malignancy. If I have cancer on the right side, I know that it isn't small, because the ridge can be readily felt and is quite large! This is frightening

.

FEBRUARY 18, 1999

I went to the doctor's office a few days after the initial biopsy to have an actual larger biopsy taken from the right breast. It was a horrible ordeal. They said they would give me a local anesthetic and I would be fine. However, it was very painful and scary, like having major surgery without anesthesia! It felt like my body went into shock. The doctor removed about a one-and-a-half-inch piece of tissue that looked white. They put it in a bottle to take to the lab. I was shaky and weak afterward and had to sit in the car for quite a while to recover before I could drive home. I guess I should have brought somebody to drive me.

The doctor called the following Monday in the middle of a very busy morning, about eleven o'clock. He said, "The biopsy showed conclusively that you have cancer in your right breast. Come in tomorrow, and we'll have a long talk about your options." I couldn't believe what I had just heard, a sentence that will change my life drastically. Monday was so busy all day that I hardly had time to think about the terrible news I had just received. Yes, I did have breast cancer! I felt my world would never be the same again. Although I was home with the kids, I told no one. I didn't cry but kept my emotions in tight rein.

That night I told Mike we needed to go for a ride. I told him the news in the car. We talked for about an hour, especially about how we would have to have me relax more and have the kids do more chores. When we got home, we talked to Robert and Matthew at length. We told them I had cancer and would probably live several years but may not have such a long life. We told them we needed for them to be more responsible and self-starting. Richard was asleep, and Seth was gone to church Institute class.

The next day, as I cried in worry and sadness about my health and about my kids, I decided to listen to one of Michael's music tapes. As it began to play, I realized, to my surprise, that it was an actual recording of Michael playing Vivaldi's violin pieces "Winter" and "Summer" from *The Four Seasons*. These were songs on which I had accompanied him on the piano when he was alive. I found the piano music and played along with the recording, as we had done so many times in his life. As I played, it seemed as if Michael had come to visit me and comfort me. And I haven't cried since. I have felt strong physically and emotionally.

FEBRUARY 19, 1999

I went to see the surgeon today to talk about my options following the results of the biopsy. I was shocked to hear that I, not the doctor, must be the one to decide what sort of surgery I will have for my cancer. I can either have a mastectomy with complete removal of my breast or a lumpectomy combined with six weeks of radiation later. I was told that the statistics of survival are the same with either choice. I eventually chose the lumpectomy with radiation option.

MARCH 19, 1999

Four days ago I had surgery for the breast cancer—the large cancer that the mammogram did not detect. How is that possible? It was found accidently by the doctor's physical exam and by my suspicions. I am also surprised it has taken two months to get to this point. I would think the doctors would have acted more quickly. The doctor had to remove about a quarter of the breast. It was not a lumpectomy but a segmental mastectomy. He also removed the lymph nodes under my right arm to learn if any of them have cancer in them. Before the operation, Mike gave me a priesthood blessing. I felt very little fear, and all went well. I stayed in the hospital overnight. I was kind of scared and lonely after the operation, and I was so glad when Mike came to be with me.

I have come home with a drain—a tube coming from the area of my lymph nodes that drains fluid into a small rubber bulb. It is strange to have this hanging from my side. My upper arm feels very strange— both numb and painful, like wires sticking me. I am getting used to the feeling, but it is not fun. I am supposed to do exercises to reach my arm up high, which is difficult to do. The removal of the lymph nodes is causing me more pain and discomfort than the actual breast surgery.

MARCH 24, 1999

Mike and my sister Wendy went to the doctor with me to find out the results of the operation. The doctor pulled the drain out of me with a quick jerk, which felt funny. Then he told us that two out of the fourteen lymph nodes removed were positive for cancer, so that means I will need to have chemotherapy. He said, "This is not early breast cancer. It is middle breast cancer." The tumor type was invasive ductal comedocarcinoma, which is relatively aggressive. The tumor was approximately twelve centimeters or about three inches long— not small at all. Because there is cancer in the lymph nodes, cancer cells may have spread through the bloodstream to other areas of the body. That is why systemic chemotherapy is necessary to kill any cancer cells left in the body. Can all of this really be happening to me?

I have no history of breast cancer in my family, but I have eaten a rather high-fat diet, which is a risk factor. I was pleased to hear that only two lymph nodes were positive. On Friday I will see the oncologist, who will prescribe the chemotherapy.

MARCH 26, 1999

I went to see the oncologist today with Mike. She is a young doctor with long dark hair and seems very intelligent. From the lab tests, she has learned that my cancer is mildly ER (estrogen-receptor) positive. Thirty percent of my cancer cells are ER positive. That is good but not as good as they would hope. It means that tamoxifen, an antiestrogen pill, might help some. She asked me if I have any aches and pains, which I do. She said she could not make a decision on treatment until more tests were done to determine the likelihood of other metastases or spots of cancer in my body. She ordered a CBC, CEA, CA 27/29 (cancer antigen tests), and also a bone scan and abdominal CT scan, to look for cancer in bones and vital organs. She also ordered a chest x-ray to look in the lungs. If all of these tests are okay, it means the cancer is stage 2, which she said is early cancer.

MARCH 29, 1999

Today is the anniversary of Michael's death five years ago. Today was the time for the boys' IVIG. The nurse, Melanie, said about my cancer that we should just leave it in the Lord's hands. I feel strong right now, and maybe the cancer will be an avenue for me to grow and also help other people.

I have spent a lot of time reading books from the library about cancer, cancer diets, herbs, and exercise. Probably my greatest hope for recovery and long life is the diet found in the Word of Wisdom, the health code of Mormonism. This diet consists of eating grains, fruits, and vegetables and meat sparingly.

APRIL 4, 1999

I got the bone scan today, a rather frightening experience. As I lay on the table after getting an intravenous dose of radioactive fluid, I saw several areas of my body light up on the screen. *Does this mean that I have cancer in all those bones, or does it mean I have arthritis?* I wondered. Afterward, I learned that they did not see anything on the bone scan that they thought was cancerous.

My abdominal CT scan and other tests were also normal, so I officially have stage 2 breast cancer, which I have learned from research means I may have a 25 percent chance of ten-year disease-free survival and a 50 percent chance of overall survival in ten years. With tamoxifen or other endocrine medicines, my chances may be 25 percent better for surviving. Not too bad. Not too good. Doctors say they can never really predict the outcome for any individual patient.

APRIL 13, 1999

I am on the plane flying from New England to Los Angeles. Mike and I went to visit Jeremy and Maya because I probably will be in the middle of chemotherapy when it is time for their graduation from Yale. We had a great time with them, and Jeremy was very kind. Now I face the unknown with this cancer. I am preparing for the worst and will pray and work and eat for the best.

APRIL 26, 1999

Chemotherapy day. I was very scared, woke early, prayed, and read scriptures: "Let us cheerfully do all that lieth in our power and then stand still to see the salvation of God" (D & C 123:17). The oncologist had told me I could choose between eight doses of CMF, which probably wouldn't cause me to lose my hair, or four doses of AC (Adriamycin, or doxorubicin, plus cyclophosphamide), which would make me lose my hair. She said they are about the same. I chose CMF—cyclophosphamide, methotrexate, and 5-fluorouracil. Chemotherapy is putting poison into my body. But, even though I do not feel sick right now, I guess I need it to kill the cancer

When I walked into the cancer office, I saw many sick-looking people, some in wheelchairs, some with no hair. Is this how I will be in a few weeks? It was very scary, but there were a lot of people there, so I am not the only one. They took me back into a room with numerous comfortable chairs and intravenous stands. Several people are getting chemotherapy today.

Now, a few hours later after the chemo, I am in bed. I feel heavy, achy with a headache, but no nausea. I was given nausea medicine. I really feel so, so awful, however. I am tempted to say I will never have chemotherapy again. Mike gave me a blessing yesterday and said, "Pray and have faith, and you will be guided step by step to know what you need to do. Trust in the Lord only."

MAY 1999

I went to the library and read some medical books that compare the effectiveness of the two kinds of chemotherapy from which I could choose. I have chosen the wrong one! They are not the same, as the doctor told me. The strong chemotherapy is about 20 percent more effective according to survival statistics. I left the library and drove out into the desert on a dirt road. I stopped the van and thought and prayed. If I get the stronger chemotherapy (AC), I will lose my hair for sure. Because Adriamycin is also a drug that destroys heart cells, I may end up with a weaker heart. I may become much weaker in my future life because of it, but I would have a better chance of surviving to raise Richard. I prayed, "Please, dear Lord, give me at least five more years until Richard is eighteen! I will take the stronger drug for his sake, even if it hurts my health." It was a scary decision to make, but I think it is right. I must have courage.

I went to see the doctor and told her of my decision. She said that was fine. Then she said, "If the cancer comes back, you are going to die!" I was surprised and offended by her words. I felt her bedside manner was very lacking. Even though what she said is probably true, I requested that another oncologist be put on my case.

JUNE 20, 1999

Seth flew back east and met Rebekah for Jeremy's and Maya's graduation from Yale Law School! What an accomplishment! Too bad I was not able to go, since I am in the middle of chemotherapy.

Jeremy has been very active in consulting with Maya's uncle, who is an oncologist, to find out his recommendations for my treatment. Seth had a great time in the area seeing the colonial-style buildings, visiting the natural history museum, and going to Cape Cod. The sad thing was that he was not able to clearly see the birds flying in the area since his eyesight is deteriorating. He could only hear them. For Seth, who loves birds so much, that is a great loss.

JULY 1999

Seth drove to the Institute of Religion at the college for an activity and afterward went to the grocery store. While he was in the store, he started to feel very ill and sat down on the floor near a pole. An employee called an ambulance for him and called us at home to tell us about it. When we got to the store, we saw the ambulance there with Seth inside. They rushed him to the hospital. He had a high fever and pneumonia, something that has happened to him more times than I can count. He was given intravenous antibiotics and was in the hospital for several days. More than at other times, he seemed to have trouble breathing.

Later, when Seth came home, he was still sick and coughing a lot. Somehow, with the breathing difficulty, I thought he might have *Pneumocystis* pneumonia, which Jonathan died from. I gave him Septra, which we had in our cupboard. It was hard on his stomach but seemed to clear up the respiratory problem. Oh, Sethy! You go through so much!

NOVEMBER 1999

I have been through one dose of CMF and four doses of AC chemotherapy. I lost my hair. The cancer doctor's office had brochures for inexpensive wigs, and I ordered two, along with some hats. The worst days at church were the first day I wore my wig and the first day I didn't wear my wig after my hair started to grow back, short and curly. I just felt so self-conscious.

I had a portacath surgically placed under the skin near my shoulder in order to have a place in which to infuse the chemotherapy, because Adriamycin is so hard on blood vessels. At the beginning of each chemotherapy session I was given Benadryl and a drug to relax me, as well as anti-nausea medication, then the red fluid, Adriamycin and cyclophosphamide. Every three weeks was another infusion. I would feel sick for a couple of days, then weak and tired the rest of the time, feeling about back to normal before the next infusion. However, before the last chemotherapy session, I was still feeling pretty awful, but it was time to put the poison into my body again.

Overall, chemotherapy was not as bad as I expected, largely because of the Zofran I took for nausea. I still had plenty of mild nausea, some mouth sores, weakness, tiredness, and light-headedness due to some low blood counts. I was given Neupogen shots to raise my white cell count and Epogen shots to raise my red cell count. Most of the time I carried on with my motherly duties and carried on a normal life with the help of some relatives who made visits to help me. I even drove to Utah in the heat of July for the family reunion—maybe not the wisest thing to do, but I did it.

Having read that patients who are part of a support group have better survival rates, I decided to join a breast cancer support group sponsored by the hospital. There were about ten ladies in the group, which was led by a social worker. We developed a feeling of love and support in the group. However, it was sad and frightening to see a couple of the ladies die as the months went by. But their cancers were more advanced than mine. Will I be that person some day?

During the chemotherapy, as suggested in a book I read, I drew pictures of my cancer and thought about my white cells killing the cancer. I also drew pictures of family members in crayon and colored them according to my feelings and how they affected my emotional state. I tried to analyze what in my life had led me to let my immune system drop down to the point where I got cancer. I realized stress has probably played a large role, and I've done what I can physically and emotionally to reduce my stress levels.

After the chemotherapy was done, I had six weeks of radiation therapy. They made a mold for me to lie in that fit my body. In each session the radiation machine was aimed at my body for about five minutes. I experienced no skin problems or burning. Maybe the vitamin E lotion they suggested I use protected my skin. I did have fatigue during the radiation, but I was lucky to have very few side effects. Following the radiation, I was put on a daily tamoxifen pill, which I am to take for the next five years. [Note: Years later, after the tamoxifen, I took Femara for seven years.]

I was listening recently to a meditation tape, which is part of my self-styled therapy, and it said that I would see someone walking to me down a path who had a message for me. I saw Jesus coming in my mind's eye. I was so thrilled I almost cried. He came to me, sat down on the bench next to me, put his arm around my shoulder, and earnestly said to me, "There is a purpose in all of this" (my illness). This message sank deep into my soul.

I've lived through cancer treatment and have done very well. Cancer has been a blessing to me and my family in some ways. I think we are kinder to each other, and our love and service for each other have increased.

> *"Let us cheerfully do all that lieth in our power and*
> *then stand still to see the salvation of God."*
> *—D & C 123:17*

32

National Institutes of Health

JANUARY 2000

Last week I got a very unusual phone call. The caller said, "Hello, Mrs. Curzon. My name is Dr. Jain. I am a doctor at the National Institutes of Health in Bethesda, Maryland. Dr. Hans Ochs at the University of Washington Medical Center has been telling me about your family. We are doing a clinical trial here at the NIH on your sons' immunodeficiency disease, and we would like your family to come here for six months, all expenses paid, to participate in this clinical trial."

"What?" I said. "I don't understand. How can you do that?"

He said, "This is not unusual for us. We bring families here all the time from all over the country for clinical trials. Will you think about this and get back with me?"

Of course I said yes.

Mike and I have discussed this phone call at length with the family. My mother thinks it would be a very good idea to go for this amazing opportunity. Maybe there can be some real headway made on better treatments for my sons' disease. So after discussing it as a family and then talking again with Dr. Jain, we will be flying to the NIH.

FEBRUARY 2000

Our whole family flew to Washington, DC. There is snow on the ground here, not like in California. Our entire "California family"— Mike and I plus Seth, Robert, Matthew, and Richard—is being put up in the Children's Inn, a wonderful big lodge near the NIH. It has beautiful bedrooms with high ceilings and luxurious draperies. There is a huge kitchen, which we share with other families, and game rooms, computer rooms, and lounging areas. What a great place to stay, and it is all for free. Taxis picked us up from the airport. A shuttle bus takes us up to the NIH hospital to see the research doctors. The whole area here is wooded with lots of natural trees. It is a whole new wonderful world. During some time off we have been able to visit the Smithsonian museums as a family, along with the Capitol Building, the Lincoln Memorial, and so on. We traveled on the subway to see these historic sites. Even though it is cold, it is great to be here in our nation's capital.

After riding on the shuttle to the NIH hospital, we arrived at the National Institute of Allergy and Infectious Disease (NIAID) department. We met in a conference room around a big wooden table with Dr. Jain, Dr. Strober, and Shuing Liu, a Chinese nurse. Dr. Jain is a very tall doctor of Indian ethnicity, although born and raised in America.

First, we talked with the doctors at length about Seth's, Robert's, and Richard's health and medical histories. We reviewed Seth's optic nerve atrophy, brain atrophy, balance problems, and history of frequent pneumonias and infections. We told them of Robert's former history of severe, long-lasting intestinal problems. But he has done well now for several years. Richard's history is just a series of minor illnesses, quite similar to any normal child. And of course, we told them of Jonathan's and Michael's illnesses and deaths from hyper-IgM syndrome.

The doctors then explained in detail what is involved in the clinical trial, which is CD40 ligand replacement therapy. Participants in the clinical trial will have chest x-rays, abdominal CT scans, and bone marrow biopsies to assess their present health. They will receive daily injections of CD40 ligand, the actual substance that their bodies are lacking in hyper-IgM syndrome. After a few days or weeks of these injections, follow-up studies will be done to see if their immunity or health has been impacted for good or bad. Our kids are to be the first human subjects, other than some cancer patients, to receive CD40 ligand. However, in the laboratory, mice injected with CD40 ligand did show increased ability to produce gamma globulin. CD40 ligand tells the B cells to produce IgG, which contains antibodies against diseases. In a normal person IgM turns into IgG, but it does not in my sons. Thus, they at times have too much, or hyper, IgM. That is my layman's explanation, which may not coincide perfectly with medical terms.

After some consultation, we were told that Seth is too ill to participate in the clinical trials, but doctors are willing to take him here as a patient and to do what they can to diagnose and treat his symptoms. That was upsetting to us, because Seth needs help more than any of the other boys.

We told the doctors that we didn't feel we could come to stay for six months, so it was arranged that we could fly to the NIH for a week and then back to California for a week on alternating weeks for a few months. Robert will not be able to participate actively until he is out of his semester of college in June. Mike, Seth, and Matthew will be staying home since Matthew does not have the disease. Only Richard and I will be making the biweekly trips. Richard can get out of school (sixth grade) and take homework with him to work on. There is also a schoolteacher at the NIH who can help him if needed, and his California school will require him to write a report about his experiences in Washington, DC, and at the NIH.

So we are starting an exciting adventure that would not have been possible without the boys having this disease. I guess there is some compensation for the suffering we have endured over the years. Richard's sixth-grade class is preparing to go to Costa Rica in a few months. I did not feel it would be a safe place for Richard to go with his immune deficiency. So Washington, DC, will be a nice substitute for that.

MARCH 2000

I am here at the NIH with just Seth so the doctors can check him out even though he will not be participating in the clinical trial. He got a fever while he was here and was put into the hospital. The CT scan showed pneumonia. He was put on azithromycin for a few days, but the fever came back. I ended up having an argument with the doctor about whether or not he should be given azithromycin for a few more days. I told the doctor that if they didn't treat him without doing a whole bunch more tests, I would leave and take him home. The doctor finally relented and gave him more medicine. Seth is not someone you can fool around with, or he will become septic, which is life-threatening. I have seen this too many times with him. He got better with the continued antibiotic.

Before he got the fever, I couldn't help but notice how difficult it is for Seth to maneuver here at the cafeteria. He really cannot get the food for himself due to his increasingly poor vision. I have to sit him at a table and get his food for him now. He recently lost his ability to drive and even to do his job at the Devil's Punchbowl because of poor eyesight. This is so very sad for him and for all of us.

The doctors are trying a new experimental drug on Seth called pleconaril. It is to fight the supposed enterovirus that is attacking Seth's central nervous system. It is thick and oily liquid medicine that so far has seemed to make him slightly worse, a little nauseated, and more confused. So I don't know if it will be effective. Apparently, it is the only treatment that is available to offer him right now. They refuse to do a brain biopsy to see if they can detect what is really going on. I had a phone conversation with Dr. Ochs from Washington, and he suggested that a brain biopsy should be performed. But none of Seth's doctors here will take the risk of doing the procedure. Maybe they are right that it would not be wise or productive.

APRIL 2000
Seth is feeling back to normal now after returning from NIH. I have lined up a date for Seth with a girl here in the church who has cerebral palsy. She walks with a cane. Mike and I double-dated with them a couple of times. Seth walks well, and she can hold on to his arm to steady herself. She can be his eyes, as she sees better than he does. So they are a good pair in that way. It was fun for all of us. Over the past year I have also helped Seth get on an LDS online dating site so he can communicate with some girls there. I type what he tells me to say for him. He has even gone out on a few dates with our help! He also had one Hispanic girl he met at a church conference that was very interested in going out with him. I don't know what her motives are, but it's nice for him to get some attention. He does like girls.

Mike, the kids, and I went to visit Rebekah in New Mexico. She has a boyfriend and a job there, and we wanted to see where she lives. We went to the zoo and had a good visit. It was good to see her.

APRIL 30, 2000

Richard and I are now here at the NIH. I have been agonizing over Seth's further loss of sight in his "good" (left) eye, his not being able to have a driver's license, and his depression and lack of frequent socialization. He has gone downhill the last few months. I've prayed and prayed for an answer, understanding, and comfort. Finally an answer came to me last night at the Children's Inn at the NIH. I had some quiet time to myself, lying on the bed, and the answers and peace seemed to flow into my mind as from a gentle voice speaking to me and opening my understanding. I've been thinking about Richard, at age thirteen, and comparing this trip with my last experience here with Seth. I realize how much more confident I am in Richard's ability to function independently than I am with Seth's. It makes me realize more clearly than before that Seth's overall independent living abilities are very low. He is functioning in some areas of his life at a very young age level, especially in being able to safely and easily find his way and make decisions in new situations. For example, he can't negotiate preparing meals or cooking for himself anymore. He is like a young child in these ways, especially because of his eyesight.

If Seth and I could just accept the fact that he is now severely handicapped and if we would stop trying desperately to make him act in a normal way for his age, we could both have a lot more peace in our lives. I need to realize that it's okay right now if he's somewhat low functioning and doesn't do more things or if he spends long hours watching (listening) to TV. I should shower him with love and affection and not badger him about doing things that are really beyond his ability. And he shouldn't torture himself about these things either. Seth is a very special spirit sent to earth in a less-than-perfect body and mind at this time of his life. He has been sent here more to test and bless others than to be tested himself. If I can accept things as they are, I will have more peace. That is my answer.

MAY 7, 2000

Richard and I are at the NIH. Now that all the preliminary tests and CT scans have been performed, he will start the study tomorrow, getting CD40 ligand injections. We have been to the National Zoo, a carnivorous plant nursery we drove to in Virginia, and Mount Vernon, which we went to on an NIH bus yesterday. We also saw the LDS Washington, DC, Temple, which is just a few blocks from the NIH. It is so beautiful.

We have attended church here in Bethesda, which has incredible, faithful, intelligent people, including the famous Marriott family. The young people here are not ashamed to speak intelligently and articulately in church. This is a wonderful place to be—so much beauty, so much culture, and so much history. I love it here.

MAY 8, 2000

Following a picture-taking session with my thirteen-year-old Richard poised on a hospital bed surrounded by Drs. Jain, Strober, and others, Richard received his first injection of CD40 ligand in his arm. It is a subcutaneous injection, and he was watched carefully for any signs of anaphylactic shock or violent reactions from his body. It has gone okay, but as time goes on, he is getting a large red swelling around the injection site. It is not too painful or itchy but is definitely a reaction. Richard is excited to participate in the study and hopeful that this will be a better treatment in the future than IVIG (gamma globulin). He thinks it is "cool" to stay in the hospital without being sick, as he's never been hospitalized before. The CD40 ligand dosage will be increased gradually as he gets more injections the next few weeks.

JULY 2000

We went to Salt Lake City for the birth of baby Leah, Jessica's new daughter and my second granddaughter! She is such a sweetie. Jessica did a great job of having her at home in a birthing pool with Rebekah there to help. The whole family was there Friday night, including Jeremy and Maya. I helped Jessica some of the time, as did her husband, Rob. Rich and I flew from Salt Lake City back to the NIH without going home first.

JULY 23, 2000

I have been going back and forth to Washington, DC (Bethesda), to the NIH with Richard and Robert. Rob started going the end of May when he got out of school. He was found to have resistant strep pneumonia on a CT scan and was given Levaquin, a strong antibiotic. He had to have a bronchoscopy to find the organism. I love being here at the

NIH because it's medical heaven. If the doctors want to do a test on a patient, they can just do it without having to get referrals and approval by the insurance company and without bills being sent to the patient. Everything goes so smoothly and easily. Of course, they are funded by the federal government, for good or for bad. We are lucky to be able to come here.

Robert was also able to participate in a clinical trial in the dentistry department to get his wisdom teeth taken out. That was also at no expense to us. Usually that would cost us $800 as a family. He did very well with minimal swelling using ice packs. Each time the boys come, they are also in a clinical trial that involves apheresis, where some blood is taken from them, the plasma is removed, and the red cells are returned to their bodies. They have also been given bone density tests, because patients with hyper-IgM syndrome tend to have some osteoporosis. Although the boys' bones are less dense than average, it does not seem to be any problem at this point. They have also had bone marrow biopsies under anesthesia to verify the status of the blood-producing cells found there.

Richard and Robert have both been getting higher doses of CD40 ligand, causing sore arms and big red spots. Robert developed a fever one night from it, and Richard had some nausea. They had to stay in the hospital and were too sick to go into Washington D.C. that week. It was boring. Usually we have some free time each week to visit some of the historical sites.

This summer we have been able to visit more of the Smithsonian museums, the National Cathedral, Arlington Cemetery, the Capitol Building, the Lincoln Memorial, the Jefferson Memorial, and the Vietnam Veterans Memorial. All these places are free for the public to visit. We usually go on the subway and then walk to where we want to go. It has been very fun, though hot and humid. Being in Washington, D.C. has swelled my patriotism for this great country, especially when we went with a family from the church to see Fourth of July fireworks at the Washington Monument. It was awesome to be with the huge crowds, to hear the beautiful music playing, and to see the fantastic fireworks display. I love this city!

It has been neat to meet many other patients who are staying at the Children's Inn, like Sharon, a Jewish mother whose two boys have liver abscesses from a different immune deficiency; Nim from India and his mom, Samantha, who has a website for immune-deficient patients; and Charlie, a nice guy around twenty who has bone cancer. We also met a family from the Philippines who have three small sons with hyper-IgM syndrome. They will be continuing to be guinea pigs in the same clinical trial as my boys when we leave this summer. We met a chaplain intern here, a young lady named Hyja Yui. I have been typing a page a day on the Children's Inn computer recalling Michael's cancer and death. I gave the chaplain a copy to read, and she said it was wonderful and made her cry. She encouraged me to write a book.

Only two more weeks at the NIH this summer. It has been a wonderful adventure that we will never forget. Dr. Jain wants the boys to continue to come to see him every year or so, paid for by the NIH, and we'll always be able to call him when medical questions come up. So that is a great comfort. Yes, the National Institutes of Health is a medical heaven to us.

If I can accept unchangeable conditions as they are with Seth right now, I will have more peace of mind.

33

Living with Blindness

JUNE 13, 2000 (SETH'S JOURNAL)

I've been going to a lot of activities with the young adults in my area, such as dances, birthday parties, and young adult youth conference. [Maybe the pleconaril medicine from the NIH had some good effect on him?] I have also been having some depression because of my difficulties with losing my eyesight due to an enterovirus in my nervous system. One night after my brother Matt brought me home from Institute, I was sitting at the kitchen table and thinking about how I have lost my driving privileges and my ability to read as well as I used to. Thinking on these things, I felt my life was being taken away from me. I just wept for a while over my trials. I became very humbled, pleading with the Lord to help me. I prayed many times a day to receive support from my Heavenly Father. He comforted me, and I received great joy and happiness. Things are getting better, and I can read fairly well now and am getting involved with people my age, which is making me happy.

AUGUST 2000

Although Seth has had some good times with others his age, he still is bored and lonely a lot of the time. He has been seeing a psychiatrist for depression and has been put on medication for it. It is so sad for him to not function as a normal twenty-five-year-old young man. He was recently referred to a special low-vision ophthalmologist in Los Angeles. He got a pair of very thick glasses to wear and some yellow goggles to wear over his glasses that can help things appear lighter and easier to see. Not very fashionable, however.

OCTOBER 2000

A neat thing has happened. A large stray dog that is very friendly to our family and very obedient showed up in our yard. He has no collar, and Seth just loves him. Seth named him Reggie and takes him for walks in the back acre and down the dirt roads behind our home. Reggie is a good companion for Seth during this lonely time. I feel this dog is a gift from God for Seth right now. Unfortunately, Reggie is a pit bull and has some scars on his face, I assume from fighting. I hope this will not be a problem. So far, he is a great family dog who willingly stays outside on the porch and does not try to come in.

MARCH 2001

Seth was in the hospital at the end of this month for pneumonia. He was very sick and had a bronchoscopy. We are still fighting his cough.

APRIL 2001

I have learned about a wonderful institution near Hollywood called the Braille Institute. It is a school where blind people can take classes in various subjects. I have decided this would be a great opportunity for Seth. He could learn to prepare food and cook for himself using a Crock Pot and so on. Seth was able to attend a blindness conference with me in February. We stayed at the hotel where the conference was held. There were blind people there from all over California. Seth was able to meet and talk to some blind people his age. Most of them have been blind since birth and have had training throughout their lives on how to live productive lives with blindness. They confidently walk with their white canes with the red stripe signifying they are blind. We walked to a waffle restaurant at night with a group of young adults. They could confidently and safely walk down the sidewalks and cross the street. Seth tried to follow them, holding on to my arm. Maybe he can learn to live as confidently and independently as they do!

MAY 2001

Seth is going to the Braille Institute on Tuesdays and Thursdays. I drive him down to Hollywood and wait in the hallway while he goes to classes. There are dancing, bowling, cooking, and mobility classes and many others available. He takes a handwriting class where they are teaching him to write with a thin marker instead of a pencil and to use plastic guides on the paper so he can "feel" where the lines are. There are special calculators he can use that say the numbers you punch in and so on. These little tricks can help Seth maneuver in life and become more self-sufficient. All students are required to use their blind canes to find the classrooms on their own as they maneuver down the halls. This is good practice for Seth. Right now I am close by him, but he is getting better going from one hall to another and finding his classrooms independently. He also needs to learn how to push the correct buttons on the elevator. The people in the office seem somewhat surprised that Seth is not more able to do these things on his own. Is it because his cognitive ability is declining?

Having the blind cane comes in very handy at times, although Seth does not use it much outside the school. We have been going to the UCLA Medical Center to see a neurologist. It is so helpful when he has the blind cane in the busy halls, for people know to stay out of his way and to help him when he needs it. I am always there, however, for him to hold on to my arm. The neurologist gave Seth a memory test. He did quite well. His balance is off some. They are not sure what is causing his balance and tremor problems.

Seth is seeing two other doctors at UCLA—a liver specialist and a dermatologist. (It was like pulling teeth to get these referrals for specialists.) Seth's liver function tests are quite abnormal, and he will have an abdominal ultrasound this week to look at his liver. The dermatologist says he can use a laser to remove the spots (small hemangiomas) that have appeared on Seth's face since he began the Neupogen shots.

Seth's cough has just about stopped now after taking clindamycin for twelve days—150 milligrams four times a day. The pulmonologist, Dr. Ho, also gave him an inhaler to use. Seth is also getting more Neupogen, .5 cc daily. The immunologists, Dr. Lee at UCLA and Dr. Jain at the NIH, both say no to a possible bone marrow transplant for Seth. Though the transplant could potentially cure his immunedeficiency, he already has too many complications, and it could end up being a fatal course of treatment. Seth may start a full-time blind school pretty soon. Life is okay, as I have overcome many worries by faith, prayer, and fasting.

JUNE 3, 2001

Fast Sunday—my prayers are being answered. A marvelous, marvelous day. I talked to Jackie and Barbara, my sisters, on the phone, and they told me about Russ (my brother-in-law) and his appendectomy. During surgery, Russ said that my dad was holding his hand from the spirit world. Dad told Russ that he'd gotten back his "navy-blue hair," meaning he was young again. This is a well-known joke in our family. Dad had told us as little kids that his hair was not black but navy blue. He was carrying two briefcases when he saw Russ, another well-known trait of my father. My father proceeded to tell Russ many important things for our family, his children. He said he visits my mother every day and holds her hand. His greatest concern is still his family, and he said that it is very important that all the unions (marriages) in the family must not break. We all need to treat each other better. He also said that our spiritual callings are more important than our earthly vocations, which are secondary. He said, "There will not be many more generations until the Savior comes. The gospel is definitely true. There is no doubt about that. If we have obstacles regarding the gospel, we need to increase our faith."

Hearing about this experience has made me so happy! I feel as if I have heard from my dad again after all these years, and he addressed many issues, questions, and problems that have been swirling around in our families. I think it also helped to solidify Robert's decision to serve a mission. We don't know for sure if he can go with his immune deficiency and necessity of having monthly infusions, but at least he wants to put in his application papers as soon as possible.

SEPTEMBER 5, 2001

Seth's vision is getting very bad. I'm not sure he can see at all now! One night the family was at the Los Angeles Temple visitors' center with Seth. The huge lighted white temple was above us shining in the night sky. I pointed it out to him, and it seemed that he could not see it. He can no longer see to write in his journal or to read. We have had some more bad news. Seth's neurologist from UCLA said Seth may have a genetic condition that is causing his brain atrophy— Huntington's disease. He does have the symptoms of neurological decline of Huntington's. Could it be possible that he has it and that others of my children could also develop it? It is very frightening to think about. Seth is getting a blood test to check for the disease.

OCTOBER 2001

Thank goodness the blood test for Huntington's disease has come back negative! At least I don't have to worry about Seth's neurological problems developing in my other children. Still, he does have similar symptoms of Huntington's disease, especially some tremors in his left hand. I have found a Huntington's disease website where many other people complain about the same symptoms Seth has. I can relate to their fear for their loved ones and the desire of some to not prolong their loved ones' lives unnecessarily by using feeding tubes.

NOVEMBER 2001

I learned of a wonderful school where young blind people can live on campus and receive training. It is in Los Angeles and is called the Foundation for the Junior Blind. Their brochure said they could work with any disabilities and could train blind people to use computers and to become independent citizens. I was very excited about this opportunity for Seth. We got a cell phone for Seth to take with him so he could call us any time on autodial. He was nervous, but we trusted that the school would take good care of him.

Two days after Seth arrived at the blind school, he fell down some stairs and broke his hand. We brought him home, and he has not returned. The staff there told us that he doesn't seem to have the ability to maneuver his body safely enough. They said he is too disabled in other ways besides blindness. I did notice when we were there that his fingers were moving uncontrollably around the elevator buttons, so he was not able to push the correct button. Another step down in his disability.

At home, we are trying to help Seth have meaningful experiences even though he cannot see well. A family in our ward gave us a big-screen TV for Seth to watch in hopes he could see some of the picture. If not, he can listen to the programs. The church provides church magazines on tape, which we can play on the special tape recorder the Braille Institute gave us for free. We can also check out books on tape from the library for him to listen to. He has quite a few music CDs and a nice new CD player that holds three CDs. Sometimes his brothers will read him some pages from his falconry books. In spite of these things, it is still hard to feel that his life is anywhere near what he would like it to be. It is very sad for him and for us that he has lost his eyesight.

> ***We tried to give Seth as normal a life as possible, in spite of his disabilities.***

34

Mike and Israel

AUGUST 2000

Mike and I were lying on our backs on the bed one evening reading and talking. I love those times when we can talk and share our feelings. Mike casually told me that, while combing his hair in front of the mirror, he had noticed a big lump the size of a lemon under his left arm. He'd been very alarmed and had gone to see the doctor. The doctor had said that it could be a type of cancer called lymphoma.

I was so shocked and scared when Mike told me this! Just when I was getting over my cancer, Mike could now have cancer also! How could this be happening? Over the next three weeks, many tests were performed—a CT scan, a very painful bone marrow biopsy to see if the cancer had spread there, and a biopsy of enlarged lymph nodes in his neck and under his arm. Sadly, the cancer diagnosis was confirmed. Mike has non-Hodgkin's diffuse large B-cell lymphoma. It's intermediate grade, meaning that it is fairly aggressive, or fast growing. They also found some matted lymph nodes on his chest but nowhere else in his body. So his cancer is at stage 2, and he will be starting chemotherapy.

Before this time, my mother had offered to pay for all her children and Mike to take a trip to Israel, the Holy Land, at the beginning of September. We were thrilled to have the opportunity to go on this wonderful journey, and we still plan to go, knowing that Mike has cancer and will face treatments as soon as we return.

SEPTEMBER 2000

Our trip to Israel was an amazing experience. We flew to New York City, where we met my family. We flew out on a midnight flight and arrived in Israel the next afternoon. As the sun set, our bus drove into Jerusalem. The choir we were traveling with began to sing. It was a very emotional and inspiring moment to come to this holy city where Jesus taught. Over the two-week trip, we traveled to many sites. The most memorable and spiritually inspiring were the garden of Gethsemane; the Garden Tomb, where Christ's body was laid and from which he was resurrected; and the hill of Golgotha, where the cross stood. On the shore of the Sea of Galilee, Russ and Dave, my brothers-in-law, gave Mike and me priesthood blessings of strength and love to help us in the gargantuan task of fighting Mike's cancer in the next few months.

After we returned from Israel, Mike immediately began to get the chemotherapy infusions for his cancer after having a portacath surgically inserted into his chest. The first chemotherapy regimen he received was CHOP (a combination of four drugs—cyclophosphamide; doxorubicin; vincristine, or Oncovin; and prednisone), which was infused every twenty-one to twenty-eight days for six months. We were told that this treatment had a 70 percent chance of producing a long-term disease-free survival. These drugs caused Mike to lose his hair and to develop numbness and pain in his hands and feet, as well as lowering his blood count of red cells, white cells, and platelets. He was also very tired. Nevertheless, he continued to go to work most of the time and continued to serve in the bishopric at church.

MAY 20, 2001

Mike has finished his chemotherapy and has been declared in complete remission from his cancer! How wonderful! The swollen lymphnodes have disappeared.

JULY 12, 2001

It has been three months since Mike stopped his chemotherapy. All of a sudden now Mike has discovered the lump on his chest is returning, so we went to see Dr. Black, his oncologist at the UCLA Cancer Center in Santa Clarita. Dr. Black ordered a chest CT and a gallium scan. He also sent Mike to see a radiation doctor, Dr. Schweitzer, for possible radiation.

I have been reading that intermediate-grade lymphoma that relapses is especially bad if it recurs within the first year after diagnosis and if there is weight loss (Mike is losing weight), fevers (Mike had a fever the past two nights), or weakness (Mike complains of being extremely tired). Tomorrow we see the doctor for test results.

My sister Barbara and her family came last week. Her sons and my sons went to Magic Mountain. My brother, Richard, and his wife, Lee Ann, came here for food and hours of good talk on the Fourth of July. We had small fireworks out on the street. It was very enjoyable.

Since Mike may be getting radiation, we decided to go to Utah last Thursday through Monday to visit our family there. We had visits and dinners with all my extended family.

Now that we are home again, I am feeling very overwhelmed with Mike's illness, another needle biopsy for myself, and lots of doctor appointments for Seth, with the hepatologist (liver doctor), dermatologist, and neurologist at UCLA. Rob is putting in his mission papers after having his nose broken and repaired in surgery. Rob and Matt are taking summer school at Antelope Valley College. I am trying to work on some classes by mail to finish my bachelor's degree from BYU in case Mike has to retire and I have to become the breadwinner. I pray the Lord will help me. He has given me a lot of strength recently. Things will work out okay, although I feel the challenges are huge.

FRIDAY, JULY 13, 2001

This was a very bad day, as we learned that Mike's cancer has spread to his liver. Dr. Schweitzer, the radiation doctor, was the first to tell us. He said he was sorry he had to tell us such bad news. The gallium scan showed many axillary lymph glands enlarged under Mike's left arm, and the chest CT showed several nodules in both lobes of his liver that were new and assumed to be cancer metastases. Dr. Schweitzer said that Mike could not do radiation, because it would have to be pointed toward his lung, as a lot of the cancer was on the left front of his chest. This would cause unacceptable lung damage. He said that Mike would need chemotherapy again.

SUNDAY, JULY 15, 2001

Bishop Wyatt came to our home to give Mike a blessing, but he seemed very nervous and concerned. I told him I had a feeling my dad would be there in spirit to help him. I feel this gave him courage to give the blessing. In the blessing he said Mike would be given time to do what he needed to do for his family, and strength to go through the chemotherapy.

After the bad news from the doctor, we had an emergency family reunion. We flew in Jessica and Rebekah to be with us, and Jeremy and Maya drove up, so the whole family was together. We had a wonderful warm day at the beach. Even Mike went in the ocean. The next day we stayed home while Mike went to get another bone marrow biopsy (very painful!) and had a CT scan. That evening, Jeremy showed us slides from his and Maya's visits to India and Canyonlands. Mike and I expressed our love for the kids. Jessica, Rebekah, and I sang "If We Hold on Together" by Diana Ross. It was very touching—a perfect reunion. The next day we flew to Idaho to visit Mike's brothers, sister, and their kids. It was good for all the Curzons to get together.

JULY 28, 2001
Mike started his new "salvage" chemotherapy on July 23, 24, 25, 26, and 27. He didn't do too badly—better than we expected.

AUGUST 12, 2001
About ten days ago, we saw Dr. Black again. It seems he always has bad news. He said the bone marrow biopsy showed cancer in Mike's bone marrow. Also, the latest CT scan showed a decrease in size of many of the spots in the liver but also several spots of cancer that had increased in size. The doctor said that maybe the chemotherapy hasn't had a chance to fully work. The plan is for Mike to have a stem cell transplant at UCLA as a last-ditch effort to fight the cancer if he responds to three or four cycles of ESHAP (chemotherapy), which he is now on. The doctor said the chance of a cure "is a long shot" but still possible. After we left the doctor, we talked about the gloomy news, which was such a big shock to us.

SEPTEMBER 2, 2001
We are still trudging along fighting Mike's cancer. He has had two cycles of chemotherapy. The doctor had to postpone his last cycle for one week due to low platelet and red cell counts. He has had two shots of Procrit to raise his red cell count. Of course, he has also had Neupogen shots to raise the white cell count. Yesterday the doctor called to say Mike's platelets were only 14,000—so low, "so be

careful." Normal is over 100,000. Mike doesn't feel too well and is very tired. He is in bed a lot. It is hard for me as well as for him. I feel alone and that I am responsible for more things that he used to take care of—like the cars and the acreage. The ward brought meals last week.

I'm listening to BYUtv, and the song "Abide with Me" is making me cry. "Oh, thou, who changest not, abide with me!" (Lyte 1998, 166). I know God loves us, but I do not understand why all this is happening to us.

SEPTEMBER 5, 2001

Richard, my youngest son, has started high school and seminary. He has a good attitude, and I'm very proud of him. He continues to enjoy growing carnivorous plants and has also built a greenhouse in the back acre in which he grows delicious tomatoes. Matt and Rob are very busy at the community college with work and classes. Robert is excelling in math, and Matthew has decided he will seek to become a doctor since he has found it to be so easy to memorize all the material for his anatomy class. They both were able to graduate early from high school with the home study program they participated in and have both been doing some tutoring of other students at the college. I am proud of their accomplishments, and happy that the community colleges here in California are so inexpensive!

Jessica, my daughter in Salt Lake City, has been having symptoms typical of multiple sclerosis with numbness in her body and vision problems in one eye. [Note: The test for multiple sclerosis ended up coming back negative. We decided Jessica had become malnourished from her pregnancies and nursing babies for so many months. With lots of vitamin D and other nutrients, she became better. She is typically a very healthy person.] It is so hard not to worry with so many illnesses in the family. Prayer gives me some strength.

SEPTEMBER 11, 2001

A terrible, frightful day as planes crashed into the World Trade Center and the Pentagon! Thousands of people were killed. I happened to turn on the TV this morning, and that is what I saw. We watched the news coverage all day and mourned with the nation for this terrible assault on our country! Is World War III coming?

SEPTEMBER 19, 2001

Mike has been going to work again since the beginning of September. I didn't think he would make it, but he has "resurrected" from his bed, and I have felt like I have my husband back lately. For the second week in a row, Mike's doctor has postponed his chemotherapy due to low platelet counts. We are glad he had no chemotherapy, but now the lymph nodes on his chest are growing again, and he's feeling more tired. He said, "What is wrong with me? I should be feeling better from not having chemo, but I am feeling worse." Of course, our concern is that the cancer is growing again and that we are losing the battle at this point.

A couple of weeks ago, I took Mike to UCLA to see a Jewish doctor about a possible stem cell transplant, which is the strongest treatment Mike can get. We waited two or more hours and finally saw the doctor at six in the evening. He said that the tumors need to reduce at least 50 percent on the chemotherapy in order to know that the stem cell transplant, with its high-dose chemotherapy, has a reasonable chance of working. A CT scan has shown that Mike's tumors have shrunk about 30 percent. Dr. Black has spoken positively about the chances of the stem cell transplant being successful since the tumors are responsive to chemo. Now I fear they are growing again. I feel Mike must get the stem cell transplant soon or else ....

SEPTEMBER 22, 2001

We are in Albuquerque, New Mexico, for my daughter Rebekah's wedding to Brian. I told her they shouldn't wait to get married if she wanted her dad to be there, for we don't know how long he will live. Our family drove down in two cars. I was expecting Mike to lie down in the back seat, but he felt better driving a lot of the time. Rebekah had a beautiful wedding at Brian's mother's modern new home. Mike, with his bald head, walked her down the aisle. She looked beautiful in her wedding gown. All our children were there. My granddaughter Ally was the flower girl. It was a very nice affair.

On the way driving down, Mike told me that he definitely does not want to suffer too long. If he is going to die, he would rather go sooner than later if he has to suffer a lot.

257

SEPTEMBER 27, 2001

We went to see Dr. Black, Mike's oncologist, today. Last night Mike was having pain in the tumors on his chest and underarm as well as in his liver. It seems the swelling is bigger than it has ever been. Dr. Black decided to give him Rituxan, an intravenous infusion of monoclonal antibodies that attacks only the cancer cells. Mike was in the office about six hours. He had fever and chills with severe shaking. Apparently, that is what Rituxan does during the first infusion.

SEPTEMBER 28, 2001

It has been over twenty-four hours since the Rituxan infusion. Mike has had extreme fatigue, some nausea and diarrhea, and more stomach pains. It is very scary for us. The doctor said that Mike may not be eligible for the transplant because the tumors have grown. So he will be starting Mike on new chemotherapy tomorrow called MACOP-B, a regimen of several different drugs, in preparation for a stem cell transplant, which we hope he can have.

OCTOBER 2001

I realize that what happens to Mike—how long he has, whether he lives or dies or is healed—is not up to me. My job is to love him, do my best to care for him well, and try not to worry. "Thine adversity and thine affliction shall be but a small moment, and then if thou endure it well, God shall exalt thee on high" (D & C 121:7–8).

DECEMBER 15, 2001

Mike had Cytoxan chemotherapy to shrink his tumors. Then he had a week of high doses of Neupogen injections to produce many white cells, which were then harvested and frozen for the stem cells to be used in the autologous stem cell transplant. That means he will be using his own stem cells after receiving high-dose chemotherapy to rejuvenate his bone marrow. Neupogen shots can cause a lot of back pain as the bone marrow revs up its production of white cells.

Since it is expected that Mike will have the transplant before Christmas, we had an early Christmas here with all our kids, some coming from out of town, and our granddaughters, Ally and new baby Leah. We had a family meeting, like we always do, and Mike bore his testimony. I spoke of the great influence Christ has had on the world. Each person took a turn to talk about his or her life and to share love.

Seth haltingly talked about his former days of catching hawks. His speech is not as good as it used to be. We then exchanged gifts and love, knowing this may be our last Christmas together as a whole family.

I cannot cure my husband. My job is to love and care for him and try not to worry too much.

35

Stem Cell Transplant

JANUARY 12, 2002

A lot has happened. Right now we are in the UCLA Medical Center in Los Angeles for Mike's stem cell transplant. It had to be postponed until after Christmas. Mike's stem cells were harvested about a month ago by taking blood from his arm after many large Neupogen shots. Finally they got enough stem cells. The past four days he has been having whole-body radiation, twice a day for about a half hour each time. He also had high doses of Cytoxan chemotherapy to kill the cancer along with Rituxan, the monoclonal antibody, at my request.

Last Sunday afternoon at home, Mike started having severe pain in his liver that required him to take a lot of morphine pills that night. The next morning he vomited violently and also on the way to the hospital at UCLA. He had been feeling quite bad for several days and was not eating well. He had lost weight, and his muscles were wasting. He was running fevers and sweating severely in spite of being on Cipro and amoxicillin. He seemed truly on the verge of death from his cancer. It was very scary to me. The time for this strong cancer treatment is long overdue.

Since he has been in the hospital, he has received vancomycin, because he was still running a fever. So he is pretty miserable. The liver pain is gone now, however. That is very good.

Mike has been quite emotional lately. It is easy for him to cry now with the great physical and mental stress he is under. This evening he was talking and crying a lot about his children, the death of his father, the suffering his mother went through in her widowhood, and the suffering Michael endured. It is so difficult to see him in such heart-wrenching anguish.

260

JANUARY 18, 2002

It is Robert's birthday, but I am at the Braille Institute near Hollywood waiting for Seth while he takes his braille and typing class here. We'll skip his bowling class today and go over to the UCLA Medical Center to visit Mike. Last Saturday they gave Mike a chemotherapy called etoposide. He had a high fever that night. They did blood cultures and put him on imipenem. He has had fewer fevers since then, so I think the antibiotic must be treating some kind of infection. They also did an abdominal and pelvic CT at three in the morning the first day he came. The report said he had multiple liver lesions, the largest of which is nine centimeters by ten centimeters. So we are fighting a big battle. The doctor says we are up against a wall and have no choice but to go ahead with the stem cell transplant even though Mike's chances of cure are not as good as most patients. The doctor said Mike now has about a 15 percent chance of a cure and could go into remission for about a year if the cancer is not cured.

It has been torturous seeing Mike suffer. I don't think he expected things to go so badly when he agreed to this treatment. Monday he got Cytoxan, which made him vomit, and he is eating only about three hundred calories a day lately. He gained twenty-five pounds of water weight the first few days he was here due to the intravenous fluids and a low albumin level, which can cause swelling in the body. Now his mouth and throat are terribly sore and swollen. He has diarrhea all the time. He is pretty miserable. I hope he can make it through this and come home, recover, and have a few good months. It is so hard—I can't tell you! But I am stoic and fairly strong most of the time.

The Spirit tells me that this is a test for both of us about how much we can love during this difficult time. We seem to banter back and forth, like when I try to get him to eat and he resists. On Wednesday he got his stem cells back through an intravenous infusion. So we'll see how they work for him in the next few days and weeks.

JANUARY 20, 2002

I went home for a day after taking Seth to the Braille Institute for the Blind. (I have been sleeping on a mattress on the floor in Mike's hospital room. He needs me there as much as possible.) It is a great blessing that Rob and Matt are home with Seth during the days so I can spend more time at the hospital. It was Robert's birthday two days ago. He is twenty years old! He and Matt went to a show.

Today (Sunday) Mike is feeling a little better since he is on intravenous Dilaudid, a powerful narcotic pain reliever. He has drunk a little water today and a little Dr. Pepper, which has become his new favorite. He is talking all the time and acting kind of drunk. Right now he is cleaning out the little refrigerator in his room. Amazing! I am fasting today for Mike and for me. We went for a walk down the hall, Mike saying hi and introducing himself to the other patients walking by. We watched some of the Legacy video about the Mormon pioneer trek to the Salt Lake Valley in 1847.

Tonight the doctors gave Mike some amphotericin B, a very strong antifungal infusion. It made him have terrible chills, and they gave him some Demerol to stop the shaking. He has some fungus growing in his mouth, but I think or hope the amphotericin is more of a prophylactic dose. He has eaten nothing for a few days. I am told that is normal on this floor. He is wrapped up like a mummy in warm blankets.

As I drove down to the hospital today from Littlerock, I listened to sermons on the radio. The preacher said that "God shall wipe away all tears" in the millennium when Christ shall come again.

JANUARY 23, 2002

Mike's mouth ulcerations continue to worsen. The dental team says this is a good sign—the beginning of healing. Really? They say he should start feeling better in a day or two. Two days ago, Mike drank two cartons of milk and a lot of water. But today he has had very little by mouth. The amphotericin he had has caused some kidney damage and acute renal failure of half of his kidney function. The doctors said he has to have a catheter in his bladder to help out his kidneys. His kidney function has improved today. I hope that continues. It scared me a lot, thinking that he might not make it. I have begged the Lord not to take Mike right now. I don't know how we would make it without his supporting our family. I am not prepared to make a living for us. Right now he has five months of sick leave from his job to see us through this time.

THURSDAY, JANUARY 24, 2002

Mike is a little better today, although his mouth is very painful. (I think the radiation and chemotherapy have caused this, as well as damage throughout his whole digestive system.) His white count is .13 (up). His red count is also up a little, and his kidney function is better. He drank half a can of pop and ate half a cup of tapioca pudding. His legs and feet are still very swollen. His electrolytes are off balance, but he was given potassium and magnesium. He has diarrhea again and is losing his hair. My poor sweetie. He is on the Dilaudid pump (like morphine but easier on his stomach). His fever is better than yesterday, but he is coughing some. I am still worried, but there is hope.

Mike is being very sweet to me. He gave me a hug and said he loved me. This hasn't happened for some time.

SATURDAY, JANUARY 26, 2002

The last two days have been a little better in some ways—Mike's fever is lower or gone, he's eating a tiny bit, and his white cells are beginning to rise. But he is worse in some ways with very painful diarrhea and very swollen feet and legs covered with blisters due to heart failure. They are giving him Lasix now to get rid of the fluid. He still has a catheter and is developing a productive cough. He is in and out of sleep and the effects of morphine.

He talks of death and of spirits appearing to him. He thinks one is his grandpa Martin. He says the Lord has been so good to us and we need to do better. He worries whether he will "qualify at being dead when he is dead." He speaks of family meetings (with spirits?). He looks like Gandhi, hunger strike and all. It is nighttime, and as I look out the fourth-story hospital window, I see the Los Angeles Temple a few blocks away, lit against the night sky. It is like a beacon of hope to me in this scary world—a reminder that our family can be together forever after this life. Mike and I have had our marriage sealed for eternity in the holy temple. That is such a comfort to me.

Mike is talking a lot about "graduation" today. His white count today is .47 (still extremely low but rising). It needs to get up to about 1.2 or 1.5. So it needs to triple. He is getting two units of packed red cells today as well as platelets.

I hope the boys are doing all right. I need to go home, but I always feel I need to stay here too.

SUNDAY, JANUARY 27, 2002

Good news—Mike's white count is above 1,000, a "very strong response," says the doctor. But Mike looks even weaker. He has a cough. The chest x-ray was okay yesterday. He has been having horrible episodes of very painful diarrhea. He is doing much worse than most other stem cell patients on this floor, (although one patient recently died!) They gave Mike platelets again today.

MONDAY, JANUARY 28, 2002

My sister-in-law, Lee Ann, lives in Orange County. She called to say that she, my mom, and Marshall (my stepfather) were going to my house to clean it up and to be with Seth for the day. I was very relieved. It was an answer to my prayers last night, as I felt so overwhelmed, like being buried under a crushing weight. I need more strength from the Lord.

They took seven liters of fluid off of Mike yesterday using Lasix, so he has lost twenty pounds of water weight. He now weighs 215 pounds. He weighed 240 pounds when we came in three weeks ago.

WEDNESDAY, JANUARY 30, 2002

We are still at the UCLA hospital because Mike got a fever last night and has a pretty bad cough. I drove home last night about eight o'clock. The traffic was good. Today Mike was given Levaquin, a strong antibiotic. He also had a chest CT scan and continues to spike fevers. Very discouraging. He still has diarrhea, though it's not so painful. His mouth pain is improving but still there. He drank Boost and pop today—350 calories. I worry about whether he will ever make it home again.

The doctor says Mike has had an episode of heart failure while he has been here. That is one reason why he has so much fluid in his legs. His heart is not pumping strongly enough. I feel like I am in a no-man's-land where bad things go on and on and never get better! I want to have faith, but I don't have much faith in him recovering soon. Is it just me, or is there no hope? I'm fighting to keep Mike here on earth. Does the Lord want to take him? We can't live without him right now.

THURSDAY, JANUARY 31, 2002

Mike had a 103-degree fever last night. Today doctor said it looks from the CT scan that he has aspiration pneumonia from aspirating something from his mouth. They are stopping Levaquin and giving him imipenem IV and oral Flagyl for the *Clostridium difficile* diarrhea, probably caused by the antibiotics. The doctor said he may go home around Monday.

Back to the here and now, Mike has a 104-degree temperature today! Terrible! He is so weak and debilitated. This is a terrible life, and he needs to go where he can be strong and useful.

SATURDAY, FEBRUARY 2, 2002

Will we ever go home from the hospital? Yesterday was very hard and scary. Mike's fever was 103.5. His oxygen saturation was low. I was told he needed to have a bronchoscopy in the morning to diagnose the pneumonia. They added more antibiotics—vancomycin, Bactrim, and fluconazole (for fungus), along with Flagyl (for *C. difficile* diarrhea) and imipenem IV. He is also on Zovirax for a possible viral herpes infection in his mouth or lungs. The radiation and chemotherapy have opened Mike up to multiple infections.

This morning's bronchoscopy was very scary for me. But all turned out okay, except that Mike was coughing so much afterward. He got a fever again in the evening. Bishop Wyatt came to visit and brought Matt and Seth with him. We had a nice visit. I ended up driving home. I got home about midnight, showered, washed clothes, said a few good words to the boys, had family prayer, and got to sleep about two in the morning.

SUNDAY, FEBRUARY 3, 2002

Up at eight o'clock. I called the hospital, and they said Mike did pretty well in the night. I attended the Fourth Ward fast and testimony meeting. The hymns, like "I Know That My Redeemer Lives," were meaningful to me in my state of anxiety (Medley 1998, 136). The Spirit was there, and the experience lifted my spirits. After church I drove back down to UCLA.

MONDAY, FEBRUARY 4, 2002

Mike has been in the UCLA Medical Center for four weeks now— twelve days longer than we thought he would be here for the transplant.

He is still very weak. At least it seems the antibiotics he is getting are working. He may have to go home on intravenous antibiotics—maybe in a few days.

TUESDAY, FEBRUARY 5, 2002

I have been telling one of the nurses about the church today. I had several pamphlets, and she wanted to take all of them home to read. She is a Christian from Armenia and has been attending several different churches trying to find the right one. She was very excited when I told her about the temple. She told me how much more conservative Armenia is. "Kids in America date so young," she said. I told her about how we don't date until at least sixteen in our church. She enthusiastically said she would like to know more about the church. It brings me some happiness in this trying time with Mike. Mike is a little better today.

FEBRUARY 6, 2002

I went home last night, went grocery shopping, and then slept. This morning I took Rich to school, did dishes, washed clothes, vacuumed, got prescriptions and more groceries with Seth, and returned to the hospital about four in the afternoon.

Tonight has been very scary. Mike was getting some platelets because he had a bloody nose. During the administration of the platelets he had severe lumbar back pain—"a twelve, with ten being the worst," he said. He was writhing on the bed and moaning in great distress for about half an hour. They gave him about five shots of morphine into his IV, which finally put him to sleep. The whole ordeal was very frightening to watch. They of course stopped the platelet transfusion.

I thought, *If this is the sort of thing we have to look forward to, then we better let God take him.* The ordeal totally drained me, and I said to the Lord, "I give up. Do what You want to do." (Later we found out that they had given Mike O-negative platelets, which should have been okay, but since his blood type is A positive, he should for sure receive that type in the future.)

SATURDAY, FEBRUARY 9, 2002

Well, we should never give up. Things have gone pretty well since I wrote last. Mike has had no more back pain, and his fever was

266

probably due to a reaction. He still has what I would call a low-grade fever. He doesn't feel great today. But he took a walk in the hall. The doctor says he might go home in two to three days. I hope so. How many times have I heard that?

Mike has been kind of down and depressed today. He doesn't want me to leave even for a short time. On TV we watched the opening ceremony of the Winter Olympics in Salt Lake City, my hometown! This is so exciting and spectacular. I walked outside tonight. It is beautiful and warm. I hope my boys at home are doing okay.

MONDAY, FEBRUARY 11, 2002

We are on a rollercoaster ride again. Mike got platelets again this morning (A positive), which went okay. Then they gave him some blood (type O), and he started getting chills and fever. He's not going home for a while. The blood bank says they will check to see if the blood was contaminated. Oh, when will this ever end so we can go home? Seth has been alone all day today. When I called today at one o'clock, he said he hadn't eaten since yesterday. Probably not true, but the elders' quorum from the church has volunteered to spend some lunch hours with Seth this week. His brothers are busy with school during the daytime.

FEBRUARY 12, 2002

Mike did end up coming home today. The doctors decided the 104-degree temperature was due to a blood transfusion reaction. We went home in the evening on Cipro, acyclovir, and Diflucan— medications that cover bacterial, viral, and fungal infections. He was still running a low-grade fever.

The stem cell transplant Mike has gone through to save him from cancer has been a horrendous experience for us. If we had known how horrible it would be, we may not have chosen to do it, but I am so glad Mike is still with us and that the sick leave he accumulated at his job for five years continues to provide our family with the income we need. This experience has obviously brought Mike to a state of deep humility and feeling of dependence upon God. I see him poring over his scriptures as he lies in bed. They give him comfort at this trying time.

MARCH 10, 2002

Mike has continued to run a low-grade fever for weeks. He has been getting platelets and blood one or two times per week at Lancaster Hospital for the past three weeks. The boys and I are getting back to almost normal life, although Mike has been in bed nearly all day every day. He has continued to lose weight (down to 195 pounds), in spite of the fact that he's taking in about 1,200 calories a day. This has been a great weight-loss program, as he has lost almost forty pounds in two months. A very bad way to lose weight, however. I would not recommend it to anyone!

I will not detail all that Mike has been through since getting out of UCLA, but in summary, he has been in the hospital again twice for fevers and pneumonia—once in Lancaster Hospital and once again at UCLA, where they put him on intravenous vancomycin, acyclovir, Diflucan, and oral Flagyl. That covers about every possible germ, including almost all bacteria, herpesviruses, fungal infections, and *Clostridium difficile* diarrhea. After all that, his fevers finally went away. A lot of difficult things to go through.

I need to remember the glorious experience I had going to the Los Angeles Mormon temple in March. Mike was still in the UCLA hospital but doing pretty well that day. I had not attended the temple for three months and felt a great need to be strengthened in these great trials. To walk on the beautiful grounds and to enter that glorious building filled my heart with peace.

Never give up! Even when the clouds are very dark,
the sunshine of hope can shine through!

36

Help!

MARCH 27, 2002

Mike has been in and out of the hospital. The doctor finally put him on Cipro, and in a couple of days his fever was gone. It was wonderful while it lasted, but now he is having occasional low fevers again—100 degrees. He is still getting platelets twice a week, blood every two weeks. His white count is not too bad but not too good either. Although the stem cell transplant may have been successful in killing the cancer (we don't know for sure yet), it is still taking time for Mike's bone marrow to become fully functional again. We are beginning to wonder if he will ever recover from this pancytopenia, or low blood cell counts. Mike still spends most of his time in bed. His muscles are wasting, and he still isn't eating enough calories most days.

If Mike was all I needed to concentrate on, that would be good. We have so many doctor, blood-draw, and transfusion appointments for him—and for Seth. Yesterday I squeezed in a bone scan for myself, as I am having a lot of pain in my hips, ribs, and so on. Not to mention Seth's ongoing physical, social, and emotional needs. I take him to the Braille Institute on Wednesdays now—an hour drive each way. Sometimes I take him to Institute religion classes in Lancaster, a half hour away.

I am also trying to get Robert's mission papers ready. He got most of the papers in at the last minute on Sunday, but he still needs to get some dental work done. Then I've got Richard to get to school each day and pick up. Not to mention cooking meals, cleaning, washing dishes and clothes, and flushing Mike's central line.

The church has brought in a lot of meals, which is really nice, but I've told them to stop for now, because I feel so stupid about it going on and on. But just as soon as I say I don't want more help, I need

269

help! I can't do it all alone, but I feel I need to learn to and need to be more organized so I can accomplish everything. It is so hard.

Back to real life. I have begun the application process to become a substitute teacher in case we get into a position where I need to work. I need to take the CBEST test. I am taking a logic class through BYU Independent Study that I need to finish. If I can get my bachelor's degree, that would be a great help to us. I am getting Mike signed up for Social Security disability and helping one son with some emotional problems. I feel like I am balancing a million things.

Yesterday Seth decided to walk up to Avenue T to the store. Brother Crawley from the church saw him and brought him home. This was surely an answer to prayer. I didn't know where Seth could be. I was worried about him walking with his poor eyesight. Wow—life is so challenging right now!

I have been trying to help Seth learn braille. How much can one person do? I need to be more organized. Maybe have my sons do more work for me or hire a teenage girl to help? And what about doing the taxes? And what about our income? Is it going to continue? Can Mike go back to work by May 20 so that we don't have to go on half pay? It doesn't seem very likely. Lord, I need Thy help so much! "O God, where art thou? ... All these things shall give thee experience and shall be for thy good" (D & C 121:1, 122:7).

APRIL 2002

General Conference is being broadcast on TV. Brother Edgley said that we would not choose today most of our heartache, but we did choose these trials in the pre-earth life before we were born. All that appears wrong will eventually be made right. "Who did sin ... that this man was born blind?" No one, "but that the works of God should be made manifest" (John 9:2–3). The atonement is for me in my suffering. (Edgley 2002). President Hinckley also gave a powerful talk about the Savior. He said:

> There stands the Redeemer of the world, the Son of God, certain and sure as the anchor of our immortal lives. He is the rock of our salvation, our strength, our comfort, the very focus of our faith. In sunshine and in shadow we look to Him, and He is there to assure and smile upon us ... He was a man of miracles. He reached out to

270

those in distress. He healed the sick and raised the dead (Hinckley 2002).

How I need these precious words of strength! Robert gave me a big hug and told me he loved me a few days ago when I was sad. Many people love me and have called to wish me happy birthday—Mom, Jessica and her kids, Rebekah, Paula, and Barbara. Mike and I had our birthdays on April 4 and 5. We are fifty-eight and fifty-five years old. We went to dinner (fish and chips) and to a show in between doctor visits and transfusions. Mike is getting a little stronger! I am grateful for these blessings and for people who care for me.

APRIL 30, 2002

Mike has had a follow-up abdominal CT scan to see how the stem cell transplant worked against the cancer in his liver. We went to see Dr. Black at the UCLA Cancer Center in Lancaster for the results. He sorrowfully told us that there is still a large tumor in Mike's liver. "Because we have done all we can to treat this cancer, this means, Michael, that you probably have only about two months to live!" This news hit us like a ton of bricks.

I begged the doctor, "Can't you give him Rituxan again?" (Rituxan is monoclonal antibodies, which fight lymphoma cells, but is not chemotherapy. It has almost no side effects.)

"I don't think it will work," said the doctor. "But we will give it a try."

I expressed my concern that Mike needs to go back to work in three weeks if we are to keep a full salary to support our family. He needs to finish a few more months to receive a retirement pension. I also gave Dr. Black forms to fill out to apply for Social Security disability payments. There is no question at this point that Mike will qualify.

Mike looks like a shriveled-up old man in his nineties now. He uses a walker to walk around the house. He has aged about forty years in the last four months. People at church are very shocked at his appearance. So am I. Is this really the man I am married to? He is so kind and sweet to me now that he has realized he can be taken away from me. He is very needy in his desire for my love and affection. I need to look at pictures of him when he was young and healthy and to tell myself that he is the same man inside that I married. He just looks different on the outside.

MAY 2, 2002 (MIKE'S JOURNAL)

The last few days I've been thinking about my probable death. (The doctor says my cancer is back in my liver and there are really no other treatments. He said I may have two weeks to two months to live. I have a hard time believing it can happen that fast, but we'll see.) When the doctor said the CT scan showed that the cancer was back, I accepted that as my answer. I wasn't too concerned—this is the will of the Lord, I surmised. I've always thought death would be wonderful—a great spiritual experience—and I still believe this will be true.

But out of the blue it struck me—I will be leaving my dear wife, Colleen. I was greatly distressed by this awareness and also by the realization that my children will be out of my life as well. I searched the Bible and read of where Hezekiah was about to die and pleaded that his life be spared. The Lord gave him another fifteen years (2 Kings 20). I am also pleading that I may not die, if it could be the will of the Lord.

MAY 10, 2002 (MIKE'S JOURNAL)

We'd decided, if I was able, to visit my family in Idaho, stopping to see the Scott portion of the family on our way up to Idaho. We needed to go up soon to finish this goal before I die (if I am going to). It had to be this weekend or not for several weeks, so we decided to go right away—this afternoon. Seth, Colleen and I went.

We stayed in Mesquite at the Oasis Motel ($105) Friday night. The next day we finished the trip to Salt Lake City, Utah. We had a family sharing time with Colleen's family in Utah. It was a gratifying and strengthening experience for me. There were many kind and uplifting remarks about myself and our family—no doubt overstated, but still nice sentiments to listen to. I bore my testimony and said that to love God is the most important thing.

The next day we traveled to Blackfoot, Idaho, in the evening to see my brother Dick. All his kids were there to say hi and talk. [Note: Mike lay on the couch and looked very ill. I think it scared everybody to see him so emaciated.] I shared some gospel thoughts with them. We stayed at a motel in Blackfoot, and then Colleen drove all the way back to California (about 950 miles), and we arrived back home at three in the morning.

> *"Oh God, where art thou? ... All these things shall*
> *give thee experience and shall be for thy good."*
> *—D & C 121:1, 122:7*

37

Resurrection

MAY 20, 2002

By sheer willpower, Mike has arisen from his bed of sickness and returned to work. He drags himself there, works slowly, and comes home late only to immediately drop into bed for the night. He has fallen a couple of times—once at the gas station, where he landed on his face, and once at work. He does not want to take a walker to work, but he will need to get a cane. He falls asleep at work sometimes, but he is working nonetheless as a school psychologist. We cannot afford in any way to believe what the doctor has told us about Mike's impending death. Hopefully, the Rituxan will be effective against the cancer, and he will be given a second chance at life!

I have been reading in some books about many natural treatments that supposedly have cured cancer for many people. Up to this point, Mike was not willing to try any of these things as long as the doctors had treatments for him. But now, with him on death's door, I convinced him that we should at least give some of these things a try. We went to the Whole Wheatery health food store to buy Essiac tea, shark cartilage, CoQ10, astragalus, and many other things—all supplemental herbs or substances claimed to combat cancer. The supplies cost hundreds of dollars but will be worth it if they can help him. Another thing we learned about was flaxseed oil, which is supposed to cure cancer. So I've decided to mix a tablespoon of it with a spirulina protein drink that Mike can drink each day. I have gathered all the herbs and vitamins into one box, and he gets about ten pills a day. We'll see how all this works.

We've had visits from Jessica and her girls and from Rebekah this month. They wanted to spend time with their dad, thinking it may be the last time to see him if the doctor's predictions are correct. Jessica worked on fixing the goat cage in the backyard while Mike, using his walker and wearing pajamas, watched. Rebekah went with us to the beach and hiked with the boys.

JUNE 5, 2002

Something good is happening to Mike. He really is gaining strength. Since we started the flaxseed oil, he is now able to walk down the hospital hall when he goes to get transfusions instead of having to ride in a wheelchair. He is getting much stronger! The claims I read about flaxseed oil said that it is full of omega-3 fatty acids, which every cell of the body needs to function properly. Maybe it is just what he needs to recover from the debilitating stem cell transplant.

The doctor was surprised to see Mike so improved and asked what we were doing. I told him about the flaxseed oil. He said to keep doing what we are doing. He was not expecting the Rituxan to help Mike. Anyway, whatever the doctor and we are doing is helping, so we will keep it up. Mike still is weak and tired but is so much better than he was. Maybe the liver tumor shown in the CT scan was in the process of dying from the stem cell treatment but just didn't show on the scan yet. Whatever! We are encouraged, and it doesn't seem that he will die anytime soon!

JULY 1, 2002

Mike's doctor has given him four doses of Rituxan and is surprised at what he feels is a very strong response to the Rituxan, which he did not expect to work. A couple of months ago I asked the Lord to prepare me for what will happen with Mike. As I thumbed through the scriptures, the impression I got was that we would have a miracle, as so many of the scriptures I came upon talked about miracles. Mike's increased strength lately has seemed miraculous. He is taking Megace, which is a medicine that has increased his appetite, and he has gained a little weight. His platelets and red and white cells are still decreased, and he is still rather weak, but he goes to everything (work, church, movies, and so on), so things are good!

AUGUST 10, 2002 (MIKE'S JOURNAL)

Last night Colleen and I had a date. After a little squabble, which we resolved, we had an enjoyable time together. Today, Saturday, the boys went to the beach. Tim Boulter, their friend from Utah, is visiting. Seth went with them. Later Colleen and I went down to pick up Seth so the other boys could go to a Dream Theater concert. Colleen, Seth, and I went to a movie.

AUGUST 14, 2002

Mike has August off from work, so we spent a week in Utah and Wyoming for the Scott family reunion at Martin's Cove. That is where the handcart pioneers of the Martin Handcart Company stayed in the cold of winter waiting to be rescued by the men from Salt Lake City in the 1850s. We had ancestors in the Martin Handcart Company. It was a nice time. Mike, Seth, and I rode in the wagon instead of walking up the trail like the rest of the family did.

During the summer Mike was assigned to work two hours away, so I drove him to and from work. Now he has been transferred to work in Santa Clarita beginning in September, only a thirty-minute drive. I think he can do that on his own. Such a blessing. Mike is still pretty weak, and a few weeks ago his electrolytes were critically low. He also had some bad liver pain last Sunday. It scared us. Mike has had four doses of Rituxan in July and August, and I started the flaxseed oil again. He needs to live! Hopefully all these things can keep him going for a long time—for the sake of our boys, our insurance, and so on. Things are definitely so much better than they were three months ago. Now if we can just keep it that way.

After we added many supplements and flaxseed oil to his diet, my husband improved dramatically.

38

Missionaries

AUGUST 14, 2002

We got a wonderful surprise today—the happiest thing that has happened in a very long time. Robert received a mission call from the church to go on the Baltimore, Maryland Mission leaving October 23! I was so excited. Robert was surprised and shocked at first. (We hadn't been sure if the church would allow him to go with his health issues.) But later he seemed happy. He told me he will go on a mission for a while to see if he feels what the church teaches is true. His mood has been up and down. His acceptance to UCLA cannot be deferred, so that was discouraging to him.

OCTOBER 23, 2002

Robert left on his mission today. We drove him to the Missionary Training Center in Provo, Utah. We stayed with my mom last night and had a family get-together. Robert looked so good and handsome but nervous. This last week Robert attended the San Diego Temple for the first time with Mike and me.

Robert's farewell meeting at church was a great occasion. Robert spoke, as did Mike and I. A highlight of the meeting was when Robert and his brothers and friends sang a song together.

DECEMBER 2002

We have had another amazing gift. Matt received his mission call to the McAllen, Texas Mission! Being right on the border of Texas and Mexico, it is both an English- and Spanish-speaking mission. Matt is very excited to be able to use the Spanish that he has learned so well in college and also by spending so much time in his friend Cesar's home. Cesar's family is from Mexico, so they speak Spanish in their home.

Robert has been serving his mission in a couple of small towns in Maryland. They have been having record snowfalls in the East, and he sent a picture of himself standing on a giant mound of snow. He is doing well and has been very healthy so far on his mission.

Seth, however, has been having more difficulty with his balance, so I bought him a dark-red walker with four wheels and a seat. He has been taking it to church lately. He was asked recently to share his testimony in church. He spoke somewhat haltingly, but his testimony of the Lord is so strong and pure. He touches everyone's heart. A friend of mine in the ward said that the first time she shook Seth's hand, she felt such a powerful spirit of love from him. She tells me that he is a very special person. I have to agree with her and have always felt that way about him. Even in his disabled state, he is a missionary for the Lord.

FEBRUARY 2003

Matthew had his missionary farewell, and then we had Cesar's family over for dinner afterward. They are Matt's good friends who emigrated from Mexico. The next day we drove him to the Missionary Training Center in Provo, Utah. He was given a language test and was told he knows Spanish so well that he doesn't need to learn it in the MTC! So he will only be staying three weeks in the MTC to learn the missionary discussions instead of the usual eight weeks to learn the language. Wow, he is so smart! He seemed happy to go into the MTC and anxious to begin his mission.

MARCH 2003

Robert has been transferred to work in the city of Baltimore. Some of the areas are in the slums. The ward there has about twelve sets of missionaries, which is surprising to me. It is a big city. Robert and his companion have had the opportunity to teach an African American woman and her son. She requested to be baptized and is grateful for the church. I hope it helps Robert in his faith also.

My daughter Jessica has been taking an online course in nursing and, after some weeks of clinical experience, has graduated with her RN degree. What a blessing that will be for her and her family! She has had such strength and determination to do this. We are proud of her!

APRIL 2003

Mike, Richard, Seth, and I flew to the National Institutes of Health in Bethesda, Maryland, to see Dr. Jain again about the boys' immune deficiency. Richard is doing well, but Seth's neurological decline has been of great concern to us. He was able to go to the neurology department at the NIH, where they did an MRI scan of his brain. In comparison to scans taken a couple of years ago, there is more cortical atrophy of his brain. The doctor said he has never seen anything like it before. The MRI shows destruction of both the gray matter and the white matter in Seth's brain. It is not clear to me exactly what that means, but I know it is very serious. The ventricles in Seth's brain are also quite enlarged because of the atrophy, or shrinking, of his brain. The doctors have no treatment for him, and their only theory is that an enterovirus is destroying the neurons in his brain, although no tests have been able to isolate the virus. This is so sad.

On our second day at the NIH, Robert was able to come with his mission president to see Dr. Jain. The Baltimore mission boundaries are not far from the NIH. Robert was dressed in some scrubs because he was going to get a bone density test in addition to other tests to make sure he's doing well. We got to visit with him and his mission president for a while but not for long enough! He looks wonderful!

The next day we decided to rent a car and drive to Baltimore. We wanted to see the city where Robert has been serving. We drove around the wharf and saw the ships in the harbor. We parked and walked a few blocks to see the Baltimore Aquarium. Seth was using his walker to help him walk. Richard was there to assist him, and I walked with Mike to make sure he did not trip on anything as we walked along with his cane. The aquarium and the surrounding area were very interesting to see.

APRIL 2003

A lot of the family goings-on are recorded these days in my emails to my missionaries and to doctors. I am including some transcripts of these emails because they convey very well what has been happening.

THURSDAY, APRIL 1, 2003 (EMAIL FROM ME TO ROBERT AND MATTHEW)

Hi, Rob and Matt,

We went to Jeremy's house in Palo Alto, California, over the weekend. We got there Friday night. Saturday we were planning to go to the beach to see the seals, but during lunch at Jeremy's house, Seth vomited some bright-red blood. So we went to the emergency room. They put a tube into his stomach and found some more blood, but later it stopped. They put him in the hospital for observation. On Monday they did an endoscopy and could find no certain site that they thought had bled, although they did find esophageal varices (big veins in the esophagus due to his liver causing blood to back up). They assumed that was the source of the bleeding. They gave him infusions to help prevent any further bleeding and also gave him two units of blood, but he's still pretty anemic. He got out Tuesday at about one o'clock, and Jeremy took us to the bird refuge so Seth could hear some bird calls. Then we drove home yesterday. Seth has really been going downhill.

While Seth was at the hospital, I heard some interesting programs on TV. One was about the scientifically proven evidence that spirituality and prayer help in healing. It was called "Medicine and Spirituality" and was broadcast on the Stanford Research Channel. It was based on studies done at John Hopkins University Hospital.

We drove home yesterday but left Richard up north to go with Jeremy to Redwood National Forest. Next week Richard goes to Scout camp, and the week after he goes to an Especially for Youth conference at Ricks College in Idaho. So he's going to be gone for a long time but home on weekends.

We love you guys. We're thrilled at the many good experiences you're having on your missions and pray for you daily. I prayed so much when Seth was in the hospital about so many things, and I felt my prayers were answered so many times. Pray always. Ask and ye shall receive.

Love always, Mom

MAY 28, 2003 (EMAIL FROM ROBERT)

Hey, family,

I just read the emails you sent. My health is adequate although not ideal. I still have a cough and sinus congestion after a ten-day course of Augmentin. The cough and congestion cleared up a good amount but returned after I stopped taking the Augmentin. I got a refill and will be on it for another ten days. After that I don't know what else I'll do. I'll survive one way or another. My patriarchal blessing promises me that I will be blessed with health enough to be able to go out and be an example to others.

We knocked on the door of a younger black woman who invited us right in. We also met her husband, who had to go out and work on his car, but he was very nice. We taught her the first discussion with Brother Freeman, a member of our church who just got married about a year ago and who is also black. Both the young woman and Brother Freeman are very well educated, so it was a good discussion. Well, hope all is well.

Love :)
Elder Rob Curzon

MONDAY, JUNE 23, 2003 (EMAIL FROM MATTHEW)
Subject: Adios muchachos
Hey, family! How's everything?

It's been really hot the past few days, like 103–105, por ahí. Rob's lucky that he doesn't have to deal with all this heat. The work's going well. Most of our investigators are just achugging along slowly. We met and gave an awesome first discussion to a guy named Rene (pronounced ree-nee) the other day. He really felt the Spirit and thought what we said was true. We have an appointment with him tonight, so we'll see how that goes.

Love, Matt

JUNE 2003
I have been very busy with Seth lately taking him to speech therapy and physical therapy as well as many doctor appointments. His speech started getting less easy to understand about a year ago. Speech therapy helps him to say the words more clearly. I also take Seth to a special gym for physical therapy to strengthen his muscles, which are becoming weaker due to his brain atrophy. He rides a stationary bike and sits on a large balance ball. Physical therapists work with him. Physical therapy gives Seth something to do with his time and

is enjoyable social interaction for him. He is also going to see a psychologist to talk about his depression issues. To lose his health at this prime time of his life is very sad and difficult for Seth and for the whole family. Seth's poor eyesight is now the least of his problems. He had his twenty-eighth birthday on June 27.

On the other hand, Mike is beginning to look a lot healthier. A man at church last week said to him, "Wow, you look great!" He has gained some weight back but not too much. He does look so much better than a year ago. Although it is still tiring for him, he is better able to handle the workload at his job. The doctor is still amazed that he continues to live and to go to work!

OCTOBER 2003

My missionaries are in my heart and in my prayers! I am so proud of their efforts to serve the Lord. I know it isn't easy, but they are doing it.

I have been taking Seth twice a week to an adult day care for a couple of hours. It gives me a chance to get some shopping and errands done, and he gets some physical therapy and social interaction.

OCTOBER 10, 2003 (EMAIL FROM MATTHEW)

Hey, family,

Everything is pretty well here in good old South Texas. General Conference was awesome, wasn't it? On the mission, conference is bigger than Christmas. It always is very inspiring and helps to build my testimony. It's also nice to kind of be in contact with the church, since out in Raymondville it's not always exactly the way you'd think church would be. The work's been pretty slow.

I just need to be patient, keep working hard, and trust in the Lord that He knows what's right for me. It sounds like things are getting hard with Seth. I wish I could be there to help out. That's good that he'll be able to go to that day care thing. It will take a load off of you. Tell him that I love him and hope that he's feeling well and happy. Well, fam, I gotta go. Keep up the good work and keep the faith!

Elder Curzon II

NOVEMBER 2003 (EMAIL FROM ROBERT)

Hey, family! How's everyone? Things are going well here. I'm still here in Edgewood, enjoying my time here. We got two families out to church this past week. We have three Thanksgiving meals planned on Thanksgiving, so no need to worry whether or not I'm being fed enough. :) I wish you all a happy Thanksgiving! Take care.

Love, Elder Rob Curzon

DECEMBER 1, 2003 (EMAIL FROM MATTHEW)

Hey, family, how's it going? Yeah, I'm in my new area, Mission. It's a cool place, right along the border. The other day Elder Holmes (my new companion) and I rode our bikes down to the Rio Grande (the border) and looked over to old Mexico. It was cool. Oh, we're on bikes now, no more car, but our area is only about eight to ten square miles, so it's not that bad. There's a lot more Spanish down here than in Raymondville, obviously, but also a lot more rich people. There are some very nice neighborhoods and big houses. I like it here, though, and I'm excited to be in a new area. Hope all is well with y'all. Talk to you later.

Elder Mottox (Matthew)

DECEMBER 25, 2003

Today is Christmas without my missionary sons. But we got to talk to them on the phone. All the family gathered around, taking turns, and we spent hours talking to them. It is so good to hear their voices. They are visiting with and being fed by families in their areas, so I am glad about that. We sent packages of food and decorations to help them have a good Christmas.

JANUARY 4, 2004 (EMAIL FROM ROBERT)

Hey there, all. How's everything? Well, this week was very good for the most part. A man named Jason Lee was just baptized here in the Frederick Ward. He's from Taiwan and has two very cute daughters, ages three and five. He's awesome. I love Oriental people! He's a very solid individual.

This past week has been extremely cold, averaging around fifteen degrees, and it's even colder with the windchill. It's crazy. Brrrrrrrrrrrrr! I stay fairly warm, though, with my new coat.

I was sorry to hear about Seth and his difficulties. It's so hard to be away knowing that he's slowly deteriorating, that I'm missing out on being able to see him before he's too far gone. But then again, it was very difficult to see him deteriorate, and even though I love him and would like to cherish the time that's left, it's almost like I don't want to have to deal with the pain of seeing him suffer. I have mixed feelings about it. Anyway, tell Seth that I love him and hope he's happy.

I'm extremely exhausted with the routine of being a missionary. I feel like I'm going crazy with it all—with everything going on with Seth, along with everything else. For now I'm just enjoying my time and loving the people. Bye for now.

Love, Elder Rob Curzon

JANUARY 28, 2004 (EMAIL FROM ROBERT)

Hey, all, what's up? Well, this week was a long one. Very cold and I've been sick with a cough as well. We spent the good part of two days in the apartment. We have been able to get out a bit and work. It's hard with all this snow and freezing rain. I don't think I had ever seen freezing rain until a couple of days ago. It's pretty but very dangerous. Our cars have been grounded for most of the week as well, which has made it all the more difficult. Well, today I'm going down to the NIH again, probably my last time for a while. I'm going down to see Dr. Rosendale.

I love you guys and hope all is well. Thanks for all you guys do! I'll talk to you next week.

Love, Elder Rob Curzon

JANUARY 30, 2004

I have been keeping in touch with a Huntington's disease online support group because Seth's symptoms of extreme tremors and the course of neurological decline seem so similar to Huntington's disease. There has been some talk on this site about the pros and cons of feeding tubes. I have thought about whether we should give Seth a feeding tube, but I am against it because it will just prolong his life, which is of such poor quality. Terri Schiavo has been on the news a lot lately involving a big fight in her family about whether to remove her feeding tube. I asked Seth if he wanted to have a feeding tube, and he said no. Seth does eat, because I feed him, but each meal takes a long time. He is slowly losing weight.

FEBRUARY 2004

Robert has decided to come home from his mission early with all that is going on with Seth and with the health, mental, and spiritual struggles he has had on his mission. When we picked Robert up at the airport, Seth gave his brother a big hug, and so did we. We are grateful for his sacrifices to serve the Lord.

Robert gave a very nice talk in church stressing the importance of service. He does seem more mature and more eager to be of service to the family. The next week Jeremy took Robert and his friend Cesar on a trip to the Everglades. They drove across the country and had a good time.

FEBRUARY 16, 2004 (EMAIL FROM MATTHEW)

Dear family,

This week was pretty good. It did rain and get pretty cold (if forty degrees is cold—I'm not sure; here it is anyway). I haven't had the cold and all that Rob had to deal with. I can't imagine working in five-degree weather with snow all around. I've been thinking a lot about Rob, about what's happened. He really has had a tough time on his mission, a lot tougher than me, I think. One of the things was that he didn't really even expect that the church would let him go on his mission due to his illness, and once the shock came that he was going, he maybe didn't really feel ready.

Thanks a lot for the Valentine's candy and letter. It's always good to hear from my wonderful family. Well, I hope everything is well with y'all still. I hope Rob and Rich had fun in Florida. Well, I'll talk to y'all later!

Elder Curzon

JULY 19, 2004 (EMAIL FROM MATTHEW)

Hey, family, how's it going? Yes, it has been very hot lately. Around one hundred right now. And we're low on miles in the car, so we've been on bikes the past couple of days. Very hot. As far as the work, things are pretty good. Jonathan, the thirteen-year-old, is getting baptized next week, and we have a new person we are teaching. Her name's Lorianne, and she's very awesome. She's already read a ton in the scriptures and came to church for the first time Sunday and loved it. She has a baptismal date for August 15. Life's good. The work is hard but good. Y'all have a good week, ya hear?

Love, Elder Curzon

JULY 2004

It has been great to have Robert home, and he does do a lot to help take care of Seth and to spend time with him. I'm sure that is one of the reasons he felt he should come home early from his mission—to have some meaningful experiences with Seth while there is still an opportunity to do so. My sister Barbara came to stay with me for two weeks to help with Seth and Mike and with my disorganized house. It was wonderful to have her here and to receive her assistance. It seems impossible to keep up on everything that is going on in my life right now.

AUGUST 2004

Robert has been here at home going to Antelope Valley College in Lancaster, California, the last few months. Now he is moving to San Diego to attend the University of California, San Diego, majoring in engineering. He found a nice apartment with a couple of guys. This will be an exciting adventure for him. His girlfriend will be attending the same school. It is clear to me now that he has decided not to be in the church anymore. Of course this saddens me, but he is old enough to make his own life choices.

NOVEMBER 8, 2004 (EMAIL FROM MATTHEW)

Hello, family!

Well, I've been transferred to the wonderful city of Hidalgo, Texas. Almost all Spanish, not one white person (at least I haven't seen one yet). Also, huge warehouses of used clothes where we can get lots of good ties for cheap. Today I got five pretty nice ones for a buck. The people here are great too. We have a great lady named Marina who's getting baptized on the twenty-first of November. We've been tracting (knocking on doors) a lot to find more people. One area we tracted is about one hundred feet from the border. It's kind of weird. We can see Reynosa (the city in Mexico) right there close. Needless to say, there are a lot of "wetbacks," or illegals, swimming across the border all the time. It's pretty interesting.

I should be coming home Wednesday of the week of January 20. I'd like to travel around the mission for maybe three days or so and see all the people I've met if you can come down to Texas to pick me up from my mission. I love y'all tons and hope everything is going well. Take care!

Elder Curzon

It brings me joy to feel of Matt's enthusiasm for sharing the gospel in Texas. Mike and I have always dreamed and planned for the time when our sons could serve missions for the church. Only one more son to go—Richard. This joy is in opposition to the sadness we have felt lately that most of our kids no longer believe in or attend church. I think this unbelief has come from many sources, one of which was Michael's unexpected early death. Why did God allow this to happen is a question that I know some of my children have asked. Also their college training in scientific thinking has made it harder for them to believe in things that may not have a good scientific explanation. Perhaps they became lax in their obedience or were not able to get answers to their prayers. Whatever the reason, their unbelief has been a great burden on my heart as it runs so counter to the dreams I had for my children when they were being raised. I see other church members my age who are also grieving their children's similar choices. I will always love my kids and strive to be close to them in spite of our different beliefs and lifestyles. I always pray that God will renew their faith sometime in the future, and I have some assurances that it may happen, but when or how is a mystery. It would be a wonderful miracle.

"I have no greater joy than to hear that my children walk in truth."
—3 John: 4

39

Death Scares

I brought Seth home from the day care center today. Sometimes when I pick him up from the care center, he seems to be staring into space—all alone. However, there is a special attendant there, a young mother about his age, who thinks Seth is so special. She gives him extra attention when she can. Seth got physical therapy at the care center today. I played some Sound of Music tunes on the piano there when I picked him up. The patients seemed to enjoy it. I guess I should share my talents when I can.

I was thinking about how far Seth has declined in the past year and a half since Matt left for his mission. At that time, Seth wore glasses, took my arm to be led around, and was speaking pretty well. Now he is almost blind and can barely stand up with the walker. We just started using the wheelchair at the care center because getting up and down from a chair is so precarious for him. The wheelchair is much safer. We have been hoping to drive to Texas to pick up Matthew from his mission, but the worse Seth becomes, the more such a trip seems like an impossibility.

Now it is almost nine in the evening, and my husband, Mike, is still not home from work. He left at seven this morning. I worry, but this has become a pattern with him, so I have to trust he will make it home safely as he drives up the Pasadena Freeway. It seems he takes so long these days to read, write, or think that it requires twice as long to do his job at work as it should. His energy level is so low. Two years ago, when the doctor thought Mike was a terminal cancer patient, he prescribed hydrocodone pain pills for Mike's chronic neuropathy pain. I'm sure this medication makes Mike sleepy. To counteract this,

288

he has been given a prescription for Dexedrine for occasional use to help him stay alert.

Last week we drove to Los Angeles to speak with a counselor about his possible retirement from the Los Angeles County Office of Education. The counselor told us that he will get much more money if he does a disability retirement rather than a regular retirement. He certainly is disabled. He has no energy, because of some congestive heart failure. He could retire now, but then we would lose the health insurance for our boys, who have high medical needs themselves. We could technically continue the insurance, but it would cost a lot more money. Mike's retirement income would be half of his present salary. It's just not enough. He needs to keep working as long as possible. But I don't know how much longer he can continue this demanding work schedule. No wonder he sleeps all weekend, day and night.

Ever since his cancer treatment he has been a different person, more like ninety years old than his actual sixty years. His walking is so slow, his balance unsteady. I fear he is developing some dementia. I no longer have a fully functioning husband, either physically or mentally, but his paychecks keep coming in, which is a huge blessing! However, I do feel like a widow in a sense. My son Richard is more of a companion to me than is my husband. It is a sad thing that cannot be helped.

SEPTEMBER 24, 2004

I'm in the waiting room of Dr. Kennedy, a psychologist. My seventeen-year-old son, Richard, is here for about the fifth time. It's for depression, procrastination in school, and low motivation. I think it has been hard for Richard to have to become a secondary caregiver to Seth, although I still do almost everything. With his dad mostly out of his life due to illness and his favorite brothers gone on missions and college, Richard has sort of been abandoned. He is the only young and healthy one in our home now. I try to act young and healthy, but I'm his mother. Since he passed the high school equivalency exam at age sixteen with a straight-A average, he has been going to college early—another challenge in a new environment where he doesn't know anyone. He is doing better now in school, and I see improvement since he started taking Zoloft and getting counseling.

Last week I returned with Seth to the UCLA neurology department to talk to the doctor about Seth's movement disorder, which started about eighteen months ago. He can't stay still except when he is sleeping. His head is constantly bobbing. His torso twists, and his hands are constantly moving. Sometimes it seems like tremors, like when he is reaching for something. Otherwise, it is movement that is called chorea. (Thank goodness we found out it is not Huntington's chorea, the inherited disease.) Anyway, chorea looks like his fingers are playing the piano. It is involuntary, caused by misfiring of electrical impulses in his brain due to brain cells dying. He also seems to have some chorea in his right leg and foot. It started in his right hand but is in his left hand now also. This movement disorder also affects his tongue and swallowing muscles. He can hardly talk at all now. When I take Seth out to the clinic in his wheelchair, people are always staring at us. It is uncomfortable to be the center of attention, but it must be obvious to onlookers that he is a very disabled person and I am his caregiver.

SEPTEMBER 28, 2004
9:00 a.m.

I am very scared and tied in knots right now as I am sitting here in the Antelope Valley Hospital emergency room watching my husband with his oxygen mask. Mike came in early this morning by ambulance. As he lay in bed at home last night, he moaned and moaned. At first I thought it was his usual leg pain, but soon I could tell it was much worse than that. "Get lots of blankets!" he said. "I'm freezing!" When I felt his head, he didn't feel like he had a fever, and his temperature was only 97.5. But I knew the signs of rigors and chills. His body was trying to raise his temperature by vigorous shivering. Sure enough, he spiked a temperature of 103.5 two hours later in spite of taking Tylenol. Mike has had diarrhea for five days and a scratchy throat. This temperature spike must be sepsis—infection that has gotten into the bloodstream.

Right now his temperature is 101.8, and his blood pressure is 81/41—low! They are giving him IV fluids to bring his blood pressure up.

The nurse asked Mike, "What month is it?"

No answer.

"What year is it?"

"1904," Mike answered.

"Where are you?"

"I'm in this room."

"Where is the room?"

"It's in this building."

"Where?" asked the nurse.

Nothing.

Mike is clearly confused. He also seemed delusional this morning before he came to the hospital. He was saying so many sentences with big academic words, but they made no sense.

The alarm just beeped loudly because Mike's heart rate fell to forty-two for a moment, causing three nurses to run in here. But now his heart rate is back up to ninety-three. His oxygen level has continually been going down to 89 percent or lower, so they just raised the amount of oxygen they are giving him. Oh, what is happening? Now his blood pressure is 75/39! The beeper goes off again. This is getting scary! He is so sick!

Now they are doing an EKG on Mike and putting him on dopamine to raise his blood pressure. The doctor just came in and said, "We don't have the blood tests back, but I think he's in septic shock. That is why his blood pressure keeps dropping. We'll put him on intravenous antibiotics—Fortaz. We can't wait for the white count."

Wow, this is really, really serious! I should have called 911 at four this morning instead of eight. Now they are putting an oxygen mask on him to replace the nose cannula and are turning the oxygen level up. Another doctor just came in with blood results. He said to Mike, "You have an infection—a big infection. You had a stem cell transplant? How's your immune system?"

"Not good," I said. "His white count is usually pretty low."

The doctor asked, "Have you had a chest x-ray this morning?" He listened to Mike's lungs with a stethoscope. "He has a lot of fluid on him. Have you had fluid in your lungs before?"

"Yes," I answered for Mike, because he's too sick to answer for himself.

291

10:30 a.m.

Well, things have stabilized for the moment—pulse 107, blood pressure 109/45. This has been a very scary hour. The nurse came in. "I'm going to access your portacath to give you more fluids," she said to Mike. I wonder if he could have gotten sick by going to the dentist last week. He really should take prophylactic antibiotics before going to the dentist. Wow, he's got three bags of stuff dripping into him right now. I hope it's not too much fluid for his heart to handle. Gee, if he didn't have all this support, he would be dying right now! I'm standing next to him and watching his pulse pounding, pounding in his neck. Pulse is 108 while he is sound asleep. That shows me he is still very sick.

12:30 p.m.

Things still seem to have stabilized somewhat—pulse 105, blood pressure 101/45, oxygen at 92. The oxygen is turned down some now, and he has a nose breather instead of a mask. The lab tech is taking some more blood from Mike. Now his temperature is 98 something. Much better. Maybe everything will be okay.

The nurse comes in again and asks Mike the same questions to test his cognition. "Can you tell me the day, month, and year, Mr. Curzon?"

"Wednesday, September 28, 2004," Mike answers.

"Pretty good. Lungs sound good. I don't think it is your lungs." She asks general questions about his health and advance directives. He is going to be admitted to the intensive care unit because of his low blood pressure. Oh, I wish I had signed up for the intensive care insurance offer we got in the mail last month. I am so relieved he is doing better than he was earlier this morning.

OCTOBER 2, 2004

Mike recovered from his sepsis after a few days, and we brought him home from the hospital. He returned to his work as a school psychologist, and life went on as normal for a little while.

NOVEMBER 6, 2004

A couple of nights ago I was so tired after feeding Seth a bedtime snack, giving him his pills, taking him to the bathroom, putting on his pajamas, brushing his teeth, giving him a Neupogen shot, and tucking him into bed. I couldn't wait to have a good night's sleep.

Shortly after I got into bed, my husband, Mike, became very ill— again. First, he was moaning with pain, saying his stomach hurt. He was clutching at his right side. I felt so reluctant to get out of my nice bed to serve him when I felt so tired. But it wasn't long before he started running a high fever and had shaking chills.

I said, "We need to go to the hospital right now."

He said, "Just wait a while until I feel better."

Since he refused to help me, or couldn't get himself up, I had to call 911. Soon the ambulance was at our house with four men and a stretcher in our bedroom. They got Mike into the ambulance, and I followed them in the car. It was another case of infection—pneumonia this time. But we caught it faster than the last episode, and within a couple of days he was much improved. Thank goodness for intravenous antibiotics. They work wonders.

NOVEMBER 27, 2004

I just got word that my mother broke her leg spontaneously while walking in a parking lot. In the course of treatment, doctors found that she has a non-Hodgkin's lymphoma tumor in her bone. They believe it originated there. She is in her eighties and too old to do chemotherapy. She will have some radiation and Rituxan, like Mike had, and hopefully she will be okay. Now both my parents have had cancer, as have my husband and I and our son Michael. It seems like an epidemic.

DECEMBER 22, 2004

Last Monday night Seth was coughing in his bedroom, or so I thought. When I walked into his room to check on him, he was vomiting, and then came huge amounts of bright-red blood—all over his bed! I kept saying, "Oh no, oh no, oh no!" The time was eleven thirty. A certain part of me was thinking, *This is it. His time to go into the spirit world has come.* All night he vomited, and then he stopped for a few hours. By six in the morning he had lost about two quarts of blood. I did not take him to the hospital, for his quality of life is so poor, not being able to walk or talk or care for himself, and he did not have a DNR (do not resuscitate) order from the doctor.

293

I called Bishop Wyatt about six thirty to see if he could come over to give Seth a blessing. It was wonderful to feel the peace brought by our religious leader. After he left, I called Pro-Care Hospice to see if they could contact the doctor and have Seth admitted into hospice and give a DNR order. We had talked about hospice with the doctors a few months earlier, but it hadn't seemed like the right time. Hospice said they would call the doctor and take care of everything.

Then there was a flurry of other phone calls, including ones to Jessica and Rebekah. Jessica called Jeremy, and he said he would fly down that day. Jessica wanted to come with her girls that night. Seth's vomiting had stopped, but we knew from our experience with Michael's death that his condition could change quickly. He vomited again about one in the afternoon, shortly before Jeremy arrived. Jeremy hugged Seth and sobbed. It was very touching.

I was so scared and uncertain as to what to do. It was torture to do nothing. I was praying constantly in my heart for guidance. I asked Seth if he wanted to go to the hospital or stay home. Around three o'clock he said he wanted to go to the hospital, so we got him ready. We went to the emergency room, and they quickly got him into a bed and ran intravenous fluids. Robert came up from San Diego. I also called Matt's mission president in Texas to tell him what was happening in case Seth passed away. He said he would call me back.

Late that night Seth was put upstairs into a hospital room. Jeremy and Robert stayed most of the night. I went home and found that Jessica and the girls were there. Lee Ann, my sister-in-law, had come up from Orange County and cleaned up, set up mattresses for everyone, and brought blankets and pillows for all the guests. She was a huge help.

We were all running on a small amount of sleep. But Seth was relatively comfortable in the hospital. That made us all feel good. In the night Seth vomited blood again. Jeremy called us and said the doctor had given Seth a vitamin K shot, which might help the bleeding to stop. We visited Seth bringing a CD player and Christmas music, food, and a cute black stuffed puppy—anything we could think of to help him to be happier.

DECEMBER 23, 2004

I am fasting and praying today about Seth and searching the scriptures: "Whoso shall ask in my name in faith, they shall ... heal the sick" (D & C 35: 9). Is it possible that Seth can be healed if we have enough faith?

We got a phone call from Matt's mission president. He said that since Matt had only a few weeks left on his mission, he was going to send him home early so he could see his brother. When Matt got home, he was very happy to be home before Christmas. However, when he saw Seth's condition, he was shocked. Seth could no longer walk or talk much, not even feed himself. He had deteriorated so much since Matt had seen him almost two years ago.

After the vitamin K shot, Seth did not vomit any more blood, so we brought him home. Later he got a transfusion of blood. It seems he will be with us a little longer! Many of us were together for Christmas, so that was wonderful.

I sent Seth's neurologist, Dr. Matthew Arnold, an email telling him about this recent esophageal bleed. He wrote me back:

Dear Colleen:

I am sorry to hear about Seth's deteriorating condition. I know it has been a long struggle with Seth and difficult to watch without being able to help him a great deal. I think that hospice is a very reasonable choice to try to maximize his comfort at this point. I think an autopsy later would be extremely helpful in trying to understand what has caused his deterioration over the last ten years. I know that at UCLA we have one of the country's preeminent neuropathologists who would be interested in brain tissue. Once again, I am sorry to hear of Seth's decline.

Dr. Matt Arnold

DECEMBER 31, 2004

Seth is recovering from his esophageal bleed. I had scheduled an appointment for him weeks earlier to see Ulrike Ziegner, an immunologist south of Los Angeles. She is a wonderful doctor with a foreign accent. She has written a paper about the possibility that IVIG

295

(intravenous gamma globulin) might actually cause neurological decline, as has been seen in a minority of patients with primary immune deficiencies. Strangely, she said Seth looked better than she expected, which surprised us. Following is an email she sent to several other doctors throughout the country concerning our visit:

To: Doctors Hans D. Ochs; Jonathan Goldsmith; Adrian Casillas; Jeff Sy
Cc: Colleen Curzon
From: Dr. Ulrike Ziegner, MD

Happy New Year everybody. On Friday, December 31, 2004, I saw Seth Curzon, accompanied by his mom, Colleen, and brothers Matthew and Richard. He seemed to be able to follow our conversation, responding and even laughing at times. His chorea-like ataxia has developed and is progressive over the last two and a half years. His brothers think that he is only able to see shadows and lights.

His abdominal CT had shown liver cirrhosis in the past; however, a liver biopsy did not confirm this. He is on a beta-blocker to control portal hypertension. The family is not sure if hepatitis C virology was done by PCR. He appeared tiring out and pale. While off hospice care, he might benefit from a platelet and red blood cell transfusion. He continues to receive low-dose granulocyte stimulating factor for his hyper-IgM related low white cell count along with IVIG.

I was happily surprised that Seth had recovered from his recent esophageal bleed and is neurologically functioning better than expected. Thanks to all of you for your interest and advice.

Best regards,
Ulrike Ziegner, MD, PhD
Riviera Allergy Medical Center
Redondo Beach, CA 90277

FEBRUARY 1, 2005

As it turned out, Seth was "healed" temporarily. We took him to the hospital last month to get a transfusion of two units of blood, and he felt a little better after that.

The other day I was in my bedroom folding clothes, and the Spirit came upon me, strongly telling me it was time for Seth to go to the temple for the first time. This is something Seth has been desiring to do for several years, and I feel now that it's very important that he receive these blessings before he dies, so that he will have more power and advantage after he leaves this life. I talked to the bishop and stake president about it. Seth was able to answer the interview questions saying yes or no. I told them that although he seems not to know what is going on, he does know what is happening. I know this because when he is listening to the TV, he always laughs at the proper time when jokes are told. He understands what is being said, although he cannot respond verbally.

FEBRUARY 7, 2005

Mike came home early today from work and said that his supervisor had found mistakes in the test scoring of a little girl he had tested. The supervisor told Mike that she feels he is no longer able to do his job sufficiently well to continue working and that he will have to be laid off. Mike was very despondent about it.

He will be able to receive full pay until August, when his sick leave and vacation leave run out. After that, he should be able to receive half pay as part of disability retirement. This means we can't afford to keep living in this house! Either we have to buy a mobile home here in California or move to Utah, where houses are much less expensive. This is really scary, but we have seen it coming. It was inevitable. In the past couple of years since the stem cell transplant and hospitalizations, he has gone downhill so much both physically and cognitively.

FEBRUARY 15, 2005

Seth wanted me to take him to visit Darla, the young caregiver his age who was so kind to him in the care center. He wanted me to give her a copy of The Book of Mormon. It was a cold, blustery day. We drove to her house. I took the wheelchair out of the trunk and helped Seth get into it, and we went in to visit her. We had a nice visit. She was kind and happy to see Seth. We left around three o'clock. I got Seth in the car and lifted the heavy wheelchair back into the trunk. It was a physical strain for me.

As we drove home, I began to feel very strange. My face, arm, and leg on my left side were feeling numb, and I felt kind of light-headed. After we got home, I took some aspirin and ate some yogurt. Still, I did not feel normal. Finally, I called my friend to take me to the emergency room. The doctor did a head CT scan and ultrasound of my carotid arteries. The right one was partially blocked with plaque, they said. By then, however, I was feeling fine and wanted to go home. They said I had experienced a TIA, or transient ischemic attack— basically a ministroke.

FEBRUARY 21, 2005

A few days after going to see a neurosurgeon about my TIA, I quickly found myself having a carotid endarterectomy. The doctor took a vein from my lower leg and replaced the carotid artery with the transplanted vein to open up the blood flow to my brain. I was in intensive care for a couple of days. It seemed like a blur of pain and discomfort, as surgery always is, but it passed quickly, and I was back home being a wife and mother, taking aspirin and Plavix to prevent further TIAs.

APRIL 2005

Mike and I drove to Utah with Seth for General Conference. We stayed with my sister Barbara and her husband, Russ. We decided this would be a good time to take Seth to the temple that was close by. We got him out of bed, got him dressed in white clothes, got him into the wheelchair, and took him to the temple. The people there seemed overcome with compassion for him. The spirit of love was so strong. We were thrilled that he was able to receive these temple ordinances before he died and that my brother, sister, and cousins could accompany us to the temple.

MAY 1, 2005

Mike's doctor ordered him to have a brain MRI to see if he has had a stroke, as he has fallen a lot, his thinking is not as clear as it used to be, and he has difficulty writing. They found that he has had a stroke in a part of the brain called the thalamus. It is an area responsible for memory and balance. We have no idea when this stroke could have happened, perhaps during one of his many hospitalizations when he was so ill that stroke symptoms would not have been noticeable.

MAY 8, 2005
We need to sell the house if possible because Mike will be retiring in seven weeks. If we get the equity out of our home, we'll be able to live more comfortably and possibly move to Utah.

JUNE 5, 2005
I go back and forth in my mind between thinking of staying in California or moving to Utah. The boys want to stay in California, but we can't afford to stay in this house.

Seth is totally bedbound now. I try to feed him very soft food or baby food about five times a day. Each meal takes about an hour because he has difficulty swallowing. He has lost a lot of weight. We put him on the portable toilet three times a day. He wears diapers sometimes. A bath nurse from hospice comes three times a week to give him bed baths. She fondly calls him "Blue Eyes." He gets his IVIG at home now instead of at the clinic, and I give him a Neupogen shot every other day so his white cell count doesn't go too low.

Mike, Rich, and Matt help me with Seth. Sometimes when I am trying to maneuver Seth, who is five feet eleven, he falls onto the carpet. I cannot get him up by myself, since I am only five feet one. I have to get Mike out of bed to help me. Once I had to call a neighbor to help pull Seth off the floor when I was alone with him. Oh, Sethy, how far you have deteriorated! I'm so sorry!

Mike is also in bed most of the time. He is spending hours studying and marking scriptures to help him overcome his feelings of sadness and hopelessness. He is exhausted and has never really regained his strength. He also spends hours sleeping. One positive thing is that we are getting a little closer to each other emotionally, as he is home all the time.

I've been working on getting the retirement papers done. Mike cannot do it himself. Two months until we have no pay—unless we get it from disability retirement.

Keep patients comfortable, respond to new symptoms promptly, and stay calm! Ask for help.
"Yea, though I walk through the valley of the shadow of death, I will fear no evil, for thou art with me."
—Psalm 23:4

40

Goodbye

Two weeks ago Seth had been running a low fever for a few days and coughing a lot, even though he was on Levaquin, so Richard and I packed him into the wheelchair, into the car, into the wheelchair again, into urgent care. Transporting him from one place to another is very difficult now. When we took Seth into triage, he started crying very hard and sliding down in his chair, like a child having a tantrum. He saw the doctor, who ordered a chest x-ray. Seth had to stay in his wheelchair while we held him still so they good get two good x-rays. We were told he had pneumonia. The doctor decided to give him a Rocephin shot since it was quick. Then the nurse set him up to have intravenous antibiotics at home for the next few days. Because of Seth's actions, I feel that I shouldn't ever bring him to urgent care or to the hospital again. He obviously did not want to be there but can no longer speak to tell us his wishes.

The next day the home nurse came to administer the intravenous antibiotics. She poked Seth seven times trying to find a good vein with no success. It wasn't until after Mike said a prayer that the catheter went in after the eighth try. Seth was also due to have his IVIG (worth $3,000), which was sitting in the refrigerator and had to be used within a few hours or it would begin to deteriorate. The nurse said she could not give the intravenous gamma, because Seth was getting antibiotics. I tried to explain to her that he needed the gamma even more now that he was sick. Finally, I called Dr. Lin at the UCLA immunology department. She told the nurse that the two medications could be given in the same day. Why do I have to argue with medical personnel?

Because Seth is so terribly disabled and unhappy with his life, I have been wondering if we should discontinue his gamma, Neupogen, and antibiotics in the future and let nature take its course.

JUNE 27, 2005

Today was Seth's thirtieth birthday, an age that few patients with hyper-IgM syndrome reach. Jeremy drove up for the occasion. Rob is also here for the summer. Matt, Rich, Mike, and I were also at the party. We had cake, chicken, Jell-O, and fruit salad. When we sang "Happy Birthday" to Seth, he started to cry and then sob uncontrollably. We all felt that he was expressing to us his distress and sadness about still being alive at age thirty but unable to function at all independently in his life. It was very upsetting to all of us. Later, we watched Star Wars, and he laughed at Darth Vader.

After Seth and Mike were in bed, the rest of us stayed up late talking around the kitchen table. We feel that Seth's crying tonight was an indication that he wants our keeping him alive unnecessarily to cease. Indeed, it is only because of continual medical intervention that Seth continues to live. We know from past experience that if we stop supporting his immune system with gamma globulin and Neupogen, it will be only a short time before he gets pneumonia. Pneumonia has been called "the old man's friend." If the pneumonia is not treated with antibiotics, it will turn into sepsis, a speedy way for him to leave this world. We kind of decided we should stop the gamma globulin in the future and give Neupogen sparingly to prevent mouth sores, so that we don't continue to prolong his poor quality of life. He is so unhappy. This was a weighty decision, but we're doing it for Seth. I know he would be so much happier if he could leave his wasted body. But still, I couldn't make this decision without a confirmation from heaven that it's right.

JUNE 29, 2005

Mike and I went to the sealing of my niece and her husband's marriage in the San Diego Temple. It was a beautiful occasion. Before the ceremony in the hallway, I was talking to a lady who had recently been the caregiver for a dying cancer patient. The patient had said to her, "I would tell my family to let me go! Don't let me linger and suffer!" Why was she telling me this in the temple? I felt it was a message to me regarding Seth. I also turned to the scriptures. I read, "He who dies in me shall not taste of death, for it shall be sweet unto him" (D & C 42:46). That is an assurance to me that death will be sweet for Seth and that he will go to heaven.

JULY 2, 2005

Matt has been doing some online dating and has been emailing a girl from Canada named Christina. He seems to be falling for her. She is of Philippine and Indian descent, and she also wants to go to medical school in the future. Her father works for the airlines, so she was able to fly down here cheaply to visit Matt. They seem to really like each other. I am happy for Matthew. It wasn't long ago that I was fasting and praying that he could find a girlfriend.

JULY 3, 2005

I've been praying about what to do about Seth but seem to get no answer. What would my father, Verl Scott, say about Seth? I think he would say to let Seth go. The spirit world is real and wonderful. My dad needs help in the missionary work there. What did my dad do when he got pneumonia on top of his cancer? He chose to go home to die and not treat the pneumonia. What did Michael do when he was dying? He chose to refuse more medical intervention. Both were less disabled than Seth. I feel comfort and connection with my dad. Thank you, Dad. I love and miss you! Last night Seth was crying and said, "Oh, Mom!" I felt again he was asking that there be an end to all his suffering.

JULY 4, 2005

Independence Day. We had a family feast with Rob, Matt, Richard, Seth, Mike, and me. Many of us helped to prepare hamburgers, hot dogs, macaroni salad, corn on the cob, and brownies. We did fireworks outside with Seth in the wheelchair on the lawn. I don't know if he enjoyed it or not.

JULY 12, 2005

Seth had his gamma infusion again. I can't bring myself to stop it. His Neupogen shot was a day late, and he got a fever and cough Sunday night, but it was gone in the morning.

My sister Barbara called me this morning before she was going to the temple. I asked her to put our names on the temple prayer roll. She said she heard we were going to stop the gamma for Seth. I said, "Well, no, he had it last Friday."

Barb asked me, "What does the Lord want you to do?"

I said, "He probably wants me to let Seth go."

"Well, then it's a tug-of-war now between you and the Lord," she said. "What does your family want you to do?"

I said that most of them think we should let him go but that I have confusing feelings. Barbara said, "Well, you could probably keep him here forever with what you're doing, but his work here is finished! He's not going to get better. He has work to do on the other side. Dad needs him over there!"

I said that I just didn't want him to suffer too much when he dies. She said, "Well, he's suffering more now. That's what we think. Do you want us to have a family fast so he can go?" I couldn't answer. I was choked up with tears. "Well, think about it and let me know," she said.

I guess I needed someone to call and say this to me. It seemed almost as if it was a phone call from God. Later, Barbara told me that she felt it was a phone call from Dad (through her). Yes, that is how Dad would have talked to me—straightforward and to the point. It was a phone call from my dad. I had asked my dad for guidance from the spirit world, and he had answered me.

JULY 30, 2005

Mike and I drove with Seth to Salt Lake City for Danny Hunter's wedding. The two weeks prior to this, Seth had no Neupogen shots, no gamma globulin, and no antibiotics. I was surprised that he did not become ill immediately. However, in Salt Lake City he began to have a low fever, which we treated with Tylenol. One afternoon, Seth felt pretty well, and Rebekah took him swimming in the pool, which he seemed to really enjoy. She said at one point he seemed to really be looking at the trees and sky and looked at her with a gaze that seemed to see her in spite of his blindness.

While we were in Salt Lake, Mike and I went house shopping for a few hours over a couple of days with a realtor. We were staying at my mother's condo, and Jessica or Rebekah stayed with Seth while we were away. We made an offer on a home in Kearns. It met all our requirements—a garage, four bedrooms, and two bathrooms, along with a storage room, family room, and laundry room. The kitchen was a little small, but I liked the high vaulted ceiling in the living room. The yard will need some work, but the price was right. We were excited to find a house, but underneath it all, my heart was aching with sadness for Seth.

AUGUST 5, 2005

Because Seth was becoming ill, we left at ten in the evening with Seth in the back seat of the car so we could get back to our home in California as soon as possible. We were doing fine until we got to Beaver, Utah, where our car began heating up.

We had to stop at three in the morning. Seth seemed very restless. I decided to take him to the emergency room of the small Beaver Hospital. They put him on oxygen, gave him fluids, and took his temperature, which was 103.3. The doctor said he had pneumonia in his lower left lung and sepsis. This was Seth's ticket to leave his stricken body, so we told them that we would not be doing any lifesaving treatments. They said he could stay for a little while but that they could not admit him under those conditions.

In the morning, we found a motel while Mike took the car to get fixed. It was nice for all of us to have a bed for a while. A while after we got there, Seth started vomiting. I called the doctor at the emergency room. He ordered some suppositories for nausea and fever. After administering those, Seth felt better and fell asleep for most of the day. We got the car going again and drove as quickly as possible, arriving in California at ten that night.

FAST SUNDAY, AUGUST 7, 2005

I attended our church testimony meeting this morning and asked the congregation to include Seth in their fasting and prayers that he might not suffer too long. On Monday Jeremy arrived on a plane. The hospice nurse and bath lady came to take care of Seth. When he was awake, he was pretty miserable because of mouth sores, and I was miserable trying to help him feel better.

MONDAY, AUGUST 8, 2005

Tonight we had a short family prayer in Seth's room around his bed. Seth was always one to remind us of this important tradition. Jeremy, Rob, Matt, Richard, Mike, and I were gathered there—our last prayer with Seth. We read a scripture about God as creator of the world. It comforted me to think that God is in charge of everything, including Seth, and will take care of all of us in this scary time.

TUESDAY, AUGUST 9, 2005

This morning was very difficult because Seth was so extremely agitated. He was sweating profusely and couldn't swallow. Even morphine did not seem to calm him down. I talked to a hospice nurse, and she told me that I could give him his muscle relaxant pills rectally. After I did that, he did finally go to sleep. Jeremy said we should try to keep him sedated. He had called Jessica, who is a nurse, and she said to give Seth enough morphine to keep him asleep and comfortable. Jeremy did this by putting morphine drops under Seth's tongue. With the morphine, it seemed as if Seth was in a coma. We were all very quiet and solemn around the house. I called Rebekah and told her that Seth might die tonight or tomorrow.

We took Seth's temperature—99 degrees without Tylenol. His blood pressure was 91/50, up from earlier. It almost seemed he might be getting better. Or was this the hypothermia that is part of late septic shock? We were trying to figure it out.

Seth's doctor, Dr. Sy, called and told me to be strong for the rest of the family and said that I was doing the right thing. It was very comforting to hear this from a doctor who had been so helpful with Seth. I told him we were using morphine very liberally and asked if that was okay. He said yes.

WEDNESDAY, AUGUST 10, 2005

We went to bed about midnight after giving Seth morphine, muscle relaxants, and antinausea medication. Jeremy was sleeping on a mattress in the hall next to Seth's open bedroom door. We could hear Seth's labored breathing. I set my alarm for 3:00 a.m. so I could check on him. Just before the alarm went off, Jeremy came in and said, "Seth has stopped breathing." We were shocked and a little scared. I started

306

crying and went in to see him. I hugged him and cried, "I love you, Sethy."

The whole family went into his bedroom. Seth was lying on his left side with his legs curled up and his back to us. I said, "We need to turn him over and straighten him out." We did so, washed him up, and put clean clothes on him. We closed his eyes and mouth the best we could and folded his hands at his waist. He felt cold. I put a blanket on him. He looked peaceful and pale. Each of us in the family took some time to be alone with him—me, Mike, Jeremy, Rob, Matt, and Rich.

Two hours later we called hospice. The chaplain came about six thirty, listened to Seth's heart, and called UCLA and the mortuary. UCLA is going to do an autopsy. While we were talking to the chaplain, Mike said that our faith gave us comfort in this difficult time. This caused some contention between him and a son, who didn't agree. We all said our goodbyes to Seth. Then the mortuary came and got him off the bed onto a stretcher, covered him up to his neck in a blanket, and took him in a van. Seth's long suffering was over!

Mike and I went to the mortuary to make funeral arrangements, choosing Seth's casket and flowers. The next couple of days we arranged for the funeral, the programs, and the obituary in the Antelope Valley Press and the Utah newspapers.

AUGUST 11, 2005

This morning a man and his wife knocked on our door. The man said he wanted to show his wife our house, as he had seen it the week before while we were in Utah. He had just driven by and seen the "For Sale by Owner" sign in the front yard. He said he wanted to buy our house—for $345,000. We were very surprised and pleased at their offer.

AUGUST 25, 2005

Three days after Seth's death, I had another episode of numbness on my left side. I went to Antelope Valley Hospital with Mike. They admitted me, did a carotid ultrasound, CT, and MRI and found that my right internal carotid artery was 100 percent blocked only a few months after my surgery to open it! I don't understand why my left carotid artery is just fine, however. I think it might have something to do with the radiation I had on my right side during cancer treatment.

The next day I felt better and spent hours reading through Seth's journal to prepare for the talk I would give at his funeral. The hospitalization was a blessing in disguise, I guess, to give me time I needed to write the talk. The doctor said they could not operate if the artery was 100 percent blocked, so they put me on Coumadin, a stronger blood thinner. I told the doctor I had to leave to attend my son's funeral. They said if I did, it would be AMA—against medical advice. But how could I miss my son's funeral? Anyway, I felt okay, so I left.

The funeral on August 16 went very well with almost all the family speaking. I read excerpts from Seth's journal showing his struggles, his joys, his faith in God, and his love for missionary work, the scriptures, and the Lord. Jessica and Rebekah sang the wonderful song "The Test" by Janice Kapp Perry. The song says:

Tell me friend, why are you blind? ...
Why must you die? ...
Didn't He say He sent us to be tested?
But didn't He say we could live with Him forevermore,
Well and whole, if we but patiently endure?
After the trials, we will be blessed.
But this life is a test! (Perry 1985)

This song truly reflected the trials Seth has gone through and his faith in his Heavenly Father. Rebekah wrote a wonderful poem about Seth that she read at his funeral. Portions are included here:

Stormy Blue

Stormy-blue eyes gaze intently for a falcon's wings piercing the sky.
Withal he taught us to love, how truly to listen,
Compassion and patience, a humble existence.
Farewell to Seth's spirit—such a bittersweet goodbye!
But we will think back on his love and those stormy-blue eyes.

We had a nice luncheon after the funeral. I was so surprised that my sisters and brother came from Utah and Arizona to attend the funeral. Such great love and support! Afterward, we went home and got ready to go to Utah for a second funeral and for Seth's burial next to his brothers Jonathan and Michael. The second funeral, held in the funeral home in Salt Lake City, was pretty much a repeat of the one in California, but it allowed our Utah and Idaho family members and friends to be there.

I did not shed as many tears at Seth's death as I had for Michael's. I think the tears for Seth had been spread out over ten years as we watched him slowly going downhill. His death was a blessing. His long, long suffering was over. It was somewhat difficult to even remember what Seth had been like when he was healthy. It had been such a long time. But we did remember. And we loved him and missed him—he was such a very vital part of our family!

After his burial in Salt Lake next to his brothers, we searched for the perfect tombstone for Seth. We decided on a plaque showing mountains, where he loved to hike, and pine trees with an eagle flying in the sky. The following scripture passage seemed perfect for Seth: "And they that wait upon the Lord shall fly up with wings as eagles ..." (Isaiah 40:31). The rest of the scripture says, "And shall run and not be weary and walk and not faint." Now Seth could fly with the eagles and run and walk! His blind eyes would be able to see!

SEPTEMBER 25, 2005
Since Seth's death, we have had a few experiences in the family where we have felt connected to Seth in the spirit world:

1. Rebekah said she saw a vision in her mind of Seth meeting Michael in the spirit world and the two of them giving each other a hug.
2. Robert woke up suddenly in the night at our house shortly after Seth's death. He said that he felt Seth's spirit come into their bedroom and lean over to comfort Matthew, who at that moment briefly awoke and talked in his sleep. Robert saw nothing but felt instinctively that Seth was there.
3. I was walking in our back acre, crying and talking to Seth, telling him how sorry I was he had to suffer so much. As the sun was setting, I felt as if Seth's spirit was big and everywhere, covering the whole sky! His influence was all around. He seemed happy, loving, and wise. He was so happy to be free! I talked to him and also prayed to the Heavenly Father. I felt peace afterward

as some ravens flew around and settled into our big trees for the night. It was fascinating to watch them, and it was as if Seth was saying, "It's okay, Mom. Don't worry. Just relax and watch these birds." Now I could experience why he loved bird-watching so much.

4. I took a drive into the desert and stopped the car in front of a Joshua tree, feeling sad about Seth's death. Suddenly, a whole flock of birds landed in the Joshua tree, seemingly saying to me, "It's okay." The birds that Seth loved so much seemed to carry his message of comfort to me.

5. I got a brain MRI to make sure I had not had a stroke. It was a strange experience where I had to lie still for so long with the loud, rhythmic thumping of the machine in my ears. I seemed to go into a sort of trance or dream. In the dream I saw both Seth and Michael. It was nice. They were dressed in white and were in the midst of other people in white on what seemed to be a bus. Michael was driving it. *How nice that he is driving now,* I thought, since he hadn't been able to get his driver's license before he died. Seth was in charge of the other people on the bus and was helping them. They were busy and doing important work. This comforted me a lot. I felt I had a glimpse of their heavenly duties.

6. Matt dreamed he saw Seth and was able to tell him all the things he wished he had said to him before he died. This comforted Matt's grieving heart.

7. When Richard started his job at the college working with someone who was disabled, he said he felt like he was helping Seth all over again, which made him feel happy and close to Seth.

8. One day Jessica was driving in the car with her daughter Ally, and Ally suddenly yelled out the window, "Sasquatch!" Jessica was very shocked. She remembered Seth had done exactly the same thing several times when riding in the car with her in years past. It had been sort of an inside joke with them. It seemed as if Seth was saying hello to Jessica. But, apparently, Ally did not know about this inside joke. She just did it.

9. At the funeral, Jeremy spoke of a sweet dream he'd had about Seth. They were riding in a car together in a beautiful green valley, and there was a sweet sadness that they would not have such sweet experiences together again.

10. Robert saw a pelican dive out of the sky into a pond as he drove up to see Seth just before his death. Robert had never seen such a thing before, and it reminded him of Seth's love for birds.

11. Seth's friend Darla, the caregiver whose home we'd visited, did not know that Seth had died. When I told her, she said that she had seen a white owl on her fence for several days looking at her. She'd known in her heart that Seth had passed away and that this was a sign for her.

12. I dreamed of Seth and my grandma Martindale. Grandma said, "I've been taking care of Seth." Seth gave me a hug and said, "I love you, Mom." It made me so happy.

My Sethy had a big, noble spirit filled with love, and he reached out to many people even after he passed away. Were these real experiences or imagined? I firmly believe that our loved ones who have died do reach out to us in dreams, in nature, and in thoughts and images in our minds to comfort and guide us if we are willing to believe these tender gifts from the spirit world.

> *The doctor said, "Be strong. You are doing the right thing." I felt that Seth was flying in the sky with the birds. He was so happy to be free of his body.*

41

Empty Nesters and Dementia

DECEMBER 15, 2005

Mike and I have moved to Kearns, Utah, a suburb of Salt Lake City just as I have felt impressed that we should do. We sold our house in California for a very good price, had lots of moving help from ward members and family, hired some people to clean out our garage and back acre, and took off in three cars to Utah. I drove one, Mike drove our old Idaho farm pickup truck, and my sister Wendy drove another car. Our household goods were transported by a moving truck in two PODS. We said goodbye to our boys Richard and Matthew. They have decided to stay in California, where they have lived for the last eight years, and to attend college in Los Angeles—Matt at UCLA and Richard at Santa Monica Community College. Robert has already been attending UC, San Diego.

On the drive to Utah, Mike began getting a painful case of shingles on his chest and back that was first noticeable in Las Vegas. Because of this, his overall fatigue, and the old truck he was driving, it took us four days to drive to Utah, a drive that normally could be made in one or two days. I was feeling very impatient over this! We had to get to Utah so we could get carpet installed before our furniture arrived!

After arriving in Salt Lake, we stayed at my mother's condo for a week while we painted our house and had carpet put in. Mike stayed in bed after getting some medication for the shingles virus and for the pain he was experiencing. My mother helped take care of him. When it came time for him to drive the truck to our new house, he got lost in the dark. When I found him, he was stopped in the truck writhing in pain from the shingles. The doctor had put him on very strong pain medication, but it still wasn't enough at times.

It has been great living here in Utah and being able to have my mother and Marshall over for dinner as well as my daughters, Jessica and Rebekah. Unfortunately, Jessica and Rob have divorced but live within blocks of each other to facilitate taking care of their girls. It has been a hard row to hoe for Jessica, but she has been amazingly strong in spite of her broken heart, and is working as a nurse at the University of Utah Neuropsychiatric Institute.

I love being able to invite my granddaughters, Ally and Leah, to have sleepovers at my house. They love our cats, although they are slightly allergic to them. We've gone to lots of family get-togethers with my sisters and brother. How great to live in the same city with them! This is where I need to be, surrounded by family, for I know Mike will have an early death and I will be forced to live alone.

I am feeling more softhearted and compassionate toward Mike with all his afflictions. I hope I can have the patience I need. It is coming. We've had some good times watching and going to movies, shopping to find furniture, and getting things set up in our house. I feel this time should be a little honeymoon time for us, if at all possible. This is the first time in about thirty-five years that we have lived without children. But, oh, how I miss my boys! I have gone from having four young adult sons living with us just six months ago to now having none of them with us. It is a huge adjustment.

JANUARY 15, 2006

We had a wonderful Christmastime with a family home evening, visiting Temple Square, seeing the *Joseph Smith* movie at the Legacy Theater, attending the Scott family Christmas party, and going to the Spaghetti Factory on New Year's Eve. A wonderful holiday season with family. Richard stayed a little after the New Year and got his wisdom teeth out in preparation for his mission. We had some good gospel discussions. He is my buddy, and I miss him when he is gone. We have gone through so much together.

I have felt kind of lost and sad lately now that Christmas is over and my sons have returned to California. It is very quiet around here, and Mike is usually in bed sleeping. But I am taking an independent study class from BYU, working toward my bachelor's degree in English. So I have something to keep myself busy.

JANUARY 29, 2006

I finally took Mike to a neurologist to see if he has some dementia and if there are treatments. His body and his brain have been through so much in the last four years, and I'm sure there has been some damage. Dr. Zimmerman did some mental testing on him, as I have been worried about his memory. He made a few mistakes, could not spell world backward, and couldn't write a sentence. He couldn't remember one out of three objects. Dr. Zimmerman told him not to drive and said, "Just to give him the benefit of doubt, we will start him on Aricept." Aricept is a medication for Alzheimer's. The doctor was very smooth and unobtrusive in telling us these things.

So now it has been determined by a doctor that Mike may have early or moderate Alzheimer's. We've never really talked about it since. I think he understands what went on. The diagnosis from the doctor gives me a feeling of not being all alone, and we are now getting some medical support for the disease. The Aricept package is very thorough at explaining the symptoms and time frame of the disease. If he does have it, he could have five more years until he might need to go to a nursing home. Is this what we have to look forward to? In the meantime, we'll just live each day the best we can.

Mike and I recently went to visit some friends. The wife's mother, who has Alzheimer's, was there too, and Mike was very nice to her because, he said, he is "now one of them." I need to help Mike have meaningful experiences, do genealogy and temple work, and write his history. Although he is ill, this could be a special time for us since neither of us is working.

We are living on Mike's half-salary pension and Social Security. The finances are definitely tight, especially with the huge amount of money we have to pay to continue our health insurance from California for us and our boys with immune deficiency. We do still have savings from the sale of the house, but we are using this money to help the boys with their college expenses.

I have also recently taken Mike to an ophthalmologist for cataracts, a cancer doctor, and an internist for diabetes and pain. I need to be more loving and patient with Mike. I have been doing a lot better, except I kind of lost it last night when I found him scratching his shingles sores again and making them bleed. His shingles could have healed two months ago, but it's getting worse and infected from scratching.

FEBRUARY 4, 2006

This morning around six thirty I woke up. It was dark. I felt on Mike's side of the bed, and he wasn't there. I remembered that perhaps two hours before he hadn't been there either. On getting up to look for him, I found him in the kitchen barefooted and shirtless. The bandage I had put around his chest to keep the dressing on his shingles was hanging with knots in it, the bloody gauze on the floor. There were three empty ice cream and Cool Whip containers on the counter. He was buttering a piece of homemade bread with a long, sharp butcher knife. He was putting huge amounts of butter on the bread and had butter on his fingers too. He had actually been standing there asleep part of the time. His fingers felt like ice. I took the bandage off over his head, led him into the bedroom with his bread and milk, and put his shirt back on. I tested his blood sugar—315. Too much sugar eaten in the middle of the night. I repeatedly asked him to take the diabetes pills, which I had put on his bedside table, and repeatedly said, "Lie down and get under the covers so you can get warm." Finally he did so.

Last night I reluctantly went to Deseret Industries (DI), a secondhand store, with him—reluctantly because he always spends too much money there. I waited for a long time in the car before he came out of the house. He eventually came out walking haltingly with his cane, carrying his briefcase loaded with books, size D batteries, and flashlights. It weighed about thirty pounds. He halted at the car door and then finally got in, squashing his briefcase beside him, unable to shut the door at first because he and the briefcase just would not fit.

"Why are you bringing all these books?" I asked.

He said, "Well, I might have some time to read at the library."

I said, "The library is closed. I told you that. I'm just going to drop off some videos at the drop box."

Then I drove to DI. I drove angrily around the parking lot, then found a parking space. I was so tired of all the strange things he does. I tried to calm myself down and asked God to please help me to do so and to please help me to find a book in DI that could help me in this difficult situation of dealing with Mike's dementia.

I went in and started looking at the books. It wasn't long before I found a book about caring for people with dementia! It seemed like an answer to my prayer, and I read several helpful ideas of things to keep in mind when caring for someone with memory loss. I am grateful to have found a book that can help me but also petrified about going through the possible course of events that such a diagnosis brings.

A few nights ago a nice salesman from Craftmatic beds came by. I asked Mike if he wanted to get out of bed and listen to the presentation since the man said he needed to speak to both of us. Mike said no. I went into the living room, and the salesman and I talked a little longer about family, church, and so on. We heard some rumbling from the bedroom closet through the wall. The man left. I went into the bedroom to find Mike fiddling with the deer-hunting rifle! He was thinking of using it if the salesman didn't leave. I was horrified by the idea. Mike said, "Well, I need to be able to defend our home if people won't leave." I need to get rid of or hide the guns.

FEBRUARY 10, 2006

I really miss my kids tonight! This is a sort of hell—living without your family. Heaven would not be heaven without my parents, my kids, and my husband. I worked on Seth's and Michael's scrapbooks because I found more items to put in them. I miss them! I don't think you ever get over it! I need to write the stories of their lives. Their lives would make great books or even movies.

MARCH 9, 2006

I really feel like I am going crazy! I don't know who to talk to—maybe an Alzheimer's support group would help me. At this moment, all is quiet. Mike is in the bathroom here at home. What am I so afraid of? The last two days have been very hard. If he would just act normal! It seems everything he does is sort of out of the boundaries of normal, but then maybe I'm judging him too harshly.

I dropped him off at Deseret Industries while I went to the library the other night. I thought we'd agreed that he would spend only about thirty dollars. When I picked him up when the store was closing, I found him with a cart full of books, dishes, clocks, and so on. He had two plastic tables in big boxes. None of this is stuff we need, at least not in my mind. I managed to take out twelve dollars' worth of church books that we already own. The eighty-five dollars he spent was not in our budget at all. I felt like I had hit a brick wall emotionally, like I was having a nervous breakdown. I was so mad. I spoke very little, but what I did say was accusing. I came home and lay on the bed. I felt like my life was over, like I couldn't go on. After a couple of hours, I started to get myself out of the feeling of frustration.

Last night Mike stayed up most of the night. Every hour or so I would ask him to come to bed. At two in the morning he was bringing stuff in from the car. At four he was eating. At six he was sitting up in the chair in the den sleeping. I finally persuaded him to come to bed. At eight o'clock he was up again eating three bananas and whipped cream—not great for his diabetes. He eats crazy. He talks crazy. He keeps mentioning how he can drive here or there, when the doctor has said he shouldn't, and it scares me to death. He talks about driving the truck back to California to pick up the rototiller we left behind. That old, scary truck is what caused me so much anguish on the way up from California. He talks about getting a job. Normal things, but he isn't normal. Am I crazy, or is he? Poor sweetie. What can he do with his life?

I try to find the old Mike in there whom I fell in love with long ago. There are occasional glimpses of him. I feel so ashamed that I haven't been able to love him as I should in all his trials. I pray and ask for help, for forgiveness. I guess I am only human, not the saint I want to be. How would Jesus treat him? Mike can't really help all his weirdness. I guess I just need to have breaks from him and do some things by myself so I'm not constantly trying to deal with his antics. I need to see the good and normal things he does and not always comment on the stupid things he does. (He did dishes the last two days, but I didn't express appreciation to him.) Maybe I need to take an antidepressant. I need to treat him as if I am a kind nurse, not an impatient wife.

Mike can't hear me half the time. I need to get him a hearing aid. He can't see well. I need to take him to get his cataracts fixed. But then he'll think he can drive, which he shouldn't do. So many responsibilities I have. His life is in my hands.

Last night in the temple, I asked the Lord how long Mike will live. I felt a question back: "How long do you want him to live?" Wow, is it up to me? It's true that I have begged the Lord before not to take him.

I guess I would say, as long as he can have some decent quality of life, after his sixty-second birthday, when he can get his Utah retirement. Not so long that he becomes completely senile and has to go into a nursing home. If we could just have some good times together and accomplish a few good things. That is my answer as to how long. Please, Lord, help us do these things. Help me to look past his aggravating behaviors. Help us to have a few more good experiences together. Help me to love him.

In spite of many frustrations, I do still love him. It is nice at times to lie in bed next to each other and hold hands and just feel the comfort of having him there with me. He understands my pain and appreciates my caring for him. At least he is still here. He is my husband.

MARCH 5, 2006

My granddaughters have been sleeping over sometimes, and we have good times watching movies and talking. Jessica just got engaged to a nice guy she has been dating named Tony! I am happy about this. I feel he is a good man and will treat her well and be a good step-father to her daughters.

Overall now, Mike seems to be more mentally alert now that he's been on Aricept (Alzheimer's medicine) for six weeks. Does that mean he does indeed have Alzheimer's? That is a scary thought, but for now things are a little better. We need to use the time we have to good advantage.

APRIL 13, 2006

After six months, Mike's shingles wounds have finally healed on his chest and back but with big scars. He finally listened to the doctor and stopped scratching them. However, he continues to have severe postherpetic pain in that area. It will likely stay with him for the rest of his life due to nerve damage from the shingles. This is a huge setback in his health and requires pain pills, which make him sleepy.

APRIL 30, 2006

Mike and I had a nice road trip to California for the week of Easter. We visited our church and friends in Littlerock, as well as our three boys and Maya in Los Angeles. We also drove to Mesa, Arizona, to see my sister Wendy and husband, Tom. On the trip, it was hard for me to carry all the heavy suitcases, but Mike couldn't do it. It snowed in Utah the day after we returned. That was hard to take after the balmy California weather.

Today Mike took two Dexedrine tablets for energy and went to church. Now he is talking on the phone to his ninety-six-year-old aunt, Lucille, in Texas about genealogy material that we want to borrow from her. He is really a wonderful person to do this. He has improved a lot on Aricept for Alzheimer's.

He has had the following doctor appointments this last week:

- *Dr. Harrison*—He says Mike is taking too much pain medicine. It will hurt his liver.
- *Dr. Zimmerman*—She says Mike has improved 50 percent on the IQ test on Aricept. He is more alert. However, he has tremors in his hands when he stretches out his arms. This is called asterixis and is a sign of hepatic encephalopathy, where the liver does not cleanse the blood sufficiently and poisons get into the brain.
- *Dr. Poku (cardiologist)*—He did a stress test on Mike's heart but had to stop because Mike's pulse was forty! He took Mike off of digoxin and Diovan HCT and increased his diuretics because his legs are very swollen due to his heart not pumping strongly enough. I have been so scared by all this!
- *Dr. Katzman*—Cataract removal went great! Mike now sees twenty-twenty in his right eye!

MAY 12, 2006

Today I am with Mike at urgent care. I have been scared stiff because Mike has been having a lot of tremors—very bad last night, a little better today. I fed him mostly carbohydrates last night because if his tremors are due to asterixis, he may need to have less protein.

Last night, I just felt that there were too many problems with his body. I couldn't diagnose and treat all of them by myself! He needs a home health or hospice nurse or needs to be in the hospital for a while to let the doctors figure it all out and get him stabilized.

MAY 25, 2006

I ended up taking Mike to the ER a week ago because he was practically comatose. He was admitted to the hospital for a few days. The doctors said that his comatose state was due to the hepatic encephalopathy—liver toxins affecting his brain, and that he needed a lot more lactulose. They gave him some four times a day, and he became more alert. Now we are adjusting to the new problem of diarrhea caused by the lactulose along with his fifteen other medications.

Taking care of Mike's physical and mental problems is very overwhelming. I burst out crying the other day when the mail came. It was the straw that broke the camel's back. I felt I couldn't handle one more bill or one more phone call to be made. I couldn't take on one more responsibility, no matter how tiny. Mike said to me, "Just go ahead and cry." So I did. He said, "I am so sorry you have to go through all of this. I know it is very hard." What a sweet thing to say! I feel better today and got a lot done on the yard, the kitchen, and the stack of papers, and I went to the library for computer time and to make copies of my BYU paper.

However, tonight I feel sad and nervous, as I have printed off a durable power of attorney, a power of attorney for health care, a living will, and papers for a family trust. The trust is in my name, because it seems obvious that Mike will die before I do. I am officially taking over all the financial and medical affairs of our marriage. I have actually been in charge of all this for quite a while, but now it is more official with legal documents. We'll put the house in my name with the trust as beneficiary. I hope I am doing the right thing. I am. It will be a relief to get it done.

JUNE 4, 2006

Life continues to be difficult as a caregiver. A couple of times this week I thought I was going to go insane! I ran away to the library. Today I talked with the bishop. I left a note for Mike before leaving. He was downstairs. I was gone about forty-five minutes and realized when I got back that he hadn't even known I was gone! Yeah! I cried and poured my heart out to the bishop. He said the congregation loved us and to hang in there. "I know it's hard," he said. He told me the young men and women of the church need service hours and could help. He didn't preach at all, just listened. It was nice. No great answers—just nice to talk to somebody, a built-in counselor set up by the Lord. Thank You!

An average day for me is like this: In the morning I check Mike's blood sugar, which is usually high from him eating in the night, and give him an insulin shot. I change the bandages on his legs. (When his legs swell, blisters form on the skin which break and become infected at times.). Then I give Mike his morning pills—glyburide, Namenda, Lasix, potassium, and cephalexin for his infected legs. I fix breakfast and serve it to him in bed. Then he takes Dexedrine or NoDoz to wake up.

Mike usually sleeps most of the day, and while he sleeps, I write checks, do bills, make phone calls, make doctor appointments, order his medication or mine, and go to the pharmacy, post office, library, bank, or grocery store. He wants to eat lots of apples with salt on them. It used to be tomatoes, peaches, yogurt, or sugar-free ice cream. He goes through phases of what he is craving. We don't eat lunch till five. Mike gets up for a few hours, and we go somewhere, like DI, the movies, the dollar store, or the library. I'm always afraid he will spend too much money or buy crazy things we don't need.

In the evening we have dinner at nine. I check his blood sugar, give him an insulin shot, bandage his legs, and give him his nighttime pills, about ten of them: Aricept (for Alzheimer's), cephalexin (for his infected legs), glyburide (for diabetes), digoxin and Diovan HCT (for congestive heart failure), Namenda (for Alzheimer's), warfarin (for the blood clot in his portal vein), and pain pills (for neuropathy and shingles pain). Then we might watch TV—BYUtv or news channels.

I have been getting the sprinkler system and swamp cooler fixed, putting grass seed down in spots, and mowing the front lawn. Mike mows the back lawn with the tractor mower. We went to Walmart last week, and Mike bought $132 worth of flowers! I was not happy about the money spent or the planting I would have to do. He also went into the garden area of Walmart where no one was working and turned on the hose. I found him watering the plants and getting water on the cement floor. I was so upset, but luckily, no one really saw this happen. Then he took a bucket, put a little water in it, and took "samples" off of several plants to take home for garden starts. I was mortified when we walked through checkout with the bucket, but the clerk didn't see what was inside. This is not normal behavior for an adult. I was upset that I would have to plant all the flowers, even though he promised me he would plant them. But he is not able to do it. A few days later, Jessica helped me plant the flowers, and they do look pretty. Before his illness, Mike used to plant flowers to beautify our yard.

JUNE 15, 2006

We flew to California again for Rich's and Robert's graduations—another hard trip. Robert graduated from the University of California, San Diego, with a bachelor's degree in applied mathematics. Richard got his associate degree from Santa Monica Community College. We went to the beach and to restaurants. We stayed with Jeremy one night and with Rich and Matt one night. Mike gave blessings to Matt for finals and to Richard for his mission preparation. He gives good blessings. We returned home leaving from the Los Angeles airport. Mike was in a wheelchair, and I had to wait for an hour for him to come out of the bathroom when we got to the Salt Lake airport.

JUNE 18, 2006

This has been a crazy week. Every day something strange happens. Mike cut his own hair yesterday—not good! We almost had to shave his head to even it out. (I should say that in past years he has been able to cut his own hair successfully.) Today he put mascara on his hair and eyebrows while I was gone to make them look better. He picked at the sores on his legs and made them bleed. He does so much self-destructive behavior. The picking and scratching goes on every day, so the sores won't heal. I put bandages and medicine on his legs, and sometimes we have to get antibiotics from the doctor because the sores become infected.

We had to take the computer and printer to Office Depot because Mike had put the ink cartridge in upside down and put the wrong CD-ROM in, so the printer didn't get hooked up to the computer. He bought a new laptop when I sent him in the store a few weeks ago to buy just a computer mouse! I was so angry—another assault on our budget.

Yesterday Mike accidently broke dishes in the kitchen, spilled juice, made messes, couldn't hold the bowl steady, and got ketchup all over his fingers when he ate french fries. He tried to write a note on the birthday card for Jessica, but it didn't make much sense. He couldn't really write a cohesive sentence. The dementia is making big inroads into our lives. I am losing the husband I used to know!

Oh, I finished my online English 292 class, Nineteenth-century English literature! I studied very hard and it was very enjoyable. I got an A in the class. My studies have helped my sanity.

JULY 24, 2006

Pioneer Day. Jessica, Tony, Ally, Leah, Rebekah, Mom, and Marshall came for a picnic in our backyard. We told pioneer stories of our ancestors who were in the Martin Handcart Company. Thomas Porritt and his wife, Margaret McCann Porritt were converted to the church in England. After the unexpected deaths of Thomas and a young daughter due to illness in England, Margaret and her three remaining children traveled from Ireland to England and across the ocean to the United States. Then began their arduous trek with handcarts across the Great Plains encountering early winter storms. After being rescued, they finally made it to the Salt Lake Valley in November 1856. I guess I shouldn't complain so much about my hardships.

JUNE 27, 2006

Today is Seth's birthday, the first since his death. I felt very sad and teary last night. Today we drove to Kinko's in the wind and rain. It was my task to copy lots of genealogy papers that we have received from Mike's great-aunt. I was tired and discouraged. Then I seemed to hear Seth's calming voice in my mind: "Calm down, Mom. This is very important information that we need in order to do our work here. You need to copy this genealogy. It is important for us. You can do it!" This gave me a lot of strength to spend the hour copying. A young lady in the Kinko's helped me a lot, and I was able to quickly copy hundreds of pages that contained many names we can later take to the temple. Mike came in with me and walked around a while but then went back to the car and slept.

I went to the Salt Lake Temple while Mike stayed home to rest. It was so good to be there. I had a strong impression from the Lord that I had promised in the pre-earth life to care for my disabled family members. Caring for them is supposed to be part of my mission on the earth. It is not an accident. This idea somehow makes things seem a little easier.

AUGUST 10, 2006

Seth died one year ago today—or last night at 3:00 a.m. He was such a great son.

Mike bought an adult tricycle today since he can't drive. He rode it around the bicycle store parking lot and enjoyed it. But riding it down the slanted sidewalk in front of our house is more problematic, and he has some difficulty controlling it when trying to turn. I hope it will work out for him, but I'm afraid it might not.

SEPTEMBER 3, 2006

Because finances are tight, I decided to see if I could get a job in the schools. I walked to the elementary school two blocks away and asked the principal if they had any teacher's aide jobs. The principal said, "Yes, we need a teacher's aide. I've been so worried about it. I've been praying all day, and you are an answer to my prayer! We needed you two weeks ago!" What could I say? I guess it was an answer to my prayer also. The job is in a severely intellectually disabled unit for kids ages five through eight, for six hours a day. I have a forty-minute lunch hour where I can go home and check on Mike and get lunch. It is perfect to be so close to home and to make an extra $1,000 a month. Mike is encouraging me take the job.

SEPTEMBER 13, 2006

It was dusk as Mike and I entered the small cemetery to place flowers on the three graves of our precious sons—Jonathan, Michael, and Seth. Today is Jonathan's birthday. He would have been thirty-seven years old today. I placed a vase of bright summer flowers on his grave marker and a flower each on Seth's and Michael's graves. "Help me to do what I should do with my life," I said to them. It seemed clear what I should do. I should not let their lives be in vain. I should tell their stories of love and faith. They are doing their work now in heavenly spheres, and I must do mine while I still have time. It all seems so simple and so clear.

I turned around toward the city, hearing the crickets sing against the silhouette of the tall trees surrounding the cemetery. A statue of Christ with his hands outstretched was silhouetted against the sunset. All was peaceful and beautiful. "Just think," my husband said. "Jonathan will be resurrected as a baby, and we will be able to raise him. Seth

324

and Michael will be ours again. We'll be able to see them married someday." *What absolute miracles those events will be,* I thought. *Miracles that I believe in. But how can it be possible?* I looked again at the statue of Christ. How joyous and peaceful I felt in that spot. Through Christ, all our fondest dreams will come true. These sons who have passed away will be ours again. The pain and sadness we have suffered as a result of their illnesses and deaths will seem as a distant memory. These boys are our "treasures in heaven, where neither moth nor rust doth corrupt and where thieves do not break through nor steal" (Matthew 6:20). They have fought the good fight and triumphed spiritually in their trials (see 2 Timothy 4:7).

NOVEMBER 14, 2006
4:45 a.m.

I just woke up to thunder outside. I was dreaming about meeting with an important doctor at a prestigious medical institution regarding Seth's autopsy. I felt almost as if it was Seth waking me up to tell me to be sure to make his autopsy results available to the many doctors I know in the field of immunology across the country. The autopsy showed that Seth died of pneumonia and hemophagocytosis, which is where white cells attack parts of the body. He had damage to many parts of his brain from a virus that destroys brain tissue. He was also found to be infected with cytomegalovirus (CMV). I will share this information with more doctors in hopes that his suffering and death may help other patients to avoid such illnesses, if possible.

10:00 p.m.

Mike and I celebrated our thirty-eighth wedding anniversary tonight. We went to eat at the Texas Roadhouse—very good food. We also went to see the movie *The Queen* about Queen Elizabeth. Pretty good time.

DECEMBER 2, 2006

Mike is in the intensive care unit at Jordan Valley Hospital after a GI bleed last night. We were at a movie, The Nativity Story, which we enjoyed very much. When the movie was over, Mike said he felt like he was going to vomit. But he didn't, so I said, "Let's try to go to the car and go home." After walking about ten feet, he said he couldn't do it, and he lay down on the carpet in the theater. *Oh dear, what should I do?* I thought. But I knew we would have to get an ambulance.

I used the theater phone to dial 911 and told the manager Mike was sick. The paramedics came and found that his blood pressure was 59/30—way too low! While we were watching him, he asked for a popcorn cup, and then he vomited into it. It was blood—a lot! Oh no, not again! "You've just won your way to the hospital," the paramedic said. They got him on a stretcher. He then seemed to almost lose consciousness. It scared me. He was obviously bleeding internally— probably from esophageal varices. They took him out of the theater to the ambulance and sped away. There was also a fire engine there. I followed them in the car. They were driving very fast with their lights flashing.

At the emergency room, doctors loaded Mike with fluids going full-bore in both arms under pressure. It seemed like we could lose him. He got two units of A-positive blood. I suggested to the doctor that he also give Mike vitamin K, as it had helped Seth stop his GI bleed. The doctor was very grateful and said he should have thought of that. (Unfortunately, I have had too much experience with GI bleeds in my family.) Mike's blood pressure was up and down all night, mostly down. They got him pretty stable at about five in the morning and took him up to the intensive care unit. I went in and watched him for a few minutes and then went out to my car to go home at about six o'clock, having been up for about twenty-three hours total. It was freezing outside. I had to scrape frost off the windshield and warm up the car before I could leave.

When I got home, I ate a little and slept for about three and a half hours, waking up around ten. I couldn't stand the thought of calling the hospital. I felt I couldn't deal with it all. I just wanted to crawl in a hole and cry. I pictured the Savior helping me, holding me, and it did give me some comfort. I read some scriptures, which indicated to me what a good man Mike is and assured me that he's not going to die right now. I need to repent of my sometimes unkind words. He doesn't deserve it. The Lord is kind and merciful to me in spite of my weaknesses.

Then I decided to call my daughters. I knew they would want to know. Jessica and Rebekah came over to comfort me for a couple of hours. We called the hospital, and they said that Mike had had an endoscopy and banding of three varices, or broken blood vessels in his esophagus. He had been combative during the procedure. They had also given him platelets because his platelet count was down to 10,000. His hematocrit, or red cell count, was about 25 percent—pretty low.

I got feeling better and went to see Mike at the hospital. He had passed a lot more blood from his bowels and was running a fever of 101.9 degrees. He received twelve units of blood overall while he was in the hospital. Mike definitely was not a happy camper. The nurses seemed pretty overwhelmed with his care, although they were so kind and nice—like I should be.

DECEMBER 15, 2006

Mike spent ten days in Jordan Valley Hospital. The heart doctor also came to see him because Mike's legs were very swollen from heart failure. Now Mike will have to have an endoscopy every two months to check on the large veins in his esophagus. If any need to be banded, that will be done, a procedure that is painful for about a week afterward. Mike has taken another step down in his health. It is very sad.

> ***Being a caregiver is difficult. Give yourself permission to take a break at times, and find someone you can talk to. Pray for strength.***

42

Family Scrambles

DECEMBER 2006

Good news! Our son Richard got his mission call to the New York North Mission—Mandarin speaking! He will be in New York City, Chinatown. I was jumping around when I heard it. Richard wanted to go on a foreign mission, but he must stay in the United States for his gamma globulin. New York's Chinatown is about as foreign as you can get in this country. I am so happy!

All our kids were here for Christmas. We had a fun party, including building a snow fort in the backyard, singing Christmas carols, having Christmas Eve dinner, making cookies, and watching a little film about Jesus. Christina, Matt's fiancée, was also here.

After Christmas, Richard went to the Jordan River Temple in preparation for his mission. He said that he felt the Spirit very strongly in the temple and that he knew he was doing the right thing.

FEBRUARY 18, 2007

On Valentine's Day I gave valentines to all my family, and we went to Sizzlers to eat with my daughter Rebekah and her husband. They are not getting along. He would like to leave the state but has to stay in Utah as ordered by a judge for several months for threatening to harm Rebekah. They will likely be getting a divorce. I feel great sorrow that Rebekah has been in an abusive marriage and had her heart broken by her husband. Rebekah asked Mike and me if Brian could live in our basement for a few months. He has a pipe-fitting job to go to, so I guess we will give him a chance. I think that is what Christ would do.

Snow is gone! Wonderful! I am enjoying a new job I got with Granite School District visiting different schools to help their special education teachers with their files. I like it quite well.

MARCH 2007

Rich left for his mission and to learn Mandarin in the MTC for twelve weeks. It's a big task and a difficult language. But I'm sure the Lord will bless him. He is such a good son. I mourn, however, for not having a better relationship with another son. But we have so little in common now, and he doesn't like me for my religious beliefs. I have to let him go, but it makes me cry.

MARCH 11, 2007

Marshall, my stepfather, my mom's second husband, died today after battling with pneumonia. He was a very good man with strong values that he strived to pass on to all of us. He will be missed.

MAY 19, 2007

The following is from a letter I wrote to Richard on his mission:

Hi, Elder Curzon,

Thanks for so many letters and pictures from you! I am going to the temple this morning. Dad is too weak to go, but I need to go and am looking forward to it. I did some academic testing on a sixth-grade boy yesterday in my job. He is only on a second-grade level intellectually and has a very hard time in school. He gets very frustrated and discouraged because of it. The teacher said his mother did meth when she was pregnant with him and that is why he is disabled. He told me he doesn't want to go stay with his mother, but he has to. It made me feel like crying. I felt so much love for him and wished I could take him home to a nice new place. It was kind of a spiritual experience for me that made me want to become a special education teacher. Uncle Richard came over two nights ago to fix my swamp cooler, which had leaking pipes. So that's fixed. Lots to do this next week to get ready for Jessica's wedding and the family coming from out of town. Wish you could be here!

Love you,
Mom

JUNE 3, 2007

Jessica married Tony last weekend in a lovely garden ceremony. She looked beautiful in her black flowered dress, and her daughters were cute in pink dresses. All our family was there (except our missionary), including Robert's and Matthew's fiancées. Tony will be a great addition to the family and a good father figure to Jessica's daughters. I tried to overlook the alcohol being served and tried to be loving and friendly to everyone I met. Use of alcohol is against the teachings of our church, so I am not used to being around it.

Today I fasted on how to help my family, and as I prayed, I pictured all of us sitting in a circle with our arms around each other, loving and respecting each other. What we drink or don't drink isn't so important. What is important is the love that we share.

JULY 15, 2007

I've been worried for a while about how to get the money we need for Matt and Christina's wedding coming up. While they were visiting here last week, their car, parked on the street, got hit by a drunk driver in the middle of the night. The car was totaled, and since we own it, we received a good amount of insurance money, which will help pay for the wedding, a blessing in disguise. (We let Matt and Christina use an extra car we have here.)

SUNDAY, AUGUST 5, 2007

This has been a sad and upsetting few days. I've had trouble putting up with Mike's poor memory and behavior. I think his Alzheimer's is getting worse. Every day in so many ways he is forgetful and acts strange. But the other day I was so upset. He rode with me in the car to run errands. Two hours later he took a package of melted ice cream bars, which he had brought with him and forgotten about, out of his briefcase. This has happened other times also. I drove to a gas station so he could throw it away. Instead, he ate it, dripping it on his clothes and hands. I went to get a wet towel in the bathroom, and I berated him for the whole thing. Then he went into the bathroom to clean up.

I was listening to Dr. Laura Schlessinger on the car radio. I actually called her on my cell phone to ask what I could do about living with someone with Alzheimer's, but I couldn't get through. Then I thought about what she would tell me if I did talk to her. She would probably say I need to realize that my husband can't help his behavior and that these happenings are part of his disease. I should treat him kindly and also take time out for myself to do things I enjoy. I am also sad because some extended family members are getting divorces. It all makes me so sad, and I wish I could fix it. But I can only pray.

I prayed and fasted this Sunday for a miracle to happen in our family—something that will shake things up. Dear Lord, please give me strength to go on. Mike is really a good man. I bore my testimony in church today and mentioned that I'm grateful for our temple marriage and for what a good man Mike has always been. I also told him so in the car after church and said I am sorry I nitpick at him all the time. I thought I better say this to him before he dies, while I still have a chance. He said he understands that caring for him is difficult for me and appreciates what I do for him. So sweet.

Richard is doing well on his mission in Chinatown. I'm grateful for that. I'm sure it is harder than he lets us know. I pray he will enjoy it and find success.

AUGUST 15, 2007
Mike and I drove up to Blackfoot, Idaho, to visit his brothers, Dick and Tim. While we were there, Mike became very enthusiastic about buying a pistol for me from a pawn shop, something that I did not want. He insisted that I needed to learn to shoot it for my protection and said that we could go shooting together. What a frightening idea! After purchasing it, he took the gun to Dick's house and was checking it out in the basement when it accidently went off. A bullet hit the cement wall and ricocheted in the basement. Dick and I were upstairs. We were horrified at what had happened and were glad Mike was not hurt. I asked Dick to please return the gun for us and to send us the money from it, which he did. I definitely see this incident as an example of poor judgment from the dementia that Mike is struggling with.

AUGUST 27, 2007
Mike and I just got back from Matthew and Christina's wedding in the Toronto Ontario Temple. As usual, it was very difficult packing for both of us, helping Mike get ready, and carrying the bags by myself.

After some airline delays, we finally made it to the beautiful temple, and the ceremony was wonderful.

The next day Christina's family held an elaborate reception at their church that lasted about five hours. Mike, however, could not endure that long and ended up lying down on a couch brought from the foyer for the last hour or two of the reception. There was dancing and food and speeches. It was a beautiful occasion.

Now we will be having another reception for Matt and Christina here in Salt Lake in a couple of days. I am in charge of it, and I have had so much to do for it—ordering the cake, the flowers, the decorations, and so on. It will be a nice affair. They will return to live in Los Angeles, where they are both applying to various medical schools around the country.

It is sad that Richard is missing these weddings. He is doing well on his mission, however. He successfully learned the Mandarin language and is able to use it to talk to people on the street. They have been pretty successful in having baptisms. He loves the Chinese people in his branch and has enjoyed his companions. He lives with three other missionaries in a third-floor apartment in the heart of Chinatown, New York City.

Robert has moved to Santa Cruz, California, and has acquired a good job with McGraw-Hill using his math degree. He will have good health insurance to pay for his IVIG. His fiancée, Stephanie, is going to school there, working on a doctorate in chemistry. Jeremy and Maya are in Southern California. My family is scattered! I'm glad Jessica and Rebekah still live in Salt Lake City, so we can see them more often.

OCTOBER 2007

I think I am learning to be more patient, and Mike has improved some in his unusual behavior since being on both Aricept and Namenda for Alzheimer's. I make sure we sit over to the side in Sunday school. He makes fewer rambling comments that way. We don't go shopping often at DI, so less money is wasted. Mike is also getting weaker as time goes on. We don't leave the house so often. I go to work and come home tired. We did visit several of our relatives in the past month in Salt Lake. Mike still does some unusual things, like putting too much food on his plate and not eating it, spreading too much butter on his bread and fingers, and dipping cookies in milk and making a mess. It is embarrassing, but oh well, that's Mike now.

We listened to the General Conference of the church on TV, and, as usual, it was very inspiring. "Wherefore, be of good cheer, for I the Lord am with you and will stand by you" (D & C 68:6). I felt the love of my Savior more than ever before.

NOVEMBER 4, 2007

Another hospitalization for Mike. We are at St. Mark's Hospital this time. Another call to 911 in the middle of the night. This is the fourth or fifth time we've done this in the past few years. Mike has no recollection of ten people crowding into our hall and bedroom from the fire department, the long fire truck outside, or the ambulance in the dark of the early morning. He doesn't remember his trying to get up to go to the bathroom, his shaky arms and legs, the inability to move his legs, the diarrhea on the floor, the fever, the ambulance ride, his two days of near-comatose state in the hospital, the huge amounts of watery diarrhea.

He finally "woke up" after two days of intravenous Zosyn and Flagyl to treat possible sepsis and possible *Clostridium difficile* infection in his bowels. Neither have been proven by lab tests—as usual. But I felt he was in grave danger, and the doctors agreed. Now he is almost back to his usual sick self, so he may go home today. Last night he was having a hard time breathing because of his big tummy swollen with fluid. All intravenous fluids were stopped, and he is on fluid restriction. Lasix was given, and he got rid of a large amount of the fluid buildup.

This all started when Mike was prescribed amoxicillin a week ago for a cough and then had an eye surgery on Tuesday morning to remove blood from the vitreous humor of his right eye (caused by diabetes). After surgery he went home and was fine, but that night he had nausea, fever, and severe diarrhea. These issues could have been from the antibiotics, food, or a virus. Who knows? He was obviously dehydrated, considering the profuse amounts of intravenous fluids he has been given. But after a few days it was too much fluid, which is what we are dealing with now. We are waiting for the doctor to send him home today, hopefully.

The doctor said he can't go home because of the ascites—the fluid in his abdomen that causes his breathing difficulty. This condition is usually caused by cirrhosis, but his liver function looks good, so the doctor says it is probably due to a blood clot in his portal vein, or portal vein thrombosis. This can be caused by many things, such as infection, cirrhosis, liver cancer, chronic heart failure, and so on. They will continue to give him Lasix to get rid of more fluid. The doctor is reluctant to do a paracentesis—taking out fluid with a syringe and needle—because there is some danger to the procedure and the fluid usually returns quickly.

NOVEMBER 14, 2007
Mike recovered and returned home. Today is our thirty-ninth wedding anniversary. We went out to eat at Applebee's and then saw the *Martian Child* movie. Will this be our last anniversary?

I have been praying fervently as to what to do about my job and career. My feeling is that I should stay with my present job with Granite School District. I am also teaching some piano lessons and working on my bachelor's degree, taking algebra.

DECEMBER 25, 2007 (RICHARD'S JOURNAL)
It's Christmas! I baptized a young man, Zheng Xiao Ban Jieme this last Sunday. We had a couple of other tender mercies too. The older Brother Zeng invited us to eat over at his apartment the other day after correlation meeting. He is actually a really good cook.

I am writing in the subway now. We just went up to the Buetikofers' right now and had breakfast and called our families. I talked to my family for about fifty minutes. It was weird but nice. Last week Brother Zeng took me and Elder Lee out to eat at a dim sum restaurant. We had lots of good food, including cow tripe (it's a separate category) and duck tongue (strange, but I ate it). Brother Zeng is great!

JANUARY 13, 2008
I went to the Jordan River Temple and had a very spiritual time. I learned and felt much. I feel as if I've been to heaven and have been given strength to triumph in my life. I need to use my time well. No murmuring—just faith.

Richard has been transferred on his mission to work in Harlem, New York, for a few months. This gives him a break from Chinatown but is very different. He is enjoying it, however, and having some success in his missionary work. He writes:

So, I am here in Harlem right now. The Harlem apartment is huge compared to Chinatown. Today was amazing. Besides the fact that our investigator Fabflia is having drug problems, she wants to be baptized soon. (She is the one that is black, from Africa, has a thick British accent, and lives in a rehabilitation center.) We tracted some really rich apartments, got kicked out, and then went to the Baldwins (a member family). We decided to tract in their apartment building. Her kids came with us. We found some great people in that building. One was named Dana, who invited us into her home (a first for me). Her son had died a few months earlier, and the Baldwins helped set up everything for his funeral. We taught her about the church, and she said she is willing to be baptized. The Spirit was there very strongly. She is the most prepared person I have seen.

FEBRUARY 2, 2008

Our prophet President Gordon B. Hinckley has died, and today we watched his funeral on TV with my mom, brother, and sisters. It was great to be with my family during this very inspiring time. President Hinckley always gave us so much hope. He said, "It isn't as bad as you sometimes think it is. It all works out. Don't worry. I say that to myself every morning. If you do your best, it will all work out. Put your trust in God, and move forward with faith and confidence in the future. The Lord will not forsake us" (Hinckley 2000). I have this quote on my bedroom door and look at it often. We loved him so much!

MARCH 30, 2008

I am at St. Mark's Hospital again—another day in the saga of Mike's lingering illness. We came to the emergency room after Dr. Harrison called to let them know that Mike has possible subacute peritonitis, an infection of the fluid accumulated in his belly due to liver disease. The doctor did a paracentesis, taking out some of the abdominal fluid, which was found to be infected. Now Mike is on intravenous antibiotics and doing a little better. My family visited and have been offering to do things for me.

Mike's blood pressure is low. He is on oxygen when lying down but not when sitting or walking. His heart rate is low, and he has diarrhea and a cough. They are having him walk up and down the halls and giving him daily bed baths. He is on a low-protein, low-sugar diet.

I went to the Jordan River Temple last week with great fear and sadness, fearing that Mike is dying. I felt that he may indeed die this year, but that it is okay. God will comfort me. I felt a blanket of love and peace as I entered the temple, as if I were coming home to my Father. Everything will be okay if Mike leaves. But also, miracles are possible if we have faith. Some friends and family are encouraging him to drink energy drinks and nutritious juices. There is a silver lining of hope in my heart but mostly fears of liver failure, coma, and death. It helps to have him here in the hospital, where there is support for his care.

Robert's wedding is in six days in California! I just hope we can get out of here and make the trip okay.

APRIL 5, 2008

Today is my birthday (sixty-one years old). Mike turned sixty-four yesterday. Today was also Robert and Stephanie's wedding in the Santa Cruz Catholic Church. It was a very nice wedding with prayers and songs. Afterward they had a nice reception with dancing. Mike and I danced one slow dance, something we haven't done forever. I didn't think he would be able to keep his balance, but he did. He said we needed to dance "for posterity's sake." Pictures were taken, and I'm sure they will be precious to us.

The trip flying to San Francisco was difficult as always. Mike was in bed at the motel most of the time except for the most important occasions of the weekend. At least he was reasonably well. I am so glad he has lived to see the three weddings of our children this past year and to see Richard go on his mission.

"It isn't as bad as you sometimes think ... Don't worry ...
Put your trust in God and move forward."
—Gordon B. Hinckley

43

An End and a Beginning

I have fasted today for greater understanding and compassion toward Mike, whose health and mind continue to decline. Today we were getting ready for church. We were going to our own church and then to a baby blessing for Brittany, our niece. Mike asked me several times where we were going, what day it was, and if we had any family activities going on today—after I had told him several times what was happening today. He could not remember. He seemed to have difficulty walking—so slow and hard to get going. He used his walker today at church because two weeks ago he fell in the chapel when we were walking in. I have been on the verge of tears, especially in church, from embarrassment.

I'm beginning to wonder if he should continue to go out in public. At church, at McDonald's, at family dinners, he often sits and sleeps. He acts like he doesn't know where he should be walking to. I get embarrassed. In testimony meeting today at church Mike got up to walk to the podium. Everybody was anxious as he haltingly walked up to the front. We were all afraid he would fall. But he didn't, and he gave a beautiful testimony (although a little long). It was eloquent and powerful. I felt this was an answer to my prayer for more understanding and compassion—*this is the real Mike!* The person I deal with on a daily basis is not the real Mike—just his body and brain ravaged by disease.

JUNE 24, 2008
Mike has been in hospitals—the University of Utah and St. Mark's—for eleven days for *Clostridium difficile* diarrhea. (I've read that some people never get over this kind of diarrhea and can die from it.) He has been treated with Flagyl and vancomycin. He has also had some chest

337

pain, heart failure, and kidney issues. He is home again now but still very weak. I cannot leave him.

I prayed and asked for guidance and read Nehemiah 9 about the Lord's tender mercies, guidance, and care to the Israelites for forty years in the wilderness. He will give us tender, loving care also, as he has in the past. "The Lord will give strength to his people. The Lord will bless his people with peace" (Psalm 29:11). "Let your hearts be comforted … for all flesh is in my hands. Be still and know that I am God" (D & C 101:16). "Care not for the life of the body, but care for the life of the soul" (D & C 101:7). "Thy days are known and shall not be numbered less" (D & C 122:9).

JULY 20, 2008

I am sitting in a hospital room again—the University of Utah Medical Center. Mike was making progress at home, but then came the terrible diarrhea again and the fever. I told him we had to go to the emergency room, and I drove him there on Tuesday night. When we got there, he said, "Colleen, where are you taking me—to the hospital? I told you I wouldn't go to the ER!" I said, "Mike, I told you that was where we were going." He wouldn't get out of the car, and I was too tired to fight with him, so I made the half-hour drive back home, and we had a difficult night.

In the morning, I knew Mike needed to go to the emergency room. I didn't want to call 911 again! But he said he wasn't going. I went in the kitchen and cried, threw dishes, and yelled, "I don't know what to do! I don't know what to do!" I was in despair. I needed help and support but didn't want to call anyone. He also had a liver doctor appointment that morning. We tried to get ready, but then he had to go to the bathroom. I called the physician's assistant and talked to her on the phone. She said she always worries if someone has a fever and diarrhea and said we should go to the ER. I was tearful as I talked to her. She asked if I had someone I could call, because I didn't sound good and it sounded like I needed support.

I did call Sister Woodward to tell her not to bring us a meal, because we were going to the hospital. She asked if she could come and help me get him into the car. I didn't answer. I told her not to worry about it and ended the phone call.

I then said to Mike, "Do you want me to call our home teacher or Jessica to persuade you to go to the emergency room, or do you want me to call an ambulance, or will you just get in the car and let me drive you? Are you deciding to die? Or do you want to go to the hospital and get well?" Poor sweetie. He was so tired of going to the hospital. He said he would get in the car. So we started getting ready to go with great difficulty. I didn't know if he was strong enough to walk to the car with the walker. Luckily, Sister Woodward showed up at my door. She came in, I cried on her shoulder, and she gave me a hug. It was what I needed. She is strong. She helped Mike get up and out to the car. What a blessing that was to me!

Right now we have this hospital room to ourselves. Mike has been getting IV antibiotics and is beginning to recover again. BYUtv is playing inspiring words and music, and all is peaceful. Mike is lying in his hospital bed talking in his sleep. He really is so weak. He can no longer get out of bed by himself. Before we came here, he could.

I heard such an inspiring message on the radio as I drove to the hospital. A pioneer widow mother, crossing the plains, was asked by the Spirit, "Do you want to obtain the highest kingdom of heaven?"

She answered, "Yes, what lack I yet?"

"Send your son with the Mormon Battalion. Sacrifice is required to reach heaven."

The commentator then went on to say, *"Where there is no cross, there is no crown"* (Penn 1842). No cross, no crown? Tears ran down my cheeks. That's what all this suffering and these trials are about! It was a comforting and inspiring moment for me.

SUNDAY, AUGUST 17, 2008

Mike was in the hospital again the first part of August for shortness of breath. An echocardiogram found that his heart ejection fraction is less than 20 percent. Normal is 60 percent. So his heart is worse than it has ever been, and he has lost more energy. The cardiologists at the University of Utah were very discouraging as they talked to me and my son Matt. They said they could not help Mike. They said to stop taking him to hospitals and to take him home, make him comfortable, and put him on hospice. I have been reluctant to follow their advice. I don't want to give up. If Mike could just get a little stronger and live

339

until Richard comes home from his mission next March! That is our goal, but I don't know if we can make it. If he can just hold on a little longer. If we can just have a little miracle to keep him going.

I have agonized over whether to take Mike home or have him go to a care center where he can get some physical therapy to help him get stronger. At the temple I felt that man should not be alone and that I should follow the counsel of my husband. Mike wants to go home, so we will give it a try. If it doesn't work out, he can go to a care center later.

So we brought him home with the help of Matthew and Robert, who were visiting from California. They got the big desk out of the den, and we had a hospital bed placed in there, so Mike can be lifted up and down. We have a bedside commode, because Mike is too weak to walk the fifteen feet to the bathroom.

Barbara and Russ brought dinner, and Russ is stressing the importance of a nutritious liquid diet to help Mike get well. "Though I walk through the valley of the shadow of death, I will fear no evil, for thou art with me" (Psalm 23:4). I am in tears as I read this scripture, but these are words of comfort to me.

TUESDAY, AUGUST 19, 2008

I was feeling very discouraged, and I asked Mike if he could say a prayer to strengthen us. I trust his communication with the Lord. In his weakness, he said a very eloquent prayer and prayed that I could realize the joy I will have after much tribulation. I asked, "What joy could I possibly have after all this?" Then in my mind's eye I saw a big grassy hill. I struggled to climb it, and at the top were those I had lost—Jonathan, Michael, and Seth—and also Mike. It was a very joyous reunion after all the tribulation. Mike is a spiritually powerful, good man. He prayed that he would have healing, strength to endure, and comfort through Jesus Christ.

In the midst of all this turmoil with Mike, I have climbed some other "cliffs." I have completed intermediate algebra, college algebra, and statistics classes at BYU Salt Lake Center during the last six months. It has been very hard but fulfilling. The Lord has helped me tremendously with encouragement and courage and even some answers during tests.

I got a C−, C+, and C, respectively, putting forth my best effort. Math is not my talent, but at least I passed.

AUGUST 22, 2008

I called Richard's mission president in New York to let him know how very sick Mike is and asked whether Richard might be able to come home for a short time if his dad gets much worse. Under the special circumstances of our family, he gave permission, and I also got his okay to call Richard (Elder Curzon) personally. Richard and I read scriptures together over the phone and decided that he should stay if possible and continue to work in his mission going forward with courage and faith. He should "keep all the commandments ... and [the Lord] will cause the heavens to shake for [his] good ... and Zion shall rejoice upon the hills and flourish" (D & C 35:24). This section also spoke of having faith, which meant to me to have faith to do things that will improve Mike's health. We decided that if his health got really bad, Richard would come home for a short visit. I feel very relieved to have talked to him about this so that there are no huge surprises for him.

I am supposed to go back to work tomorrow for the new school year, working three days a week. Jessica, Rebekah, and a home health nurse have agreed to each come one day each week to help Mike.

AUGUST 27, 2008

Jeremy's wife, Maya, had a beautiful baby girl by C-section in California. The baby is little—five pounds, six ounces, and seventeen inches long—because she was three weeks early. Jeremy is ecstatically happy. Her name is Mala, an Indian name. She has lots of black hair. Mike talked to Jeremy on the phone and congratulated him. We are so happy about this, our third grandchild and third granddaughter.

Barb and Russ came over to witness Mike signing his will and trust papers while he lay in his hospital bed. We had a notary public come to verify this. We must be prepared in all things, as we don't know how long we have. Barb and Russ also brought my mother with them and dinner for us. My sister Paula did the same another day. It's wonderful to have family to help.

SEPTEMBER 1, 2008

I took Mike to see Dr. Harrison, his primary care doctor, who felt it would be worth a try for Mike to go to a care center and have physical therapy for a while. It might help. These last few weeks have been very difficult for me caring for Mike at home—feeding him, cleaning him up, losing sleep, crying, and feeling like I'm going crazy. He has been having diarrhea again, so Dr. Harrison said to just keep him on vancomycin pills to hold the diarrhea at bay.

Dr. Harrison wrote an order for Mike to go to the Garden Terrance Care Center, a beautiful place on the other side of town. Mike doesn't want to go, but as I pray and agonize about this decision, I feel that I need to take care of myself as well as have Mike taken care of. I just can't do it anymore. It makes me feel very sad.

SEPTEMBER 15, 2008

Now Mike is a patient in the Garden Terrace Care Center. Their bus came to our house and took Mike away in his wheelchair. It was a sad day. Will he ever come home again? I followed the bus in the car and helped to get him set up in his room. I don't like the fact that he has been placed in the Alzheimer's unit with locked doors. They said they didn't have room in other areas of the care center. The room is beautiful, however, with flowing dark-pink drapes and grass and trees outside the window. When he came here, Mike said to me, "I will die here."

This has been a very painful decision for me to make, but the hope is that he will be able to get stronger and come home again so he can at least walk to the bathroom in our house. Medicare will pay for ninety days in a facility like this as long as he has been an inpatient in a hospital within the past thirty days, which he was.

Mike's oxygen saturation goes up and down between 93 percent and 85 percent. It should definitely be above 90 percent. This is with the oxygen machine turned up to three and a half to four liters. His blood pressure is 90/60. The nurse is very concerned. She said to me, "We don't know how aggressive you want to be with his care."

I said, "Well, we don't want him to be taken to the hospital. We've decided that we don't want him to be intubated or resuscitated if he passes away."

The nurse said, "He is a very sick man."

I answered, "I know he is a very sick man, but we're just going to try to keep him going for a few more months." She looked at me like I was crazy.

A few weeks ago when Mike was in the hospital, the doctor explained that doing CPR on someone seldom brings them back to a good state of health, unlike is portrayed on TV. He recommended we not resuscitate Mike, especially considering all the health problems he has.

Money has been tight with me not being paid this summer, so I sold Mike's three-wheel bike for $250 and the Ford Taurus for $900.

I need to finish my schooling by April 2009, or all my work will be for naught. So I just signed up for an independent study class, Writing in the Social Sciences. I work on writing my papers while I am here visiting Mike. I usually stay from ten in the morning till ten at night, and then I go home and type my papers on the computer. For Mike, even twelve hours doesn't seem long enough for me to visit. He has been here a week. Mike is getting physical therapy every day. Today he asked me when he is going home. It scared me. He can't go home for several more weeks, until he gains more strength.

SUNDAY, SEPTEMBER 21, 2008

I am at the care center. I went outside to walk around the grounds, feeling discouraged and burnt out. I asked for courage and strength to go on. When I came back in the room, a talk on BYUtv by Jeffrey R. Holland gave me some courage:

> However long and hard the road—if the burden is too heavy— stick with it … When days are difficult and problems seem unending, I plead with you to stay in the harness and keep pulling … Be not weary in well-doing. "Succor the weak, lift up the hands that hang down, strengthen the feeble knees" (D & C 81:5) (Holland 1983).

That is the job I have to do right now! My prayer for strength has been answered. How good God is to always continue to answer me. Ask, and it shall be given.

Jessica brought her husband Tony and my granddaughters, Ally and Leah, over to visit Mike. They enjoyed coming here, watching TV, eating sandwiches they had brought, going down the hall to see some little finches in a cage, and playing games. They found this to be an adventurous place. Mike was glad to see them but also slept a lot when they were here.

Mike is doing somewhat better. He doesn't need oxygen as much now, and he is walking better. He has been up to the bathroom by himself three times today, and he is feeding himself more. Why am I discouraged? Just that it is such slow progression. I am tired of the caretaking. (I still do quite a bit to help him here.) But look at this nice place and all the help I am getting! I need to be grateful.

SEPTEMBER 28, 2008

I came home from the care center feeling discouraged about Mike being sick for so long. I lay down on my bed with my whole soul crying out to God, "Why is this happening?" As soon as I asked the question, I felt a sense of great peace, and it was as if I could see through an eternal window as to why. I knew it was for the growth of both Mike and me, although I was looking "through a glass darkly" (1 Corinthians 13:12). I knew that God in His omniscience and wisdom had great purposes for us in this trial we were passing through. I felt as if my head was lying on my Heavenly Father's lap and He was stroking my hair lovingly. Just as I pet my cat and the cat doesn't realize my world and my thoughts and purposes, I do not understand God's reasons. "Now," I thought, "I know that man is nothing, which thing I never had supposed" (Moses 1:10, P of GP). I knew that Heavenly Father's purposes are great and beyond my comprehension but that I am safe in His arms. This was an amazing and comforting experience for me.

SUNDAY, OCTOBER 5, 2008

Mike is doing pretty well. I took him on an outing to Rich and Lee Ann's house for the usual after-conference family dinner. The men of the family lifted him up the steps in his wheelchair. *Maybe this will be the last time my family sees him*, I thought.

OCTOBER 7, 2008

Mike continues to do physical therapy, walking up and down the halls with his walker. He also does occupational and speech/memory therapy with two sweet young ladies. We told them about his life and family, and they talk to him about these things. Mike has tried to share the gospel at times. One of the nurse's aides told me that he had discussed the gospel with her, and as a result she is returning to the temple again. She thought he was a wonderful man. Yes, he is.

Mike has been getting up for therapy, but the rest of the time he is usually in bed, while most of the other patients are up for meals and daily activities. He is so tired, and he doesn't eat much unless I feed him. I have been upset with the food he is being served here because it has too much salt in it. I am surprised they do not provide low-salt meals like a hospital does to protect his heart. But, I have been bringing low-salt food from home for him as much as I can. He has been losing weight except for his belly, which is huge from the fluid (ascites) caused by liver failure.

Being in the Alzheimer's unit is an interesting experience. Occasionally other patients come into the room. One patient walked in and said, "I came to fix your car." I told him we didn't have a car for him to fix, and he was upset with me. The nurse came to take him out. The staff has put a big stop sign on the door to prevent such visits from Alzheimer's patients.

FRIDAY, OCTOBER 10, 2008

Today Mike was up walking with the physical therapist, but then he said he didn't feel well and would have to stop. "Can't you just walk a little farther?" I asked. He said, "Colleen, what did I say? I don't feel well." So he went back to bed. Later in the day I noticed that his catheter had no urine in it. He has had a catheter for a month, since he's not able to make it to the bathroom. We tried to have him drink lots of fluids today, but to no avail. He was still not producing urine. Obviously, his kidneys have shut down.

SATURDAY, OCTOBER 11, 2008

When I arrived this morning, I was determined to take Mike to the hospital. Perhaps they could put him on dialysis. When I told him this, he said, "No, *it's time*." A little later, I said, "Come on, Mike—we need to take you to the hospital." Again he said no. I talked to the care center doctor on the phone. She said that if he is not making urine, he could die within hours or within two days. What? I was in shock!

Could this really be the time he is going to die? I knew it was coming, but now? Could this really be happening? Today?

I prayed to know if this was the time for him to die. All the scriptures I randomly turned to were about people dying. Again, I prayed silently in my heart, *Heavenly Father, is it really time?* I walked over to the window and looked out on the grass, where I saw an amazing sight. There was a dead mourning dove on the grass with its mate walking around it. The light-brown speckled bird was walking near its dead mate, touching it, and then flying around close by. I could not believe it. Was this a sign, a symbol of Mike and me—he dead and me scurrying around him in sorrow and panic? (Later, I was told that mourning doves mate for life.) I guess it really is time for Mike to leave this world.

What should I do now? I need to call all the kids. I hate to tell them the sad news, but at least there may be time for them to say goodbye. I called our daughters, Jessica and Rebekah, who live in town. (They have been so good to come and stay with Mike and take care of him in every possible way while I was working.) After they arrived, we called all the boys. We first called Robert, who lives in California, and Matthew, in the Caribbean. Both boys had visited Mike in August. We called Jeremy in California, whose wife had the new baby, and learned that Maya's family was visiting from India. The boys all talked to Mike on the phone and said their goodbyes to him, as they were unable to come at this time. I called Richard's mission president, and they arranged for Richard to fly home on Monday.

SUNDAY OCTOBER 12, 2008
Still no urine is being made. Mike has had many visitors—old friends, ward members, and his brother and niece and nephew from Idaho. Also, my brother, sisters, and other family members who live in Salt Lake City stopped in.

MONDAY, OCTOBER 13, 2008
Mike was very weak and tired. With great difficulty and earnestness he said to all the children, grandchildren, and relatives that were visiting, "Remember, remember God loves you. I love you! Remember your grandpa. Follow the prophet. Remember, my children, Jesus Christ is the way. God loves you! Come back to God." Some people in the

room may have ignored his words, taking them as the ravings of a sick old man, but I knew he was expressing his heartfelt feelings as strongly as he could in his last hours.

During this time, we tried not to feed Mike or give him liquids too much, because if his body wasn't getting rid of wastes, eating and drinking would just make things worse. But he did say once, "I want food!" I got some cake from the kitchen for him to eat, which he was very happy about. He showed some enthusiasm when some visitors came. Our missionary son, Richard, flew in from New York City and was able to spend some time with Mike while he was still able to visit with people.

TUESDAY, OCTOBER 14, 2008
This was a very hard day. Mike woke up moaning with every breath. He seemed to be in pain and also short of breath. The doctor had said he may go into a coma or become short of breath—maybe from all the poisons and fluid in his abdomen. This moaning and pain went on for hours. My daughters and I gave him sips of juice, put ChapStick on him, and asked for more pain medication for him—and then more. It wasn't working. He was still in pain. We were all crying. It was agonizing to watch.

The nurse suggested I sign him up for hospice, since only hospice is authorized to give the kind and level of pain medication that he required. So at five o'clock we called hospice, and they came over and signed him up after having me fill out many forms and answer many questions. The switch to hospice had to be done as quickly as possible.

The hospice nurse gave him subcutaneous Dilaudid, along with lorazepam and Haldol for anxiety. Because of his profuse sweating, the aide gave him a bed bath, hurting him even more. He was in pain everywhere! I couldn't even touch his arm without him moaning. I ran outside and walked around the building, praying, *Please, please take him tonight! He is suffering too much! Please, please!* I called my brother, Richard, and asked him to come and give Mike a blessing.

When my brother arrived, my son Elder Richard Curzon anointed Mike, and my brother pronounced the blessing as my daughters, grand-daughters, and son-in-law looked on. In the blessing, given by the priesthood in the name of Jesus Christ, my brother said, "The Lord loves you, Mike. Your work on earth is completed. You have served the Lord. You have kept your covenants. Your next step in life will be glorious and wonderful, and you will have a wonderful reunion with Jonathan, Seth, Michael, and your parents. You will go in the Lord's time." After the blessing, Mike got more medication and finally fell asleep. The difference was night and day.

The hospice nurse gave me an intravenous push to administer pain medication to Mike every fifteen minutes subcutaneously, and she administered a pain shot every two hours. I slept in the adjoining bed in his room. After sleeping for a while, I woke up as the nurse gave him a shot at two thirty in the morning. He was breathing loudly. I fell back asleep, woke again at three thirty, and looked over at Mike. This time there was silence. He had stopped breathing.

His back was to me. I went around the bed to look at him. His eyes were closed. I was surprised, as I had expected him to live through the night or longer. No one but me knew he had passed away. I walked out into the hall and saw the nurse with her head on her desk sleeping. I did not want to wake her. I wanted to be alone with Mike during this peaceful time. I caressed him and expressed my love to him as we had some time alone. In my mind's eye, I pictured him leaving his body and rising into glorious light, and I felt that his mother was there to greet him.

I called Jessica, Rebekah, and Richard and asked them to drive over to see their dad. I walked into the outer hall and looked out the glass doors. A full moon was in the dark sky, and there were Christmas lights on in the hallway. (Why in October, I don't know.) They were beautiful. It seemed like a magical, peaceful, beautiful time that Mike's spirit had left his body. The kids arrived and had their time alone with their dad. All was calm. I lay down beside Mike's body for a while and hugged him, feeling his warm tummy, his hair, his ears, his chest, his hands. My husband—how I loved him. I didn't want to lose him!

As the sun began to rise, the nurse became aware that Mike had died. The doctor and the mortuary were called. The doctor wrote on the death certificate that Mike had died of kidney failure, liver failure, and heart failure. He died about three o'clock on October 15, 2008, a beautiful autumn night. On my calendar I drew a heart and wrote, "Mike died." Could it be true?

OCTOBER 18, 2008

Today was Mike's funeral. My mind is muddled. The last three days have been a whirlwind of activity. Matt and Robert arrived as well as Jeremy, Maya, and their new baby, Mala. We went to the funeral home to choose the program, flowers, casket, and so on. My stomach was hurting, and I didn't feel like the man working at the mortuary was very sympathetic to our loss. Just another funeral to him. Not to me. We were able to help dress Mike in his temple clothes. Our kids spent a few private moments with their dad. Last night we had a viewing and displayed some of Mike's paintings and memorabilia. Afterward, I persuaded the boys to play their guitars and sing Dream Theater's "The Spirit Carries On," about life after death. I believe Mike heard that song sung by his sons, a song that he had heard many times in our home.

Today, after the family prayer given by my son Matthew, before the casket was closed, I kissed and hugged Mike. I wanted so much to get in the casket with him, in the beautiful white silk, and just be there with him forever. I don't want to be alone. I feel like I have been torn in half.

The funeral was very nice. Robert performed a song he'd written entitled "Fields of Gray." It was concerning Mike's words to Robert the last time Robert saw him in the hospital as he was approaching death. Robert played acoustic guitar and sang, and Rebekah accompanied on her cello. Other members of the family sang along. The song sounded beautiful and went like this:

> Waking up to your smile makes me think back to when you were a child.
> But that was so long ago. Now, pray for me, my son.
> I have no time left. This life has taken all I have.
> Now I go towards the distant door, far away across the fields of gray. But the fields turn to green as I remember all I've felt and seen. As I see my family, I know together forever we will be.
> Through my heart flows the love and peace for those I leave behind.
> Remember, remember, my family dear, God's pure love divine.

All my kids participated in some way during the funeral with prayers, songs, talks, or readings. Our missionary, Elder Richard Curzon, talked about Mike's life. Jeremy read the obituary, and Jessica and Rebekah talked about memories of their dad. Russ, my brother-in-law, gave a good talk, titled "Turn up the Mike" about the hours they had spent discussing the gospel together. Mike's brother and sister had traveled from Idaho and Washington to give the prayers.

At the cemetery, all six of our living children were the pallbearers. The military soldiers played taps, folded the flag, and gave it to me. Mike was proud of his ten years of service in the US Army as a medic and as a chaplain. He was buried near Jonathan, Michael, and Seth on a gorgeous, warm fall day with beautiful golden leaves on the trees.

After the funeral the Relief Society women served a meal in the cultural hall of the church. Then we had more time to admire and hold little Mala, the newest member of our family. She was so tiny and sweet with her long black hair. We all love her very much. How kind of heaven to send her to us just when our daddy had to leave us. I'm sure Mike can also see his granddaughter. An end and a beginning—"The Lord gave and the Lord hath taken away. Blessed be the name of the Lord" (Job 1:21).

> *"However long and hard the road—if the burden is*
> *too heavy—stick with it ... When days are difficult*
> *and problems seem unending ... keep pulling."*
> *—Jeffrey R. Holland*

44

Widowhood—Who Am I?

OCTOBER 2008

I am sixty-one years old—too young to be a widow! Mike was too young to die at sixty-four. Am I really a widow? A terrible word. A word for women in their eighties, not for me. A widow at church in her eighties invited me to sit with her. I don't want to be in the over-eighty club. I don't want to be in the widows' club!

When I fill out a form at the doctor's office and it asks for marital status, how can I put "single"? I've been married for almost forty years. How can I be single? These are difficult adjustments. Where do I belong? Nowhere. In thinking about Mike's death and searching scriptures and books, I've written down the following smattering of random quotes and thoughts that have been healing to my heart:

- "She hath done what she could" (Mark 14:8). I did all I could to care for and save Mike.
- Mosiah (in the Book of Mormon) died at age sixty-three, so it's okay to die in your sixties (Mosiah 29:46).
- Mike's recorded blessing from a patriarch says, "In the afternoon of life, no unkind hand will ever minister unto you. You will be surrounded by friends and loved ones for as long as you live." That promise certainly did come true.
- At the cemetery I told Mike I was sorry I was unkind to him at times. I seemed to feel him put his arm around me and say, "Oh, I love you, Colleen."
- The book *The Journey Beyond Life: Volume 1* describes the spirit world. It says, "There are flowers of numerous colors … The recurring theme is that no one seems anxious to leave … Everybody appear[s] perfectly happy" (Sorenson and Willmore 1992, 119). I hope Mike is happy in the spirit world.

351

OCTOBER 23, 2008

I felt so empty after work today. I didn't want to go home. I went to the bank, put some money in, went to UPS to fax claims to life insurance companies, went to Harmons and bought a few groceries, and came home to an empty house. I find as I am driving that I suddenly discover I am on the wrong road and am not paying attention. My thoughts and heart are just so far away, thinking of Mike and of all that went on with his death. I feel like I'm not in reality. If I can just have a meaningful schedule after I get home and keep busy, maybe I can stay away from the sadness and loneliness.

I check the phone messages and email. Nothing there. No one contacting me to let me know I am special to them. Okay, I'll watch the news—no, too conflicting. *Little House on the Prairie*—that will make me feel better. I think about disparaging remarks I made to Mike at times. How could I have been so cruel? I didn't have enough love and compassion. I've failed. Will he ever forgive me?

The phone rings. I want it to be Mike. I wish I could talk to him or go to a movie with him. It is my brother-in-law, Tom. He will visit me tonight. Later I realize that, because of Christ, Mike will forgive me, and I will forgive him. We do love each other and always will, no matter what, no matter how we may have hurt each other through the years. Our eternal marriage will last because of the atonement of Christ.

Tom came to visit me. We talked about Mike's death and my experiences and feelings about it and also about Mike's illnesses and the good health he now has in the spirit world. Tom said, "Mike is happy. I know it. And he forgives you and appreciates so much how you took care of him and were there for him. And your eternal marriage is intact. You will be able to reclaim your children into the celestial kingdom because of your marriage." (His words were especially meaningful as he and my sister have divorced.)

"Is he happy?" I asked.

"I'm sure of it," he said.

I needed to hear these words tonight. I feel that Mike was speaking to me through Tom. Tom talked about the happiness and the blessings that Mike and I have to look forward to after our many tribulations.

I looked at Mike's funeral program again. It has scriptures printed on the back that meant a lot to him. One of Mike's favorite scriptures was 1 Corinthians 2:9: "Eye hath not seen, nor ear heard, neither have entered into the heart of man, the things which God hath prepared for them that love him." I'm sure Mike is in a more glorious place than I can imagine.

OCTOBER 27, 2008

I went to the temple with my sister Barbara and thought a lot about Mike. Mike and I suffered so much this last year, but we were given warnings of his coming death. Things couldn't keep going on as they were. Yes, it was time for him to go. Things will be okay. And in the eternities, they will be glorious.

I felt in the temple as if someone spoke to me from the other side and said, "You have five years to write your book and to finish the genealogy work." Does that mean I will die in five years? Or what? I don't know. But this work is urgent to do in the time I have given to me.

Barbara reminded me of *Emma Smith: My Story*, a movie we saw together about Joseph Smith and his wife, Emma. They went through so many trials for their faith and lost several children to death. They loved each other, and they suffered. And finally it was time for Joseph to die. In some ways, I feel like it is also my story. I went home and watched the DVD again, and I asked Mike to please come and watch it with me. I felt that he did and that he was very close by.

SATURDAY, OCTOBER 30, 2008

I went trick-or-treating with my daughters and granddaughters around their neighborhood, crunching the fallen leaves on the sidewalk. Rebekah was dressed as Sarah Palin and talked like her all night, and we laughed a lot. It was fun and strange to do this, which I could not do when Mike was so ill.

I have spent a lot of hours filling out forms and making phone calls about Mike's life insurance, which we have been paying toward for years. I also got his Social Security and pension money put in my name. It is sad to tell people my husband has died. Suddenly, however, I am richer than I have ever been in my life. It scares me. I don't know what to do with so much money. A couple of salesmen have tried to sell me annuities. I don't feel good about it. I do know I want to share this fortune as much as I can with my children and some to my siblings if they need it.

SUNDAY, OCTOBER 31, 2008

My sisters and brother have been so good to me. Nearly every Sunday, someone invites me to their home for dinner. They are trying to ease my pain of being a widow. It was definitely right to move to Utah close to my family and not stay in California as we had considered doing.

NOVEMBER 8, 2008

While driving in the car, I heard a wonderful new song on the radio. I found myself crying and sobbing. The song was "To Where You Are" by Josh Groban. It reminds me of my husband and the longing I feel to be with him. I bought the CD, took it home, and played the song over and over again in the darkness with tears running down my cheeks. It speaks of a person longing for their loved one who has passed on and feeling that their loved one is so near. Many times listening to love songs on the car radio, I think of Mike and the love we shared, and I shed more tears. I remember all we have gone through and wish he was still here, healthy and strong.

NOVEMBER 14, 2008

Today is Mike's and my fortieth wedding anniversary, and I went to the Salt Lake Mormon temple to feel close to Mike. It was there that we were married. I had a little vision in my mind of Mike dressed in white with power, health, and priesthood, looking over our family and being able to save them. The celestial room was so beautiful with its intricate carvings and meticulous workmanship—forty years of it— for the glory of God.

The altar in the sealing room where we were married reminded me that we had knelt there and pledged our love to each other and to God. Beautiful memories. I weep as I think of it. Looking at the reflections in the parallel mirrors, I pledged to Mike that I will do nothing major with my life unless it is okay with him.

After the temple I met my daughters, granddaughters, sister, and mom at Mike's grave. I put flowers on his grave and stuck a little

"Happy Anniversary!" sign in the ground. Then we went to a Chinese restaurant and later to my mother's condo. We talked about special experiences. I read a poem I'd written and played some music I'd composed on the piano for Mike.

My sister Barbara shared with us her experiences of the three babies she miscarried due to lupus. One was five months along. Shortly before she lost this baby, she had a dream where she saw our Grandpa Scott. He had so much love for her and said, "Everything will be okay." It was two days later that the ultrasound showed that her baby was dead. It was such a sad story but inspiring.

It was so good to get together and share our unique family memories and the love we have for each other.

DECEMBER 1, 2008
I went ice-skating with my grandchildren Ally and Leah at the Utah Olympic Oval for a special children's night. It was fun. Now I am free to spend more time with them doing what they like to do.

DECEMBER 30, 2009
I had all my children in town for Christmas except for my missionary, Richard. It was fun and hectic. We had a nice family home evening on Christmas Eve. I had prepared copies of many pictures from Mike's life for the kids along with a short autobiography he had written. We watched the family video of Mike and Michael in Denver. Rebekah and her boyfriend, Josh, made a spaghetti dinner for us. My mother was also here and shared some poems she had written about Christmas and gave the family prayer. On Christmas Day many of us exchanged books—our favorite gift to give.

The Friday after Christmas, we bundled up and drove in several cars to St. George, Utah. We stayed in the Hilton Inn, a very nice place. It is nice to have the money to pay for this for the family. The next day we visited a dinosaur museum and then went to Zion Canyon and climbed over some snow-covered trails. It was beautiful but cold. Jeremy carried baby Mala all bundled up in her yellow snowsuit. Later we went swimming at the hotel and saw *Sleepless in Seattle* on TV. On the way home we stopped at the St. George Temple and ate at In-N-Out Burger.

For Ally's birthday, shortly after Christmas, we went to Leah's piano recital and then to Chuck-A-Rama to eat. Many fun times since Mike has gone, but I still feel so sad and empty inside. I especially miss him when I go to bed and he is not sleeping next to me. I can't reach over to touch him. That is a very sad thing, so I bought a big stuffed tiger to hug. It helps a little bit.

JANUARY 9, 2009

I went to the temple tonight, Friday night. It was very crowded. So many couples and me by myself. I cried quietly, tears streaming down my face, remembering our lives together, me and Mike. I thought about what Mike would say to me now. He would say, "I love you. Be strong and don't be afraid." The Savior would say, "Be diligent and faithful in keeping the commandments of God and I will encircle thee in the arms of my love. Behold, I am Jesus Christ" (D & C 6:21). He would also say, "Thou shalt not remember the reproach of thy widowhood any more. For thy maker, thy husband, the Lord of Hosts is his name. For the Lord hath called thee as a woman forsaken and grieved in spirit … with everlasting kindness I will have mercy on thee" (3 Nephi 22:4–8, B of M, emphasis added). The Lord is so gracious and kind to me. I love these soothing scriptures I read while in the temple.

JANUARY 12, 2009

Michael Bryan, an old friend of Mike's, called me today from Idaho. He said he felt it was the right time to call. It was very nice to talk to him, as he is a spiritual person. He told of seeing his mother-in-law in a dream after she died. I told him of when Russ saw my dad after his appendectomy. Spirits are there! At times, they can communicate with us. Michael Bryan said, "I have one message for you—keep your chin up!" Maybe that was really a message from Mike!

JANUARY 24, 2009

I have been missing Mike so much. I even typed his name into the computer to see if the internet had anything about him or if, in some magic way, I could communicate with him. His obituary came up, as well as some information about our buying the home in Salem. I typed in "coping with widowhood" and read some posts by several widows.

I also ordered a couple of books about widowhood and the spirit world to help me adjust to this difficult time of my life.

Tonight I went to my mom's house to watch some old videos from our trip to Israel. Mike was in the film several times. He looked so healthy and alive. It was good to see him again. I desperately wish I could have a dream about Mike and see him again as a spirit being. I pray for this often. There is nothing as devastating as losing a mate. Mike was my other half, and now I do not feel complete.

In church today, I thought about how it really was the Lord's will that Mike die at this time. I should try not to fight His will in my mind but accept it more. If it was His will for Mike to go, then it is His will for me to be alone for a while. There must be a purpose for it and important things I should be doing with this time I have been given as a single woman. I know I need to do the genealogy work that is in the big box Mike got from his aunt Lucille. It scares me, though. I do not know how to do it with the modern computerized methods.

FEBRUARY 3, 2009

I went to stake temple night tonight. In the celestial room I sat down and immediately felt a great sense of peace and calm. Mike's spirit and mine connected with unity and love. No words, just love and peace. I also seemed to see Seth and Michael coming in the room to surprise me, in somewhat of a jovial mood. I cried wholeheartedly, though quietly, as I walked out to the car in the crisp night air to go home.

As I walked across the crunchy frozen grass, I felt like I was back in the dreary world. I drove to Wendy's and bought a small chocolate milkshake and sat in the car at eleven o'clock at night listening to classical music. There was no hurry to go home—no one to go home to. I realized I had not really taken even one full day to allow myself to grieve the loss of my husband as I should. I always have other things on my mind, like school, work, finances, kids, Christmas, and so on. Although those things distract me, I need to take more time for myself. Tomorrow I could take a day off. I went to sleep thinking of Mike and prayed I could dream of him in the night.

FEBRUARY 4, 2009

I awoke about eight thirty this morning and realized that finally I had received the dream I wanted—seeing Mike face-to-face and talking with him! In the dream I was working at a large school with no ceilings—like in a large, dark cloud with partitions of rooms. (This school was similar to a school where Mike had worked with severely handicapped children.) I was working with small handicapped children. There were many children. I fed a hungry boy some bread, and he was very happy about it. Later, I fell asleep in a bed in the school, and when I woke up there, Mike was sitting in a chair at the foot of my bed watching over me, as if I were in a hospital. He had on his dark-blue shirt and his horn-rimmed glasses. He appeared to be in his thirties, looking healthy and young. I was pleasantly surprised to see him. He had been watching over me in my sleep. (Now I was the one in the bed, and he was taking care of me.)

Mike didn't say anything to me. Finally I asked him, "What is it like in the spirit world? Is it wonderful?" He said, "Well, you'll just have to be patient." Somehow I sensed that he wanted our family to read from the important writings of the apostle Paul in the New Testament. (Paul talks a lot about the Lord's help in tribulation.) I felt that Mike had been very busy and that was why I hadn't seen him before this time.

It was kind of a strange dream, but it has lots of meaning to it. I was wondering yesterday if I should work as a teacher in special education. From this dream, I feel the answer is yes. Now Mike is the strong one, and he is watching over me.

APRIL 2, 2009

I had another dream. This morning I dreamed that Mike and Seth were at first very sick. We were in a big complex that had a carnival atmosphere, but it had a room for sick people. I was gone for a while, and when I came back, I totally expected that Mike would have died. But to my surprise, I saw him walking down the hall, talking and giving orders (in a good way) to other people. He was totally healthy and in charge of something going on—a leader with 100 percent vitality. I was so surprised and so happy! Seth was also walking around and was okay. So I know that Mike and Seth are alive in the spirit world and are engaged in a good cause.

Although I am lonely living without them, I do have a lot of freedom as a widow living alone. I don't have to hurry home after work (but I usually do anyway, just out of habit). A couple of times I have gone out to eat by myself, and I even went to a movie by myself once. It's okay but not ideal. I have also gone with a girlfriend or a sister. Mostly, I am becoming used to being a single person.

The hardest thing is figuring out what to do when something breaks in the house. Lately, I've been wiring and nailing the wooden fence around the backyard to keep it from falling down. Men in the ward help me fix things, or I call a repairman. My next-door neighbor or ward members often clean the snow off my sidewalk with a snowblower, but I have found some joy in doing some shoveling on my own. Luckily, I can still do so. It gives me a feeling of strength and independence.

Losing my other half, my husband, was very difficult. But many small miracles helped to heal my broken heart.

45

I Can Fly

APRIL 30, 2009

I have had many wonderful experiences in the past couple of weeks. Richard was released from his mission, and I paid for myself and my two daughters, Jessica and Rebekah, to fly to New York City to pick him up from his mission. We spent a few days touring New York. It was wonderful! We saw Chinatown and met some of the missionaries and church members there, as well as visiting church members in Harlem. We went to Central Park, the Metropolitan Museum of Art, and St. Paul's Chapel, across from Ground Zero. We traveled on many subways and saw Times Square and a couple of Broadway plays. We were amazed as we watched Richard speaking Mandarin to people on the street in Chinatown. Richard and I attended a session at the Manhattan Temple—so quiet and beautiful amid the bustle of the city. It was a great experience for all of us.

Shortly after we returned, I graduated with my bachelor's degree from BYU! What an achievement that was for me after taking one class at a time the past couple of years to finish. As I was walking with my cap and gown, I felt Mike close beside me. I felt he was aware of this special moment and was proud of me. My sisters and children came to my graduation.

My sisters gave me a beautiful gift for graduation—a silver-and-glass music box that plays the song "I Believe I Can Fly" by R. Kelly. The words portray my feelings and opportunities at this stage of my life. After caring for my children and husband for forty years, I now have the "opportunity" of lots of free time. After helping Mike obtain three college degrees, I now have been able to get my bachelor's degree. I now have the chance to have a career and work in education, as my patriarchal blessing says I should do. I now have time to do

Mike's genealogy with no encumbrances. If I look at it in the proper way, this time alone is a great blessing to me, and so I should try to see the bright side of it and be grateful, instead of always looking at it in a negative light. I have so many blessings right now! I need to take advantage of this opportunity to fulfill my life's mission and fly!

Two days after my graduation, we had Richard's homecoming talk in church and a family get-together afterward at our house. Richard gave a beautiful talk and testimony and talked about the love of God, which he has experienced. All my children were here. It was great to have everyone together again.

MAY 2009

I have bought a nice newer car, a Ford Taurus with low mileage, with my insurance money. It is very dependable. I've been able to give some life insurance money to each of my children at this time for remodeling, publishing a book, and pursuing education. Money from Mike has blessed our family greatly. He suffered and died in order for us to have so many material blessings now. I have to wonder if he decided in the pre-earth life that he would be willing to die that we might be so blessed. I don't know, but I honor and love him for his sacrifice.

AUGUST 2009

I look back on a very busy summer. My son Richard spent the summer at home after attending spring term at BYU. He was a big help to me in battling loneliness and also in doing some projects on the house. We have done a lot of dejunking in the house and garage. Rich built a greenhouse in the backyard and planted a garden. I had some remodeling done on the house. New siding was put on the exterior, the bathroom was remodeled, and the exterior doors and kitchen sink were replaced. It's beautiful.

Richard has put in a lot of effort trying to decide where to go to school in the fall—BYU, the University of Utah, or a California school? So we flew to Santa Cruz to see Robert and to visit the University of California, Davis campus. Richard also participated in the choir at the BYU Stadium of Fire Fourth of July celebration, and I took Jessica and her family to see it. We later went to the Salt Lake Arts Festival for Jessica's birthday.

I drove my mother and Richard to Pocatello, Idaho, for the Marler family reunion, and we visited my husband's family and saw his mother's old farm. It was very nostalgic. Another time I went to Red Butte Garden with Jessica and her girls and had a Curzon girls' sleepover. I attended the celebration of my dad's ninetieth birthday anniversary at my brother's house. Richard and Robert flew to the National Institutes of Health near Washington, DC. A busy, busy summer running all over the country!

A very overwhelming thing happened to me this summer. I was called by the stake presidency to serve as a church-service missionary for twelve hours a week at the Family History Library downtown across from Temple Square. This is my opportunity to learn how to do the genealogy work that Mike left for me. It is a great blessing. I have worried about how I can fit this service in with my working and going to school, but I have felt I need to put the Lord's work first in my life and make it happen. I will work there Friday evenings and Saturday days. Mike has his mission, and I have mine.

I feel like I am healing from Mike's death almost a year ago. I don't feel quite so sad and empty. But I still feel very married to him and miss him and think about him often. I read a scripture lately that I felt was written to me from Mike:

> Without ceasing I have remembrance of thee in my prayers night and day, greatly desiring to see thee, mindful of thy tears, that I may be filled with joy. When I call to remembrance the unfeigned faith that is in thee . . . wherefore I put thee in remembrance that thou stir up the gift of God that is in thee by the putting on of my hands. For God hath not given us the spirit of fear; but of power, and of love, and of a sound mind (2 Timothy 1:3–7).

Richard and I both were unsure as to what we would be doing in the fall. After applying for many jobs, I decided to give up my job as an eligibility specialist to work in the classroom directly with special education students. I was hired as an aide in a unit of severely handicapped kindergarten children. I had to humble myself and realize that if I "do it unto one of the least of these, my brethren, [I] have done it unto [Him]" (Matthew 25:40). These intellectually disabled young children are celestial beings in broken bodies. Richard decided to accept his admission to attend Brigham Young University in Provo, Utah. I'm very happy he will be only sixty miles away and will be able to socialize with some of the people he met on his New York mission who also attend BYU.

SEPTEMBER 4, 2009

Each day this week I got up at six o'clock to be in the Joseph Smith Memorial Building in downtown Salt Lake City for genealogy training by seven forty-five. Then, in the afternoon, I went to my teacher's aide job at Truman Elementary in West Valley. A pretty exhausting schedule. The mission is inspiring and challenging as I am training in the computer program for family history.

Thursday night is my night to take dinner to my mother's condo across town. All my siblings and I are taking turns cooking her dinner because it seems that she is now unable to cook a meal on her own. Some of the grown-up granddaughters are coming during the day to make lunch for her and to do some housework. It is a major family team effort to make sure she is taken care of and able to stay in her own home.

OCTOBER 15, 2009

Today is the one-year anniversary of Mike's death. I decided to be sad. I got some videos that were about loved ones dying, such as My Life, ate chocolate, and cried. I'm not sure if it was the best decision, but sometimes I just want to revel in sadness. However, I don't let it last too long.

OCTOBER 29, 2009

This month I decided to use my UEA (Utah Education Association) break from school to fly to St. Maarten, an island in the Caribbean, to visit my son Matt and his wife, Christina. They are both attending the American University of the Caribbean medical school there. It was an awesome experience. I even got to attend medical school classes with them for one day and sit among the students in the lecture room. I knew what they were talking about to a large extent because of all the medical things my family has been through. Matt and I went snorkeling. We all went out to dinner in the dark, warm night. It was wonderful.

When I got back to Salt Lake City, I immediately started to attend my first class of a master's degree program in special education at the University of Phoenix. I go to school Monday nights from 6:00 p.m. to 10:00 p.m. The rest of the week, I read, study, and write papers in the evenings to prepare for the next week's class. It is kind of expensive, but again, I can afford it at this time. I am in a class with about twenty other students. We work in teams to accomplish some of the assignments. I really am enjoying it.

NOVEMBER 12, 2009

It seems every night I am dreaming of being with my kids when they were growing up and Mike being there as a healthy, helpful husband—just living regular life. Then I wake up and I am alone. It seems impossible that I no longer live with any of my family.

Last night I dreamed we were all staying in this fabulous hotel on a tropical island surrounded by gorgeous turquoise water and white sand. Mike was taking care of baby Richard. I think Mike is saying to me that he would have liked to do this with the family. So I think I will take the family on a beach vacation after Christmas! The Caribbean is too far, but we could go to San Diego, which is much closer. I'm excited!

NOVEMBER 26, 2009

We all went to Grandma's condo for a big Thanksgiving dinner. Jessica and Rebekah were there. My sister Wendy and I played an old piano duet. Rich played the guitar, and Ally and Leah played the piano for us. Friday night I took dinner to my mom, and we were all together again and watched a video in the living room. Nice family times. But when it was all over and we all went back to our own homes, I felt so alone again. Another day of work and school tomorrow. Where is my hubby? I miss Mike.

JANUARY 7, 2010

We just got back from our fabulous family vacation to San Diego with all my children, their spouses (except Christina), and my grandchildren. The weather was in the sixties, great for swimming in the heated hotel pool with my granddaughters. We also went to SeaWorld and the San Diego Zoo. We had a nice warm day at the beach, where my artistic kids sculpted a big sea turtle in the sand. It was a work of art! We had a lot of fun, and it was definitely worth the money spent. Thanks for your idea, Mike! Wish you had been there.

JANUARY 8, 2010

Christmas is over, the San Diego trip is over, and school and work have started again. I have felt out of place, out of sorts this week, starting a bland, boring new year. The other night I broke down in tears, missing Mike, feeling a little strange and uncomfortable with my new class at the University of Phoenix. I prayed for God to help me. It has been a struggle to not watch TV too much when I get home from work and to instead do the housework and my homework.

I went through my keepsakes drawer today, seeing many letters and cards from Mike and the kids from over the years. Some made me happy, some sad. I shed some tears and wondered at my life, my character, and my faults over the years.

MARCH 2010

Rebekah has decided that she needs a new start in life and has decided to move from Salt Lake City where she has been working as a CNA at the U of U Medical Center to Santa Cruz, California, where Robert lives. I am sad to see her go, anxious that all will go well for her, and hopeful that she can find a job that she will enjoy in the medical field. I hope she will find the happiness that she is looking for.

APRIL 4, 2010

It is Mike's birthday and Easter. I am happy because, in spite of the snow here, underneath it flowers are blooming, grass is turning green, and spring is coming—a time of new life. It reminds me of the resurrection. I will see Michael, Jonathan, Seth, Mike, and my dad in their healthy bodies again.

MAY 2, 2010

Three weeks ago I came down with a very painful case of shingles. The first week was just bad pain in my left side and lower rib cage area. I thought I had a kidney stone or tumor, but when the skin lesions came out a week later, I knew it was shingles (which Mike had also suffered from very badly). It has put a dark cloud of pain over my days—or a cloud of pain pills' effects. I took a pain pill four times a day, but even then I had a hard time getting to sleep. I immediately got antiviral medicine, and the lesions did not spread any more. I also got some large lidocaine patches from the doctor to place over the painful areas.

At church, I was surrounded by kind, loving people. One sister came up to me and said, "How are things at your house? I've been thinking about you all week." I told her things were bad because of my pain. She gave me her love, and three other sisters were especially concerned about me also. I knew that the Savior's arms were encircling me with His love through these sisters.

MONDAY, MAY 3, 2010

I started having some shingles pain again, so the doctor gave me three days of low-dose steroids, which I told him I had read about on the internet. I also took some antibiotics I had for kidney infection, because it felt like I did have one. These medicines relieved my symptoms, and my pain was gone for good. What a relief! I am always proactive in researching about physical problems that I or my family members have. I don't put all my trust in doctors. I simply can't after all I've been through.

Yesterday I took Mom to my sister Paula's house for a delicious turkey dinner, and then we went to see a nice assisted living place. Later we stopped by the graveyard to visit the graves of my family. My little white-haired mom said, "No one should have so many graves!" But that is my life and my cross to bear. I was very tearful telling Mike in my mind how much I love and miss him, and the same with Michael, Seth, and Jonathan. I told Mike to come and visit me in dreams.

JUNE 15, 2010

I don't have to go to work now, because school is out for the year. Now I can concentrate on my college work and my family-history mission. My son Matthew is also staying here with me this summer for a while studying for his medical tests coming up. It's great to have his company.

I am now working my hours at the Family History Library on Tuesdays and Wednesdays so that I can have my weekends free for family activities. My family history work is becoming very satisfying. I found a book in the library listing burials in graveyards in Tyrone County, Ireland, where my Scott ancestors came from. This was a very exciting adventure, and I also read about the wars and so on happening at that time. The Scotts, my ancestors, may have been flax farmers who later immigrated to Canada in the 1800s. It is like living in another world to put my imagination into what their lives may have been like.

JUNE 27, 2010
Today is Seth's thirty-fifth birthday, or would be if he was still living. Church was very inspiring. Later, Matt and I talked a lot about Seth's autopsy report and further studies to be done on his brain tissue to find out if it was an astrovirus that caused his neurodegeneration. Another patient was found to have contracted an astrovirus from mink. Rebekah, my daughter, has reminded me that Seth used to go visit a mink farm in Salem. I was not really aware of this. I wonder if Seth could have contracted this deadly virus from there. I have sent copies of Seth's autopsy report to several immunologists whom I know around the country as I felt Seth wanted me to do. I hope it will be helpful in some way to future patients.

Last Friday, Matt took his big United States Medical Licensing Exam (USMLE) for eight hours. Then we and Rich went to eat at the Red Iguana, watched Napoleon Dynamite at home, and had a good time. I love being with my fun boys. Richard is enjoying his time at BYU. Rebekah got two jobs in Santa Cruz recently—one as a CNA and another as an urgent care receptionist! My prayers have been answered. I have great joy to know my children are doing well.

JUNE 28, 2010
It is Jessica's birthday. We went to see The Karate Kid, and then the boys went with Jessica's family to the arts festival. I came home to work on a lesson plan for my college class. I notice my grass is yellow despite lots of watering. It is getting hot after a very cool and wet spring.

JULY 16, 2010

It was great to see Robert this last week. He came up from California, and he, Matt, and Rich went backpacking in the Uinta Mountains and had a great time, although both Richard and Robert got a little sick after returning from the trip. Their immune systems are fragile, and overexertion in the wilderness may not be the best thing for them. Matthew was fine.

JULY 17, 2010

I am now in Southern California with my granddaughvter Mala and her mother, Maya. My son Jeremy is out of town promoting his amazing book. I've spent the weekend here. We went to the beach and the aquarium. We played in the tide pools and jumped in the waves. Little Mala and I explored the backyard together and had a good time. We went to open houses in the neighborhood since Jeremy and Maya are looking for a house to buy. Mala is a lively, smart, sweet, demanding little two-year-old girl, delightful and precious. She has lots of stories read to her at nap time and bedtime. She likes to watch Planet Earth. She knows all about the wildebeests in Africa and knows different kinds of cacti. Such a smart little girl—like her parents.

I went to the temple today. I felt I need to relax, doubt not, and fear not. God is in charge. "Fear not to do good" (D & C 6:33). Other concerns I had were answered too. I have felt good about going to college, although at times I doubt and wonder if I should continue. Yes, I should. What about buying my mother's condominium? Now that she has moved to assisted living, I feel that I should consider it. It would be closer to Jessica and all my family. Doctrine and Covenants 82:17 says, "Have equal claims upon the property for managing your stewardship according to your wants." If I buy the condo, my siblings will be able to receive their equal share of the property. We would all be able to receive this part of our inheritance from my mother's estate. It could be a great blessing to myself and to them.

I do feel that Mike is very close to me in all I do with my kids, my work, and my genealogy. I love you, Mike. Seth and Michael, I love your wonderful spirits and lives that I spent with you. I cry tears of love and sorrow for the suffering you all went through and also for my precious baby Jonathan. I pray for all my children. Dear Lord, please hear and answer my prayers of faith, and forgive me of my blunders. Help me to know what I should do in the future.

"For God hath not given us the spirit of fear, but of power, and of love, and of a sound mind."
—2 Timothy 1:7

46

Life Goes On

JULY 20, 2010

All the adventures, trips, and achievements of the last year and a half
have been fun, fulfilling, and healing for me. Now I feel like saying
to Mike, "Okay, the joke is up. It's time to come home again!" Can
it really be that I won't see him again in this life and that I might be
alone for many more years? The thought is unbearable at times.

I have wondered lately if I should think about dating. The truth is, I
do think about it. But nothing clicks with anyone. Maybe if I get my
teeth fixed, color my hair, lose weight, and so on and so on. Many
times when I have prayed about this subject, I seem to be told that it
is better for me to be single right now. I can accomplish much more in
my family history work and in my education if I am not "cumbered"
by a relationship. I am free. My time is my own.

I should look forward to the distant day when I will see Mike again
and we can be husband and wife in the eternities in celestial realms.
That will be a glorious day. But so far away, it seems. For now, I must
concentrate on being a good mother, grandmother, and daughter of
Heavenly Father. Perhaps Mike would be happier if I did not marry
again.

SEPTEMBER 10, 2010

I went to talk to the bishop about my concern over wanting to remarry.
He thought that even though Mike usually seemed jealous of the idea
of my remarrying, he would feel differently now. The bishop gave
me a blessing, and I felt Mike was there at his side. The bishop said
my husband was very near. He expressed how much Mike loves me,
misses me, and wants me to be happy. He said angels are with me
both here and beyond the veil. I was told to prioritize my life and put
important things first.

I asked my ninety-one-year-old mother what she thought, since she had remarried after my father's death. She said it certainly complicates things. She said I should not actively pursue anyone, but if someone shows up in my life (like happened with her), then it would be okay. I take this as gospel from her and as my answer. In the meantime, I must be content to tackle life alone and to wait—perhaps until I die and see Mike again. For now, I am alone and free, and I can fly and do whatever I want to do! I should appreciate this blessing of time.

OCTOBER 31, 2010
I have started a new job that is twenty-seven hours a week. I am teaching reading, math, and writing to kindergarten through third-grade special education students at an elementary school. I am not a full-fledged teacher yet, just a resource aide. It is very challenging and sometimes frustrating, but I love the kids. I have wondered if I should continue with my family-history mission on Friday nights and Saturdays, but I feel I should. It is very important. I am also attending a Monday-night class and doing homework nightly toward finishing my master's degree. A big load to carry.

NOVEMBER 6, 2010
At the Family History Library, as I was looking for microfilms, I suddenly felt a sweet, peaceful understanding that if I am single, I am better able to devote myself to God's work, as I have fewer influences to keep me away. As I drove home, the sunset was gorgeous! This was a reminder to me of the glories of the afterlife and celestial realms where I can go and meet Mike, if I fulfill my mission in genealogy work.

NOVEMBER 14, 2010
My forty-second wedding anniversary. I listened to the CD of Mike's funeral, and as I did so, I felt peace. Mike is where he is supposed to be! He is with his family on the other side. The Lord was with him in his life. He was a hard worker and did not complain. He was always serving his family, his church, and other people. I need to become more worthy and feel comfortable with doing God's work so I can live with him again. *Accept God's will that it was time for Mike to go! Be grateful for your opportunities at this time of your life!*

DECEMBER 7, 2010

Elizabeth Edwards died of breast cancer today. She was the wife of John Edwards, a Democratic candidate for the US presidency. Of course, I always wonder if my breast cancer will return and if I will die of it also. On TV they played a previous interview with her before her death. I appreciated her calm demeanor and the faith in eternal life that she expressed. My faith is also what gives me hope for the future.

I realized that I could accomplish more in work, school, and my mission if I was single. I should be grateful for the opportunities I have.

47

Oh, That I Were an Angel

My dear mother, Arline Martindale Scott Brinton, passed away rather unexpectedly five days ago on March 20, 2011. She was ninety-two years old and was anxious to join my father on the other side of the veil. Having lived in an assisted living home for just ten months, she had been adjusting to the idea that it was her new home. It was a very beautiful place—the best in the valley. But still, I know she missed living in her own home, even though one of her children visited her almost every day. I saw her last Tuesday night, and she seemed fine.

A few months ago she was treated in the hospital for pneumonia. Within a couple of days her health returned, and she went back to live in assisted living with some physical therapy help. She was very healthy overall with a strong heart and lungs and no major diseases. But her mind was getting too weak for her to care for herself, her knees were painful, and she walked with a walker. She needed assistance in dressing. It was very difficult to see my mom in such a weakened condition when she had been so strong all her life. I visited her every Friday or Saturday. We usually watched a movie and talked. She was so sweet and kind. I began to assume that Mom might live to be one hundred. We would enjoy her time on earth as long as she lived and leave it in the hands of the Lord as to when He would take her.

On Friday the assisted living staff could not wake up my mother, and they called my sister. The nurse said Mom was running a fever from cellulitis in her leg and pneumonia. Mom was able to talk later in the evening as all her children gathered around her bed. She sat up on her pillows and told us that she was ready to go—"Let's get it over with," she said. She had decided to let nature take its course without medical intervention. The hospice nurse was called. She said

373

she wished all her patients had it so easy, as she assumed my mother would pass away within two or three days if she had no treatment, especially considering she was not eating.

On Friday, Mother was in a heavy sleep but could occasionally be aroused to say hello to somebody who came to see her. This was exactly the way my mother would have wanted it. A quick illness and quick exit from this world. We called all family members and close friends. Grandchildren began to call from around the country to say their last goodbyes to her on the phone. Her best friend of many years came to see her from downstairs in the same assisted living building. This friend had Alzheimer's disease and was able to speak very little, but she seemed to know what was happening. She held my mother's hand and said, "Oh, Arline! Oh, Arline! I hope you have a happy landing!" How sweet and what a great way to say that she hoped my mother landed happily in the spirit world.

For three days there was a great feeling of love and spiritual peace in my mother's room. Later Saturday evening many of us gathered around my mother's bed. We sang hymns and family songs that Mom and Dad used to sing. We laughed. We cried. My mother was sleeping soundly. But soon she began to shake or shiver. I said I thought it was because her fever was spiking.

The hospice nurse gave her some medication under her tongue to calm her and a Tylenol suppository. After a few minutes she was calmly sleeping again, breathing quickly. Her oxygen level was going down, as well as her blood pressure. Each hour brought lower levels. The time was getting closer. It was now about three in the morning. The nurse said it could still be several more hours, and most of us decided to go home for some sleep. My sister Barbara, however, would not leave and wanted to stay by Mom's side.

I went back home for an hour or two of sleep. Suddenly my phone was ringing. It was Barbara saying that Mom had just passed away. I had missed it! I quickly got dressed and returned to the assisted living facility to Mom's room.

There she was on the bed with her eyes closed and a pleasant look on her face. Barbara told us that when we all left, she also had decided to fall asleep next to Mom. Suddenly she woke up at eight o'clock. She went to the other side of the bed to see Mom's face and saw her take her last breath. Before Mom did so, she said "Hi," even though she had been unconscious for hours before. Her speaking to Barbara was such a tender mercy from God. She had been ill for only three short days. Her death could not have been planned better. It was just how my mom wanted it to be. She had lived ninety-two and a half productive years and was returning to her Heavenly Father and to her husband.

It was a beautiful spring morning—a Sunday. In fact, it was the first day of spring, March 20, 2011. How symbolic. The first day of spring and the first day of my mother's new life beyond the veil! Now she was free of discomfort and pain, free of her old, frail body and now in her spiritual body, which was full of energy and health. She was with my dad, whom she had been waiting to see again for more than twenty-two years! A joyous day for her!

The next few days were full of busy times arranging the funeral program, cleaning out my mother's apartment, and having the viewing with displays of pictures and artifacts from my mother's life.

The funeral was perfect, just as my mom had planned it, with lots of the music she had written performed by her children and grandchildren. All Mom's children spoke about her long life of love and service to the Lord and to her children. She had served four missions for the church and had left a posterity of seven children, forty-one grandchildren, and over twenty great-grandchildren. Her legacy of faith and love was remembered by all. My sisters and I sang the family traditional song, "Oh, That I Were an Angel," written by Wanda West Palmer: "Oh, that I were an angel, and could have the wish of my heart" (Alma 29:1, B of M). Finally my mom did have the wish of her heart—to be an angel and to reunite with my dad in heaven. She was a sweet, kind lady to all who knew her. I will miss her sweet presence. I love you, Mom!

It was the first day of spring and the first day
of my mother's life beyond the veil.

48

Struggling to Finish College

JANUARY 14, 2011

I have had two days of fearing I might die. Silly but true. I had a TIA yesterday (a ministroke), with numbness and tingling on the left side of my body, because I had gone off of my blood thinner to have a tooth extracted. So then I had to go to urgent care and get shots of heparin to overcome my TIA symptoms. I went to Walmart after the extraction and felt so extremely tired, which scared me. Then I watched a TV show about a man whose family had been killed in an accident. He said, "There are reasons God didn't take my life. I am supposed to be here for a reason." That is true of me also, I suppose. But my life could be short, and it is precious. I must use the time I have left wisely.

SUNDAY, JANUARY 23, 2011

I went to see my brother, Richard, to counsel with him and to get a priesthood blessing. I am feeling worried and burdened down. I have questions about continuing my graduate studies. Is it worth it? Should I continue my family-history mission? Richard asked me if I have time to do all these things. Yes, I really do. He said that I have huge burdens on my shoulders in my life because I have the strength to carry them. In the blessing he said, "You have come to a new phase in your life where you have been given an opportunity to work with handicapped children in your job because you have compassion and the ability to understand them. You can have a great influence upon them, not only academically, but also by being an example. They can sense your love. Be patient! Your prayers will be answered as you feel the Lord's guidance day by day." This blessing was very strengthening to me. I must press forward.

I came home with a sweet spirit and read again the scriptures on the back of Mike's funeral program. One says, "After much tribulation come the blessings" (D & C 58:4). Mike went through much tribulation—even more than I—but I am ready for some more blessings.

SUNDAY, FEBRUARY 2011

The condo issue—whether I should buy my mother's condominium or not—has come to a head in my family. The family feels the condo needs to be sold soon. I went to see it tonight. I walked around the beautiful grounds and felt very sentimental thinking of all that had happened at this place where my parents had lived—family reunions, my father's death, and some of Michael's and Seth's final days. It just felt right that I should buy it. After thinking and praying about it, I felt I should trust the Lord in this endeavor. At the condo, I will live closer to Jessica and her family and also nearer to my siblings. The only problem is that I have so much stuff to get rid of in my house, especially in the basement and garage. But I can do it! If there's a will, there's a way, and I will have help.

FEBRUARY 17, 2011

I'm worried about buying the condo, but after figuring the numbers, I think it will work, and the scriptures continue to encourage me to move to the condo closer to the mountains. "Press forward, Saints. Zion shall flourish upon the hills and rejoice upon the mountains and shall assemble together unto a place which I have appointed" (D & C 49:25).

The condo is the best place for me now that I am getting older. It will be closer to my family. It is like long-term care insurance, which I have not otherwise been eligible to buy, because of my history of cancer and mini-strokes. It is also a great chance to dejunk. Now is the best time.

FEBRUARY 22, 2011

Today was a very bad day at work because of a misunderstanding about my teacher's expectations for me. I have been working many more hours than I have been paid for because she requires that I record the scores after school. I talked to the office about this, and they said I will be fired if I work extra hours. I am in a bind between the teacher and the principal. I am also worried about selling my house, as housing prices are dropping.

Two brothers from the church came to visit tonight. They suggested that I try to sell now while the interest rates are low. They also advised that I should communicate with the teacher about my side of the story. Their advice was a tender mercy to me today, and I don't feel so alone and vulnerable. A very bad day, but maybe things will be okay.

APRIL 3, 2011

I felt the love and spiritual presence of my mom and dad and Mike tonight—subtle but comforting. Angels are around watching over me. I just need to "be still, and know that I am God" (D & C 101:16). It's lonely living by myself. So many challenges in work and school and moving! But I am doing okay.

SUNDAY, APRIL 10, 2011

I called Jeremy and Robert, and I may be going to Florida with them to see Jeremy speak about his book. I have written seventeen pages of chapter 2 of my research proposal this last week for college. I don't know how I did it. I thank the Lord for His help and tender mercies to me. Life is good!

APRIL 30, 2011

I went to Florida over spring break with my son Robert, and we met my other son Jeremy there. Jeremy gave an excellent presentation about his book. Then he drove us to the Everglades two days in a row to see the many sights. We stayed in a wonderful motel, had delicious meals, and had a great time. In my spare time, I asked Robert to help me understand a little more about statistics, as I am writing a statistical chapter in my research proposal for school.

MAY 10, 2011

Since I will be student teaching soon, I needed to quit my job and also my mission at the Family History Library. It has been difficult the past twenty months to do this mission with all that has been going on in my life. But I knew I was supposed to serve and learn by accepting this mission call, even though it seemed overwhelming. It has been a huge blessing in my life, and I hope to continue doing family history research. Considering that I was originally signed up to serve for only six months, I feel grateful that I was able to serve for twenty months. It has been a great experience.

JUNE 9, 2011

I thank the Lord for helping me to finish my research proposal on the subject of positive discipline for my master's degree program. The proposal is about sixty pages long and has required a lot of mental work and research. As I read it, I am impressed with the quality and scholarship of the writing. Did I really write this? The Lord has indeed boosted my writing ability to finish this degree as I have asked for His help.

I also put my house up for sale a couple of months ago, and now it is under contract to be sold. I have started my student teaching at Beehive Elementary, where I help to teach kindergarteners through third graders in a special education resource classroom. I teach seven small groups a day in reading, math, and writing. Some of my students have major behavior problems, but I have learned to manage them and have a good rapport with them. I just got an A on my midterm teacher evaluation.

In July I plan to move to the condo. As always, moving is an overwhelming task to think about and to do! The condo has a smaller square footage and less storage than my current home, so I need to simplify and throw away a lot. I pray the condo will work out and be a nice home for me and my family when they visit.

JUNE 19, 2011

It is Father's Day. I took a red rose to Mike's grave and told him I wished I could come and be with him! I seemed to hear him say, *"Yes, but you still have work to do!"* I thought about our lives together, the births of our nine children, and deaths of three children—all we have been through in our special lives together. Yes, I need to finish writing about the unique challenges we have experienced. Mike and my boys in the spirit world are depending on me to tell their stories. I am the only one who can do it.

JUNE 26, 2011

As I was finishing my last two days of student teaching, I got up Thursday morning and couldn't think straight or remember. I called

Paula, my sister who is a nurse, and she called 911. I only have a vague recollection of calling her and of riding in the ambulance to St. Mark's Hospital. After that I remember almost nothing that happened for eight hours. Paula told me that I talked to her a lot during the day and kept asking about over and over again what had happened and why was I in the hospital.

I started to feel more normal that evening. But what went on in the hospital during that day is very unclear to me. The rest of my sisters, my brother, and one of my brothers-in-law came over to see me in the evening. Russ and Richard prayed for me. The doctor told me that this was a case of transient global amnesia (TGA). It can be brought on by emotional stress in people who have a history of migraine headaches. Yes, I have been under emotional stress, and yes, I have a history of migraines. I am told it is not likely to happen again and there should be no major consequences from this. I hope not.

I returned home the next day and seemed to be okay. This whole experience has scared me a lot. Now I think much more about how I am getting older. I'm sixty-four, the age that Mike died. I know it's relatively young, but it's definitely older than the majority of people I work with.

In my heart and spirit, I still feel young, but I don't have as much confidence in myself as I did before. I am not sure that my body will always cooperate with the goals I want to accomplish. I am scared about my health. I really need to eat healthy, reduce stress, exercise, relax, and not worry so much. And go to counseling? Should I really try to teach or just write my book? What is most important for me to accomplish? The doctor gave me a prescription for antianxiety pills. I guess I should take them.

JULY 18, 2011

Well, I have moved into the condo in the Sugar House area of Salt Lake City with a lot of help from my kids, siblings, and men I hired. Church members also helped. My daughter Jessica and her husband, Tony, helped for hours on the Fourth of July. I heard the fireworks outside but could not enjoy the festivities, as I was washing out the garage with a hose.

Now everything I have chosen to keep is at the condo. So many boxes to find places for and to sort through! I have gone through everything I own in the last month, finding so many treasures, such as cards, papers, and pictures from earlier and happier days. It has been quite a sentimental experience.

The Lord has been with me in all of this. He told me to move closer to my family and to share my wealth with my siblings by buying their shares of the condo. My family is happy I have kept the condo within the family, and they feel less worried about my security and welfare. It certainly is secure here. I have to use three keys just to go from the garage to inside my condominium! When I forget my keys, I'm in trouble.

There have been a lot of family activities this month. It was definitely the right choice to move to Salt Lake City from California to be surrounded by so much family. However, I am feeling so worried and strange and stressed living in this new place! The condo board of directors has special rules about a lot of things, including pets. I still have the two cats we got in California. I have to get a note from the doctor saying I need my pets for emotional reasons. Do I? The doctor was able to truthfully write that I have severe anxiety (because of my hospitalization two months ago). I would have anxiety about getting rid of the cats, because my sons love them so much. This is all very stressful to me. I've decided I better start taking Zoloft to calm my anxiety. However, the medication makes me feel sick and weird. Maybe if I take a smaller dose, it will be okay.

"You still have work to do," Mike told me.
"After much tribulation come the blessings."
—D & C 58:4

49

The Time Is Far Spent

AUGUST 29, 2011

I have finished all the work for my master's degree program! I have received my transcripts and have officially graduated with my master's degree in special education! I now have a teaching certificate and a mild/moderate endorsement. Yesterday my son Rich and I drove with Jessica's family high into the mountains to see wildflowers and have a picnic. Jessica brought a delicious apple pie for my graduation. I didn't want to go through the actual graduation ceremony. Just give me the piece of paper! (And a job!)

I am feeling anxious now that Rich has returned to BYU. I have no job or homework to occupy my time. I'm uncertain about the future. There have been a lot of expenses with college starting, and then there is the new dishwasher I had to buy, hospital bills, and taxes coming up. I can afford these things over time, and I hope not to have to use my savings. A small job would be nice. As I read the scriptures, the message was to be patient. I pray for the Lord's guidance and comfort and pray that whatever is best for me may happen. I will have a lot of time to write my book for now. I need to stop feeling sorry for myself. Jump in and enjoy life!

SEPTEMBER 28, 2011

I have a job now! Not as a teacher, but as a behavioral health assistant at Orchard Elementary. The job is for three days, nineteen hours a week. When the principal called asking if I wanted to interview, I remembered a dream I'd had in which I was working with children with behavior problems, so I said yes. Just like the dream, I was hired the same day that I interviewed.

I work with a difficult third grader right now who has Asperger's syndrome, or high-functioning autism. He had his teacher in tears the first day I arrived. I helped him write an apology letter to her. He does not scare me. I will strive to help him make progress. I love the team of people I work with, and I feel this is the perfect job for me right now—not too overwhelming.

OCTOBER 14, 2011

Three years ago this night, Mike was dying in the Garden Terrace care facility, passing away at three thirty the next morning, October 15. As I went to the Salt Lake Temple tonight, I wanted to feel closer to Mike. My memory of him is fading. I was reminded of the importance of following my husband's counsel, remembering the Savior's sacrifice, and giving my own sacrifices to preserve our eternal family.

OCTOBER 16, 2011

Richard has moved home and is going to commute to BYU in a carpool. We are hoping this change will help him to settle down more in his studies and remove the distraction of roommates.

I took some beautiful, fragrant white lilies to Mike's grave this evening to remember his death date. My breath was taken away by the beauty of the bright sunlight shining on the rugged mountain ahead of me as I drove while the sun was setting. There were many patches of red from autumn oak brush on the mountain. It was ethereally gorgeous! All the nature around me was beautiful—green grass, gold fall leaves on the trees, and many birds flying and chirping.

At the grave, I remembered the two messages I have specifically received from Mike: "Be patient" and "You have work to do."

NOVEMBER 14, 2011

Today is Mike's and my forty-third wedding anniversary. Mike has been gone three years now. A poem has come to me as follows:

To Mike, for Our Forty-Third Wedding Anniversary
Dear Mike, I love you, miss you, want your warm embrace,
Cry for it, try for it, pray for it. Then it comes.
The memories so dear, the years and years, our love, our tears.
Once so young and strong, now I'm older, and you're gone.
How long, how long?
Please be with me, stay with me, visit for a while—

Your smile, your strength. (I know you must go at length.)
Heal me emotionally with your warm heart.
Kiss me, miss me. Remember how we were at the start?
Walking in the rain, no sorrow or pain,
Love's light sublime. Babies came in time,
Sweet and precious—oh, how they blessed us!
Our wedding anniversary—so special to me.
Our marriage bond—so strong. It goes on.

DECEMBER 27, 2011

I had most of my family here for Christmas. My son Jeremy and his
wife Maya and daughter Mala came from California. Mala danced
around the living room in her ballerina tutu on Christmas Eve. It was
very cute. We had a nice time for the most part. I had prepared for my
granddaughter to play in the snow by buying boots and a coat for her.
Alas, there was no snow, not even in the canyons! But we did have
some good times going out to dinner and to a natural history museum
with some cousins.

JANUARY 24, 2012

Rich and I went to eat at Jessica's tonight, and she said to me, "Mom,
it's time! It's time for you to start dating!" I am making friends with
a few nice gentlemen from church. Nothing big. But then I read in
1 Corinthians 7 where Paul counsels widows not to remarry (see 1
Corinthians 7:8). In all the priesthood blessings I have received from
my bishop and others, there has been no mention of remarrying, just
that I will be a teacher, that I am to do good, and that I have a lot of
work to do. But for how many years? I would prefer not to be alone
for the rest of my mortal life. I miss Mike and wish I didn't have to
go on without him. I'm sad that I have to keep chugging along, doing
it alone. Please help me, Mike and Heavenly Father. The road is long
and hard and scary. Please help me.

MARCH 20, 2012

"The time is far spent, there is little remaining" (Snow 1998, 266).
These are words of a hymn I turned to today. I feel like I am running
a marathon against the deadline of five years since Mike died. There
is only one and a half years left until what? Until I die? Until I get

married again? Until I become disabled? At any rate, I feel very driven to complete my book, write family histories, and do more genealogy within the next year and a half, after which point I may not have time or health to accomplish these projects. That is what I feel.

APRIL 22, 2012

I have been called to be an ordinance worker in the Latter-day Saint Temple Salt Lake Temple. Yesterday as I stood in one of the beautiful temple hallways for an hour, I felt the strong, sweet Spirit of the Lord with warmth and peace down to my bones. I definitely felt that this was the Lord's house, because His power and peace were there.

I keep thinking about dating because I have been so lonely, but I feel the Lord wants me to just be grateful for each moment, the here and now. I feel I am supposed to just love Mike, my kids, and my grandchildren and write my book. To fulfill these tasks is my life's mission. Thy will be done, not mine. Do not covet other people's lives.

MAY 3, 2012

I had a terrible job interview today with Jordan School District. In the middle of the interview my head seemed to be deprived of blood supply. I couldn't even remember the questions when I was in the middle of answering them. Afterward, I felt disoriented and could barely figure out how to drive home. I think it was another episode of transient global amnesia (TGA), which sent me to the emergency room last summer. I just drove home, took two aspirin, and went to bed, for I felt that I knew what was happening and that it would pass. It did.

That night I crawled into my bed feeling vulnerable, sad, and tearful about being rejected from jobs and by some people. After reading some scriptures, however, I felt assured of God's love for me. I pulled my covers around me and over my head and felt safe in the womb of God's love. I didn't ever want to come out again.

MAY 7, 2012

Richard and I had the wonderful opportunity to fly to the tropical island of St. Maarten in the Caribbean. My son Matthew and his wife, Christina, have been attending medical school there, and we attended their graduation! We drove our tiny rental car on narrow winding roads to find their university, the American University of the Caribbean. The island was a beautiful place to visit with turquoise ocean waters surrounding green islands where native black people, descendants of the old slave trade, work. They sell beautiful items for tourists to buy and construct buildings—some humble, some magnificent. Our hotel looked out onto the ocean, where white-sailed boats floated, framed by tall palm trees. A beautiful paradise that I felt truly sad to leave.

MAY 15, 2012

As my son Richard said our family prayer before leaving for Idaho for summer work, I felt how important is my obligation to him right now. He is my number one priority until he graduates from college and gets fully settled into his own life. I went to Mom's grave for Mother's Day and then to Mike's grave. I felt again my obligation to finish my book.

An older lady who works in the temple told me not to be afraid to remarry, as she has done. She said our relatives in heaven may even send someone for us to meet. I also had a feeling in the temple that Mike would like me to marry a certain old friend of ours. Really? Is it getting closer to a time when I could remarry? I am obviously confused about all this.

JUNE 7, 2012

Another vacation trip to Santa Cruz, California. Why do I complain about my life? I am so blessed! Richard and I flew there to witness my son Robert's graduation. Robert got his master's degree in statistics, and his wife received her doctorate degree in chemistry. What smart children I have! We also enjoyed visiting with his wife's parents and siblings and enjoying the cool but sunny California air. The beach was close by with sand cliffs in sight of a lighthouse. We rode a train up to the redwood forest in the mountains and down to the wharf, where there is a carnival of shops and amusement park rides. Beautiful!

AUGUST 2012

Richard and I drove to Tennessee with our car filled with Matt and Christina's belongings, which I have stored for the last five years of their schooling. Now that they live in a bigger townhouse with a garage, they can store these things for themselves. The trip was interesting. We drove across the middle United States, going from drought conditions in Kansas to very green surroundings in Tennessee. We had an old-fashioned creole dinner on the river in a beautiful restaurant and visited the Smoky Mountains National Park. The drive home seemed to take forever. But overall, it was a nice little vacation to see their new location. Matt is beginning his residency in pathology, and his stories of autopsies he has helped to perform were very entertaining.

AUGUST 15, 2012

One last chance before I start back to work to visit Jeremy's family in Southern California. I flew there, and Maya picked me up. I had a nice visit with her and their four-year-old daughter, Mala, while Jeremy was out of town. Visits to the aquarium and to the beach were fun. Also, they have a charming blue-tiled swimming pool in their backyard that we enjoyed. Their city is always such a beautiful green place to visit with perfect temperature year-round.

SEPTEMBER 1, 2012

I have applied for many teaching jobs during the summer with no success. So I have returned to my old job as a behavioral health assistant. The principal and counselor have moved on to other schools, so I am orienting new people as to my responsibilities. It is very fulfilling to work with the children.

Travel and enjoy life as much as you can,
especially in times of loneliness and stress.

50

Culmination

NOVEMBER 2012
Today, while going through some papers, I ran across a recent issue of the IDF Advocate, the national newsletter of the Immune Deficiency Foundation—always a reminder of the challenging genetic disease my sons have battled with. At the back of the newsletter are names of people who have had contributions made to the foundation in their names. Seth's name was on that list in 2005.

I noticed with interest the recent Think Zebra! campaign that the Immune Deficiency Foundation launched to publicize to the medical community the prevalence of primary or genetic immune deficiencies. The newsletter says:

> When doctors go to school they learn the saying, "When you hear hoof beats, think horses, not zebras." However, sometimes people get sick a lot, their illness doesn't get better, or they have an unusual infection. When this happens, doctors should wonder whether the person might be a zebra with an unusual condition, like primary immunodeficiency disease, and not a horse with a common infection. People with primary immunode-ficiency diseases are the zebras of the medical world! Questions? Contact IDF to learn more. www. primaryimmune.org or 800 296-4433. (Immune Deficiency Foundation 2012)

I am so happy that my two younger sons, Robert and Richard, have reached adulthood and graduated from college in spite of their immune deficiencies! Robert has even married and his wife is expecting a baby in December. This is such a blessing! Last year Richard considered having a bone marrow transplant, which could be a possible cure for hyper-IgM syndrome, but the doctor and I discouraged him, because he could die from the treatment or go through great suffering. The chance of a bone marrow transplant being successful decreases as one grows older, we have been told. Babies and young children have the best chance of success. We will probably wait for gene therapy in the future, a treatment that involves using the patient's own stem cells, but inserting a normal gene to replace the defective gene. Such a treatment is on the horizon. I am impressed that the knowledge of primary immunodeficiency disease has come so far since we first learned of it with Jonathan in 1970.

NOVEMBER 10, 2012
I have finally, for the first time, been hired to do a job that requires my teaching certificate! I've applied for about one hundred teaching jobs, and this is the first one that has worked out. I have become a long-term substitute for a teacher who will be on maternity leave for four months. I am teaching special education resource classes for mild to moderately impaired children from kindergarten through third grade. They look and act like normal children but have learning disabilities that make it more difficult for them to read or do math.

Each day I teach five small groups around a kidney-shaped table in direct-instruction reading, language, or math programs. The teaching is scripted, fast-paced, and intense. The students are constantly reading, answering questions, and being corrected if they make a mistake. The groups range in size from only one child to up to five children. Each group time lasts about a half hour, and then the students return to their general education classroom in a regular elementary school.

The school is within just a few blocks of my condominium. I am saving money on gas and earning more money per hour than I have for the past six years. This is such a blessing to me! This is what my education has prepared me to do, and I am really enjoying it—except when my alarm goes off in the morning. I do hate to get up early five days a week. And I am very tired when I come home. Energy is at a premium.

After the first few challenging days of this job, I am feeling comfortable, successful, and full of love and compassion for these students. Our school has children from about thirty different countries and languages. I have two rambunctious Hispanic boys who are eagerly learning to speak and read English. My most flamboyant and humorous student is a third-grade African American boy, also enthusiastic to improve his reading skills. Two girls have fathers who are in jail. They timidly and slowly sound out each word. One short third-grade boy has not yet learned to recognize all the numbers between one and five, in spite of three years of schooling. Yet all the teachers love his personality. One day he hugged me after I praised him for learning numbers one, two, and three with a score of 100 percent. He has some problems with his speech and obviously problems with his memory. But he is charming and somewhat street savvy.

As I walk down the long halls to pick up my students with my badge hanging from my neck, I feel important and happy to be doing a professional service for these children. This is my career. It may not last too long, but this is the teaching I have wanted to do since I was a little girl playing school with my sisters and teaching them to read when I was just six years old.

SATURDAY, NOVEMBER 2012

Today I woke up reluctantly, feeling very tired and uninspired even though it was my day to serve in the Salt Lake Temple. I didn't know how I could inspire others in the temple when I felt so depressed. I dragged myself out of bed, got ready, arrived later than I should have, hurried to change into white clothes, and made it to the temple chapel to play the organ reasonably well as the congregation sang. The instruction from the temple presidency was amazing, as it always is.

Still, I felt slightly depressed and bereft of the Spirit. However, as I performed my assignments that day, I was greatly blessed. As I looked into the eager and believing eyes of sisters coming to the temple—sometimes eyes that were filled with tears of gratitude—my eyes too filled with tears of joy.

One temple session had over one hundred sisters attending, in addition to the brethren. There were all variety of women dressed in white—old sisters in wheelchairs, young sisters in the bloom of their beauty, overweight sisters, thin and frail sisters, sisters with foreign accents and strange names, Hispanic sisters, Asian sisters, Caucasian sisters, and African American sisters. All of them were happy to be there. I was overcome with joy that so many had come to God's temple.

What a privilege! I did not need to inspire all these people. They were inspiring me! They were uplifting me! What a joyous time this day has been for me, to serve in the Lord's house for several hours! It is not a sacrifice but a blessing.

NOVEMBER 2012

I spent the day cooking with Jessica and Richard for Thanksgiving, but tonight I have felt so alone. I belong to nobody now that Mike is gone. I prayed about it and turned to some scriptures, which again point my mind to the stewardship and duty I have to write inspirational words and have them published to the world. This duty is important, but it is a sacrifice for me. It is hard to go on. Work, work, work! That is how I have avoided sadness these last few years, along with the Lord's guidance and comfort. I can do this writing, and I must.

Being able to work in a position to help others brings satisfaction. Service leads to joy!

51

Let Your Hearts Be Comforted

NOVEMBER 18, 2012

Four days ago was Mike's and my wedding anniversary, on November 14. It would have been forty-four years if Mike was still living. Today is thirty-five years since my son Michael was born. Richard and I got out the video of our family meeting from a few weeks before Michael died. It was a wonderful experience to watch this video in commemoration of his birthday. I felt inspired as Michael said in that meeting, "Follow my example. Whatever you are interested in, dig into it. Get involved in everything you can. Use your time wisely, and don't be afraid to have fun. Don't waste your time, because you don't know how much time you have! Just have great lives and live them the best you can, because I want to see all of you again. Don't worry about me, and I promise that if I can, I will visit you often. I am happy to do what the Lord wants me to do."

In that meeting, which we are so fortunate to have on videotape, my husband, Mike, had many wise things to say to help our family meet the challenges of Michael's upcoming death. I think his words could help anyone dealing with the death of a loved one. The following are excerpts of Mike's uplifting words spoken to our family in March 1994:

> Through my tears in the hospital I told Michael about his cancer, and it was wonderful to see his faith. He told me that if he died, he felt worse for us but that he would be okay. What great faith you have, Michael!

> We take our faith for granted until a time like this comes to us. These situations are very hard. We have to reach deep in our hearts and cry to Heavenly Father, who loves us all and knows

all things. The scriptures say, "For whosoever among you are sick ... and [are] not appointed to death shall be healed ... and if they die, they shall die unto me, and if they live they shall live unto me ... Those that die in me shall not taste of death, for it will be sweet unto them" (D & C 42:43–48).

If Michael is not appointed unto death, he will be healed. If he is appointed unto death, it is a mission call for him to the spirit world to perform a great work. We accept the will of our Heavenly Father, but this will be very hard for us. I have shed many tears. But we have a lot of people on the other side of the veil—Grandpa Scott, Jonathan, and my dad, Grandpa Leo, whom Michael was named after. I haven't seen my dad since I was eight years old when he died. But when I was seventeen in the army, far away in Korea and feeling afraid, I felt him close to me.

Michael, we love you. You are very special. I honor you for your intelligence, your goodness, and your talents. I remember playing with you when you were just a little boy. *I will never get over you.* I will always love you, and I look forward to seeing you again when I die! The Lord has taught, "Eye hath not seen, nor ear heard, neither have entered into the heart of man, the things which God has prepared for them that love him" (1 Corinthians 2:9). "Let not your hearts be troubled ... In my father's house are many mansions ... I go to prepare a place for you" (John 14:1–2).

Mike's words were full of faith, assurance, and love. I miss that strength in my life now. But to see all my children and my husband on the video, sharing our love and unitedly singing songs of faith, made me feel for a moment that we were all together again in our wonderful family. To see Michael alive; to see Seth there also, healthy and talking well; to see Mike, my steadfast husband, in the prime of his life, speaking words of testimony and wisdom—this was a dream come true for me. All of us were there—father, mother, and every child (except our baby Jonathan). To be all together again in unity is my hope for the future.

DECEMBER 31, 2012

As I think of all the experiences of my life, I realize how death or illness of a loved one is a very difficult, heart-wrenching passageway to knowledge and understanding. None of us ever wants to go through such a trial, but when such a challenge comes to us, we can know that our Heavenly Father is there to weep with us, to comfort us and to give us hope that we can be reunited with our deceased loved ones again. We need only reach out to Him and cry for His love and help. To turn our back on Him at these times of deepest sorrow is to turn our back on solace and peace. This I know from multiple trials. The Lord has said, "Verily, I say unto you, my friends. Fear not, let your hearts be comforted; yea, rejoice evermore, and in everything give thanks; waiting patiently on the Lord. All things wherewith ye have been afflicted shall work together for your good, and to my name's glory, saith the Lord" (D & C 98:1–3).

My afflictions have been for my good and for my growth. I feel safe in God's love and know that all my dreams will someday come true because of Him. I will see my lost family members again and embrace them in heaven. God does not lie, and He will bring to pass all His promises.

Five days ago I saw my fourth grandchild for the first time—Susanna Melody Curzon. She was almost two weeks old, the daughter of my son Robert (after all his illnesses!) and his wife, Stephanie. As I held the baby in my arms, listening to the tiny squeaking noises she made as she breathed, her head lying on my shoulder, her soft body wrapped in flannel, it took me back to when I snuggled my own babies and cradled their downy heads in my hands. So newly fresh from God. So dependent. So sweet. She is a little miracle. Life begins again. I have seen it come. I have seen it go.

As my husband often used to say, little miracles, small feelings of peace and love from heaven, are like snowflakes falling. At first as we look at the ground, the snow may be imperceptible. Snowflakes melt so quickly. The evidence of a snowflake is so small. But as they continue to fall, more and more, they pile up. The ground becomes white. The trees are frosted with their sparkles. Now we know for sure. It has snowed! Many small flakes—many small miracles, many small and tender mercies from a loving Heavenly Father—pile up. After a while we cannot deny their reality. We cannot deny it has snowed. We cannot deny there is a God. We cannot deny what we have felt, over and over again. In a thousand small ways, day by day and occasionally in big ways, God shows us that He cares!

As we turn to Him in our need, "God shall wipe away all tears from [our] eyes," and in the end when Christ returns, "there shall be no more death, neither sorrow, nor crying, neither shall there be any more pain: for the former things are passed away" (Revelation 21:4).

"All things wherewith ye have been afflicted
shall work together for your good."
—D & C 98:3

Epilogue

FEBRUARY 2013

The ugly head of hyper-IgM syndrome has again raised itself into our lives. My son Robert has been quite ill in the last two months. He told me on the phone that he can hardly walk up the stairs because he is so weak. I wondered if I needed to go to California to help him out. We were worried about serious long-lasting illness, but eventually, over a couple of months, it was discovered that he had "walking" pneumonia. After a couple of rounds of strong antibiotics, he was nearly back to normal. Now he is battling abdominal pains and weight loss, which have been going on for a while. I worry that these symptoms could be the beginning of long-term problems like he had twice as a child. I don't dare let my fears get too out of hand, but they are bubbling under the surface. Please, no more illness and sad times!

FATHER'S DAY, JUNE 16, 2013

Four months have passed. What can I say? So much has happened since I wrote last. So many surprising blessings and answers to prayer! So much happiness! For one thing, Robert is doing better than he was and is gaining weight! Also, I prayed very earnestly in February that the Lord would send me a companion, if it was right. Almost immediately I met a wonderful man named Gary Openshaw, and we will be married in one month! My time of lonely widowhood is over! Through the wonders of modern technology, we met online, on a religious dating site. We soon learned that we both work in the Salt Lake Temple on Friday nights.

We have been amazed at the many similarities and coincidences in our pasts. His wife died of pancreatic cancer, as did my son Michael. His son deals with blindness, as did my son Seth. We both have sons who married Filipino girls from Canada. We both cared for our ill spouses for many months. We both love working in the temple. And we have both felt impressed from spiritual sources that now is the time to move on in our lives and find a marriage partner, for "it is not good that … man should be alone" (Abraham 5:14, P of GP).

I am impressed with Gary's well-balanced personality. He is strong physically, socially, and spiritually. He is well loved by the people in the Sugar House area of Salt Lake City, where he has lived for forty years. There he had a successful career in the employees' health system of Union Pacific Railroad, raised four good sons with his wife, served as a leader in church callings, and kindly looked after the needs of elderly neighbors by taking out their garbage cans and shoveling their snow. He is organized and strong where I am weak, and he shows me great concern and kindness. Gary makes me laugh, records beautiful music CDs for me, and looks after my needs. I will be honored to be his wife and to serve the Lord by his side. I feel that God is telling me now to rejoice and be happy! The time of my blessing has come!

AUGUST 5, 2013
Gary and I were married three weeks ago on July 12, a simple ceremony in the chapel where he served as bishop for five years. It was a small but beautiful wedding with our immediate family and a few close friends.

I feel my life has come full circle and that it makes sense. I am so pleased to be married to this wonderful man and so happy that we can serve together in the Salt Lake Temple, the worldwide symbol of The Church of Jesus Christ of Latter-day Saints. I am happy that I am no longer alone in the world and that Gary and I can bless each other's lives and labor together in the Lord's kingdom. I look forward to many more years of peace and happiness. The Lord has again wiped away my tears, and I thank Him for this time of renewal and joy. I pray the happiness Gary and I feel will also extend to our children, for indeed, our families constitute our greatest eternal prize.

MAY 29, 2016
Three years have passed. There have been many happy days, and some sad days as two more divorces have occurred in the marriages of my children Jessica and Robert. I have mourned to see their anguish of heart. It has also been sad to lose in-laws whom I have come to love

over the past few years, but now must let them go. Nevertheless, life goes on, and there is hope for better days in the future.

My youngest son, Richard, has been working in Virginia as a horticulturalist for two years after graduating from BYU. He works for a nonprofit organization, Meadowview Biological Research Station, where he grows and sells the natural-growing carnivorous plants of the area and helps in the restoration of many acres of land to their natural habitat. He visited doctors at the nearby National Institutes of Health recently, in Bethesda, Maryland. The bone marrow transplant team there is encouraging him to participate in a clinical trial testing the safety and efficacy of bone marrow transplants to heal primary immune deficiencies. We are carefully considering this so that he may be cured from his hyper-IgM syndrome but are still worried for the ill health and even possible death the transplant could cause.

We have recently discovered a Facebook page where patients and families from around the world can connect and discuss their challenges with immune deficiency: the Hyper IgM Syndrome Group. It has been thrilling for us to become acquainted with many other people who struggle with the same disease we have had in our family. We have been saddened to see that some bone marrow recipients have died from the treatment, but other patients have indeed been given a long-term cure after the harrowing ordeal of stem cell transplants. So it is a very difficult decision that we are still considering. My older son Robert is against doing a bone marrow transplant for himself and is content to let nature take its course with his disease. Perhaps the best option is to wait for the less invasive gene therapy or gene editing that may be coming in a few years. I hope and pray that both Robert and Richard have many more years of quality life.

JULY 24, 2016

An amazing day, Pioneer Day in Utah, where we celebrate the arrival of the Mormon pioneers into the Salt Lake Valley on July 24, 1847. Gary and I went to an early breakfast, drove to my sister's house for a potluck lunch, went to see a carnival, and then watched fireworks in the evening. I recently heard of two individuals who have had near-death experiences in their own lives. The fireworks, with their heavenly beauty and beautiful patterns of light, made me think of the beauty of the spirit world. I have been reading some books lately about people who have had near-death experiences. Their spirits left their bodies during times of medical crisis, they saw the spirit world, but were then revived and brought back to life. I was reminded of a lady I knew years ago who told me of her visit to the spirit world when she was very ill. She was asked whether she would be strong enough to withstand the many trials of life through which she would be required to pass if she returned to earth, as she desired.

The accounts I have read discuss the unspeakable peace and love that is felt in the spirit world. People who have these experiences often see their loved ones who have already died, and some say they have seen the Lord. As mentioned before, I have at times sensed around me the spirits of my loved ones who have died. They have guided me, comforted me, and given me their love. The veil can be very thin at times. For me, I have had these experiences at times when I have been able to unhook from the world through solitude, prayer, devotion, and being in quiet, holy places.

I hope that if you mourn the death of a loved one, you may feel comforted with the hope that there is life after death. I wrote the following poem to express my faith in the life hereafter in regard to those we have lost in my family:

Curzon's Crucible

March 29, 1994,
The day that rocked our world—Michael died!
How could it be? How could this happen in our family?
It hurts so much!
Our hearts are touched with love so sweet.
With tears we weep.
A wound so deep—how can it heal?

Michael's blood was shed, but he said, "Thy will be done.
I look forward to experiences new."
He was a faithful son, asking for bishop's blessings
Until he felt the peace he sought.

"Live your lives so true, so I can again see you"—
His last words in our family meeting

399

As we were all around him seating,
Each one of us clinging to faith, to hope,
To temple blessings sealing us forever.
We felt, we knew these things were true.
It was the glue that bound us together.

Now, twenty-two years later,
Our lives have divided, and multiplied with new family members.
Separate homes, some loves lost embers,
But, hey, the sun still shines!
The planets still turn!
The galaxies still swirl!
All cannot truly be lost in this crazy world,
Though our lives may seem tempest-tossed.

Remember that special place in our hearts,
Where we felt God's loving care
And knew that He was there?
Michael, Seth, and Dad are waiting,
And little Jonathan, anticipating our return to them!
Hope is not lost!
Our lives have purpose,
And so did theirs.
It will all make sense, you'll see,
When we meet them in eternity—
Our beloved Curzon family.

There is life after death, and we will see our loved ones again. This great mystery can give us peace.

APRIL 5, 2017
Today is my seventieth birthday! Hard to believe when my spirit feels so much younger. But my body does feel seventy years old. These last few years have given me aches and pains I never knew existed from arthritis, bursitis, and sciatica. My blood pressure goes too high and then too low. I have a hiatal hernia that causes chest and stomach pain. The doctor says I need surgery, but I am reluctant to do so right now. Some days I feel well, but if I overdo it, my body definitely lets me know!

I had a very helpful surgery a year ago involving the removal of a cyst near my spine. The cyst was pressing on the nerve going to my leg, causing severe pain. What a relief it was to feel the pain gone when I woke up from surgery! But recovering took several months of taking things easy and not bending over. Gary, my husband, was a great help. We have both had our turns taking care of each other. He broke his ankle two years ago and was in a wheelchair when we went to New York City with some of my family. I was in a wheelchair last year when we were visiting Disneyland with Gary's family. At least we have been healthy enough to take several trips together, including to Canada, California, the Bahamas, and Florida. (How sad it has been to see the devastation that has occurred from the recent hurricanes!)

I have asked myself why God would let me have these bouts of pain, fatigue, and anxiety. I feel that pain causes me to be more humble. It takes the wind out of my sails for a while and lets others around me shine, rather than myself. My family shone today as they gave me a surprise birthday party at Chuck-A-Rama! Gary organized it. It was very sweet of all of them.

Looking back on my life, I know I have not been a perfect person or mother or wife, although I have sincerely sought to do what I felt was right. I have many weaknesses. Now I more fully realize my faults. I have to wonder if the present atheism of some of my children and the divorces which some have gone through could have been prevented if I had been a better mother and teacher of my children as they were growing up over the years. I certainly had my weaknesses, but my strength of having faith in God through my many trials is what I have to offer to the world. In spite of my frailties, I have presumed to write this book, thinking that it will somehow be meaningful or helpful to other people going through illnesses and deaths of loved ones. I hope it will.

I dread getting even older with probable further health issues. But recently I helped serve at a funeral luncheon at the church. Most of the sisters I served with were near eighty and still going strong. It gave me hope that I can be as lively as they are in ten years if I take care of my health. My cardiologist says I need to eat a diet high in vegetables with little or no meat and dairy in order to improve my circulation. Trying this diet lately has made me feel better with less chest pain and brain fog. It certainly goes along with the Word of Wisdom which my church teaches—to eat grains, vegetables, and fruits along with eating meat "sparingly" (as well as avoiding alcohol, tobacco, tea, and coffee) (D & C 89.)

I aspire to become more mild and kindly as I age and to feel closer to God. I like what Robert Browning, a nineteenth-century poet, wrote about aging:

> Grow old along with me! The best is yet to be,
> Our times are in His hand,
> Who saith, "A Whole I planned,"
> Youth shows but half; trust God; see all, nor be afraid! (Browning 1864, 1257).

AUGUST 5, 2017
In May of this year, I flew to San Jose, California, with my daughter Jessica and granddaughters Ally and Leah to attend my daughter Rebekah's nursing graduation. It was a wonderful occasion, and it was very evident how much Rebekah has matured and how hard she has worked to graduate with honors from the RN program at Hartnell College. The affection the faculty and class members have for each other was very evident as well. The red caps and gowns added to the atmosphere of this joyous occasion. We are so proud of Rebekah's accomplishment. Afterward, we ate at a beautiful restaurant built on a vinecovered cliff. It was amazing. My son Robert and little Susanna came for the dinner, after she too had graduated—from preschool. We stayed at a nice motel surrounded by tall redwoods. Overall, this experience filled me with joy. Now all my children have college degrees and are on their way to good careers and successful lives!

Now that all my children are in their thirties and forties and I can get a clearer view of what their lives will be, do I have any regrets that I brought them into the world? Do I think I had too many children or that the vicissitudes of life we experienced were too much to bear? Why did I have so many kids, especially when some of them had a genetic disease? These are questions I know that other people may wonder about. Some people, even in my own family, may be angry that I chose to have children who could possibly suffer and even die.

Why did I make the choices I did? I instinctively felt that my babies were asking me to let them be born. I love large families, being born the oldest of seven children. Most of the families in our rural Utah town had between four and thirteen children. Thus, it seemed pretty normal for Mike and I to raise our eight kids in Salem, Utah. My husband was supportive, and we had a large house and yard. We had some difficult times, but we made it through and were able to help our kids get their college educations.

People were shouting in other parts of the world about population control, but it did not seem terribly relevant to me, living where there was a lot of open land nearby where my children could explore. I am not sorry that I chose to bring each special child into the world. Although my sons with hyper-IgM syndrome had the interruptions of doctor appointments and hospital stays, they spent the majority of their lives enjoying the normal experiences of childhood—playing with friends, attending school and church, and pursuing their varied interests and talents.

I do not regret my decisions about motherhood, but I do feel very sad for the physical and emotional suffering endured by my kids during their times of illness. I truly did not expect that my sons would die, since the prognosis of their particular disease was not explained to me until my youngest was thirteen years old in the year 2000. I am sad for the anguish that Mike, my other children, and I went through in seeing our sons or brothers suffer and pass away. Hopefully, there will be compensating blessings of strength of character and compassion that will bless my children's lives because of these tragedies they have seen up close.

It is common for Mormons to have big families but not common that they would have many children if there was a genetic defect that could be passed on. Doing so was my interpretation of my faith, as I believed God would provide for and bless us, and indeed He has, both temporally and spiritually.

My six living children are amazing, talented adults. Jeremy has a law degree and is an award-winning author and photographer. Matthew is a medical doctor of pathology. Robert is a statistician and investor. Richard is a wildlands conservationist. Both Jessica and Rebekah are nurses, and Jessica has also added a thriving vegan doughnut business,

Big-O Doughnuts, to her life. My children also have other talents in music, art, drama, drafting, debate, biology, and in just loving people. All are sensitive, passionate, strong-willed, and educated human beings. Those with children are dedicated parents. And my granddaughters—Ally, Leah, Mala, and Susanna—are charming and creative individuals. I am glad I had the opportunity of bringing all my children into the world. We have a great time when we are together with our varied and interesting personalities, and we love each other in spite of our differences.

Jessica was recently engaged to a charming man named Zak from Salt Lake City. He has two nice teenage kids, Abby and Noah, whom we have enjoyed getting to know during the past year. Recently I was excited to meet (on Skype) Richard's fiancé, Siru. She is a beautiful intern from Finland whom Richard met at work. They plan a wedding next September, 2018 in the Salt Lake Temple. We are thrilled with the prospects of welcoming her as a future member of the Curzon family. Our family continues to grow as time goes on.

AUGUST 10, 2017

Today marks twelve years since Seth passed away at age thirty. I posted this on Facebook and received some wonderful comments from people in Utah and California who knew him. They said that he was missed by them, that they had good memories of his missionary service in California, that he changed their lives for the better, that he was remembered for his testimony and faith, that he was a sweet soul and an incredible young man. Such nice comments from people outside the family! Yes, Seth became blind, had difficulty speaking, and was in a wheelchair near the end of his life. But those disabilities did not hide his amazing spirit, and people loved and admired him. Should he not have been born because he had to suffer? Some people would say yes. But I feel that the sum total of his life and personality and his contribution to our lives certainly outweigh the pain he, and we, had to suffer due to his disease.

The same can be said of his brother Michael. Michael's wonderful violin music, his striving for excellence, and his contagious joyful personality were a gift to all who knew him. And the strength that both Seth and Michael demonstrated in their illnesses was a great example.

Their value as people cannot be measured, and it was my woman's right to choose to bring them into the world. Although Michael and Seth died at ages sixteen and thirty, they were great young men— talented and full of faith, giving their gifts to humankind. I do not apologize that they were born, and I am glad people were able to know them! And, of course, Jonathan, my firstborn, was an innocent sweet baby who radiated love and wisdom to those around him. We had no knowledge that he carried a defective gene until he became very sick and passed away before his first birthday.

March 2023

Robert and Richard, my other two boys with hyper IgM, made it safely through the Covid pandemic. Richard and Siru were married in 2018 and now have a baby, Maija Josephine, named after her parents' grandmothers. She is such a smiling, cute baby! They live in Tennessee. Robert and Nicole were married in 2021 in California. Nicole is a wonderful addition to our family! She is super friendly and caring to all of us and is a positive influence. God has blessed me and my children exceedingly. There is much to be thankful for!

I thank God for His loving kindness and comfort to me in my many trials of life. It is a gift to believe in spiritual things that are usually not seen with our eyes but only felt with our hearts. (Although, to see the wonder of life and the order and beauty in the universe is evidence to me of a higher power.) For those who don't have faith, I would say, "Ask, and it shall be given you. Seek, and ye shall find" (Matthew 7:7). "Whosoever will, let him take the water of life freely" (Revelation 21:17).

It seems almost as if I was born with faith in a loving God and Savior. I am grateful for this belief, as it has indeed been a strength to me since I was a child. "Faith is the substance of things hoped for, the evidence of things not seen" (Hebrews 11:1). It is evidence that can be strongly felt, but not seen or proven to others. That faith assures me that Jonathan, Seth, Michael, and Mike and all my family members who have died are actually still living in the spirit world and that I will surely see them again. They are happy and busy and doing wonderful things. They are even watching over us and encouraging us in our difficult mortal lives. In one hundred years it will all make sense to us, and the agonies we have passed through here on earth will seem like a distant memory, like a mother's pain before her beautiful baby is born. Our suffering will be in the past and won't matter anymore. Mortal pain is already over for those who have died, which is a very comforting thought to me.

As mortals we cannot clearly see the blessings awaiting us across the veil of death. In the eighteenth and nineteenth centuries, society in general held a belief in heaven, as reflected in the works of writers and poets of that time. As I studied their works in my college literature classes, I was inspired by the belief in the Divine that existed in that era. Not being distracted by electric lights and electronic gadgets, they were much closer than we are in their daily lives to the natural world and to the wonders that God has created. Although they experienced illness and death more often than we do, they seemed to find more peace than our society does, because of their sure belief in life after death. In 1807 William Wordsworth wrote the following as part of his poem "Intimations of Immortality":

> Our Souls have sight of that immortal sea
> Which brought us hither …
> What though the radiance which was once so bright
> Be now forever taken from my sight,
> Though nothing can bring back the hour
> Of splendour in the grass, of glory in the flower;
> We will grieve not, rather find Strength in what remains behind …
> In the faith that looks through death.
> (Wordsworth 1993, 192–93)

Johann Wolfgang von Goethe, a famous German author, wrote of the eternal nature of the spirit. He said, "The thought of death leaves me in perfect peace, for I have a firm conviction that our spirit is a being of indestructible nature. It works on from eternity to eternity. It is like the sun, which though it seems to set to our mortal eyes, does not really set; but shines on perpetually" (von Goethe 1830).

Faith in God, in the immortality of the spirit, and in a paradise to come can give us strength to plow through our terrible trials of life, including the hardships of broken relationships, disease and death. Regarding the future days when Christ returns, the Bible says: "And

I saw a new heaven, and a new earth, for the first heaven and the first earth were passed away. . . . And I saw the new Jerusalem, coming down from God out of heaven. . . . God himself shall be with them, and be their God. . . . And God shall wipe away all tears from their eyes; and there shall be no more death, neither sorrow, nor crying, neither shall there be any more pain (Revelations 21: 1-4)."

What wonderful things we have to look forward to!

God loves all of His children! He will give each person the lowest penalty and the highest rewards possible according to their works on earth. May we believe in Him and love Him, and seek to live His commandments as long as we live! He is merciful and kind to those who seek Him!

Old age may bring pain and physical ailments. These help us to be humble and to let the rising generation shine in their strength. Aging can also bring satisfaction as we see our posterity take their places in the world and as we reflect upon our own accomplishments. It is comforting to know as we come closer to death that it is simply a door to a glorious new life in eternity!

References

Bell, James P., and Faust, James E. 1999. *In the Strength of the Lord: The Life and Teachings of James E. Faust*: 250. Salt Lake City: © Deseret Book Company. Used by permission.

Brown, Hugh B. 1967. "Father, Are You There?" @ https://speeches. byu. edu/talks/hugh-b-brown father/ ©Intellectual Reserve Inc. Used by permission.

Browning, Robert. 1993. "Rabbi Ben Ezra." In *The Norton Anthology of English Literature*, Sixth Edition, Vol. 2. Edited by B. H. Abrams, 1257. New York: W. W. Norton & Company.

Candlelight Media Group. 2008. Emma Smith—My Story. DVD.

Clayton, William. 1998. "Come, Come Ye Saints." In *Hymns of the Church of Jesus Christ of Latter-day Saints*, 30. Salt Lake City, Utah: The Church of Jesus Christ of Latter-day Saints, © Intellectual Reserve Inc. Used by permission.

Davidson, Karen Lynn. 1998. "Each Life that Touches Ours for Good." In *Hymns of the Church of Jesus Christ of Latter-day Saints*, 293. Salt Lake City, Utah: The Church of Jesus Christ of Latter-day Saints. © Intellectual Reserve Inc. Used by permission.

Donne, John. 1609. *Death, Be Not Proud*, Holy Sonnet 10. www. poemhunter.com

Edgley, Richard G. 2002. "For Thy Good." *Ensign*, May 2002, © By Intellectual Reserve, Inc.

Faber, Frederick W. 1998. "Faith of Our Fathers." In *Hymns of the Church of Jesus Christ of Latter-day Saints*, 84. Salt Lake City, Utah: The Church of Jesus Christ of Latter-day Saints. © Intellectual Reserve Inc. Used by permission.

Faust, James E. 2001. "The Good That Can Grow out of Tragedy," *Stories from My Life*: 21. Salt Lake City: © Deseret Book Company. Used by permission.

Flint, Annie Johnson. 1919. *The Poetry of Annie Johnson Flint*, "What God Hath Promised," www.homemakerscorner.com/annie/htm.

Gardner, Ruth M. 1998. "Families Can be Together Forever." In *Hymns of the Church of Jesus Christ of Latter-day Saints*, 300. Salt Lake City, Utah: The Church of Jesus Christ of Latter-day Saints. © Intellectual Reserve Inc. Used by permission.

Groberg, John H. 1993. *In the Eye of the Storm*. 101, 114. Salt Lake City, Utah: © Deseret Book Co.Used by permission.

Gordon, Grace. 1998. "Called to Serve." In *Hymns of the Church of Jesus Christ of Latter-day Saints*, 249. Salt Lake City, Utah: The Church of Jesus Christ of Latter-day Saints. © Intellectual Reserve Inc. Used by permission.

Hinckley, Gordon B. 1993. "The Peaceful House of God." *Ensign*, May 1993. © By Intellectual Reserve, Inc. Used by permission.

Hinckley, Gordon B. 2000. "Latter-day Counsel: Excerpts from Addresses of President Gordon B. Hinckley." *Ensign*, October 2000. © By Intellectual Reserve, Inc. Used by permission.

Hinckley, Gordon B. 2002. "We Look to Christ." *Ensign*, May 2002. © By Intellectual Reserve, Inc. Used by permission.

Holland, Jeffrey R. and Holland, Patricia T. 1983. "However Long and Hard the Road," BYU Devotional, January 18. @ https://www.google.com/url?q=https://speeches.byu.edu/talks/jeffrey-r-and-patricia-t-holland however-long-hard-road/ © By Intellectual Reserve Inc. Used by permission.

Immune Deficiency Foundation. 2012. IDF Advocate. *The National Newsletter of the Immune Deficiency Foundation.* Spring, No. 69. Towson, Maryland. Used by permission.

Immune Deficiency Foundation. 2013. *Patient and Family Handbook for Primary Immunodeficiency Disease,* 5th Edition. Towson, Maryland. www.primaryimmune.org. Used by permission.

Jackson, Linda Jo. "I Am Free." http://www.abundantfun.com/poems/poemn48.html#.WqMWjjEwuYM

Keen, Robert. 1998. "How Firm a Foundation." In *Hymns of the Church of Jesus Christ of Latter-day Saints*, 85. Salt Lake City, Utah: The Church of Jesus Christ of Latter-day Saints. © Intellectual Reserve Inc. Used by permission.

Lyte, Henry F. 1998. "Abide With Me." In *Hymns of the Church of Jesus Christ of Latter-day Saints*, 166. Salt Lake City, Utah: The Church of Jesus Christ of Latter-day Saints. © Intellectual Reserve Inc. Used by permission.

Medley, Samuel. 1998. "I Know That My Redeemer Lives." In *Hymns of the Church of Jesus Christ of Latter-day Saints*, 136. Salt Lake City, Utah: The Church of Jesus Christ of Latter-day Saints. © Intellectual Reserve Inc. Used by permission.

Maxwell, Neal A. 1981. "Grounded, Rooted, Established and Settled." BYU Speeches, September 15 @ https://speeches.byu. edu/talks/neal-a-maxwell grounded-rooted-established-settled-ephesians-317-1-peter-510/ © By Intellectual Reserve Inc. Used by permission.

Moore, Thomas. 1998. "Come Ye Disconsolate." In *Hymns of the Church of Jesus Christ of Latter-day Saints* 115. Salt Lake City, Utah: The Church of Jesus Christ of Latter-day Saints. © Intellectual Reserve Inc. Used by permission.

New York American Bible Society. 1900. The Holy Bible: *Containing the Old and New Testaments, Translated out of the Original Tongues and with the Former Translation Diligently Compared and Revised.*

Penn, William. 1842. *No Cross, No Crown. A Discourse Showing the Nature and Discipline of the Holy Cross of Christ*. London: Harvey and Darton, Gracechurch Street.

Perry, Janice Kapp. 1985. "The Test." In *The Light Within*, 18. Provo, Utah: Prime Recordings. Used by permission.

Rankin, Jeremiah E. 1998. "God be with You Till We Meet Again." In *Hymns of the Church of Jesus Christ of Latter-day Saints*, 152. Salt Lake City, Utah: The Church of Jesus Christ of Latter-day Saints, © Intellectual Reserve Inc. Used by permission.

Rodgers, Ralph; Dayley, K. Newell; and Huffman, Laurie. 1989. "I Feel My Savior's Love." In *Children's Songbook*, 74. Salt Lake City, Utah: The Church of Jesus Christ of Latter-day Saints. © Intellectual Reserve Inc. Used by permission.

Scott, Verl F. 1982. Personal communication. (Not copyrighted.)

Smith, Joseph. 2007. *Teachings of Presidents of the Church: Joseph Smith*, 176. Salt Lake City, Utah: The Church of Jesus Christ of Latter-day Saints. © Intellectual Reserve Inc. Used by permission.

Snow, Eliza R. 1998. "The Time is Far Spent." In *Hymns of the Church of Jesus Christ of Latter-day Saints*, 266. Salt Lake City, Utah: The Church of Jesus Christ of Latter-day Saints. © Intellectual Reserve Inc. Used by permission.

Snow, Eliza R. 1998. "Though Deepening Trials." In *Hymns of the Church of Jesus Christ of Latter-day Saints*, 122. Salt Lake City, Utah: The Church of Jesus Christ of Latter-day Saints. © Intellectual Reserve Inc. Used by permission.

Sorensen, Michele R. and Willmore, David R. 1992. *The Journey Beyond Life, Volume I*, 119. Sandy, Utah: Sounds of Zion. Used by permission.

The Church of Jesus Christ of Latter-day Saints. 1990. *The Book of Mormon: Another Testament of Jesus Christ*. Salt Lake City, Utah. © Intellectual Reserve Inc. Used by permission.

The Church of Jesus Christ of Latter-day Saints. 1990. *The Doctrine and Covenants of the Church of Jesus Christ of Latter-day Saints*. Salt Lake City, Utah. © Intellectual Reserve Inc. Used by permission.

The Church of Jesus Christ of Latter-day Saints. 1990. *The Pearl of Great Price*. Salt Lake City, Utah. © Intellectual Reserve Inc. Used by permission.

Thoreau, Henry David. 1854. *Walden, or Life in the Woods*, 98. @ https://archive.org/details/waldenorlifeinwo1854thor

Top, Brent L. and Wendy C. Top. 1993. *Beyond Death's Door*. Salt Lake City, Utah: © Deseret Book Company. Used by permission.

Wade, John F. 1998. "Oh, Come All Ye Faithful." In *Hymns of the Church of Jesus Christ of Latter-day Saints*, 202. Salt Lake City, Utah: The Church of Jesus Christ of Latter-day Saints, © Intellectual Reserve Inc. Used by permission.

Walker, Charles L. 1998. "Dearest Children, God is Near You." In *Hymns of the Church of Jesus Christ of Latter-day Saints*, 96. Salt Lake City, Utah: The Church of Jesus Christ of Latter-day Saints, © Intellectual Reserve Inc. Used by permission.

Wordsworth, William. 1993. "Intimations of Immortality." In *The Norton Anthology, English Literature*, Sixth Edition, Vol. 2. Edited by M. H Abrams, 190. New York: W. W. Norton & Company.

Von Goethe, Johann Wolfgang. 1830. @ http://likesuccess.com/857397

About the Author

 Colleen Scott Curzon Openshaw was born and raised in Salt Lake City, Utah. She has a BGS degree from Brigham Young University with an emphasis in English literature and an MS degree from the University of Phoenix in special education. She and her husband Michael G. Curzon had nine children, three of whom died at various ages due to hyper-IgM syndrome, a genetic immunodeficiency disease. Colleen has lived in California, Georgia, and several other states, but most of her married life was spent in the small town of Salem, Utah. Colleen enjoys doing research on religion, nutrition, and medicine while seeking solutions to her family's medical problems. Colleen's husband died in 2008 from complications of cancer. After his death, she finished her education, served a volunteer mission at the Family History Library in Salt Lake City, and worked for the Granite School District in special education. In 2013 Colleen married Gary G. Openshaw. They reside in Salt Lake City, Utah, and have been able to volunteer in the temple of the Church of Jesus Christ of Latter-day Saints in past years together. Colleen has six living children - four boys and 2 girls, as well as five granddaughters.

Readers may contact Colleen at her email address (curzons@msn.com) to order books.

www.ingramcontent.com/pod-product-compliance
Lightning Source LLC
Chambersburg PA
CBHW060851120626
46553CB00001B/46